The Economy

ELEVENTH EDITION

National and Sectoral Policy Issues

6

Edited by

John O'Hagan

and

Carol Newman

GILL & MACMILLAN

Gill & Macmillan
Hume Avenue
Park West
Dublin 12
with associated companies throughout the world www.gillmacmillan.ie

978 07171 4973 5

Index compiled by Cliff Murphy
Print origination in Ireland by TypeIT, Dublin
Printed by GraphyGems, Spain

The paper used in this book is made from the wood pulp of managed
forests. For every tree felled, at least one tree is planted, thereby
renewing natural resources.

A CIP catalogue record for this book is available
from the British Library.

For updates and more information go to
www.gillmacmillan.ie/economyofireland

Contents

Section V
POLICY ISSUES IN THE NON-MARKET SECTOR

Preface

It is only three years since the last edition of this book went to print, but how things can change so dramatically in such a short time. The 'storm clouds' discussed in the Preface to that edition developed into a tornado. The pace of the decline in economic activity was almost unprecedented. Output (GNP) declined by 3.5 per cent in 2008, and by a further 10.7 per cent in 2009, a quite staggering turnaround from the heady days of 1994 to 2007 (see Chapter 7). Output declined again in 2010, by 2.1 per cent, marking an aggregate drop in output of around 15 per cent in three years.[1] Such a decline had almost no peace-time parallel in the developed world since the 1930s. Related to this was the huge increase in unemployment, up from 4.5 per cent in 2007 to over 14 per cent in early 2011. Large drops in employment occurred and there was a dramatic decline in gross in-migration, with gross out-migration now exceeding it by perhaps 40–50 thousand, although no reliable figures are yet available (see Chapter 6).

The drop in economic activity led to a huge fall in tax revenues for the state and this in turn has led to a fiscal crisis, with the general government deficit set to exceed 10 per cent of GDP again this year (see Chapters 3 and 4). This is despite three major corrective budgets between 2008 and 2010. The problems do not end there. The collapse in the property market created a huge banking crisis, the scale of which was not fully realised until early in 2011. The cost to the taxpayer of rescuing the banks now stands at an astonishing 40 to 50 per cent of national output. The combination of the fiscal and banking crises meant that Ireland could not access money, except at exorbitant rates, in the bond markets by end 2010. As a result an EU/ECB/IMF 'rescue' package had to be put in place and now influences how economic policy will evolve in years to come.

IRISH ASSET 'BUBBLE' AND FINANCIAL CRISIS

The Irish economy would have shrunk anyway because of the recession in the USA in 2008 and 2009, as the financial sector experienced a credit squeeze and investment from the USA slowed considerably. This recession spread to Europe in 2009, but in 2010 the large European economies of France and Germany pulled strongly out of recession, and both have booming economies in 2011. This was and is not the case for Ireland. The property price bubble here was exceptional. The scale of building activity was unsustainable, largely because the price of houses had to drop, and substantially so at some stage. What few, if any, realised was the scale and speed of the adjustment in house prices and related to this the price of development land. A major banking crisis in Ireland was inevitable.

Having been caught up with the euphoria of the boom years the media ran opinion pieces with regard to how severe the collapse in house and development land prices might be, with what appeared at the time as apocalyptic predictions coming true. A series of books on the causes of the collapse ensued. However, it was not until March 2011 that a detailed, professional assessment of the causes of the financial collapse emerged. The Nyberg Report spread the blame widely,[2] and put it down essentially to collective 'madness', as evidenced by the following:

> Much points to the development of a national speculative mania in Ireland during the period, centred on the property market. As in most manias, those caught up in it could believe and have trust in extraordinary things, such as unlimited real wealth from selling property to each other on credit. Even obvious warning signs went unheeded in the belief that the world had changed and that a stable economy was somehow automatically guaranteed. Traditional values, analysis, and rules could be gradually less observed by the banks and authorities because their relevance was seen as lost in the new and different world. When it all ended, suddenly and inexplicably, participants had difficulty accepting their appropriate share of the blame for something in which so many others were also involved and that seemed so reasonable at the time.[3]

The main point to make here is the enormous dangers that result from the build-up of asset prices and their subsequent collapse, something to which few macroeconomists either here or elsewhere were to any major extent alert. Economists everywhere had largely forgotten their economic history.

The Irish banking system was very much linked to those in the USA and Europe, but it was only a tiny cog in the overall scheme of things. In this regard, it could be argued that the Irish banks were simply following practice elsewhere. As such, the broader focus for criticism is perhaps the larger banking and regulatory system which Ireland had eagerly embraced and was, indeed, initially lauded for so doing. However, some banks in Ireland took this to extremes and many other countries equally linked into the international banking network did not encounter anything like the problems Ireland did.

What is remarkable perhaps is that during the boom times few questioned this policy and/or practice, even though the warning signs, it is now evident, were there as early as 2002. With hindsight some are arguing that they foresaw the banking crisis coming, but no serious agency was 'calling from the rooftops' of a pending financial collapse. Indeed, many 'stress tests' by, for example, the Central Bank and the IMF were indicating that there were no unambiguously serious problems in the housing and banking sectors, even though the boom in expenditure on property was funded by huge private debt, financed largely from overseas. There was probably more worry in the late 1990s when many commentators could not foresee the boom lasting, including the rise in house prices. A microcosm of this is that many parents will tell you that they strongly advised their children to defer the purchase of a house as the levels at that time were unsustainable. How foolish they looked, they say, when house prices doubled or trebled in the succeeding years. It did appear that there had been a paradigm shift in market economies, with the old indicators of asset bubbles, it was argued by some eminent economists, no longer applicable.[4]

The emphasis now has switched to who will pay for the banking crisis and the huge bill resulting from this. At present, under the EU/ECB/IMF Memorandum of Understanding it is Irish taxpayers who will by and large foot the bill. There is an understandable desire of Irish people to have this bill shared by other euro zone taxpayers or by the banks which lent the money, but as several chapters in this book outline (see Chapters 2, 3 and 7 in particular), the economic and political implications of any euro zone solution are much more complex than the vast majority of media commentators seem to imply. The future of the European banking system, and hence the whole euro project, is at stake and as such the solutions have to be Europe-wide and acceptable to all euro zone governments. As discussed at length in Chapter 3, due to increasing economic integration and globalisation, many economic issues today transcend national boundaries and can only be addressed at a higher level of government. Recognition of this fact by all can eventually lead to a better, shared outcome for Ireland and Europe in dealing with the banking and fiscal crises. What these crises have also highlighted beyond doubt are the fault lines in the institutional underpinnings of the euro, something that in mid-2011 remains very much a work in progress.

FORECASTING FAILURES

It might reasonably be argued that we cannot predict what the likely outcome for the economy in the next few years might be, given that all of the major forecasting units in Ireland and elsewhere did not with any force predict how serious the recession of 2008–9 was to turn out. Take for example, the ESRI, arguably the most respected forecasting institution in relation to the Irish economy. Let us look at the forecasts of the ESRI for 2009 in relation to three key economic indicators, from Quarter 1 in 2008 to Quarter 2 in 2009. The purpose of this exercise is not in any way to criticise the ESRI, but to give an indication of how *all* forecasters, including the Department of Finance, IMF, OECD and Central Bank, failed to predict the extent of the recession in 2009, even as late as Quarter 2 2008.[5]

Let us start with forecasts for GDP growth. The ESRI in Quarter 1 2008 still expected the economy to grow by 3 per cent in 2009. This prediction fell to 2 per cent by Quarter 2 2008, to *minus* 3.7 per cent by Quarter 4 2008, to *minus* 7.9 per cent by Quarter 2 2009. In relation to unemployment, the situation was the same. The ESRI in Quarter 1 2008 predicted an unemployment rate in 2009 of 6.2 per cent, but raised this to 9.4 per cent by Quarter 4 2008. By Quarter 1 2009 the predicted unemployment rate for 2009 was 13.2 per cent, but this was reduced to 12.6 per cent by Quarter 2 2009 in response to evidence that more people were emigrating in search of work and hence not joining the unemployed in Ireland. Finally the ESRI looked at the general government deficit; in Quarter 1 2008 it predicted that it would be around €4 billion in 2009. By Quarter 4 this figure had risen to around €18 billion and by Quarter 2 2009 to over €20 billion. These are remarkable changes in forecasts and for many they raise doubts about the ability of forecasters to predict the likely outcomes in 2012 and thereafter.

While forecasting the economy failed spectacularly in the 2008 to 2010 period, and not just in Ireland, it should be pointed out that in the previous 15 years or so the changes in the economy had been predicted with reasonable accuracy. As such some credibility must attach to most forecasts today which see little prospect of an upturn in 2011 and only modest growth for several years thereafter.

WHERE NOW? THE WIDER CONTEXT

This book is not and never was concerned primarily with shorter-term economic issues. It generally takes a much longer-term historical perspective, a perspective that is salutary in reminding us that booms come to an end and, in the present context, that the 'bad times' do not last forever. Indeed, in some cases they can end much more rapidly than expected, as in the mid-1970s or early 2000s, or last much longer than is necessary, as was the case in the 1950s and 1980s. This book is also much more about general policy issues, thereby providing the context for debate, be it in the short, medium or long term.

There is no reason why Ireland cannot prosper in years to come and remain one of the high-income countries of the world. The country has a healthy, stable democracy and a well-established rule of law. The people and the level of human capital therein are the same as they were prior to 2008. There is an openness to competition and entrepreneurship that simply did not exist in the 1980s. Ireland has the security of membership of the euro zone, and a strong commitment to the EU, and thereby free trade, international competition, a cleaner environment, and all that the EU stands for on the world stage.

All democracies are flawed to some extent and economic debates are often fraught and misinformed, Ireland being no exception. The debate in 2011 on budgetary reform in the USA is a salutary reminder of this. Predictions of economic decline can be altered within months. An example of this is the earlier forecast by some in 2009 of a long Japanese-style relative decline in Germany to be followed six months later with the reality of Germany pulling out of recession faster than the USA or UK and now booming on all fronts.

The last three years have seen a slowing down and then a significant reversal of the boom times from 2003 to 2007; about that there is no doubt. But there has *not* been a disaster. The standard of living and the numbers in employment may have fallen back to 2004 levels but these are still some of the highest in the world and represent a huge increase in living standards over, say, 1994 when Ireland was already a very wealthy country in a global context. There will still be 80 per cent more in employment in 2011 than in 1994, a huge increase when seen in a historical context.

It is true that the distribution of losses in the last three years has been markedly skewed. Tens of thousands of people have lost their jobs, and in all income categories; social welfare payments for the unemployed, though, are at high levels compared to other countries and for those who were in relatively low-income employment they are a major cushion against the income loss arising from unemployment. However, unemployment can involve not only a loss of income but also a loss of status and self-esteem, and there is little doubt that the newly unemployed and the involuntary emigrants are the great losers in the recession of 2008–10. This is especially so if these same people bought property at the height of the boom and as such are part of the substantial section of the population experiencing negative equity. For some people the consequences are stark and very disturbing.

Others have lost their entire life savings or pension funds as a result of the collapse in asset prices. Many of these were not wealthy individuals but people who invested, either personally or through a life assurance company, their relatively small savings for retirement. The vast majority of people, though, are still in employment and have experienced a fall in the cost of living, as prices in some years have declined, thereby cushioning them from the full effects of the drop in incomes experienced by nearly all. There are others who sold at the peak of these prices and are now wealthy beyond their wildest dreams; remember, every billion euro 'lost' by someone was a gain for someone else, either in Ireland or overseas. The vast majority of households do not have any mortgage or negative equity problems.

There is also a strong intergenerational inequity dimension being played out resulting from the crisis. It is the younger age groups who almost certainly bought houses at the top of the boom, with most of the older generation having long paid in full for their properties, purchased at times of much lower real prices. Besides, to pay for the debt the burden again will fall mostly on the younger generation, through reduced incomes for those starting out at work, fewer promotional opportunities, particularly in the public sector, and longer working lives. A disturbing reflection of this is the exercise of 'grey power' in recent years, where as a result payments to the over-65s, regardless of their circumstances, have been protected while those to other younger groups have been cut.

There are other potential disasters that should continue to concern us and will do so well beyond the present setbacks, such as the threat of a major terrorist attack, especially if it involves the use of biological or nuclear weapons, or indeed a war initiated by the aggression of a nation state. There is also the possibility of a major environmental disaster leading to the loss of hundreds of millions of lives and the danger of major water shortages for tens of millions of others: events in Japan in 2011 reminded the world starkly of this (see Chapter 10). There is also the possibility of severe energy shortages, either because the world runs short of the exploitable natural resources required or because of the actions of some states in cutting off supply. On all of these issues Irish interests and concerns are best voiced at an EU level and through the EU on the global 'stage' (see later).

As urgent and pressing as are the decisions of the next few years, they must be seen in this context. These global problems are outside the control of Irish policy-makers acting on their own, yet they could have catastrophic consequences for Ireland. The problems we face in the years ahead – resolution of the problems of the banking sector, restoration of balance to the public finances and a return to competitiveness – are all largely within our own remit and can be resolved, given the political will and an informed and realistic public debate. In relation to the former, the vociferous objections of special interest groups (and often those who suffered least in the recession) must be resisted; and in relation to the latter, alternatives must be presented, especially by those whose job it is to sift and present information/arguments in a balanced way, so that informed decisions can be made. EU/ECB/IMF intervention may have altered the dynamic of the policy response to the crisis, but it has not changed its substance. What is being put in place by the so-called 'troika', in consultation with the Department of Finance and the government, would have had to happen anyway. Once you borrow large sums of money, no matter from whom, you automatically become dependent on this source and must comply with the conditions attaching. It is perhaps part of the present malaise that the blame may now be shifting to outsiders, thereby providing temporary excuses for avoiding necessary and sweeping reform.

LONGER-TERM ECONOMIC POLICY FRAMEWORK

Ireland is now a region of the euro zone, the euro having replaced Irish notes and coins in January 2002. As such, there are no chapters in this book on monetary policy or on balance of payments and exchange rate policy in Ireland, although the future of the euro in its present form came under serious question at a European level in 2010 and 2011. Indeed, its future remains in doubt unless the institutional underpinnings of the euro are greatly reformed, something that is encountering primarily political as opposed to economic difficulties.

The policy emphasis now at an Irish level, though, is almost exclusively on the competitiveness of the EU region, 'Ireland Inc.', and this is reflected in many chapters throughout the book. Even in relation to this Ireland must operate within an agreed competition and regulatory environment determined, with Ireland as a voting member, at an EU level. Competitiveness is a key determinant of our attractiveness to foreign direct investment: the scale of US investment has been such that Ireland might be viewed in an industrial sense as a region of the American economy, despite the fact that in a monetary sense the country is an integral part of the euro zone. International benchmarking in terms of competitiveness is now commonplace and the *Annual Competitiveness Reports* published by the National Competitiveness Council each year since 1997 are some of the most talked-about reports produced.

Despite the industrial connection with the USA and the economic, monetary, and political links with the EU, the euro zone in particular, the relationship with the UK is for Ireland still very important, for a variety of reasons (see Chapter 1). While the nature of this relationship may have altered significantly, its substance has remained the same. In terms of simple geography, Ireland is a tiny country, an island to the west of Britain, which in turn is a somewhat larger but much more densely populated island to the west of mainland Europe: its population is over 15 times that of Ireland. Ireland and the UK have a common labour market, a common language, and huge trade and tourism flows in both directions; by and large people in both jurisdictions watch the same TV programmes and follow similar key sports and cultural events. These are inescapable facts, which, as shall be seen throughout the book, are important to an understanding of the Irish economy, past and present.

Moreover, the island of Ireland consists of two political units, the larger portion of which forms the Republic of Ireland and the smaller portion Northern Ireland, which is part of the UK. This too has had an impact on economic, social and political life in the Republic. This book is about the economy of the Republic of Ireland, and henceforth the terms 'economy of Ireland' and 'Irish economy' refer to this economy, unless otherwise stated. Some reference is made to the Northern Ireland economy, but since Northern Ireland's economic policy is largely determined in London, it is difficult to devote much attention to policy there without also reviewing British economic policy in general. There has been, though, as Chapter 3 points out, greatly increased cross-border co-operation on the economic front since the Good Friday Agreement of thirteen years ago.

The links, economic and cultural, to continental Europe are strengthening, something that low-cost air travel and the use of the euro has facilitated. Irish people are now much more familiar than they were even twenty-five years ago with political developments in Europe, and with European sporting and cultural events. Indeed, as a result of the earlier boom in incomes, many own second homes there. But Ireland and the EU have also to look at the wider world, as issues and problems that are truly global in nature must be addressed. Top of the list is the environment and the danger of serious global warming. Not far behind are terrorism, free trade, sharply increased world food prices resulting from new demands for food and land use, increased migration (legal and illegal) and international crime. As Chapter 2 points out, concerns about environmental degradation must qualify any endorsement of economic growth as a policy objective. Chapter 3, though, highlights the governance difficulties faced when dealing with environmental issues that extend beyond national boundaries. This, as seen already, also applies to many financial issues. Later chapters discuss various policy measures being adopted to address such issues, both within Ireland and internationally.

The rise of China and India in particular is an economic reality that has affected not just small countries like Ireland but also the two largest trading blocs in the world, namely the EU and the USA. It has led to a huge increase in competition, for both goods and investment flows. It has also of course led to a huge increase in trade and investment opportunities. China hosted the Olympic Games in 2008, its military prowess is growing, and Mandarin is the mother tongue of by far the largest number of people in the world. As such, its influence will soon extend well beyond the economic to the cultural and military spheres. Ireland, as part of the larger EU, will have to learn to adapt to such seismic geopolitical changes in the global economy.

STRUCTURE OF THIS BOOK

This book has grown out of an earlier book, first published thirty-six years ago. The Irish Management Institute published the first six editions, Macmillan what in effect was the seventh edition and Gill & Macmillan the eighth and current editions. The broad structure and purpose of the book have remained the same over the years, but in terms of content there have been sweeping changes, even since the last edition. For example, Chapters 4, 5, 8, 9 and 10 are new since the last edition. Apart from updating, major changes have also been made to the remaining eight chapters, bar Chapter 1 on the historical background, to reflect the rapidly changing circumstances and policy issues facing the Irish economy.

As mentioned, the overall structure of the book has been unchanging over the years. Part I provides the key policy context, namely the historical evolution of the economy up to the 1990s (Chapter 1) and a discussion of the key policy objectives and issues for a regional economy such as that of Ireland (Chapter 2). It is important to know what we want from the Irish economy before asking how to achieve these aims and how well we have done in so doing. These are the questions looked at in Parts II and III. Chapter 3 sets out the role of the state, in terms of rationale, levels of government and size of the state sector. It also addresses the recent fiscal crisis in Ireland and the euro zone. Chapter 4 examines how state involvement is funded and the issues to which taxes give rise. Chapter 5 examines the issues of competition and regulation, paying particular attention to banking regulation. Part III consists of three quite lengthy discussion of Ireland's success or otherwise in meeting the three objectives outlined in Chapter 2, and the policy issues to which these give rise, namely employment (Chapter 6), growth in living standards (Chapter 7) and social justice (Chapter 8).

Part IV contains a detailed discussion of policy issues and performance in the market sector and builds on much of the earlier material. Chapter 9 examines the market sectors perhaps of most importance to the success of the future economy, namely manufacturing and traded services. Chapter 10 looks at the importance of physical infrastructure to an economy, in the transport, energy and environment areas in particular. It also contains a much broader discussion of other policy issues in the energy and environmental areas. Chapter 11 looks not only at the agricultural sector but also the issues of food distribution and consumption and food safety. Part V concludes the book with an examination of two key areas of the public sector, namely health (Chapter 12) and education (Chapter 13).

ACKNOWLEDGMENTS

There are many people we would like to thank who have facilitated the publication of the eleventh edition of this title. We would like to thank staff at Gill & Macmillan for their central role in bringing this book to publication. We would also especially like to thank our copy-editor Jane Rogers; she was a pleasure to work with.

The book would not of course exist without the contributed chapters. As always, it was most enjoyable work liaising with each of the contributors, at each step of the process. In particular, it was rewarding seeing chapters take shape and mesh into the overall structure of the book following comments and suggestions. We very much appreciate the input and co-operation of each and every contributor.

We would also like to thank the many lecturers and students who have used this book over the years. This has made the book both financially viable, despite the small size of the potential market, and a very satisfying experience for us. The book is also read widely outside academia, and indeed beyond these shores, and we hope that this will continue to be the case. This is the type of book, and related courses, which students seem to enjoy immensely and we are sure lecturers in other colleges have also found this to be the case. It does, after all, deal with the political economy of one of the most interesting case studies in recent decades in world economics!

John W. O'Hagan and Carol Newman
Trinity College Dublin
May 2011

Endnotes

1   The figures for GDP were less negative: declines of 3.5, 7.6, and 1.0 in 2008, 2009, and 2010 respectively. See Department of Finance, *Monthly Economic Bulletin: April 2011*, at
http://www.finance.gov.ie/viewdoc.asp?DocID=6780&CatID=2&StartDate=1+January+2011.

2 One of the most informed and balanced economic and political commentaries in Ireland throughout the period since 2008 has been provided by Stephen Collins, Political Editor, *Irish Times*. For example, recently he stated that the negative reaction to the Nyberg Report 'on the basis that it failed to name a small group of "guilty men" who could be blamed for the country's economic collapse, epitomises the desire of large sections of Irish society to avoid facing up to the underlying causes of the crisis ... There is still a deep reluctance at all levels of Irish society to absorb the simple lesson enunciated by Nyberg that Ireland lived beyond its means for a decade and is now going to have to live below its means for a few years.' S. Collins, 'Cheerleaders of boom among hardest Nyberg critics', *Irish Times*, 23 April 2011.

3 *Misjudging Risk: Causes of the Systemic Banking Crisis in Ireland* (Report of the Commission of Investigation into the Banking Sector in Ireland) (Nyberg Report), Dublin, March 2011, p. i, at
http://www.finance.gov.ie/documents/publications/reports/2011/nybergreport.pdf.

4 See for example the 18 July 2009 issue of the *Economist*, whose subheading was 'Where it went wrong – and how the crisis is changing it', the 'it' referring to modern macroeconomic theory. See a critical response to this issue by Robert Lucas in the 8 August 2009 issue of the *Economist*. Contributors to the *Financial Times* also mused about the state of macroeconomics, none more so than Paul De Grauwe in his 'Warring economists are carried along by the crowd', *Financial Times,* 22 July 2009.

5 Indeed, the ESRI *Medium-Term Review* of 2008 was expecting a favourable economic outlook for Ireland up to 2013.

SECTION I

POLICY CONTEXT

CHAPTER 1

Historical Background

Jonathan Haughton

1 WHY ECONOMIC HISTORY?

Why take the trouble to study history, and particularly the economic history of a minor European island? Five good reasons spring to mind.

History tests theory. The propositions of economics are often best tested by exposing them to historical evidence. Was Malthus right when he argued that population growth would inevitably outstrip food supply? Irish experience, even during the Great Famine, suggests not. Do farmers respond to changes in the prices they face? Evidence from late nineteenth-century Ireland confirms that they do. Does emigration serve to equalise wages between Ireland and Britain? Data for this century indicate that, broadly speaking, it does.

History gives perspective. Standard economics textbooks typically provide a short-run and partial approach to economic problems. While this may be appropriate for tracing the immediate effects of a shift in demand, or a monetary expansion, it provides fewer insights into the fundamental determinants of economic growth or of income distribution, since these may only be observed over long periods of time. The historian Joe Lee has made the point forcibly, writing that 'while contemporary Irish economics can be impressive in accounting for short-term movements, it has contributed relatively little to understanding the long-term development of the Irish economy'. He argues that most economists are 'blind to either long-term perspective or lateral linkage' and that 'with the exception of a handful of superior intelligences, Irish economists are far more impressive as technicians than as thinkers'.

An important lesson from economic history is that it provides a sense of the fragility of economic growth, and of its intermittent nature. For instance, many look back to the 1960s as a golden era of Irish economic growth. Yet Kennedy, Giblin and McHugh, in their interesting study of Irish economic development in the twentieth century, argue that 'a sense of historical perspective would have encouraged greater modesty about the achievements of the 1960s by recognising that they depended heavily on a combination of uniquely favourable external and internal circumstances'. In the same vein, it is important to recognise that the remarkable boom of the late 1990s has also passed, although not without dramatically changing the country in the process.

History fascinates. While the study of any subject may be justified on the grounds of its intrinsic worth, economic history is particularly interesting. The visible remains of the past are everywhere – ports, houses, crooked streets, abandoned fields and ruined cottages. It is natural to wonder about their origins. Less visibly, our view of history informs our view of who we are, and what our culture stands for. These roots merit exploration. History also has its share of intellectual puzzles: why was economic growth in the 1950s so anaemic? How did per capita incomes rise faster in Ireland between 1850 and 1920 than anywhere else in Europe? Was the tariff regime of the 1930s a failure?

History debunks. Ideologues of all stripes invoke history to bolster their claims. When John Mitchel argued that 'The Almighty, indeed, sent the potato blight, but the English created the famine', he was revisiting history to support his nationalist position. Marxists turn to the land question as evidence of class conflict. An appreciation of history is essential if one is to make an informed judgement about the solidity of such ideas. Once again, Lee states it well, arguing that 'the modern Irish, contrary to popular impression, have little sense of history. What they have is a sense of grievance, which they choose to dignify by christening it history.' He concludes that 'it is central to my argument that the Irish of the late twentieth century have still to learn how to learn from their recent history'. Although written only a few years ago, this view may already be outdated, prey to what F.S.L. Lyons refers to as the dilemma of the contemporary historian – recent events may still be too close in time to allow for enough historical perspective.

History instructs policy. Ireland has tried laissez-faire (1815–45); import substitution (1930–58); export promotion with foreign direct investment (1958–80). It has had budgetary discipline and chronic deficits, fixed exchange rates and floating, price controls, incomes policies, free trade zones, and public and private enterprise. Out of this varied experience there are lessons. While, in Santayana's famous words, 'those who ignore history are condemned to repeat it', the study of history is not merely to avoid making mistakes, but also to learn what works well and merits copying. The Irish experience is of particular interest to most Less Developed Countries, which are typically small open economies with a colonial past. Ireland in the twentieth century was a tardy bloomer, and a major theme of this chapter, indeed of this book, is to try to understand why.

The main focus of this chapter is on how Ireland has developed economically. Crotty defines such development as 'a situation where (a) more people are better off than formerly and (b) fewer people are as badly off'. By this yardstick it is necessary to look at population growth, since an economy whose development is accompanied by massive emigration has in some sense failed. This parallels the suggestion of the 1948 Emigration Commission, which proposed that 'a steadily increasing population should occupy a high place among the criteria by which the success of national policy should be judged'.

Economic development also requires that incomes rise (growth), including, or especially, those of the least well off (equality), and this is presumably facilitated by an efficient use of resources (notably full employment).

The starting point, arbitrarily chosen, is 1690, with the consolidation of the Protestant ascendancy. The subsequent years are divided into sub-periods – growth and early industrialisation during 1690 to 1815, rural crisis between 1815 and 1850, the population decline that accompanied increasing prosperity from 1850 to 1921, and the intermittent economic development between independence and about 1960, when the story of modern Irish economic growth begins – as discussed in more detail in Chapter 7.

2 FROM THE BATTLE OF THE BOYNE TO 1815

Eighteenth Century
At the time of the Battle of the Boyne the Irish economy was predominantly rural, although it was no longer a woodland society. Population stood at a little under two million, roughly double the level of a century before, and was growing at a historically high rate of at least half a per cent per year. With the spread of population the forest cover was rapidly disappearing, giving way to both grazing and tillage. The largest town, Dublin, had about 60,000 inhabitants.

The country was an important exporter, especially of grain, beef, butter, wool and, to a lesser extent, linen. Presaging the situation of three centuries later, almost half of all exports went to Continental Europe, notably to France. Earnings from these exports were spent on items such as coal and tobacco, and a surplus on current account amounting to perhaps 10 per cent of exports allowed for the remittance of rents to absentee landlords. Petty, visiting the country in 1672, commented on the large number of people who rode horses, and the high standard of clothing relative to France and most of Europe. He also noted the shabbiness of the houses, of which he reckoned only a fifth had chimneys. The implication was that Ireland was not significantly poorer, and was possibly better off, than most of Continental Europe at that time, although less affluent than most of England.

Income was distributed unevenly. Land was owned by perhaps 10,000 landlords, and six-sevenths of the land was held by Protestants. Much of this was let out to farmers, who in turn frequently sublet small plots to cottiers, or hired casual labour. By one estimate, a little over half of the population constituted a rural proletariat, with minimal access to land and close to the margin of subsistence. The potato had been introduced early in the seventeenth century, but was only an important part of the diet of the poor, although its spread allowed for rapid population growth throughout the eighteenth century.

Growth and Structural Change
The essential features of economic growth during the period 1690–1815 were a rapid recovery from the war, a period of relative stagnation (1700–20), twenty-five years of crisis that included two famines (1720–45), and a long wave of sustained and relatively rapid economic growth (1745–1815). The evidence for

these is indirect, since few economic statistics were collected at the time, but trade data show a steady increase in exports, with relatively rapid growth between 1740 (£1.2 million) and 1816 (£7.08 million). The structure of exports changed, as shipments of cattle and sheep gave way to beef, butter, grain, and linen.

These changes were driven in part by policy. In 1667 the Cattle Act excluded Irish cattle, sheep, beef, and pork from England. The country responded by exporting wool rather than sheep, and by searching for new markets for meat, notably the important provision trade, serving transatlantic ships and the West Indies, and the extensive French market. It also shifted resources from dry cattle to dairying, and butter exports grew rapidly. This process was speeded by the Woollen Acts, passed in 1699, which prohibited the export of wool from Ireland or England to other countries, and imposed a stiff duty on Irish wool entering England. More positively, the granting of duty-free access to England for linen helped that industry.

The significance of English laws for Irish economic growth is a matter of controversy. Writers in the nationalist vein have stressed the ways in which English law handicapped Irish growth, for instance by hampering the development of the wool industry. However, Cullen has argued that the negative effects were minimal, as producers shifted rapidly and effectively into new lines of production.

The changes in the structure of production during the eighteenth century also occurred in response to an increase in the relative price of agricultural commodities, especially grain. Increasing urbanisation in Britain raised the demand for food, and Ireland was favoured as a source of supply during the Napoleonic wars. The most important effect of this improvement in Ireland's terms of trade (price of exports relative to imports) was to raise the incomes of farmers. Ireland continued to export grain until the late 1860s, when the falling costs of shipping, coupled with the opening up of the American mid-west, brought cheaper grain to Europe.

Agricultural structure was also influenced by the diffusion of the potato. An acre of potatoes could support twice as many people as an acre of grain. Moreover, potato cultivation does not reduce soil fertility, and potatoes contain substantial amounts of protein and essential minerals. Cullen argues that as the eighteenth century progressed, cottiers increasingly ate potatoes instead of butter or oats, and sold these instead, using their earnings to buy other goods; thus the shift towards the potato is seen as 'related to commercialisation and the urge to increase cash incomes … for luxuries'.

The expansion of potato cultivation contributed to the dramatic expansion of Ireland's population, from a little more than a million people in 1600 to over eight million by 1841. It was checked briefly by a severe famine in 1740–41, which was caused by a cold summer and led to as many as a quarter of a million deaths. But population growth accelerated after 1750: better nutrition reduced the death rate, and the availability of conacre may have contributed to a reduction in the marriage age. The population rose despite substantial emigration from the north-east, which began early in the eighteenth century and became self-sustaining, and may have been as high as 12,000 annually in the difficult years of the 1770s.

Industry
Industrial change was dominated by the rise of the linen industry, which Cullen calls 'perhaps the most remarkable instance in Europe of an export based advance in the eighteenth century'. From a low base in the 1690s linen exports rose rapidly, accounting for a quarter of all exports by 1731. The first linen weavers were mainly skilled immigrants, especially Huguenots who fled France after 1685. Duty-free access to the English market helped, and in 1711 the Irish Parliament set up the Linen Board to regulate the industry, spread information and subsidise projects. Based solidly in the rural areas, an elaborate network of merchants bought the raw linen and undertook the more capital-intensive activities of bleaching and finishing. By the early nineteenth century linen was increasingly spun and woven under the 'putting-out' system; cottiers would be provided with raw materials, and paid in cash for the amount they spun or wove.

Even as late as 1841 an astonishing one person in five stated their occupation as being in textiles, and most of these lived in rural areas. Fully a third of all counties reported in 1821 that more individuals were occupied in 'manufacture, trade and handicrafts' than in agriculture. It has been argued that this type of 'proto industrialisation' is usually a prelude to full (i.e. factory-based) industrialisation, fostering as it does entrepreneurial skills, monetisation of the economy and commercial links. In the Irish case no such evolution occurred, although it is not clear why.

Other industries also expanded and modernised, notably those based on the processing of agricultural products, such as brewing, flour milling, and distilling. After 1800 the cotton industry flourished, albeit relatively briefly.

It is important to realise that the Industrial Revolution did in fact come to Ireland, initially. The organisation of many industries was radically changed, with the establishment of breweries, textile factories and glass works large enough to reap economies of scale. At first these factories were located where water power was available, but steam power was introduced early too. In the eighteenth century the road network was greatly improved and expanded, at first by private turnpikes and later by local government (the 'Grand Juries'). The first canals were built.

By 1785 Pitt and others saw Ireland as a viable competitor to English industry. But by 1800 this was not the view in Ireland, and it is ironic that the areas that most favoured union were Cork and the south, with their strong agricultural base; opposition was strongest in Dublin and the north.

Distribution of Income and Wealth
The benefits of economic growth in the late eighteenth century were not spread equally. The most evident rift was that between landowners and the large rural proletariat. Rents of a third of the gross output were probably normal. In 1687

Petty estimated rent payments at £1.2 million, of which £0.1 million was remitted to absentee landlords abroad. Rents thus came to approximately double the level of exports, or almost as much as a quarter of national income. It was this surplus, and tithes paid to the Church of Ireland, that financed the magnificent country houses, churches, Dublin squares, university buildings, paintings and follies that stand as monuments to the eighteenth century.

Most farmers were tenants of large landlords, and in turn rented out land to cottiers. Frequently such plots were confined to conacre (potato land), whose quality improved as they were planted in potatoes. Cottiers also performed work for the farmers to which they were attached. Labourers did not have even the security implied by access to a plot of land. The position of these groups did not improve in the fifty years prior to 1745. There then appears to have been a period of rising real wages, which probably stopped in the 1770s, and may never have resumed.

A second divide was between Catholic and Protestant. The Penal Laws placed restrictions on the right of Catholics to purchase land, to worship, to run schools, to vote, to take public office, to enter the professions, to take long leases and to bequeath property. Barred from the professions and politics, able Catholics often turned their energies towards commerce, and the expansion of trade helped create a significant Catholic middle class. By 1800 the wealthiest Dubliner was Edward Byrne, a Catholic businessman. Presbyterians and Quakers, faced with similar restrictions, also turned to commerce and industry, with some success. Over time most of the restrictions were removed or fell into disuse, and by 1793 Catholics could vote and attend Trinity College, but could not stand for office or fill certain government positions. At times the friction boiled over, as reflected in the strong sectarian component of the insurrection of 1798.

The third divide was between town and country. Dublin grew to be the second town of the UK by 1800, with a population of about 200,000. Cork, basing its role on the profitable provision trade, had 80,000 inhabitants, or approximately the same population as a century later. Third came Limerick, with a population of 20,000; Belfast was still a minor town. That the country was able to support such a significant urban population, and to export increasing quantities of food, reflected a growing agricultural surplus and rising agricultural productivity.

3 FROM 1815 TO INDEPENDENCE

1815 to 1850

The period 1815 to 1850 was one of rural crisis, culminating in the disaster of the Famine. The crisis was reflected in rising emigration. This was also the period when Ireland most clearly failed to participate in the Industrial Revolution that was then in full spate in Britain.

The census of 1841 enumerated 8.2 million people in Ireland, a higher level than any measured before or since, and over half the level of Britain. Since 1750 the population had risen at an average rate of 1.3 per cent per year, which was well above the annual rates recorded in England (+1 per cent) or France (+0.4 per cent).

Yet by the 1830s the growth rate had fallen to 0.6 per cent, due almost entirely to massive emigration, mainly to North America; these emigrants accounted for a third of the free transatlantic migration of the period. Without emigration, the pre-Famine population would have grown at a rapid 1.7 per cent per annum, due in part to a very high rate of marital fertility. Life expectancy at birth was 37–38 years, lower than in Britain or Scandinavia, but higher than in most of the rest of Europe.

Living Standards

On the eve of the Famine, Ireland was one of the poorest countries in Europe, as the comparative figures in Table 1.1 show. Per capita income was about 40 per cent of the British level, and contemporary visitors were particularly struck by the shabbiness of clothing and the poor state of rural houses.

Yet if the country was poor, it was also well fed, on grain, potatoes and dairy products. Peter Solar estimates that in the early 1840s potatoes and grain alone provided a substantial 2,500 calories per person for direct consumption, two-thirds of it from potatoes. Observers at the time generally thought that the Irish were healthy and strong; they grew taller than the typical Englishman or Belgian. Also compensating for low incomes was the wide availability of cheap fuel, in the form of peat.

Table 1.1

Real Product Per Capita (UK=100)

	(1) 1830	(2) 1913	(3) 1950	(4) 1992	Population growth (%) 1919–92
UK	100	100	100	100	31[1]
Ireland (South)	40[2]	53[3]	51	73	13
Ireland (North)		58	68		27[5]
USA	65	119	170	142	
Denmark	61	80	99	112	57
Finland	51	47	66	96	60
Greece	39[4]	26	27	52	109
Italy	65	49	53	102	60
Portugal	68	22	23	61	54
EU-15			69	102	

Sources: Adapted by the author from K. Kennedy, T. Giblin and D. McHugh, *The Economic Development of Ireland in the Twentieth Century,* Routledge, London 1988, pp.14–15; J. Lee, *Ireland 1912–1985,* Cambridge University Press, Cambridge 1989; and R. Summers and A. Heston, *Penn World Tables Version 5.1,* National Bureau of Economic Research, Cambridge MA 1995.

[1] GB only. [2] 1841, all Ireland. [3] 1926. [4] 1841. [5] 1984.

Industry and Agriculture

It has become common to consider the 1815–50 period as one of 'deindustrialisation', during which the importance of industry in the economy fell. This is only partly correct. For the island as a whole industrial output appears to have increased. Large-scale and more efficient production methods were applied to milling, brewing, shipbuilding, rope making, and the manufacture of linen, iron, paper and glass; the road system was improved and reached a good standard; banks were organised along joint stock lines. But rural industry declined. Thus, for instance, while in 1829 Bandon boasted over 1,500 handloom weavers, by 1839 the number had shrunk to 150.

The first cause of rural deindustrialisation was that the woollen and cotton industries wilted in the face of competition from Britain. This prompted Karl Marx to write, 'what the Irish need is … protective tariffs against England'. On the other hand Ireland was not denuded of purchasing power or exports, for otherwise it could not have afforded to buy British textiles.

A second blow to rural industry was the invention of a method for mechanically spinning flax, which made hand spinning redundant. It also led to a concentration of the linen industry in the north-east. The weaving of linen was still done by hand, and was boosted by the development. In 1841 Armagh was the most densely populated county in Ireland, testimony to the importance of cottage-based textiles as a source of income.

Despite the rapid fall in prices after 1815, agricultural exports continued to rise, notably livestock and butter and, most dramatically, grain and flour. By the 1830s Ireland exported enough grain to feed about two million people annually, testimony to the dynamism of the agricultural sector, which increasingly used new technologies such as improved seeds, crop rotations, better ploughs, and carts.

The Famine

The most traumatic event of the period was the Famine. After a wet summer, blight arrived in September 1845 and spread over almost half the country, especially the east. Famine was largely avoided at first, thanks largely to adequate government relief. But the potato crop failed completely in 1846 and by December about half a million people were working on relief works, at which stage they were ended. The winter was harsh. By August 1847 an estimated three million people were being supported by soup kitchens, including almost three-quarters of the population of some western counties. The 1847 harvest was not severely harmed, but it was small because a lack of seed. The blight returned in 1848, and in 1849 over 900,000 people were in workhouses at some time or another. After 1847 the responsibility for supporting the poor had increasingly been shifted from the government to the local landowners who, by and large, did not have sufficient resources to cope. Noting that a few years later Britain spent £69 million on the (futile) Crimean war, Mokyr argues that for half this sum 'there is no doubt that Britain could have saved Ireland'. It is also unlikely that an independent Ireland, with a GNP of £85 million, could have saved itself without outside support.

As a direct result of the Famine about one million people died, representing an excess mortality of about 3 per cent per annum during the famine years (and 4 per cent in the north-western counties); this was well above the excess mortality rates seen in the Netherlands (2 per cent) or Belgium (1 per cent), but comparable to the situation in the Scottish highlands. Three-fifths of those who died were young (under 10) or old (over 60), and labourers and small farmers were hit most severely. These unequal effects have led Cullen to argue, controversially, that 'the Famine was less a national disaster than a social and regional one'.

In the course of the Famine, the output of potatoes fell by about three-quarters, the use of potatoes for animal fodder ceased, and food imports rose very rapidly. As a result the amount of calories available for direct consumption barely fell, on a per capita basis. This gives credence to Amartya Sen's contention that famines are rarely caused by an absolute lack of food, but rather by a change in the food entitlements of major groups in society. So, for instance, labourers were unable to find employment when blight reduced the need for harvesting and planting potatoes; without income they could not buy food, and so became destitute.

Distribution

Pre-Famine Ireland probably had a 'very unequal distribution of income by West European standards'. According to the 1841 census, 63 per cent of the population had access to less than five acres of land, or were 'without capital, in either money, land or acquired knowledge'. Just 3 per cent were professionals and rentiers, and these included the approximately 10,000 proprietors, or 0.12 per cent of the population, who owned at least 100 acres.

Rent, including payments in kind, accounted for about £15 million, or almost a fifth of the national income of £80 million. Presumably the bulk of this rent accrued to the wealthiest 3 per cent or so of the population, implying a very great degree of income inequality. Rough calculations suggest that this group probably had per capita incomes averaging over £100 per annum, compared to a national average of £10, and an estimated £4 for poor households.

By 1845 a rudimentary welfare structure was in place, with the completion of 130 workhouses having a total capacity of 100,000. In practice the numbers living in the workhouses rarely exceeded 40,000, except during the Famine.

There is no shortage of hypotheses as to why Ireland remained poor, and hence uniquely vulnerable by European standards to the chance failure of the potato crop. Thomas Malthus, writing in 1817, considered that population growth was running ahead of food production; however, the more densely settled countries were not necessarily the poorest ones. Other writers blamed the insecurity of tenancy for low agricultural investment, although it is not clear how insecure tenancies really were. Some have pointed to agrarian violence, or the lack of coal deposits, or inadequate financial capital, or insufficient human resources (especially entrepreneurs) as barriers to economic development. None of these explanations is waterproof, and Ó Gráda wrote recently that 'exactly why comparative advantage dictated industrial decline for Ireland is still unclear'.

Fewer but Richer: 1850 to 1921

The seventy years following the Famine witnessed enormous changes in Irish society and saw the emergence of the modern economy. Over this period per capita income more than doubled and came closer to the British level, while the population fell by a third. A rural middle class emerged, replacing the landlords and squeezing out the rural labourers. Within agriculture tillage declined, and the production of dry cattle increased. The north-east became industrialised.

The dominant demographic fact of the period is that population declined, from 6.6 million in 1851 to 4.2 million by 1926. Without emigration the population would have risen, by about 1 per cent annually in the 1860s, and by 0.5 per cent annually at the turn of the century, a decline largely explained by a falling marriage rate. Almost 2 per cent of the population left annually in the 1850s; the pace slowed markedly to less than 1 per cent after 1900. The early emigrants were drawn from all areas of the country, but in later years the bulk of the emigrants came from the poorer, mainly western, districts. Over the period 1820 to 1945 an estimated 4.5 million Irish people emigrated to the USA, comparable in magnitude to the flows from Italy, Austria and Britain.

Living Standards

Astonishingly, between 1840 and 1913 per capita incomes in Ireland rose at 1.6 per cent per year, faster than any other country in Europe. Where Irish incomes averaged 40 per cent of the British level in 1840, this proportion had risen to 60 per cent by 1913. During this period Irish incomes came from behind, and then easily surpassed, those of Finland, Italy and Portugal.

Part of the explanation is statistical. The Famine, and subsequent high levels of emigration, removed a disproportionate number of the very poor; even if those who remained experienced no increase in their incomes, average income would have been higher than before. The poor were more likely to leave because the gap between Irish and foreign wages was greatest for unskilled labour. In 1844 the wages paid to a skilled builder in Dublin were 14 per cent *higher* than in London, but the wages paid to an unskilled building labourer were 36 per cent lower. A comparable gap persisted until at least World War I.

Incomes also rose because of dramatic increases in output per worker. The north-east became highly industrialised; in the rest of the country agricultural productivity rose rapidly. Almost all of the expansion of the modern industrial sector was in the north-east. While linen output increased slowly, it was increasingly concentrated in factories in Belfast and the Lagan valley: between 1850 and 1875 employment in linen mills and factories rose from 21,000 to 60,000 as power weaving replace the cottage industry. The manufacture of boilers and textile equipment needed in the mills helped diversify the industrial base; it also provided the skills and infrastructure that were important for the growth of shipbuilding. Harland and Wolff, the celebrated firm that built the *Titanic*, grew from 500 workers in 1861 to 9,000 by 1900. The shipbuilding industry also provided an impetus for other upstream activities, including rope making, paint and engineering.

Benefiting from 'external economies of foreign trade' – regular trade links with markets and suppliers, and a financial system geared towards supporting such links – Belfast rivalled Dublin in size by 1901, when it had about 400,000 inhabitants. Londonderry became the centre of an important shirt-making industry, employing 18,000 full-time workers and a further 80,000 cottage workers at its height in 1902.

By 1907, industrial activity in Ireland as a whole employed a fifth of the workforce, making the country at least as industrialised as Italy, Spain and Portugal. Half of all industrial output was exported, Ireland had a worldwide reputation in linen, shipbuilding, distilling, brewing and biscuits, and the volume of trade per capita was higher than for Britain.

It is sometimes wondered why Ireland did not become even more industrialised, more like Clydeside than East Anglia. And, related to this question, why did the north-east industrialise while by and large the rest of the country did not? Put another way, why did Irish labour emigrate, rather than capital immigrate?

There was no lack of capital; indeed from the 1880s Irish residents were net lenders of capital to the rest of the world, investing in British government stock, railways and other ventures overseas. Irish banks may have been cautious about lending, but in this they were no different from their counterparts in England, where industrial development was rapid. Nor is there evidence that skills were lacking. The primary school system expanded rapidly, enrolling 282,000 pupils in state-subsidised schools in 1841, and 1,072,000 by 1887. Whereas 53 per cent of the population was illiterate in 1841, this fraction had fallen to 25 per cent by 1881 and 16 per cent by 1901. Enterprise may have been lacking, although clearly not in the Lagan valley. The absence of coal probably had some effect, not because this raised costs of production unduly, but because coal itself was a big business; in 1914 a quarter of the British labour force was directly employed in coal or iron and steel. Ireland was next door to, and had free access to, the world's most affluent market.

Perhaps the explanation rests largely on chance, the idea that once Belfast grew as an industrial centre, accumulating skills, capital and infrastructure, it became an increasingly attractive location for further investment – an argument that might also be made about the unanticipated growth spurt of the 1990s.

Agriculture
Between 1861 and 1909 gross agricultural output rose by a quarter; since the rural population fell sharply, output per capita in agriculture more than doubled, a performance comparable to that of Denmark, which was considered to have done exceptionally well over the same period.

This growth masks an important change in the structure of agriculture, which shifted from crops to cattle in response to a fall in the price of grain relative to cattle. Tillage, including potatoes, shrank by two-thirds between 1845 and 1913. Farmers were not, as is sometimes supposed, slow to change or innovate. For instance, when circumstances demanded, they adopted the creamery system rapidly. Faced with changing prices and technology, wrote Hans Stahl, 'the response of the Irish agriculturalist ... was rational and normal'.

Distribution

Between 1870 and 1925 the landed proprietors 'surrendered their power and property' to an increasingly 'comfortable, educated, self confident rural bourgeoisie', thereby effecting one of the most extensive, and most peaceful, land reforms in history.

As late as 1870, 97 per cent of all land was owned by landlords who rented it out to others to farm. Just 750 families owned 50 per cent of the land in the country. About one landlord in seven lived outside Ireland, and another third lived outside their estates; the remaining half were not absentees. Two-fifths of all landlords were Catholic.

The agricultural crisis of the late 1870s meant lower agricultural prices and this, coupled with fixed rents, squeezed tenant farmers. By now they felt confident enough to agitate for the 'three Fs' – fair rent, fixity of tenure, and free sale of 'tenant right'. Michael Davitt's Land League forged a link with Parnell and the Irish Party in parliament. Their efforts resulted in the Land Act of 1881, which established land courts to hear rent appeals. The courts reduced rents by an average of about 20 per cent, and later courts reduced rents by about another 20 per cent after 1887. In a formal sense this diluted the power of the landlord – Moody refers to it as 'dual ownership' – although it is noteworthy that during the same period real rents fell by comparable amounts in England.

Further efforts prompted legislation that provided tenants with government loans with which to purchase their land, including the Ashbourne Act of 1885, and the Wyndham Act of 1903, and paid 12 per cent bonuses to landlords who sold their entire estates. The result was that 'by 1917 almost two-thirds of the tenants had acquired their holdings'.

With rural depopulation, land holdings increased in size. The number of cottiers working less than five acres fell from 300,000 in 1845 to 62,000 by 1910. The same period saw the 'virtual disappearance of the hired labourer from Irish agriculture', as the number of 'farm servants and labourers' fell from 1.3 million in 1841 to 0.3 million in 1911.

The distribution of income can be considered in other dimensions too. Thus, for instance, Protestants maintained their share of national income. This largely reflected the growth of the industrial north-east, which was dominated by Protestant interests, and the fact that Catholics were more likely to emigrate (and more died in the Famine). Catholics did come to fill an increasing proportion of government and professional jobs, although not in proportion to their numbers. The Catholic Church itself grew rapidly, with a spate of church building between 1860 and 1900, and churchgoing became much more common. The number of Catholic priests, nuns and other religious rose from almost 5,000 in 1850 to over 14,000 by 1900; this made it one of the fastest growing professions during this period.

The small towns stagnated, and so did Dublin until late in the century. In contrast to the rest of the country Belfast grew rapidly. The zenith of its prosperity came during and immediately after World War I, with a boom in shipbuilding and engineering; as David Johnson put it, 'in economic terms the last years of the Union were the best ones'.

4 FROM INDEPENDENCE TO 1960

When it finally achieved independence, the Irish Free State could count some important assets. It had an extensive system of communications, a developed banking system, a vigorous wholesale and retail network, an efficient and honest administration, universal literacy, a large stock of houses, schools and hospitals, 3.1 million people, and enormous external assets. By the standards of most of the world's countries Ireland was well off indeed.

On the other hand, the new state faced some serious problems. It had to establish a new government, the civil war had been destructive and had helped prompt 88,000 people to emigrate in 1921–22, the dependency ratio was high – Catholics marrying before 1916 had an average of 6.0 children per family – and the post-war boom had run its course. We now document its subsequent achievements, and evaluate its performance as an independent country.

1921 to 1932: Agriculture First

The growth model pursued by the Cumann na nGaedheal government was based on the premise that what was good for agriculture was good for the country. Patrick Hogan, the Minister for Agriculture, saw the policy as one of 'helping the farmer who helped himself and letting the rest go to the devil'. This emphasis on agriculture was not surprising. In 1926 agriculture generated 32 per cent of GDP and provided 54 per cent of all employment. The government relied heavily on the support of the larger farmers. The expectation was that agricultural growth would not only raise the demand for goods and services from the rest of the economy but would also provide more inputs on which to base a more substantial processing sector. The three major industrial exporting sectors at the time – brewing, distilling and biscuit making – were all closely linked with agriculture.

The essential elements of the policy, which has come to be known as the 'treasury view', were free trade, low taxes and government spending, modest direct state intervention in industry and agriculture, and parity with sterling. Free trade was seen as essential if the cost of farm inputs was to be kept low.

The support for free trade was perhaps surprising given that Griffith had argued that one of the main benefits of independence would be that the country could grant protection to infant industries. On the other hand, the government was cautious about making such changes, perhaps for fear of upsetting the financial community, whose opposition to protection was well known, or perhaps because they were, in the words of Kevin O'Higgins, 'the most conservative revolutionaries in history'. The government sought to deflect pressure for stiffer protection by establishing the Tariff Commission in 1926, and appointing members who were, in the main, in favour of free trade. The onus of proof was on any industry wishing to be protected, and the Commission moved slowly on requests, granting few tariffs other than for rosary beads and margarine.

Government spending was kept low, the budget was essentially balanced, and revenues came to just 15 per cent of GNP in 1931. This was a remarkable achievement, given that military spending had trebled during the civil war. One serious consequence was that welfare spending remained low, and in the absence of major government assistance, housing for the less well off remained scarce.

Ideologically the government did not favour taking a very active role in promoting economic development. Despite this it intervened pragmatically in several ways. The Department of Agriculture was greatly expanded, although the impact of this on agricultural output has been questioned. The Congested Districts Board was replaced by the Land Commission, which transferred 3.6 million acres, involving 117,000 holdings, to annuity-paying freeholders during the period 1923–37. Laws were passed to improve the quality of agricultural output, by regulating the marketing of dairy produce (1924) and improving the quality of livestock breeding by registering bulls (1925). The Agricultural Credit Corporation (ACC) was set up to provide credit to farmers. The government subsidised a Belgian company to establish a sugar factory in Carlow, and provided incentives to grow sugar beet.

A major innovation was the establishment of the Electricity Supply Board (ESB) in 1927. This, along with the ACC, represented the first of the state-sponsored bodies (SSBs) that were established during the ensuing years. The ESB successfully undertook the Ardnacrusha hydroelectric scheme, which boosted both its and the country's prestige, and was the most visible accomplishment of the first decade of independence. In due course SSBs were set up in many fields, including air, train and bus transport, industrial credit, insurance, peat development, trade promotion and industrial development. By the early 1960s, when the most important of these bodies had been established, they employed about 50,000 people, representing about 7 per cent of the total labour force. The SSBs were not the outgrowth of any particular ideology, but were rather 'individual responses to specific situations'. This, along with their ability to attract good managers, may help explain why they are generally considered to have been successful agents of economic development, especially in the first few decades after independence, when the private sector did not appear to be very enterprising.

Parity with sterling was the final ingredient in the development model pursued. Few countries at the time had floating exchange rates, and it seemed logical to peg the pound to sterling since 97 per cent of exports went to, and 76 per cent of imports came from, Britain. The Currency Act of 1927 established an Irish currency, fully backed by British sterling securities; until 1961 Irish banknotes were inscribed 'payable in London'. By linking the currency with sterling the Free State gave up the possibility of any independent monetary policy, in return for greater predictability in trade with Britain.

The economic policy of the Free State in the 1920s was comparable with the typical prescription given by the World Bank to Less Developed Countries in the 1980s: get the prices right, using world prices as a guide; reduce budget deficits; keep government 'interference' to a minimum; and follow a conservative monetary policy. Did it work?

The simple answer is 'in the circumstances, yes in most respects, eventually'. The young nation got off to a rocky start. Between 1920 and 1924 agricultural prices fell 44 per cent; the civil war, which only ended in 1923, arrested investment; after independence, a significant proportion of the skilled labour force left; and the recession in the UK after sterling's return to the gold standard in 1925 reduced the demand for Irish exports. However, between 1926 and 1931 real per capita GNP rose about 3 per cent per annum; exports rose 20 per cent, reaching a peak of 35 per cent of GNP in 1929, and a volume that was not exceeded until 1960. Industrial employment rose by 8 per cent.

1932 to 1939: Self-Sufficiency, Economic War, and Depression

Fianna Fáil came to power in early 1932, with an economic policy that differed in two fundamental ways from its predecessor; it was ideologically committed to a policy of greater economic self-sufficiency, and it reneged on paying land annuities to Britain. It also came to power during the darkest hour of the Depression, a time when most countries were erecting tariff barriers.

Why self-sufficiency? The case for limiting economic interactions with the rest of the world is more cultural than economic, but it attracted some intellectual support. John Maynard Keynes, lecturing at UCD in April 1933, said, 'I sympathize with those who would minimize ... economic entanglement between nations. ... But let goods be homespun whenever it is reasonable and conveniently possible'. Perhaps these oft-quoted remarks are out of context, for he went on to argue that only 'a very modest measure of self-sufficiency' would be feasible without 'a disastrous reduction in a standard of life which is already none too high'.

How self-sufficiency? The main instrument used was more and higher tariffs, which rose to a maximum of 45 per cent in 1936, dipping to 35 per cent by 1938. In Europe only Germany and Spain had higher levels by then; Irish tariffs were twice as high as in the USA, and 50 per cent higher than in the UK. They were introduced piecemeal and so formed an untidy pattern that, in FitzGerald's view, had 'no rational basis'; Meenan considers that they fell more heavily on finished goods, and so provided an incentive for domestic assembly using imported raw materials. The pursuit of self-sufficiency would justify indefinite tariff protection; in this it differs from the views of Griffith, who saw a role for temporary protection to encourage infant industries to take root.

Self-sufficiency was also pursued by introducing price supports for wheat, which was instrumental in raising the acreage planted to wheat from 8,000 hectares in 1931 to 103,000 by 1936. Somewhat inconsistently, bounties were paid for exports of cattle, butter, bacon and other agricultural products in order to expand the volume of exports, and this resulted in a significant rise in the share of government spending in national income. To foster Irish involvement in industry the Control of Manufactures Act (1932) required majority Irish ownership, although in practice exceptions were usually granted upon request. The Industrial Credit Corporation was set up to lend to industry, and issued £6.5 million in its first four years of operation.

It is difficult to assess the effect of the policy of self-sufficiency because it became inextricably tangled with the effects of the economic war. Previous Irish governments had recognised an obligation to pay land annuities to Britain, to cover the cost of money lent under the various pre-independence land acts. These came to about £5 million annually, or about one-fifth of government spending and almost 4 per cent of GNP.

On coming to office in March 1932, de Valera refused to continue the annuities. In July Britain retaliated by imposing special duties, initially at 20 per cent and later at 40 per cent, on imports of livestock, dairy products and meat, and also imposed quotas, including halving the number of cattle permitted to enter the UK. The Free State countered with tariffs on British goods, including cement and coal – surprising choices for a country bent on industrialisation. After these escalations tempers cooled. Under the Cattle–Coal pacts Irish cattle had easier access to Britain, and Ireland agreed to buy British coal. Initially agreed for 1935, the pact was extended and renewed in 1936 and 1937, and the Anglo-Irish Trade Agreement ended the 'war', with Ireland agreeing to pay a lump sum of £10 million and Britain ceding control of the 'treaty ports'. Given that the capitalised value of the annuities was close to £100 million, this was considered a major diplomatic and economic victory for de Valera.

The combined effects of protection and the economic war were initially dramatic. Industrial output rose 40 per cent between 1931 and 1936. Population stabilised, standing at 2.93 million in 1931 and 2.94 million in 1938 – the first period since the Famine when there had not been a substantial decline – but unemployment soared, almost quintupling between 1931 and 1934 to about 14 per cent of the labour force by 1935. In large part this reflected reduced opportunities to emigrate to the United States. Despite rapid industrial growth, agriculture stagnated, as exports fell sharply. Where exports and imports together amounted to 75 per cent of GNP in 1926, they constituted 54 per cent in 1938, although this decline pales beside the two-thirds reduction in trade which the USA faced in the early 1930s. The existing manufacturing export industries also suffered some decline. By 1936 import-substituting industrialisation had run its course, and industrial output only rose a further 4.5 per cent between 1936 and 1938. It is widely accepted that the slow growth of the economy in the 1950s was largely because of the inefficiency of the industrial sector which developed during the 1930s.

One other event of this period merits a brief discussion. With the onset of the Depression, Britain erected tariffs on a wide range of items, including beer. This prompted Guinness to establish a brewery at Park Royal near London. Beer had been Ireland's single most important industrial export, and brewing had accounted for 30 per cent of manufacturing value added in 1926. Once the Park Royal brewery was established, there was little incentive to return to the earlier pattern of concentrating Guinness's production in Dublin. In this case British tariffs led to the establishment of an efficient new factory in England, at the expense of Ireland. It is possible that some Irish tariffs did the same in the other direction, although with a smaller internal market it is less likely to have been common. Using tariffs to promote investment and industry in this way has come under increasing scrutiny by economists in recent years, under the rubric of strategic trade policy.

Historical Debate: Was the Drive for Self-Sufficiency a Mistake?

Joseph Johnston, writing in 1951, argued that but for the economic war 'our real National Income might well have been 25 per cent more in 1939 than it actually was and 25 per cent more today that it actually is … The process of cutting off one's nose to spite one's face is sometimes good politics, but always bad economics.' He might have noted that between 1931 and 1938 Irish GNP rose about 10 per cent, compared to 18 per cent in less protectionist Britain. He might also have questioned how many industrial jobs were really created, noting that while the 1936 census enumerated 199,000 individuals 'involved in industrial occupations', this was only 11,000 higher than the number enumerated in 1926.

Johnston's estimate of a 25 per cent decline has been sharply questioned. Recent research, which tries to recreate what might plausibly have happened in the absence of tariffs, by constructing a computable general equilibrium counterfactual, suggests that the total cost of protection might have been 5 per cent of GNP per year, or £7–8 million annually during the late 1930s, of which perhaps two-thirds is attributable to the economic war. Against this, Ireland gained the treaty ports and received a £90 million write-off on its foreign debt. The expansion of the industrial sector may have provided experience in business management, which was valuable in later years.

Having built high tariff barriers, Ireland was slow to reduce them later, and the average rate of effective protection of manufacturing was still an exceptionally high 80 per cent in 1966. If some of the economic sluggishness of the 1950s was the result, then the protection of the 1930s may appear more damaging; perhaps had Johnston been writing in 1960 he would have been closer to the truth. One may also wonder whether a policy of more selective protection, perhaps along the lines favoured by Taiwan or South Korea, might not have proved more valuable.

1939 to 1950: The War and Rebound

The most important economic result of World War II was that it opened a wide gap between Northern Ireland and the Republic. Between 1938 and 1947 national income grew just 14 per cent, compared to 47 per cent in the UK and 84 per cent in Northern Ireland. Where incomes, north and south, were broadly comparable before the war, by 1947 incomes per head in the Republic had fallen to about 40 per cent of the British level, while in the north they had risen to close to 70 per cent. Why did the south perform so poorly?

Between 1938 and 1943 the volume of exports fell by a half, and imports fell even more. During this period industrial output fell 27 per cent, and industrial employment dropped from 167,000 to 144,000. The main reason was the scarcity of raw material inputs for industry, and the shortage of shipping capacity. Completely reliant on outside shippers until 1941, the government founded Irish Shipping, and moved rapidly to purchase ships, which soon proved their worth. Because of the difficulty of obtaining imports, the country built up significant foreign reserves, and by 1946 residents had external assets totalling £260 million, approximately equivalent to GNP in that year.

The total value of agricultural output fell during the war period, but net agricultural output (i.e. total output less the cost of non-labour inputs), rose, by 17 per cent between 1938–39 and 1945. This reflected the drastic fall in the use of fertiliser and other inputs, and is generally acknowledged to have significantly exhausted the soil. The structure of agriculture changed, as the area planted in grain and potatoes almost doubled, due in part to the introduction of compulsory tillage.

During the war real GNP fell, especially initially. Living standards fell further as households, unable to find the goods they wanted, were obliged to save more. The stock of capital in industry became run down. With emigration to the USA blocked, population rose, by 18,000 between 1938 and 1946. The unemployment rate stood at over 15 per cent in 1939 and 1940, but declined thereafter to a little over 10 per cent in 1945. The decrease was due to a sharp rise in migration to Britain, reaching near record levels in 1942, as people left to work in factories and enrol in the armed forces.

The war was followed by a rebound, and per capita real GDP rose by 4.1 per cent per annum between 1944 and 1950. This occurred despite the fact that agricultural output stagnated, with gross volume falling between 1945 and 1950, and net output shrinking by 5 per cent. Not surprisingly, 70,000 people left agriculture between 1946 and 1951; yet during this period the unemployment rate fell and population increased. Much of this is attributable to the expansion of industrial production, which more than doubled during the same period.

Government spending rose rapidly in the early war years as the army was increased from 7,500 to 38,000 men. After the war, government spending grew far faster than national income, increasing its share of GNP from 23 per cent in 1945 to 39 per cent by 1951. In large measure this increase occurred as Ireland sought to emulate the 'social investment' of the Labour Party in Britain, by expanding welfare spending.

1950 to 1958: Decline or Rebirth?
It had become standard to consider the 1950s as a period of stagnation and failure. This is a half truth. Between 1951 and 1958 GDP rose by less than 1 per cent per

year. Employment fell by 12 per cent, and the unemployment rate rose. Irish GDP per capita fell from 75 per cent to 60 per cent of the EU average. Half a million people emigrated. Yet between 1950 and 1960 real product per capita grew at 2.2 per cent per year, possibly the fastest rate recorded up to then, and industrial output expanded at 2.8 per cent per annum. Output per farmer grew at a respectable 3.4 per cent per year. Rural electrification spread, and the housing stock improved appreciably. Was the glass half full or half empty?

The key to understanding the 1950s is to note that this was the decade when Europe rebounded; Ireland's performance looks disappointing only by the standards of neighbouring countries, not by historical standards. Much of the emigration reflected the lure of improving wages elsewhere, notably in Britain.

Why did output not grow faster in the 1950s? FitzGerald believes that the key problem was a 'failure to re-orientate industry to export markets', considering that 'the naïveté of the philosophy that underlay the whole protection policy was not exposed until the process of introducing protection had come to an end'. By the 1950s Irish industry was supplying as much of the domestic market as it reasonably could, and in order to expand had no option but to seek markets overseas. But since much of the industrial sector could only survive because of protection, it was too inefficient to export successfully, although it was certainly strong enough to lobby against any liberalisation.

To help provide incentives to industries to switch to exporting, export profits tax relief was provided in 1956, and in 1958 the Industrial Development Authority (IDA), which had been set up in 1949, was granted more powers to provide tax holidays for export-oriented companies. The Shannon Free Airport Development Company was set up in 1959.

One might better view the 1950s as a period of transition than as one of failure, much as it was in Taiwan and South Korea. It has been argued that the economy was in fact in the process of re-orienting itself towards export markets, but that any such change was bound to be slow. As J.J. McElligott put it in the 1920s, when warning of the dangers of protection, 'to revert to free trade from a protectionist regime is almost an economic impossibility'. Exports of manufactured goods rose quite rapidly, accounting for 6 per cent of all exports in 1950 but 17 per cent by 1960. Dramatic as this change was, the increase was from a very low base, and the export sector simply was not large enough to be a potent engine of growth.

An entirely different explanation comes from Kennedy and Dowling, who state baldly that 'the chief factor seems to us to be the failure to secure a satisfactory rate of expansion in aggregate demand', most notably unduly restrictive (in their view) fiscal policy in response to the balance of payment crises of 1951 and 1955. This argument provides an intellectual underpinning for the highly expansionary, and ultimately disastrous, fiscal policy experiment of the late 1970s and early 1980s.

Whatever the causes, the poor overall economic performance created a feeling of pessimism, and this in turn probably deterred investors. As T.K. Whitaker, then secretary of the Department of Finance, put it, 'the mood of despondency was palpable'. In 1958, at the request of the government, he wrote the report *Economic Development*, best remembered now for the optimistic note that it struck in pessimistic times. The report proposed that tariffs should be dismantled unless a clear infant industry case existed, favoured incentives to stimulate private industrial investment and proposed expanded spending on agriculture. On the other hand, it warned against the dampening effects of high taxes. With such measures, it suggested, GNP could grow 2 per cent annually, although it stressed that this was not a firm target. These measures were incorporated in the First Programme for Economic Expansion which appeared in November 1958, but generally not implemented.

Economic growth during the period of the first plan exceeded anyone's wildest expectations, reaching 4 per cent per annum instead of the anticipated 2 per cent. At the time much of this increase was attributed directly to the impact of the First Programme, and support for such indicative planning increased. The Second Programme, introduced in 1963 and designed to run to 1970, was far more detailed and ambitious, forecasting an annual increase in GNP of 4 per cent per annum; industry was to expand 50 per cent and exports 75 per cent during the plan period. When it appeared that these targets would not quite be met, the Second Programme was allowed to lapse. A Third Programme was produced, but quickly sank into oblivion, along with most of the enthusiasm for indicative planning.

5 FROM 1960 TO 1999

1960 to 1973: From Protection to Free Trade

Between 1960 and 1973 real output increased at 4.4 per cent per annum, the highest rate sustained until then. Immigration began. Per capita incomes rose by three-fifths, kept up with income growth elsewhere in Europe, and significantly outpaced growth in Britain or Northern Ireland.

This first wave of substantial economic growth has been largely attributed to the strategy of export-led growth that the government, heeding the recommendations of *Economic Development*, pursued; less publicised, but important nonetheless, were a notable improvement in the terms of trade (39 per cent better in 1973 than in 1957), expansionary fiscal policy, the boom in the nearby European economy, and the fact that solid institutional foundations had been laid in the 1950s.

The policy of export-led growth stood on two legs – trade liberalisation, and the attraction of foreign direct investment (see Chapter 8). Trade liberalisation called for reducing tariffs; these, by making inputs dearer and by drawing resources away from other sectors of the economy, had worked to inhibit exports. Foreign investment, it was hoped, would bring new skills to the country, and help raise the overall investment, and hence growth, rate.

Trade liberalisation was begun in the 1960s as Ireland unilaterally cut tariffs in 1963 and 1964, negotiated the Anglo-Irish Free Trade Area Agreement in 1965 and subscribed to the General Agreement on Tariffs and Trade (GATT) in 1967. These moves also prepared for eventual membership of the European Economic Community (EEC) as it was then called.

With a panoply of tax breaks and subsidies, Ireland successfully, although at considerable expense, induced foreign companies to set up branches in Ireland, and by 1974 new industry accounted for over 60 per cent of industrial output. The 10 per cent tax on profits in manufacturing also made the country something of a tax haven, although it did require at least a fig leaf of manufacturing presence.

The final thrust of government policy was wage restraint, viewed as necessary, especially with a fixed exchange rate, to help keep industrial costs at a competitive level. In the 1960s government efforts amounted to exhortation. In the 1970s wage bargaining was centralised, under the National Wage Agreements. Given the option of emigration, the scope for manoeuvre here was small. If real wages were pushed below the British level they would simply stimulate faster emigration, and so could not be sustained.

Into Europe: Trade, Investment and Subsidies

In 1973 Ireland, along with the UK and Denmark, joined the European Economic Community (EEC, but referred to here as EU).

Membership immediately led to a reduction in trade barriers. The EU was founded as a customs union, with low internal barriers to trade and a common set of external barriers. By joining, Ireland was committed to trading freely with the other member countries, and by 1977 all tariff barriers had been removed. Many of the remaining, less obvious, restraints on trade within the EU were dismantled as part of the effort to create a Single European Market. Officially these changes came into effect in 1992, although the full elimination of barriers remains a work in progress.

With lower trade barriers, it was recognised that some of Ireland's industry would wither under the competition, but it was also expected that Ireland would become a good platform from which companies from outside the European Community could serve the European market.

These expectations were met. While Irish exports amounted to 34 per cent of GDP in 1963, and 38 per cent in 1973, the proportion had risen to 94 per cent by 2002, one of the highest in the world (see Chapter 7). This burst of exports paralleled a similar increase in intra-EU trade that took place in the 1960s, and shows how even small reductions in the cost of trading can have a large impact on the volume of trade.

Membership of the EU also led to a net inflow under the Common Agricultural Policy (CAP), which subsidises farm prices. Higher farm prices help farmers at the expense of consumers, but as a net exporter of farm produce, Ireland was a net beneficiary (see Chapter 11).

Although about two-thirds of EU transfers to Ireland are farm-related, the remaining third consists mainly of transfers from the Structural Funds, including the Regional Development, Social and Cohesion Funds. In principle these funds might have added to investment and thereby boosted economic growth, but in practice they mainly appeared to have substituted for projects that the government would otherwise have had to finance; they thus made a more important contribution to living standards than to growth. Net receipts from the EU peaked at 6.5 per cent of GDP in 1991, and stood at 0.8 per cent of GDP in 2006.

1979 to 1986: Growth Interrupted

Between 1979 and 1986, per capita consumption in Ireland actually fell slightly and GDP rose very slowly. What went wrong?

Membership of the EU coincided with a fourfold increase in the price of oil (from $3 to $12 per barrel) that resulted from the first oil shock in late 1973; a sharp worldwide recession followed.

The government's response was thoroughly Keynesian. The higher price of oil meant that spending was diverted towards imports, thereby depressing aggregate demand for Irish goods and services. The solution adopted was to boost government current spending, and as a consequence the current budget deficit rose from 0.4 per cent of GDP in 1973 to 6.8 per cent by 1975. For a while the policy worked: despite a difficult international situation, GDP growth during the first six years of EU membership was robust.

Then came the mistake, the source of the failure of the fiscal experiment: successive governments were unwilling to reduce the budget deficit, and continued to borrow heavily, so the ratio of government debt to GDP rose from 52 per cent in 1973 to 129 per cent by 1987, by then easily the highest in the EU. By 1986 the cost of servicing this debt took up 94 per cent of all revenue from personal income tax (see Chapter 4). Although efforts were made to solve the problem by raising tax rates, especially in 1981 and 1983, these changes hardly increased tax revenue, suggesting that the country was close to its revenue-maximising tax rates. Much of the additional spending went to buy imports, and the current account deficit widened to an untenable 15 per cent by 1981. Partly as a result, the Irish pound was devalued four times within the European Monetary System (EMS) in the early 1980s. In 1986 an estimated IR£1,000 million of private capital left the country, anticipating a devaluation; the smart money was right, and the pound was devalued by 8 per cent in August.

In 1987 the Fianna Fáil government introduced a very tight budget, cutting the current budget deficit to 1.7 per cent of GDP through reductions in real government spending that made Margaret Thatcher's efforts look gentle. Capital spending was also sharply cut, especially on housing, and by 1992 the ratio of debt to GDP had fallen below 100 per cent.

The 1987 reform worked. Economic growth resumed, as confidence (and investors) returned, and exports boomed, thanks in part to the devaluation of 1986 and to continued wage restraint. But the lessons of the failed fiscal experiment are important and have been largely internalised: fiscal rectitude is important for long-term growth, and taxes cannot be pushed too high.

1979 to 1999: From Sterling to EMS to Euro

In 1979, in a move which was hailed at the time as farsighted, Ireland broke the link with sterling (which dated back to 1826) and joined the EMS. The reasoning was straightforward. Ireland had experienced inflation averaging 15 per cent between 1973 and 1979, necessarily the same rate as in Britain, and it was believed that the key to reducing the inflation rate was to uncouple the Irish pound from high-inflation sterling and attach it to the low-inflation EMS, which was dominated by the Deutschmark. Some also argued – correctly as it turned out – that sterling would appreciate with the development of North Sea oil, and that this would hurt Irish exports. Although over 40 per cent of exports still went to the UK in 1979, about a quarter went to the other EU countries and so a change in exchange regime was considered feasible.

The adjustment to the EMS was slow and rocky. In the early 1980s inflation actually fell faster in the UK, which stayed out of the EMS, than in Ireland. The slow reduction in Irish inflation towards German levels meant that the Irish pound became overvalued, and had to be devalued within the EMS. The standard explanation is that wage demands – which often respond to recent inflation – were slow to change, so wage increases continued to be too large to be consistent with very low inflation. The lesson here was clear: economic growth and macroeconomic stability can all too easily be undermined if wage increases get out of line.

By about 1990 Ireland could boast of low inflation, a tight budget, and a falling ratio of government debt to GDP, and it looked as if, after a decade of relative economic stagnation, the decision to join the EMS was finally paying off. Then in late 1992 the EMS fell apart. High interest rates in Germany, resulting from that country's need to finance reunification, caused the Deutschmark to appreciate. Sterling devalued, and the Irish pound ultimately followed, because 32 per cent of Irish exports still went to the UK, and in the absence of a devaluation, Irish competitiveness in the important British market would be too severely compromised.

After the collapse of the EMS, it became clear that a regime of 'fixed but flexible' exchange rates is an oxymoron. Without a viable middle way between floating exchange rates and a single currency, the EU opted for the latter. The schedule was set out in the Treaty of Maastricht, signed in 1992 and ratified the following year. Ireland easily met the criteria for graduating to the euro, and the exchange rate was locked at €0.787564 per Irish pound on 1 January 1999. Ireland, like the states of the USA, no longer has the option of an independent monetary policy. This is not a radical break from the past; an independent monetary policy was not possible when the Irish pound was linked with sterling, and was severely circumscribed during the period of the EMS.

The combination of macroeconomic stability and good access to the EU market – first under the Single Market Act, and then as a member of the euro zone

– contributed mightily to Irish economic development. By the mid-1990s, US companies favoured Ireland as a platform for supplying the European market, particularly in pharmaceuticals and information technology. By the time this wave of export-oriented labour-using investment subsided – about 2000 – Irish consumers were able to maintain their demand due in part to the cheap credit that arrived with the euro. This sparked a building boom that contributed to the robust expansion of output and employment until 2007. A fuller economic analysis of this period is left until Chapter 7.

6 CONCLUDING OBSERVATIONS

The significant events of Irish economic history have been marshalled to support a number of different interpretations.

Nationalists emphasise the ways in which the links between the Irish economy and Britain have worked to Ireland's detriment. Writers in this vein have stressed the damage caused by the plantations, the Navigation, Cattle and Woollen Acts, the solid growth during the years of Grattan's Parliament, the lowering of tariffs in the years after the Act of Union, the ineffectiveness of relief efforts during later years of the Famine, and the costs of Ireland's inability to protect its industry from British goods during the second half of the nineteenth century. This approach has typically been used to lead to the conclusion that Ireland would be better off economically with independence.

Support for the nationalist interpretation waxes and wanes with the performance of the economy of the Republic. When independence did not bring a dramatic improvement in growth, and when the import-substitution policy of the 1930s created an inefficient industrial base which stagnated in the 1950s, the advantages of independence came to be seen as less obvious, especially as Northern Ireland appeared to be prospering at the time. However, from 1960 to 1980, when growth in the Republic was faster, and dependence on the British market reduced, the nationalist view became respectable again despite, or perhaps because of, the dismantling of tariff protection.

Outside the Irish context, this view is comparable to the approach of *dependency theorists*, who emphasise the harmful results of links between peripheral areas and the major industrial powers. The main weaknesses of this approach is that it has tended to neglect the potentially beneficial effects of links with the metropolitan area, and has overestimated the ability of independent states to make wise decisions, as exemplified for instance by Ireland's disastrous fiscal experiment in the late 1970s.

Membership of the EU has not made the nationalist view completely obsolete, but it has been stripped of its anglophobic character. There remains space for a nationalism, or perhaps localism would be a better term, to counteract the tendencies of the EU to regulate from the centre what would be better done at a much lower level of government.

Marxists stress the role of the conflict between different classes within the country. Thus, for instance, the Famine and subsequent emigration swept away the greater part of the rural proletariat, paving the way for the emergence of a rural bourgeoisie, which in due course wrested control over land from the aristocracy and provided the leaders of a conservative independent state. In this view the labouring class, whether agricultural or industrial, never achieved enough strength to effect significant social or economic change, and the indigenous capitalist class failed in its mission of creating a dynamic industrial base, thereby forfeiting its right to the perquisites that it continues to enjoy. The conclusion most commonly drawn is that the state needs to take a more active role in filling this entrepreneurial function. Foreign investment by footloose companies is seen as conveying few benefits.

The Marxist view fails to explain why largely non-class conflicts, such as that in Northern Ireland, can persist. It typically overstates the ability of the state and public enterprises to create sustainable jobs; once this prop falls, it is not clear what prescription for economic growth remains.

In reaction against the weaknesses of the nationalist and Marxist interpretations, most recent writers have tended to view economic events as having a significant life of their own, being 'substantially independent of political and constitutional issues'. Hence the role of the Cattle Acts, or the Act of Union, or the replacement of tenant farmers by smallholders, are seen as minor. Economic actors are believed to redirect their energies fairly quickly, and seize the available opportunities. This perspective, epitomised in the large body of revisionist writings of Cullen, could be labelled the *classical economics approach*. In the hands of a new generation of economists this approach to history has become increasingly quantitative.

This view too has its faults, in that it can go too far in neglecting political events and institutional arrangements. In the words of Douglass North, 'institutional change shapes the way societies evolve through time and hence is the key to understanding historical change'. North originally believed that inefficient institutions would be weeded out over time, but in his more recent writings he is less sanguine about this prospect. The *institutional approach* complements rather than supplants the classical economics view, and we have drawn on these two perspectives in writing this chapter.

The most interesting lessons from Irish economic history are about growth strategies. Economic growth comes from a multitude of sources such as new technology, capital investment, education and training, land reclamation, enterprise, shifting prices, higher aggregate demand and chance. However, these are only the raw ingredients, and must be combined to sustain growth. It is easy to see these ingredients at work. The new technologies of potato growing, railways, power weaving and computers have all been influential. Capital spending is essential at all times, although it rarely needs to be above a fifth of GDP. Higher levels of education and improved training have boosted labour productivity. Chance brought the potato blight and two world wars. Land reclamation helped fend off famine in the early nineteenth century. Enterprise was at the heart of the introduction of shipbuilding in Belfast. A secular increase in wheat prices radically changed agriculture in the eighteenth century. Low aggregate demand reined in growth in the 1950s.

Recognising the role of these elements is important, but holds few lessons. The study of growth *strategies* is more illuminating. The policy of laissez faire need not guarantee growth, as experience from 1815 to 1850 demonstrates. Nor does a strategy of import substitution necessarily fare better, for while it may have been helpful in the short run in the 1930s, protection left a legacy of inefficient industry in the 1950s. An approach which favours agriculture-led development, such as followed by the Free State in the 1920s, may succeed in raising real incomes, but given the small size of the agricultural sector (5 per cent of GDP) it is no longer a realistic option. An industrialisation strategy based on attracting foreign capital also has some advantages, but is expensive to implement initially, and risks leaving a country more vulnerable to decisions outside its control.

As a practical matter Ireland has less and less room for pursuing independent economic policies. Fiscal restraint is needed because persistent expansionary fiscal policy does not work well in a small open economy, as the experiment of 1978–87 shows. With the euro in place, monetary policy is not an option. Industrial policy is increasingly circumscribed by the rules that have applied since 1993 to the Single European Market. Recognising the need for greater efficiency, the country has privatised or closed down several state-owned enterprises. Ireland now has only a little more autonomy than a typical state of the USA.

That leaves a narrower and more difficult field for local economic policy. The focus will have to be on the factors needed to maintain 'competitiveness' – what Michael Porter calls the 'microeconomic foundations of prosperity'. This includes bending to such tasks as gearing society to produce entrepreneurs, vitalising indigenous enterprise, providing adequate and appropriate education and training, evaluating public investment more thoroughly, introducing flexibility into the labour market, reducing the disincentives to do unskilled jobs, and fostering competition among firms. Affluence requires efficiency in the public arena – in the provision of services and the formulation and targeting of policy – in addition to efficiency by businesses.

Since wages in Ireland are closely linked with those in Britain (and, increasingly, the rest of Europe), once individuals have been equipped with education, economic policy has remarkably little influence on the standard of living they will enjoy in Ireland. What it can still influence, perhaps more thoroughly than was commonly believed just a few years ago, is the number who enjoy that standard of living in Ireland rather than elsewhere.

Suggestions for Further Reading
The literature on Irish economic history is already enormous. A few suggestions for further reading are given here, and much of the information in this chapter comes from these sources.

General History
R. Foster, *Modern Ireland 1600–1972*, Allen Lane, London 1988.
J. Lee, *Ireland 1912–1985*, Cambridge University Press, Cambridge 1989.
F. Lyons, *Ireland Since the Famine*, Weidenfeld and Nicolson, London 1971.

Economic and Social History
R. Crotty, *Irish Agricultural Production*, Cork University Press, Cork 1966.
L. Cullen*, An Economic History of Ireland Since 1660*, Batsford, London 1972.
M. Daly, *Social and Economic History of Ireland Since 1800*, Educational Company, Dublin 1981.
K. Kennedy, T. Giblin and D. McHugh, *The Economic Development of Ireland in the Twentieth Century,* Routledge, London 1988.
J. Mokyr, *Why Ireland Starved*, Allen and Unwin, London 1983.
C. Ó Gráda, *The Great Irish Famine*, Macmillan, London 1989.
C. Ó Gráda, *Ireland: A New Economic History 1780–1939*, Oxford University Press, Oxford 1995.
C. Ó Gráda, *A Rocky Road: The Irish Economy Since the 1920s*, Manchester University Press, Manchester 1997.

CHAPTER 2

Policy Objectives for a Regional Economy

*Dermot McAleese**

1 INTRODUCTION

The primary policy objectives of a regional economy and a national economy are very similar. Both are concerned with achieving higher living standards, a fair distribution of income, full employment and decent environmental standards. Likewise, the secondary policy objectives, meaning by this the means to achieving the primary objectives, are broadly similar. Regions and nations both want price stability, both in consumer prices and in asset prices. Both worry about competitiveness. And the balance of payments has implications for both the region and the nation state, though, as we shall see, these implications are far more transparent in the case of a nation.

The main difference between a region and a nation is the *policy context*. A region has no independent currency and no control over its monetary policy. Its trade policy is determined by outside forces and balance of payments issues have to be radically reinterpreted. It has limited discretion in the use of fiscal policy. Seen in this context, a region's approach to policy has a dual dimension. First, it has to consider how to use its limited influence on policy developments where key policy decisions are being made. In the case of the Republic of Ireland, this might be Brussels, Frankfurt or Strasbourg, depending on the issue being decided; in Northern Ireland, London would figure prominently. Second, in areas where they do possess policy autonomy, regions must ensure that this degree of policy discretion is used effectively.

As Ireland becomes increasingly integrated into the European economy, the Republic is losing many of the trappings of a national economy. The completion of the single market and the establishment of economic and monetary union constitute important turning points in this respect. Hence, the focus in this chapter is on the policy objectives from the perspective of a regional economy. This perspective is of special interest at present because the Irish Republic is a comparative newcomer to regional status, unlike, say, Northern Ireland or Scotland, and it has had to acclimatise itself rapidly to the economic limitations of regional dependence. At the same time, as a nation state, the Republic could, if it managed its economic affairs well, exert more influence at the centre of European policy-making than many European regions of much larger size.

The plan of this chapter is as follows. In Section 2 we explain why growth is regarded as the primary objective of economic policy and how it is related to employment. In Section 3 the limitations of this objective are analysed by taking account of leisure and the environment. The goal of equity and the relationship between economic growth and happiness are considered in Section 4. In Section 5 we discuss price stability and general security as objectives of policy. Competitiveness is discussed in Section 6; the search for ways of restoring competitiveness has become the *leitmotif* of economic policy in recent years. Section 7 concludes the chapter.

2 GROWTH AND EMPLOYMENT

Introduction
Rapid, sustained growth is a primary objective of economic policy. Fast economic growth means higher living standards, and is associated with an expanding and dynamic business environment. Slow or zero growth is perceived as stagnation. Confronted with the record of a slow-growing economy, we instinctively ask what has gone wrong. Policy-makers are always on the lookout for advice about ways of promoting economic growth. An advance in living standards is something that most people want, enjoy and expect to be delivered.

Economic growth is desired for many different reasons. Affluent countries see growth as an essential contributor to ever higher living standards, full employment and healthy government finances. They also perceive faster growth as a way of maintaining their economic and military position relative to other countries. Not long ago, Americans worried about being overtaken by the Japanese; and the Japanese in turn worry about their economic standing relative to China. By contrast, governments of developing countries see faster economic growth as a means of escaping from poverty and material want, and in particular from the vulnerability and sense of inferiority that, rightly or wrongly, attaches to low economic development. For them, 'catching up' with the living standards of the affluent countries is a key policy imperative. All countries appear to view growth as an indicator that resources are being employed efficiently, and faster-growing economies are often taken as models for slower-growing economies to copy and learn from.

Growth and Efficiency
Economics generally endorses the idea that efficiency and growth are related. Most fast-growing economies are efficient, and most efficient economies tend to grow faster than economies of similar size and scale that are inefficient. The meaning of efficiency and growth in an economic sense is illustrated in Figure 2.1.

Figure 2.1

The Production Frontier

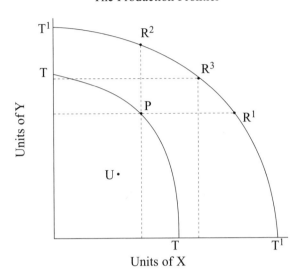

Units of X

Imagine an economy that produces only two goods, X and Y. We set up a list of combinations of X and Y that the economy could produce if its resources were utilised in the most efficient way. In other words, for any given level of X, we find out the maximum amount of Y that can be produced in the economy. The various combinations of X and Y derived in this way are known as the *production frontier*. The production frontier is TT in Figure 2.1.

Provided production takes place on the production frontier, where resources are fully employed, more of good X implies less of good Y. In other words, in order to produce more of X, scarce resources have to be transferred from industry Y to industry X. One can go further and define the cost of X as the amount of Y that has to be sacrificed in order to produce one extra unit of X. This is called *the opportunity cost of X*. The opportunity cost concept has many practical applications and serves as a reminder of the obvious point that 'free' education, or 'free' transport and other 'free' goods offered by the state are not costless. The resources used to supply these goods and services could have been used to produce automobiles or holidays instead. Hence the well-known maxim; in economics there is no such thing as a free lunch.

An *efficient* economy is one that operates on its production frontier (i.e. at a point such as P in Figure 2.1). At any point below the production frontier, society could have more of X and Y simply by moving to the frontier. By definition, this would not be an efficient outcome. Thus point U is not an efficient outcome. At that point, some productive resources are either being used inefficiently or, worse, not being used at all. If they were mobilised, a point P could be attained which is obviously superior. In addition to *productive* efficiency as above, one must have *allocative* efficiency. This means that the goods and services produced on the frontier represented by points such as P must be distributed between consumers in an efficient manner. Allocative efficiency is achieved when there is no feasible redistribution of the fixed bundle of goods P such that one person is better off without leaving anyone else worse off. At that stage, an economy is said to have achieved Pareto efficiency. Hence, efficiency is certainly an important objective of economic policy.

Why Growth is Important

Over time, however, growth will be the main force in determining living standards. A gross national product (GNP) growth rate of 4 per cent maintained for seventeen years will result in a doubling of the original GNP level. Even a more modest 2 per cent growth rate will translate into a doubling of living standards every thirty-three years. Figures such as this indicate the potential gains from raising the growth rate. In terms of Figure 2.1, outward shifts in the production frontier will over time dominate the effects of movement to a given frontier from off-frontier points, such as U. However, since countries that are efficient normally grow faster than those that are inefficient, the objectives of efficiency and growth are in practice complementary.

To illustrate the benefits of growth, we can depict it as a series of outward shifts in the production frontier, such as that represented by the move from TT to T^1T^1. The T'T' frontier shows the expanded range of options growth provides to society. Economic growth is a 'good thing', in so far as it enables the consumers in the economy to enjoy:

- more of X and the same amount of Y– at a point such as R^1;
- more of Y and the same amount of X – at a point such as R^2;
- more of both X and Y – at a point like R^3;
- any other desired combination of X and Y – on the expanded frontier.

Growth extends the range of consumption possibilities, and people choose between these different possibilities through the market system, supplemented by government intervention.

The production frontier can be shifted outwards by two forces: first, increases in the *quantity* of productive factors and, second, improvements in the *productivity* of these factors. Since we are primarily concerned with growth per person rather than total growth, it is common to abstract from the increase in growth that is attributable solely to the increase in the population. Growth in living standards, or GNP per person, depends on (see also Chapter 7):

- the *amount* of productive factors at each person's disposal (the more machinery and the more hectares of land at the disposal of an employee, the more will be produced per employee);

- the *productivity* of these factors of production (better machinery, better seeds and fertilisers, better technology);
- the knowledge, skills and motivation of the workforce (see Chapters 6 and 13).

Growth and Employment

Full employment means that there is work available for everyone willing to seek it at prevailing pay levels. This is obviously a desirable objective of economic policy. There is a strong empirical association between full employment and economic growth and this explains why one of the major perceived benefits of faster growth is that it provides more job opportunities and reduces the unemployment rate.

Yet in strict logic there is no reason why growth should be a necessary condition for full employment. To see this, go back to Figure 2.1. Assume a situation where TT is fixed (i.e. zero growth). At point U, there is unemployment. As noted above, this is an inefficient point, indicating waste of resources. The solution is to implement policies, such as greater labour market flexibility, that address the unemployment problem. As more people are employed, we move towards a point like P on the production frontier TT.

The necessary policies might take any of the forms outlined in Chapter 6. Hence full employment can be regarded as an indicator of efficiency. In moving from U to P, there will be an increase in output and therefore some faster economic growth will be recorded. But once attained, there is no reason why full employment should not be maintained at P. Faster growth at that stage makes no difference one way or another. Hence the 'classical' conclusion: *full employment is always attainable irrespective of the level of output or of the growth of output.*

Intuition and empirical fact, however, suggest that full employment is easier to attain when an economy is growing. Also, when growth declines, unemployment rises. For example, Korea, long used to near zero unemployment rates, found itself facing unemployment of an unprecedented 7 per cent following the 1997–98 currency crisis. In a similar manner, Ireland's unemployment rate has risen from 4 per cent to over 14 per cent following the property crash and the collapse in its gross domestic product (GDP). The amount of unemployment caused by a fall in output has varied across EU countries. Ireland has been especially affected because of the decline in the construction industry, an exceptionally labour-intensive activity. This explains why growth is desired not just for its own sake but for the indirect benefits it provides, such as helping to keep unemployment low.

Growth of GNP per Person as a Policy Objective

The focus on income per person rather than total income (GNP) as the policy objective has profoundly important implications.[1] Suppose one had to choose between three growth profiles as indicated in Table 2.1.

Total GNP is increasing fastest in situation A. If total GNP were the policy objective, A would be the preferred situation. If GNP per person were the policy objective, situation C would be chosen. Ranking A and B would be more difficult. The only difference between them is that there are more people around in A to share a given GNP per person growth rate. Suppose these additional people happened to be immigrants from Africa. The economy's faster growth means that they can be accommodated without impairing average living standards of the existing population; while at the same time the immigrants' living standards are much higher in the host country than they were at home. Also if the host country had a large national debt, this debt could be shared among a larger population. This would suggest a preference for A over B. But there may be other effects to consider, relating to the broader social impact of immigration and effects on income distribution. An influx of unskilled immigrants, for instance, would tend to reduce earnings of native unskilled workers, but would tend to benefit the middle and upper class generally by reducing the cost of unskilled labour that these more affluent people employ (domestic help, catering staff, building workers and so on). Clearly personal values and one's position in the income distribution ranking influence preferences between the various growth and population combinations.

Table 2.1

Growth: Illustrative Example

Growth profile	Total GNP (% p.a.)	Population (% p.a.)	GNP per person (% p.a.)
A	5	3	2
B	4	2	2
C	3	0	3

In the above example, population growth is treated as if it were independent of GNP growth. A crucial question is whether and how population growth interacts with GNP and the consequential effect on living standards per person. Take, for example, a country such as Uganda with an annual population growth of 3.2 per cent. Its population has grown from 19 million in 1990 to 38 million in 2010 and it is estimated to reach 61 million in 2030. Output growth of over 3 per cent will be needed simply to prevent living standards from falling. Many argue that population growth at that rate has a negative effect on total GNP growth and hence can depress income per person. An expanding population of young people and large family size reduces national savings and consequently limits the volume of investment. Simultaneously, a burgeoning population puts pressure on a country's natural resources. If the rate of population growth interacts negatively with GNP per person, a vicious circle of economic decline can be generated. At the other end of the spectrum, excessively low population growth can be equally problematic. The 'greying' of Europe's population has led to concerns about the financial viability of pension schemes, escalating medical costs and an erosion of social dynamism and innovation. This line of reasoning reinforces the case for GNP per person, not total GNP, as the primary policy objective.

Affluent households tend to have smaller families than poor households. Likewise, developed countries have lower population growth than poor countries. Thus, since 1980, population has grown in higher-income countries by only 0.6 per cent per annum, compared with 2 per cent in low-income countries. Ireland too has experienced the same phenomenon. As Chapter 6 will show, with increasing prosperity its birth rate has declined. But have we become better off because of a low birth rate, or is the birth rate low because we are more affluent? There is no definitive answer to this question, but many governments in less developed countries now believe that lower population growth would help to raise living standards and have introduced strong family planning programmes to encourage smaller family size. Irish governments have never gone as far in this direction as governments in developing countries such as India and China. One reason for this is that Irish people, unlike many in the present developing world, had the option of emigration.

Migration and Growth

The impact of emigration on living standards has long been a controversial topic. Some argued that increased population would have raised living standards in Ireland. Patrick Pearse believed that the country could support a population of 30 million. With greater population would go larger domestic markets, greater economies of scale, higher productivity and, eventually, more growth. Higher living standards and a more dynamic local community would in turn induce skilled and talented Irish people to stay at home, thus reinforcing faster growth. This is a rather rosy view of what might have happened to living standards in the absence of emigration. Demographers, however, agree that if there had been no emigration since 1841, the population in the Republic would be in the region of 20 million instead of 4 million.[2] Some argued that a growing population was a good thing in itself, irrespective of its effects on material welfare.

An opposite viewpoint was that emigration acted as a welcome safety valve, enabling the amount of land and capital per person remaining in Ireland to be increased, with beneficial effects on Irish productivity. At the same time Irish emigrants were able to find more productive employment and acquire valuable work experience and skills abroad. A win–win outcome for all parties, just as predicted in John Kenneth Galbraith's famous dictum that 'emigration helps those who leave, the country they go to, and the people they leave behind'.[3] Underlying this approach was the idea that the primary focus of economic policy should be the living standards of the Irish people wherever they happened to live, not just of those residing in the Irish state. Thus the policy objective should be to encourage Irish people to go to where their productivity was highest and their material rewards greatest. According to this logic, Ireland's access to the comparatively prosperous labour markets of the USA, the UK, Australia and Canada has been a tremendous boon and the Irish government's main responsibility is to provide education to its citizens and equip them to make maximum use of the opportunities open to them at home *and* abroad.

Which of these differing perspectives is 'correct'? Research on this question remains inconclusive. A comprehensive National Economic and Social Council (NESC) study found convincing evidence that emigration did not impair the long-run growth in living standards of those remaining in Ireland, but was unable to go further and assert that emigration actually improved living standards.[4] During Ireland's boom, the focus of interest changed to the effects of immigration rather than emigration. For the first time in centuries foreigners came each year to work in Ireland. At a broad level, this change in demographic pattern was benign. Higher output growth involved both significant net immigration *and* an improvement in living standards. Now the pendulum has swung back and Ireland has reverted to being a country of net emigration. At one level the close correlation between total GNP growth and growth in GNP per person suggests that in Ireland's case opting for growth in GNP per person as the primary policy objective need cause no special angst.[5] At a broader societal level, however, migration, inward and outward, brings its own set of problems and opportunities that the policy-maker must not overlook.

Optimal Growth, not Maximum Growth
While growth is a primary policy objective, it does not follow that the aim is simply to *maximise* growth. One reason for this is that growth involves a degree of intergenerational distribution. By cutting down on its consumption and investing more, any present generation can raise economic growth rates. Japan's average investment/GNP ratio during the period 1960–95 exceeded the investment ratio in the European Union and the United States by more than ten percentage points (31 per cent as against 22 per cent and 18 per cent respectively). Not surprisingly, Japan's growth rate of 6 per cent per year was twice the rate of most industrial countries. China and some other fast-growing emerging economies put aside as much as 50 per cent of their GDP for investment. By investing so much, the present generation sacrifices its material welfare in the interests of future generations. But for how long can, and should, this process be maintained? Clearly different societies place a different premium on the future relative to present living standards. Authoritarian societies are often able to record extraordinarily rapid growth, but at serious cost to the people who had to produce the necessary saving.

Another reason for not choosing maximum growth as a policy objective relates to its potential undesirable spill-over effects. These became apparent in the early 2000s in Ireland. Traffic congestion worsened markedly; water quality declined; hospital resources were overstretched. Another spill-over effect was the inflow of job seekers from abroad. Initially the decline in emigration was widely welcomed. No less welcome was the inflow of former emigrants returning to a buoyant domestic market. These immigrants helped to sustain the boom by moderating pay growth and plugging vital gaps in labour supply. Generally there is no problem with immigrants of similar nationality and background to the host country. Difficulties arose, however, when unskilled immigrants of more diverse backgrounds entered the picture. There were also income distribution effects to consider. Middle- and upper-income groups gained from the entry of the unskilled into the Irish labour market, but those at the lower end of the income profile tended to lose out. Finally, excessively rapid growth can often lead to inflation and to escalating property prices. Inflation can cause many problems, as we shall see below.

One important, intangible benefit of growth is the influence and power that it brings with it. We can learn from the dominance of the USA in the world economy how economic success and political and military power are closely linked. In Ireland's case, economic growth boosted our reputation abroad. Successful countries tend to be listened to with respect. Economic success engendered a palpable air of self confidence and a virtual disappearance of the grievance mentality that blighted the country in the past. Economic decline has led to the opposite: a severe reputational loss and exposure to criticism and mockery, all deeply discouraging to a country that had become used to taking praise and admiration for our economic achievements as a matter of course.

These advantages and disadvantages must be weighed in determining a country's optimum growth rate. Choosing an optimum growth path requires careful consideration of the broader socio-political factors mentioned above, as well as of the limitations of GNP as an indicator of welfare, a subject to which we turn next.

3 GROWTH AND HUMAN WELFARE

So far we have discussed economic growth as if growth, as measured by GNP in the numerator, were the sole objective of economic policy. Growth is taken to be desirable because it enlarges the range of consumption possibilities available to society. But it is well known that growth is an inadequate indicator of human welfare. As one critic expressed it:

> The Gross National Product does not allow for the health of our children, the quality of their education or the joy of their play. It does not include the beauty of our poetry or the strength of our marriages; the intelligence of our public debate or the integrity of our public officials. It measures neither our wisdom nor our learning, neither our compassion nor our devotion to our country; it measures everything, in short, except that which makes life worthwhile.[6]

GNP does not account for many of the things that make for the good life and some items are included in GNP that may worsen rather than improve human welfare. Four specific criticisms of GNP have been made on this account. First, that it puts no value on leisure and the household economy. Second, that it ignores income distribution (discussed in Section 4). Third, that it takes no account of resource depletion and degradation of the environment. Fourth, some items are recorded as outputs although in reality they are inputs or costs.

Leisure and the Household Economy

Leisure is a good like any other, so theoretically it should be included alongside other goods and services when choosing growth as a policy objective. The difficulty arises because of the way growth is measured. For various reasons, changes in leisure hours are not taken account of in the GNP statistic. Hence if GNP growth is rising but everyone is working harder and working longer hours, the net improvement in human welfare may well be much lower than it appears. In 2009, the average American worked 1,768 hours per year; the average German 1,390 hours per year. Americans have more goods and more GNP per head, but they have miserably short vacations. Irish employees work 1,549 hours per year (see Chapter 6).

A feature of rich societies is that employees are well paid. They are well paid because they are productive and that in turn means that the opportunity cost of leisure increases as economies become more prosperous. Hence the widely observed phenomenon that people in affluent societies tend to be more harried and harassed, have less time for talk and a chat than their counterparts in poorer countries. The process of economic growth inherently tends to accentuate this problem.

To take another example, suppose that a person takes a second job. This makes large inroads into leisure time. The GNP measure includes all the output generated but ignores the welfare cost of the loss of leisure. Human welfare has presumably increased as a result of this decision – otherwise the second job would not have been taken – but the net increase in welfare will be much less than the increase in GNP indicates. The individual is likely to be more harassed and to have less time for enjoying domestic life.

GNP includes only transactions that involve a monetary exchange. Hence leisure is excluded. But this is not the only excluded output. Housework done by members of a household, being unpaid, is not recorded in GNP. As members of the household enter the workforce and household tasks such as repair, maintenance and care of children are passed over to paid professionals, GNP rises. Yet all that is happening is that these functions have been shifted from the traditional realm of the household and the community to the monetised economy. Welfare has presumably increased, since the decision to work outside the home was taken voluntarily. But the increase in GNP will grossly exaggerate the increase in welfare. These examples help to explain why economic growth will bring fewer real benefits than appears.

Growth and the Environment

Conventional GNP measures do not deal satisfactorily with environmental and ecological factors. Higher GNP has implications for the environment on several levels that fail to be recorded in the statistics. Three aspects, in particular, merit attention: (a) higher levels of pollution; (b) depletion of natural resources; and (c) global warming.

First, no deduction is made in GNP statistics for the higher levels of pollution and chemical waste that often accompany economic growth. Some countries have attempted to compute 'green' national accounts that allow for these negative effects, but there is as yet no consensus on how the pollution effects should be computed.

Second, depletion of a nation's stock of non-renewable resources such as oil and coal is not accounted for in GNP calculations. Even in the case of renewable resources, problems can arise if economic growth leads to their being exploited in excess of the replacement rate. For example, the serious decline in the water table caused by increased economic activity in the countries bordering the Aral Sea, in Northern China and Israel-Occupied Palestine is ignored in the national accounts.

Third, economic growth is associated with deforestation, change in land use and, most notable of all, with burning fossil fuels. As a result the concentration of greenhouse gases has risen alarmingly – the current level is higher than at any time in the last 650,000 years – and there has been an accompanying rise in world temperatures. Already, an increase of 0.6°C has been recorded since the mid-1970s. A change of this magnitude may appear small, but its effects over time could be enormous (see Chapter 10). Long time lags between today's green gas emissions and future damage to climate and the environment mean that the adverse effects will not be reflected in GNP for many years. Although Ireland might not be as badly affected as other countries by global warming, we will be expected in the interests of EU solidarity to pay carbon taxes (see Chapter 4), to restrain energy consumption and, in short, to become much more 'green' than before (see Chapter 10).

Inputs Recorded as Outputs
By a perverse quirk, the cost of moderating the adverse effects of pollution is sometimes included in GNP as an output (service provided) instead of as an input (a production cost to society). For example, the medical attention given to a victim of air pollution will be recorded in the national accounts as an addition to GNP instead of as a deduction from it. This is part of a more general criticism of GNP relating to inputs misclassified as outputs. For example, military spending is included as a positive contributor to GNP, even if that spending is undertaken at the behest of reckless political leaders and with disregard for the needs of the people. Likewise the inclusion of expenditure on crime prevention as an output in GNP has been criticised. To be sure, such spending could represent improved living standards in so far as the community obtains greater security and more orderly traffic. But it could equally be a sign of diminished quality of the social environment and hence a cost of securing higher GNP (e.g. if more police were needed to maintain the same level of security and traffic movement).

39

GNP and Human Development Indicators

Making GNP per capita a primary objective is really shorthand for something much more complex. In evaluating a country's economic performance, account must be taken of the quality of the lifestyle enjoyed by the population as well as the quantity of goods and services consumed. Thus, imagine two countries. One has a lower GNP per person than the other, but it happens to have a healthier, more literate and less crime-ridden society. In this instance, GNP is an inaccurate measure of the relative welfare of the two countries, and making GNP growth a primary policy objective may not be an appropriate response. Instead of economic growth, can we find a way of measuring human development and making it the primary policy objective?

In an effort to develop a more comprehensive socio-economic measure than GNP, the United Nations has developed the Human Development Index (HDI). The HDI is a composite index and consists of a weighted average of data on GDP/GNP per person, income distribution, life expectancy and educational attainment of the population (see also Chapter 7).

As one would expect, such exercises lead to some changes in ranking. The 2010 *Human Development Report* reveals an HDI ranking higher than the GDP per person ranking for Sweden, Portugal, Greece and the UK; the opposite is the case for Singapore, China, and South Africa.[7] Ireland is placed fifth of 169 countries in the HDI league; a position that flatters and is unlikely to last. By adding to the list of indicators, and measuring them in different ways, more radical alterations in ranking can be computed. Experimentation and analysis along these lines is continuing.

Yet the limitations of GNP as a measure of welfare must not be exaggerated. For all its defects, a higher output per person gives society the *capacity* to achieve a better quality of life. This explains the close positive correlation between the HDI and total output per person. Also there is a strong positive correlation between GNP per capita growth and some important empirical measures of the quality of life. Countries with higher GNP per capital tend to be healthier and better educated than those with lower GNP per capita. They also tend to be better policed and are more secure in a financial and physical sense. London is safer than Lagos, Manila or Sao Paolo. Affluent Tokyo is one of the safest cities in the world. While many forms of recorded crime have increased since 1945, prosperity has tended to result in a reduction in crime and disorder. During the nineteenth century, industrial nations became less crime-ridden as they became more industrialised. Indeed, as pointed out in Chapter 1, these two factors are interrelated: the rule of law and good governance are essential prerequisites of a prosperous market economy.

Faster growth makes it easier to reduce unemployment, to lessen poverty, to improve education and health services and to provide all the other good things that constitute prosperity. There are, of course, negative aspects of growth, such as damage to the environment, erosion of community life and destruction of rural values. Since the birth of the Industrial Revolution in the late eighteenth century, economic growth has had its critics, some of the most trenchant of whom have been economists. The tradition of scepticism, verging on hostility, towards growth remains active to this day. Despite these downsides, governments and those who elect them evidently believe that the positive effects of growth outweigh its negative effects, and both continue to accord it a high priority.

4 EQUITY, INCOME DISTRIBUTION AND HAPPINESS

Policy Debate

GNP per person, being an arithmetic average of total output divided by total population, reveals no information about the distribution of resources within a society. It could rise, even though the majority of the population may be getting worse off. For example, if the income of the most affluent one-third of a population rose by a total €50 billion, and the income of the poorest two-thirds fell by a total €30 billion, GNP would increase. But does it follow that society as a whole is better off?

Some argue that the long-run sustainability of growth depends on income being shared on an equitable basis. Successful policy-making requires change, and such change can only be achieved if the majority of people believe that they have a stake in the economy and will benefit from its continued growth. But this still leaves open the question of what is meant by sharing income on an equitable basis. Since Chapter 8 is devoted to this topic, a brief outline of the main parameters of this debate will suffice at this stage.

The value judgements underlying modern economics are derived from a philosophy of individualism and liberalism. *Individualism* means that what ultimately counts is the utility every individual attains and that the utility of each individual should be given an equal weight. *Liberalism* signifies that individuals should be free to decide what provides the greatest utility. Individual preferences are taken as given. The task of the economist, in this view, is to devise market structures that will enable individuals to satisfy their preferences, not to pass judgement on them.

Utility and income must be distinguished in this analysis. The standard assumption underlying economic reasoning is that the marginal utility of income is positive but decreases as income rises. Individuals always prefer a higher income to a lower one, but the intensity of this preference diminishes as income rises. A systematic relationship thus links utility to income. On the face of it, the individualist principle of treating the utility of every person equally, coupled with the assumption of declining marginal utility for all individuals, would imply that the total utility in society is maximised when income is distributed perfectly evenly. But there are two reasons why even committed utilitarians do not push the argument to the extreme of total income equalisation.

First, different people derive different amounts of satisfaction from the same income levels. Material wealth does not matter equally to all. However, utility is

41

difficult (some would say impossible) to measure and compare among individuals, hence it is not possible to redistribute income on the basis of assumed differences in capacity to enjoy income.

Second, the adverse effect of policies to achieve greater equality on incentives to work and enterprise may, after a point, lead to a fall in total income. Arthur Okun described the process of redistributing income as akin to transferring water from one barrel to another with a leaky bucket.[8] The more we try to increase equity by the redistribution of income, the more we reduce efficiency. In transferring income from the high-income group to the low-income group of society, the authorities levy taxes on individuals' income from employment and capital holdings. The former gives people an incentive to work less and the latter entices people to save less. Both effects lead to a reduction in the amount of income available for redistribution. The less well off in society may well lose rather than benefit from such policies in the long run.

The assumption of decreasing marginal utility implies that when we take a given amount from the rich to give to the poor, the rich will suffer less of a utility loss than the utility gain enjoyed by the poor. If asked to choose between a perfectly equal distribution of income and an unequal distribution of *exactly the same total income*, a utilitarian would favour the equal distribution. Egalitarian predispositions also emerge from other philosophies and schools of thought. Some argue that society should give the utility of the poor greater weight than the utility of the rich on grounds of need, regardless of fine points about diminishing utility. Others, such as the philosopher John Rawls, have pushed this line of judgement to the extreme, arguing that any economic change which increases inequality would be acceptable only if it also makes the poorest better off. This implies that the utility of the worst-off individual takes precedence over all others and that a fair distribution of income is one that makes the poorest person as well off as possible after taking all costs of income transfers into account.[9]

Irish policy objectives have a Rawlsian flavour. Thus governments have tended to prioritise social inclusion as a strategic objective in its own right, the primary objective being to ensure that 'the benefits of economic growth and related social improvements are shared by all sections of the Irish population'.[10] Social inclusion has been a major theme of successive agreements with the social partners (see Chapters 3 and 8). Does the same principle apply in the case of economic decline? Should the losses in income be shared by all sections of the population? Not much explicit consideration has been given to how the losses of economic decline should be shared – until 2008, this type of problem seemed almost inconceivable.

In opposition to the egalitarian presumption, Robert Nozick argued that the idea of fairness as an outcome could not be justified. Fairness must be based on rules, not outcomes.[11] Two rules are crucial: (a) the state must enforce laws that establish and protect private property; and (b) private property may be transferred from one person to another only by voluntary exchange. Provided markets are open to competition and there are no major market 'failures' (a hugely unrealistic assumption), the resulting distribution of income is, by Nozick's definition, fair. It does not matter how unequally this income is shared provided it is generated by people each of whom voluntarily provides services in exchange for market-determined compensation. The entrepreneur who accepts business risks and has succeeded deserves to be rewarded. Redistribution of these earnings is unjustified. By the same token, in times of recession, business losses are solely the responsibility of the entrepreneur and no government bailouts are justified. From this perspective the key issue is equality of opportunity, not equality of outcome. Indeed given an uneven distribution of skills, motivation and willingness to work, equal opportunities will inevitably entail unequal outcomes.

So far the discussion has focused on *vertical equity*. This refers to the proposition that differently situated individuals should be treated differently. The well off, in other words, should be taxed in favour of the poor because they can afford to pay these taxes with less pain. *Horizontal equity* is also important. The underlying principle is that people with the same incomes and the same circumstances should be treated in a similar fashion. For example, families with the same number of dependants and the same income should pay the same rate of tax (see Chapter 4). Horizontal equity requires that property developers, farmers and PAYE employees should be subject to the same tax unless there is a clear demonstration of different circumstances. Perceived breaches of this equity principle can be a source of major grievance. By extension, people in different circumstances should not be asked to pay the same taxes. This principle is the motivating force of many income distribution policies (see Chapters 4 and 8). The case for regional grants and incentives, for example, is based on the idea that people in less developed regions do not enjoy the same access to infrastructure as those living in richer regions.

Equity, Economic Growth and Happiness

We have already referred to the debate about the relationship between economic growth and equity. The proposition is that to achieve income equality some sacrifice in growth is necessary because equality requires high taxes that can damage enterprise and investment. Some find this line of argument persuasive. Others doubt that such a trade-off exists. They point to the many studies showing that countries with more evenly spread income grow faster than countries with a large gap between poor and rich. Also faster-growing economies have lower unemployment rates. Since the incidence of unemployment is highest among lower-income groups, these groups in particular will benefit. In Ireland's case, the virtual disappearance of unemployment brought about a decline in levels of deprivation. There was also evidence of considerable escalation of gains at the top of the income distribution: see Chapter 8 for a discussion of this and the more recent period.

The relationship between equity and growth depends ultimately on individual attitudes and culture. Income inequalities are more acceptable and financial work incentives valued more in some societies than in others (see Chapter 8). The combinations of growth and equity attainable in a competitive market economy full of individualistic materialists will be different from those attainable in a co-operative economy run by and for ascetic altruists! In practice, governments have voted with their feet on this question. Comparison of income distribution before and after tax and state benefits shows that major transfers take place from richer to poorer income groups in all industrial economies (see Chapter 8).

In recent years, the research agenda has been widened even further by tackling the much broader question of how GNP per capita is related to happiness. Do higher standards of living, whether defined on broad or narrow definitions of the term, translate into greater happiness? Economists have had a long and abiding interest in this correlation. In the light of our discussion of GNP per capita as a measure of welfare and of the importance of income distribution, the reader will not be surprised that economic research has come up with some complex findings.

A first step is how to measure happiness. The main source of information comes from large-scale citizen surveys that ask individuals to report on how happy they feel, how satisfied they are with their lives and/or with their jobs. Sometimes this is supplemented by data on suicide rates and health status as proxies for (un)happiness. Defined this way, happiness is clearly dependent on many variables other than the level of income – contrary to the much-quoted adage that 'anyone who says money can't buy happiness doesn't know where to shop'. The key methodological challenge is to identify the specific contribution of increases in GNP per capita, and by extension an individual's income level, to the happiness index.

Research over the past decade enables us to draw several broad conclusions.[12] First, for any one individual, more income leads to more life satisfaction, everything else being equal. Within a single country, at a given moment in time, those in the highest income groups are happier than those in the lowest income groups. Second, citizens of very poor countries tend to be happier as living standards increase. Studies of former Soviet Union countries, for instance, show a clear positive correlation between income per capita and reported happiness. Third, beyond a certain level of income, the average person does *not* become significantly happier as income increases. At an aggregate level there has been no increase in reported happiness over the past thirty years in Japan and Europe, with, if anything, a decline in the USA. This is called *the Paradox of Happiness*. Fourth, *relative* income matters as much, if not more, to most people than *absolute* income levels. People's definition of what constitutes an 'adequate' level of income seems to depend as much on the level of income enjoyed by their neighbour as on the absolute value of their own income (see Chapter 8). Fifth, virtually all studies show that being unemployed has a strongly negative effect on happiness. Joblessness depresses well-being more than any other single characteristic, including divorce and separation. Not only those who are made redundant suffer, but the spread of job insecurity lowers welfare among those still in employment. For this reason, those working in the private sector tend to be affected more strongly by economic downturns than those working in the public sector.[13]

In Ireland, too, the relationship between happiness (measured as percentage of the population who described themselves as 'very satisfied with their life') and material welfare is decidedly weak. The annual *Eurobarometer* survey showed that 40 per cent of Irish people fell into the very satisfied 'Happy' category in 1980. There is no evidence of the proportion of happy people rising since then, notwithstanding the huge increase in material income. Curiously, even after the trials and tribulations of the economy and society post-2007, Irish people were still ranked eighth in the EU-27 in terms of life satisfaction, according to the Autumn 2009 *Eurobarometer* survey. A surprising 88 per cent of those surveyed described themselves as 'very satisfied' or 'fairly satisfied' with life. That state of satisfaction went hand in hand with a grim assessment of the situation of the national economy – 84 per cent (compared with an EU average of 26 per cent) described the national economic situation as 'very bad', and 72 per cent considered that the impact of the crisis on the job market was likely to get worse.

One element on the happiness spectrum *did*, however, change. The number of people who were acutely *dis*satisfied with their life declined consistently since 1990. The fall in Ireland's unemployment since that time was most likely a key factor in this development. Hence, to the extent that fast economic growth has helped to reduce unemployment, we can conclude that economic growth in Ireland may not have added much to the happiness of already happy people, but it made those at the bottom of the happiness league feel less dissatisfied. As unemployment rises, a reversal of this tendency must, alas, be expected.

Archbishop Whately, who established the Chair of Political Economy in Trinity College in 1832, took an interest in a related question of whether economic growth has an impact on moral behaviour. Unlike a modern social scientist, he had to rely on deductive reasoning instead of mass opinion surveys. As a general rule, he concluded, 'advancement in National Prosperity, which mankind is by the Governor of the universe adapted and impelled to promote, must be favourable to moral improvement'.[14] Whately championed the cause of teaching and research in economics because he believed that economic growth would lead to moral improvement, and moral improvement would in turn bring as much 'happiness' as we can reasonably expect in this life. This is an alternative perspective on the GNP/happiness correlation that would no doubt prove controversial in modern Ireland.

The literature on happiness continues to grow. It is a subject that requires cross-disciplinary research involving economics, statistics, psychology and philosophy. As yet results are tentative, but the general thrust of the findings suggests two conclusions. One is that it would be a mistake for economists in the twenty-first century to focus excessively on ways of increasing the level of GNP per capita, or to accept too readily that slow economic growth necessarily indicates 'failure'. A second conclusion is that, as prosperity increases, more emphasis should be placed on the provision of public goods than on facilitating the output of more private goods and services. The 'well-being' of an individual includes much more than income: access to decent public amenities, pollution-free air, good education, secure employment and a fair distribution of income, and a crimeless environment contribute more to happiness than any monetary measure can adequately convey.

5 PRICE STABILITY

A regional economy has a strong interest in price stability. However, a region will experience price stability only if the centre provides it. In the Republic's case the centre is Frankfurt, the headquarters of the European Central Bank (ECB), while for Northern Ireland the relevant policy centre is the Bank of England. Policy in the regional economy must therefore focus on supporting the establishment of solid financial institutions at the centre and setting clear objectives for them.

Definition and Measurement
Price stability is a relatively new phrase in the policy-maker's lexicon. But it is not a new concept. In the past, inflation was so rampant and endemic that the analysis usually proceeded in terms of the costs of inflation. The Irish price level, for instance, increased by a factor of ten between 1972 and 2007; a basket of goods that cost the equivalent of €10 in 1972 would have cost more than €100 in 2007. This constitutes a huge erosion in the purchasing power of the currency. Deflation (declining prices) means that the purchasing power of the currency is increasing. This is good news for those with cash balances but it has serious damaging side-effects. Hence price stability is the objective; avoiding both inflation and deflation.

Price stability is defined as the absence of any persistent and pronounced rise or fall in the general level of money prices. The general level of prices is measured by the Consumer Price Index (CPI). This index is defined by reference to the price of a fixed 'basket' of consumer goods. In the Republic, the selection of items for the basket is made using results of the national Household Budget Survey. Every five years new weights and new items are introduced into the index. Each month some 50,000 price observations are made by the Central Statistics Office. The results are aggregated into 613 items. These include staple goods such as food, clothing, cars and petrol, and also items such as mobile telephones, medical insurance, bank charges, child-minding fees, and wedding and funeral expenses.

Three factors tend to impart an upward bias to the price increases recorded by the CPI. First, the number of goods in the sample basket is an incomplete inventory of the economy's goods. Delays in incorporating new products give rise, for technical reasons, to an upward bias (*composition bias*). Second, improvements in quality are an important feature of new goods and services, ranging from high-technology goods to medical services and drugs, and they tend to be insufficiently allowed for in CPI price data (*quality bias*). Third, the CPI may fail to take full account of people's ability to substitute low-priced goods for higher-priced goods or to shift purchases from high-priced outlets to cheaper retail outlets when prices are rising (*substitution bias*). A doubling in the price of potatoes, for example, would raise the Irish CPI by over one-third of a percentage point (potatoes carry a weight in the basket of 0.33 per cent), but this takes no account of the availability of close substitutes such as rice and pasta. As time goes by, people switch their buying to products which have increased less in price: but the base weights (the CPI is a Laspeyres index) take insufficient account of this switch.

The empirical importance of these measurement biases is not known with precision. Even a bias of +1 per cent is large compared with an average inflation rate of, say, 2 per cent. Because of these upward biases, the objective of price stability is not defined as a zero CPI rise, but rather as CPI increases in the range of 1 to 3 per cent. The ECB defines it as year on year increases in the CPI of the euro zone *below but close to* 2 per cent, maintained over the medium term; the Bank of England adopted a similar definition in December 2003. In February 2009 the US Federal Reserve announced a long-term inflation target of 1.7 per cent, while the central banks of Sweden, Norway, New Zealand and Canada have opted for the wider 1–3 per cent range. Central banks use different measures of consumer prices. Thus, the ECB inflation target refers to the Harmonised Index of Consumer Prices (HICP), which excludes mortgage interest and credit charges and some other costs related to dwellings; the CPI, by contrast, includes them and is thus a more comprehensive measure of the cost of living.

Asset Prices and Price Stability

The issue of whether *asset prices*, and in particular house prices, should be included in the CPI has been much debated in recent times. The issue arose because in many countries (Ireland, the UK and Spain, for example) house prices were rising well above the CPI rate for several years. While housing costs are included in the CPI (they have a weight of 7 per cent in the Irish CPI), some believe that the index took too little account of the implications of escalating house prices on long-run disposable income.

The case for not making a special adjustment is based on the argument that the aim should be to measure the cost of *housing services* rather than the price of the house itself. Thus the CPI includes rent payments on rented accommodation, the cost of housing repairs and mortgage interest payments on owner-occupied housing. The reasoning behind the focus on housing services is that what matters for living standards is not so much the price of a house *per se* but the cost of owning a house (i.e. interest payments) and of renting it. Imagine the case of a house costing €100,000 when the mortgage rate is 10 per cent. If the buyer borrows the entire capital sum, mortgage interest payments will amount to €10,000 per annum. Now let the mortgage rate fall to 5 per cent. Suppose this leads to a doubling of house prices. The price of the house rises to €200,000, but the interest cost of the mortgage remains exactly the same as before, namely €10,000. True, annual mortgage payments will increase because of capital repayments and this may impose a strain on the borrower's discretionary income. But this effect is likely to be much less than the 100 per cent increase in house prices. The house price increase will in due course also lead to a rise in rents, but these will rise in line with total mortgage repayments. The same logic applies to other assets as well as houses (e.g. stocks and shares). If assets were to be directly included in the CPI, it would be difficult to decide how to weight them relative to prices of non-asset goods which are weighted on the basis of the share of the average person's total spending allocated to them.

Whether asset prices should be included in the CPI is in a sense a technical issue. A more important matter is whether a central bank should focus exclusively on the CPI as an indicator of how well it is doing its job. With the benefit of hindsight it is clear that it should not. Asset price bubbles can inflict terrible harm on the economy – as much as any deviation from price stability narrowly defined. Hence a central bank must concern itself with the evolution of asset prices as well as the CPI and explicit account should be taken of this. Leaving asset prices to market forces and ignoring the damage they might cause was a grave mistake made by central banks in recent years. Asset prices are highly relevant to both price stability and to economic and financial stability.

Central banks should act pre-emptively, raising interest rates and/or curbing property loans when asset markets are generating a boom, and expanding credit and reducing interest rates to limit the effects of an asset market collapse. Furthermore they should be vigilant in ensuring that banks remain liquid and solvent and do not lend too much in the good times.

In practice, this policy prescription is not so easy to implement. Thus, in Ireland's case the Central Bank saw its role as limited to giving advice. It claims that it issued repeated warnings of the dangers of excessive property lending; and this is indeed correct. Studies of house prices and commercial property lending by the banks were published in the Central Bank's annual *Financial Stability Reports* and the results were analysed in meticulous and scholarly detail.[15] These studies show a clear understanding of the potential damage to the macro-economy and to banks' balance sheets from a property bust. From its perspective the problem was that its advice was ignored by the banks and other relevant parties (such as the Financial Regulator and the Department of Finance). But giving advice and issuing warnings is relatively easy. The difficult part lies in deciding who should do something about it, when they should intervene, and what form of intervention is likely to be most effective (see Chapters 3 and 5).

What state body in Ireland was responsible for actually doing something about these warnings? Some argue that the Financial Regulator was responsible. The Financial Regulator in turn pointed out that it had taken action to restrain borrowing (by requiring higher reserve ratios for higher-risk property investments and suchlike) and attributed the collapse in the banking system to external factors, i.e. the extremely unlikely and unforeseeable combination of simultaneous collapses across Europe and the USA. The Department of Finance has a key role as adviser to the Minister of Finance on all matters relevant to the economy. It argued that responsibility for regulation lies with the Financial Regulator and the Central Bank and that it had to respect the independence of the Regulator and that it 'did not try to do the job itself'.[16] With the benefit of hindsight it is clear that all parties were unaware of the scale of the risks being run by the Irish banks and of the drastic dangers facing the economy.

In assessing the immediate danger of a price collapse, one problem familiar to all those who have studied economic cycles is that of premature warnings. This applied in the Irish case, where early warnings of an asset bubble as far back as 2003 did not materialise and hence undermined the credibility of future warnings. The key point is that it is very difficult to identify, and to anticipate the consequences of, an asset price collapse, even with the support of a strong economics research team. In retrospect, we see that Ireland suffered a near-perfect example of what Nassim Taleb defines as a Black Swan: an event or combination of events that (a) lies outside the realm of regular expectations, (b) carries an extreme impact and (c) can be explained retrospectively after the event but not prospectively.[17] Banks are particularly prone to Black Swans. They can hide explosive risks in their portfolios and in just one day can lose the profits of decades. In future the financial authorities will have to be given more explicit responsibility for dealing with asset price volatility and be provided with stronger policy instruments and controls to ensure that this responsibility can be effectively discharged (see Chapters 3 and 5 for further discussion of this issue).

Why Consumer Price Stability is Important

Failure to achieve consumer price stability impacts adversely on both economic growth and income distribution. Quantifying these adverse impacts can be difficult. But the key point is to understand why deviations from price stability are bad for economic welfare. Such deviations could take the form of inflation or deflation. Of the two, inflation is the more common and persistent danger and for this reason most of the following analysis relates to the costs of inflation.

Deflation, defined as a persistent decline in the general price level, has been a rare phenomenon. In common with most developed countries, Ireland experienced virtually no sustained deflation since 1948. Prices fell, however, in 2009 and 2010 as a result of the fall in aggregate demand. The most traumatic case of deflation was the 25 per cent decline in US prices during the Great Depression of 1929 to 1933. Another case has been the deflation in Japan after the mid-1990s.[18] Japanese consumer prices have fallen in every year since 1999.

Anticipated Inflation

Suppose we focus on inflation, or upward deviations from price stability. Theories of inflation distinguish between anticipated inflation and unanticipated or 'surprise' inflation. The principal welfare costs arise only when inflation is not fully anticipated. If inflation were to proceed at a steady (or otherwise predictable) rate that the public would learn to anticipate, and if institutions adapted fully to this anticipation, people could adjust their economic behaviour accordingly. There would have to be, in effect, a fully indexed economy implying, among other things, a comprehensive system of wage and salary indexation, indexing of tax brackets and allowances, taxation of real rather than nominal returns on assets, etc. In brief, all prices for goods and services, including labour services, would be perfectly adjustable. This would be an example of what has been called the 'flex-price' economy. In such an economy, the welfare cost of inflation involves only two types of cost: 'shoe leather' costs and 'menu' costs.

Cash balances yield an implicit social return by virtue of the convenience they afford in making transactions. Inflation can be regarded as a tax on cash balances: the negative yield on cash balances is equal to the rate of inflation. The higher the rate of inflation, the larger is the negative yield and the opportunity cost of holding cash. Holders of cash balances will, therefore, shift into less liquid and convenient, but income-yielding, assets. This substitution involves a further loss of efficiency in so far as cash balances, which are virtually costless to produce, are economised on in favour of more frequent transactions in less liquid and intrinsically valuable assets. Anticipated inflation also imposes the so-called menu cost of actually changing prices in what have been called 'customer markets' (i.e. those markets in which prices are set and, in the normal course of events, kept unchanged for some time, such as labour markets, retail and wholesale trade, pay telephones and parking meters). Both shoe leather and menu costs increase rapidly with the magnitude of the inflation rate.

Unanticipated Inflation
The costs of anticipated inflation may appear rather theoretical. Yet research shows that they are empirically significant, even at relatively low rates of inflation. Far more important, however, are the costs arising from unanticipated inflation.

First, uncertainty about the inflation rate undermines the role played by money in economising on transaction costs. Fixed-price orders, leases and other explicit long-term contracts, fixed-time schedules for price changes and the broad general commitment to continuity of offers by suppliers are important ways of assisting forward planning. Uncertainty about the future price level shortens the time horizon of such agreements, thus imposing a welfare loss on society.

Second, uncertainty about future price levels results in an arbitrary redistribution of income and wealth. A faster than expected inflation rate, for instance, will tend to discriminate against creditors in favour of debtors. It will also harm those whose incomes are fixed in nominal money terms or which are indexed only after a lapse of time (pensioners), in contrast with those whose incomes are more easily adjustable to inflation, such as unionised wage earners and owners of capital. Another effect is the redistribution of real wealth from the old (who have accumulated assets) to the young, who are, in general, net borrowers. The haphazard nature of the income distribution effects can lead to social unrest and general discontent as people find it increasingly difficult to estimate the growth in their real incomes and to predict what their real earnings will be in the future. In a period of 1 per cent inflation, people who receive pay increases of 4 per cent recognise clearly that they have gained in real terms. In a world of 15 per cent inflation, those receiving pay increases of 18 per cent are likely to be much less confident about how they are faring. That loss of information is a genuine subtraction from welfare. Prices cease to fulfil their signalling function as the effects of relative shifts in prices are blurred by the general rise in the price level.

Third, inflation can have adverse consequences for economic growth. Efficiency losses, though small in any one year, can accumulate over time into a significant aggregate loss. In addition, inflation has a tendency to shorten investment horizons. It attracts capital to 'inflation hedges' such as property at the expense of long-term investment in industry.

Empirical evidence indicates that very high inflation (in excess of 40 per cent per annum) is bad for growth. The evidence is less compelling when it comes to identifying the consequences of one low level of inflation relative to another. Does it matter that much if inflation is 5 per cent rather than 2 per cent? Central banks perhaps need to be more flexible in pursuing their mandate to provide price stability and they need to be given adequate leeway to take a long-run view of an economy's needs. Price stability is good for growth; but it is a secondary, not a primary, objective for economic policy.

Inflation, Deflation and Stability
The above analysis has focused on inflation. Deflation brings similar welfare costs in its train, but for subtly different reasons. Thus, the menu costs apply in the case of anticipated deflation, with the added problem that nominal interest rates cannot be negative (the zero interest rate constraint), an inflexibility that can lead to excessively high real interest rates. At a macroeconomic level, anticipated deflation can prolong a recession by giving consumers and investors an incentive to postpone spending. It benefits lenders at the expense of borrowers and, because downward adjustments in nominal pay are often problematic, it can lead to real wage inflexibility. Like inflation, deflation tends to be self perpetuating and deflationary spirals are difficult and costly to reverse.

Opinion surveys suggest that the public values price stability for its own sake, apart from the economic costs outlined in this section. One could argue that stability in general, and not just price stability, should be given high priority among a region's policy objectives. Of primary concern in this context is the security of the financial system. Central banks have been justly criticised for neglecting this component of their responsibilities. Lending to the property and construction sector became excessive and banks became disastrously over-exposed to a downturn in the economy. The cost of this neglect to many economies, not just Ireland, has been enormous. Too much weight was given to the price stability objective and too little to the stability of banks and credit institutions. A major shake-up of regulation is under way in the EU with the aim of protecting the integrity of the financial system and preventing a recurrence of the crash.

Sustained economic growth in a context of price stability brings with it the capacity to provide many benefits, just as they in turn make growth and stability more sustainable. Economic growth has rightly been defined as a process of cumulative and circular causation. No single policy objective can be pursued in isolation; each objective interacts with the others.

6 COMPETITIVENESS

Small regional economies are largely 'importers' of price trends abroad. Thus if the CPI is rising in Continental Europe and the UK at around 2 per cent, inflation in both parts of Ireland will also approximate 2 per cent. This is a valid generalisation over the long run. But it is not universally the case and significant short-run deviations between a region's inflation rate and the national/area average do occur. During the period 1999–2008 Irish prices rose twice as fast as average euro area prices. As a result, Ireland became one of the most expensive countries in the euro zone. The excess has been only partially reversed by the decline of 6 per cent in the Irish price level up to 2010. Theory indicates that there will be *mean reversion* (i.e. that sooner or later price levels in Ireland will revert to the euro area average), but serious damage to the economy has been done in the interim.[19] Why do cost divergences occur and what can or should be done about them?

Price and Cost Divergences
One reason for the divergence in price trends stems from Ireland's rapid growth relative to the euro zone. Faster growth translates into higher pay. This is non-inflationary where productivity rises in line with pay. Thus a 5 per cent pay rise matched by a 5 per cent productivity increase leaves unit cost, and hence prices, unaffected. However, in those parts of the economy where productivity growth is relatively modest, employers will have to increase wages in line with other sectors (or else their workers will leave for better pay elsewhere). Hence unit costs and prices will tend to rise. Non-traded services are particularly prone to price inflation in such situations: restaurant meals, medical services and building and construction. Here higher pay translates into higher prices. Prices of services have risen consistently faster than prices of goods in recent years.

A second source of inflationary pressure has been the inflationary spiral. In a booming economy the normal restraints on pay rises weaken. Employees, observing higher inflation, seek compensatory pay rises. This leads in turn to further increases in services prices and a process of self-defeating catch-up. The process is further stimulated by a boom in property prices that feeds into pay claims.

Third, changes in the euro exchange rate have had a strong effect on domestic prices. A 20 per cent decline in the value of the euro has been estimated to lead to only a 1 per cent rise in the average euro zone price level. However, because of the Republic's higher trade dependence and the higher proportion of trade with countries outside the euro zone, the impact of such a depreciation of the euro on the Irish CPI is far higher. The weakness of the euro for several years after 1999 imparted a strong 'imported inflation' push on Irish prices which the subsequent strengthening of the euro has been unable to reverse.

Implications of a Loss of Cost Competitiveness
When one region's prices/costs rise relative to other regions, this is termed a loss of cost competitiveness. One immediate impact of such deterioration is a decline in exports as they become more expensive to foreigners. For the same reason, domestic goods become more expensive relative to imports and the import bill rises. The balance of payments on current account then runs into deficit.

For a country with an independent national currency the next question is the effect of the deficit on the exchange rate. If the exchange rate devalues, this offers a short-run solution to the loss of competitiveness. But the resultant rise in domestic prices could set in motion an inflationary spiral, with devaluation causing domestic price increases, which lead to compensatory pay claims. This is the classic downside of devaluation as a policy response to deficits induced by cost-competitiveness problems.

In the case of a small regional economy, the exchange rate is fixed and it will not change in response to the region's loss of competitiveness. If Northern Ireland loses cost competitiveness and runs a deficit, this will not materially affect the value of sterling. Likewise the Republic's competitiveness will have no impact on the fortunes of the euro. In each case the region is too small to affect the bigger picture.

The region may thus be left with a situation where imports rise and exports lose momentum. A balance of payments deficit on current account appears. This means that the region is spending more on foreign goods and services than it is earning from exports. In this sense, a deficit signifies that a country is 'living beyond its means'. The deficit will have to be matched by foreign borrowing, and the corresponding capital inflow will eventually have to be financed and repaid. This will entail a future stream of current account surpluses spread over many years. The level of GNP available to future generations will thus be affected.

An adverse movement in a region's cost competitiveness cannot be indefinitely sustained. As regional prices increase, the region's cost structure becomes more and more out of line with its competitors. It will begin to lose export markets and will become less attractive as a location for investment. Eventually growth will slow, labour demand will decline, and pay pressures will ease. The speed of this process was a much-debated issue in Ireland prior to the crisis. Ireland's price level had risen by 40 per cent above the euro zone average. In a situation like this, booming regions hope for a 'soft' landing, whereby rising costs will gradually be restrained to more sustainable levels over time. Unfortunately, the historical experience provides many examples of 'hard' landings where adjustment takes place abruptly, property markets collapse and unemployment rises. Ireland was to prove no exception to this rule. We suffered an exceptionally hard landing; and the slow, painful process of restoring competitiveness had to begin in earnest after 2008.

This suggests that the major concern of any region must be to safeguard its competitiveness, achieving its economic potential while moderating booms and avoiding busts along the way. The importance of avoiding deviations from competitiveness in a common currency union has long been accepted. In 2011, Angela Merkel, the German chancellor, floated the idea of a Competitiveness Pact among euro area members whereby price deviations from the euro area average on the part of a member state would be monitored and would trigger a collective response to correct them. The aim would be to ensure much closer economic and fiscal co-ordination in the euro zone.

Thus for a region lacking an independent exchange rate and with largely downward-inflexible labour costs, domestic competitiveness policy is an instrument of major importance.

Broad Definition of Competitiveness

Competitiveness has become something of a global preoccupation since the 1990s. Every region worries about it and governments everywhere feel compelled to do something to improve it. Practically every country in Europe has set up competitiveness councils. The *World Competitiveness Report*, and its rival, the *Global Competitiveness Report*, are published annually and attract worldwide publicity. Their findings are scrutinised with a fine-tooth comb by development agencies and government commissions. In short, maintaining competitiveness can now be described as a key secondary policy objective, with improvements in competitiveness seen as crucial to achieving growth and full employment.

Competitiveness has been a well-established theme in economic debate in Ireland. In the Republic, the National Competitiveness Council was set up in 1997. Its *Annual Competitiveness Report* is a rich source of information on competitiveness indicators (see Chapters 9 and 10, for example). The council's remit is to examine key competitiveness issues and to make recommendations on policy actions required to improve Ireland's competitive position.

Competitiveness can be defined in a narrow sense or in a broad sense. The narrow definition focuses on trends in pay, productivity and unit costs. These components are aggregated into a cost competitiveness index and movements in the index are tracked over time and compared with trends in competing countries. For many years, emphasis was placed on this narrow definition partly because of data limitations (information on the components of the broader definition has only recently become available) and partly because Ireland's performance on the cost competitiveness definition was exceptionally poor. The harmonised competitiveness indicator recorded a 40 per cent worsening between 2000 and 2008, the result of a stronger euro and escalating domestic costs. By early 2011, a recovery of some 15 per cent of this loss had been achieved, due to a combination of pay cuts, productivity gains and movements in the euro (see Chapters 6 and 9).

The broader definition includes price and non-price factors such as product quality, reliability of supply, back-up marketing services and taxation, and extends to consideration of human resource development, business services, infrastructure and public finance and administration. A country's long-run competitive position can also be profoundly influenced by its policy on research and development (R&D), and by its success in product innovation and technology. Innovation and R&D are the key ingredients of a region's infrastructure (see Chapters 7 and 9). Competitiveness authorities in both parts of Ireland currently use the broader definition of competitiveness.[20] In this they are in line with international practice. For instance, the World Economic Forum defines competitiveness as 'the ability to achieve sustained high rates of growth in GDP per capita'. Thus competitiveness measures the degree to which a nation or a region can, under free market conditions, produce goods and services that meet the test of international markets while simultaneously expanding the real income of its citizens.

Competitiveness is a relative concept. Success in the competitiveness league depends on how well an economy is progressing relative to others. It is possible for all countries to grow faster, to generate more employment, to export more; but by definition only some countries can become more competitive. In other words, the process of striving to be more competitive, in so far as it improves economic growth and efficiency, is a positive-sum game. But in terms of ranking in competitiveness leagues it is a zero-sum game: one region advances in the ranking order only if some other region declines. Failure to recognise this point can lead to competitiveness becoming what has been called a 'dangerous obsession' instead of a stimulus to improved performance.

Strategy to Improve Competitiveness

Policies to improve competitiveness constitute the theme of many chapters of this book. These policies change over time and according to circumstances will differ across regions and nations. To date the policy objective has focused on creating an environment that would encourage (see Chapter 9 in particular):

- the growth of export-oriented firms, especially Irish-owned firms;
- the retention and attraction of foreign direct investment in knowledge-based sectors and activities such as electronics, pharmaceuticals, biotechnology, and software;
- the development of linkages between existing and new green-field firms;
- a balanced location of economic activity within the island.

This ambitious programme has involved several policy dimensions and instruments, which will be analysed throughout this book.

The context of Ireland's competitiveness challenge has changed markedly in recent years. First, in the past Ireland has benefited significantly from the Structural and Cohesion Funds. With rising prosperity, however, the Republic's net receipts from these funds have diminished.

Second, policy measures taken at the centre (Brussels/Frankfurt/London) are becoming increasingly important. Monetary and exchange rate policy is the obvious example. The centre also exerts major influence over fiscal, competition, transport and agriculture policy as well as state aids and taxation. The European Commission is concerned about competitiveness at the EU-wide level, and action taken to improve it will have important implications for Ireland.

Finally, the scope for regional policy initiatives, though declining, remains of crucial importance. A key fiscal incentive in the Republic is the 12.5 per cent tax rate for all corporate income from 2003 and the Brussels-approved 'grandparenting' of the 10 per cent rate up to 2010 for all companies already in operation (see Chapters 4 and 9). In addition, domestic authorities have some degree of discretion in the payment of capital grants, training grants, R&D support and so on. The extension of these fiscal and financial concessions to internationally traded service industries has proved to be a significant incentive to the development of the Irish Financial Services Centre and the attraction of major multinationals to Ireland (see Chapter 9). Provision of a good physical environment and human capital structure (education) is also an intrinsic part of a strategy for improving competitiveness (see Chapters 9, 10 and 13).

7 CONCLUSION

The first priority of economic policy is to ensure high and rising standards of living. In practical terms, this means that economic performance is judged mostly by reference to changes in GNP per person. People want economic growth because of what it can do for them in terms of higher purchasing power and also because of the other good things that often accompany growth, such as full employment, generous safety nets for the poor and greater security.

Growth is a primary objective, but there are limits to what it can deliver. Growth at any price is not a sensible objective, nor is the attainment of maximum growth, particularly when this would involve environmental damage, an excessively large increase in immigration, and other undesirable spill-over effects. In setting medium-term targets, rather than targeting the maximum growth an economy can reach and then working out the implications of this for policy, we should instead be asking what growth we wish to obtain and work backwards from there.

GNP per capita has many limitations as an indicator of human welfare. It leaves out of account leisure, the environment and global warming, and misclassifies many inputs as outputs. Another limitation is that GNP per capita neglects important indicators of human welfare such as education and life expectancy. Despite its many failings, however, the GNP per capita statistic serves as a remarkably good proxy for more sophisticated measures of human welfare, as comparisons between rankings based on GNP per head and the United Nations Human Development Index demonstrate.

Equity in the sense of a fair distribution of income and an adequate level of income to all individuals is an important policy objective. The issue of equity is indeed a central aspect of most economic problems. In the Irish political domain, concerns with equity and income distribution often outweigh concerns with economic efficiency in discussion of policy alternatives. Policy-makers seek to reduce social exclusion and long-term unemployment by widening opportunities for education and work. Care should be taken, however, when deciding on the degree of redistribution to avoid penalising the achievers and stifling economic growth. Protecting the vulnerable is good, but encouraging those who will restore the Irish economy to health must, for the next decade at least, be paramount.

It is also important to consider the 'well-being' or happiness of the community in the broadest sense when formulating economic policy. The weak association between a country's GNP per person and happiness gives pause for reflection. We do not know if this relationship applies when income is falling, but with good management the painful effects of the loss of income can perhaps be moderated. This reinforces the need for policies that will seek to maximise societal welfare and that will deliver a full-employment, pollution-free, low-crime and safe society.

Price stability is a policy objective that is desired both for its own sake and as a means to the end of attaining growth. There is now more conviction among politicians of the electoral advantages of running an economy in a way that maintains price stability. As a population ages, it is likely that the constituency in favour of price stability will grow. Politicians seem increasingly content to leave monetary policy to independent central banks. This new approach is helpful for price stability and good for the overall economy, since low inflation and output growth complement one another in the long run.

Has the adoption of price stability as a policy target been associated with a demonstrable improvement in economic efficiency and social stability? Many argue that it has. They would agree with Keynes that deviations from price stability, whether in the form of inflation or deflation, have inflicted great injuries; 'both evils are to be shunned'.[21] Hence the importance of ensuring that price stability, once restored, is thereafter maintained.

Experience over the past few years has, however, taught a further important lesson. Price stability (in terms of consumer prices) is not enough. Stability of the financial system is an even more important objective that, we see in retrospect, was given all too little attention in the lead-up to the banking crisis. The remit of central banks and the financial authorities will need to be expanded and refined and the process of finding an agreed formula for doing this at a European level is now the subject of intensive consideration.

As we advance into the twenty-first century, we can expect competitiveness to occupy the high ground as a major secondary policy objective for the economy. Competitiveness covers a wider spectrum of economic variables. Irish policy-makers used to focus on standard comparisons between cost and price indicators here and in competitor countries. These indexes continue to be relevant. Within the space of a few years, the Republic became a comparatively expensive location for visiting or doing business, and prices and pay rates converged towards the higher end of the European spectrum. The detrimental effects of this loss in competitiveness became apparent as the post-2008 crisis evolved. In the longer run, it will clearly be necessary to justify these higher earnings by higher productivity. It is here that the broader definition of competitiveness comes into play. Competitiveness in this broader sense includes R&D, education, quality improvement, marketing and physical infrastructure – the intangible and often difficult to measure aspects that impact crucially on an economy's ability to perform well.

Endnotes

* The author wishes to thank the editors for percipient and helpful comments. He has drawn on Chapters 2 and 12 of D. McAleese, *Economics for Business*, Financial Times Prentice Hall, London 2004.

1 See Chapter 7 for a discussion of the difference between GNP and GDP, an issue of particular importance in Ireland. In most countries they give the same numbers but in the case of Ireland GNP (income) is around 15 per cent less than GDP (output) and hence we will use GNP for the remainder of this chapter.

2 See National Economic and Social Council (NESC), *The Economic and Social Implications of Emigration*, Stationery Office, Dublin 1991.

3 J. Galbraith, *The Nature of Mass Poverty*, Harvard University Press, Cambridge MA 1979.

4 NESC, *The Economic and Social Implications of Emigration*, Stationery Office, Dublin 1991.

5 In the words of the Whitaker Report, 'emigration will not be checked nor will unemployment be permanently reduced until the rate of increase in national output is greatly accelerated', Department of Finance, *Programme for Economic Expansion*, Stationery Office, Dublin 1958, p. 7.

6 R. Kennedy, quoted in *Finance and Development*, Washington, December 1993, p.20.

7 United Nations Development Programme, *Human Development Report*, Oxford University Press, New York 2010.

8 A. Okun, *Equality and Efficiency: The Big Trade-off*, Brookings Institution, Washington DC 1975.

9 J. Rawls, *A Theory of Justice*, Harvard University Press, Cambridge MA 1971.

10 NESC, *Opportunities, Challenges and Capacities for Choice*, Stationery Office, Dublin 1999, p. 51.

11 R. Nozick, *Anarchy, State and Utopia*, Basic Books, New York 1974.

12 A readable and enlightening overview of the literature is provided in R. Layard, *Happiness: Lessons from a New Science*, Penguin Books, New York and London 2005.

13 B. Frey and A Stutzer, 'Happiness: a new approach in economics', *CESifo Report*, Munich Winter 2010.

14 R. Whately, *Introductory Lectures on Political Economy*, London 1831.

15 A. Kearns and M. Woods, 'The concentration in property-related lending: a financial stability perspective', *Financial Stability Report 2006*, Central Bank and Financial Services Authority of Ireland, Dublin 2006.

16 Parliamentary Debates: Joint Committee on Economic and Regulatory Affairs' Discussion with the Department of Finance, 8 July 2009.

17 N. Taleb, *The Black Swan: the Impact of the Highly Improbable*, Penguin Books, 2007. Taleb has many interesting insights into the riskiness of banks. An Irish reader, for instance, will appreciate the following paragraph: 'If they [banks] look conservative, it is because their loans only go bust on rare, very rare, occasions. There is no way to gauge the effectiveness of their lending activity by observing it over a day, a week, a month, or ... even a century! In the summer of 1982 large American banks lost close to all their past earnings (cumulatively), about everything they ever made in the history of American banking. They had been lending to South and Central American countries that all defaulted at the same time – "an event of an exceptional nature"... . All the while bankers led everyone, especially themselves, into believing that they were "conservative". They are not conservative: just phenomenally skilled at self-deception by burying the possibility of a large devastating loss under the rug' (p. 43).

18 Deflation brings serious problems in its train and it is important to keep these in mind in evaluating policy options for the European Central Bank. Because it is a new institution, many feared that its urge to establish sound price-stability credentials might lead it to give too much weight to inflation and pay too little attention to the dangers of deflation. The ECB asserts that its commitment to price stability is 'symmetric'; deviations on either side of its price target are equally undesirable.

19 See P. Lane, 'Ireland and the deflation debate', *Irish Banking Review,* Winter 2003; and D. McAleese, *Economics for Business,* Financial Times Prentice Hall, London 2004, Box 12.1.

20 See D. O'Brien, 'Measuring Ireland's price and labour cost competitiveness', *Central Bank Quarterly Bulletin*, Vol. 1, 2010; and A. Gray, G. Swinand and W. Batt, *Economic Analysis of Ireland's Competitive Advantages for Foreign Investment,* Indecon, Dublin 2010.

21 J.M. Keynes, 'Economic consequences of the peace', *Collected Economic Writings*, Macmillan, London 1971, p. 149.

SECTION II

POLICY IMPLEMENTATION

CHAPTER 3

Role of Government: Rationale and Issues

Philip R. Lane

1 INTRODUCTION

Chapter 2 established economic policy objectives for Ireland. The government, on the premise that it indeed cares about national welfare, is responsible for the attainment of these goals, either directly or in tandem with its international counterparts. The government's ability to achieve its policy goals is facilitated by the special powers assigned to the state, most notably its powers of compulsion. In this chapter, the role of government in pursuing these policy objectives is addressed.

The chapter is organised as follows. Section 2 reviews the theoretical basis for government intervention in the economy. The allocation of responsibilities across different levels of government is described in Section 3. In Section 4, the central role played by public expenditure and taxation policies is analysed. Section 5 addresses other policy instruments available to the government, while Section 6 discusses the economic and political factors determining the size of the government sector. Section 7 concludes the chapter.

2 RATIONALE FOR GOVERNMENT INTERVENTION

There are a number of classic arguments that provide a rationale for government intervention in the economy. The starting point is to recognise the absurdity of a no-government economy. A central authority and a *legal system* are necessary to permit the (implicit or explicit) contracts that govern all economic activity, for example through the design and enforcement of corporate and labour laws. Cross-country evidence and historical examples show that anarchy and the absence of a 'rule of law' result in very poor economic performance (and the emergence of private contract enforcement systems, such as Mafia-style organisations): the evidence from 'failed states' lends considerable support to these concerns.[1] Put another way, we can interpret economic activity as an elaborate game: as with any other game, a set of rules and a referee are required. The government is responsible for designing and enforcing the rules that determine permissible behaviour on the parts of firms and consumers: the anarchic alternative would be unstable and highly deleterious for economic performance.

A second function relates to the efficient allocation of resources. A laissez-faire economy will not efficiently provide *pure public goods* (e.g. national defence). A public good is non-rival (it can be collectively consumed) and non-excludable (its benefits cannot be easily withheld from individuals): examples include the provision of national security and basic scientific research (a new mathematical formula can be used by everyone and, once published, is non-excludable). Non-excludability prevents market provision, since no one has an incentive to pay for a good if it can be freely consumed. The state must step in to provide such public goods and raise the resources required by levying taxation.

Similarly, market prices do not reflect *external effects*, with the result that activities generating positive externalities are under-produced and those generating negative externalities are over-produced. A good that produces a positive externality is similar to a public good, in that some of its benefits are non-excludable and accrue to others than just the direct consumer. However, such goods may be rivalrous and may be partially excludable, so that some private provision occurs even if the level of production is inadequate.

The road network is a good illustration of a positive externality: the gain to building an extra kilometre of motorway increases the productivity of other parts of the road network that become more accessible. One obvious example of a negative externality is environmental pollution. A second example is provided by commonly held resources such as fisheries, whereby individuals are not responsible for the maintenance of a sustainable stock. To promote goods that generate positive externalities, the state may engage in direct provision or offer subsidies. In contrast, it may impose quotas or taxes on goods that generate negative external effects.

Other sources of market failure include *monopoly power* and *imperfect information*. The former means that prices will be too high and output too low relative to the competitive outcome. The latter means that many credit and insurance markets are missing or incomplete, since it is impossible for private firms to adequately evaluate projects, accurately calculate default risks and monitor the behaviour of individual agents. Such market failures provide a *prima facie* case for some kind of government intervention, either by direct provision or through subsidisation.

However, the desirability of actual intervention is tempered by 'government failure': it is not clear that, in many cases, governments can deliver a more efficient outcome than that generated by even imperfect markets. Electoral pressures, interest group lobbying, perverse incentives in administration, corruption, restrictive practices and inflexible procedures in the public sector, and poor management skills may all lead to welfare-decreasing interventions in the economy. Accordingly, the optimal degree of government intervention must balance the prospective gains against potential implementation problems.

Even if free markets delivered a perfectly efficient outcome, *distributional considerations* would still justify government intervention. The income distribution attained by a market economy is conditional on the initial distribution of endowments (both monetary and individual characteristics such as intelligence, good health and family background). Being lucky in one's choice of parents is an important determinant of success in a market economy: for example, in Ireland and elsewhere, educational attainment levels are highly correlated with family income levels and social background (see also Chapter 13). Moreover, economic outcomes have a random element. The weather influences the success or failure of many agricultural projects and many entrepreneurs recognise the role played by fortune in creating viable new businesses.

Accordingly, voters typically demand that the government redistributes income in order to protect the poorly endowed and the unlucky. However, the ability of the government to redistribute income is constrained along two dimensions. First, excessively high taxation depresses incentives, reducing the level of income and growth rates. Second, mobile factors (capital, highly skilled workers) may leave jurisdictions that impose harsh tax burdens.

Finally, it should be clear that government performance is an important determinant of international competitiveness. An efficient government enhances the ability of domestic firms to compete in international markets, by reducing the taxation and other costs of attaining policy objectives; in international empirical studies, an efficient government is highly correlated with strong growth performance.[2]

3 LEVELS OF GOVERNMENT

Different levels of government can intervene in the economy. Although the traditional focus has been on national governments, global, European and local levels of government are increasingly important.

Global Governance

For some issues, global levels of government are better placed. Ireland participates in the World Trade Organisation, is a member of the International Monetary Fund and World Bank, and subscribes to various international policy agreements, such as on climate change.

The driving force behind global levels of governance is that the globalisation of many economic activities enhances efficiency and is facilitated by a common set of international rules. For instance, it would be an extremely tedious procedure for each country to negotiate bilateral agreements with all its potential trading partners: the World Trade Organisation and the various regional trade agreements greatly reduce the transaction costs in ensuring trade liberalisation.

Similarly, in tackling problems that are fundamentally global in character, non-co-ordinated national policy responses make little sense.[3] The most obvious example is the climate change problem: carbon emissions in each country symmetrically affect the global climate. However, similar considerations apply in the domain of public health: high levels of air travel mean that a virus that emerges in one area (such as SARS in East Asia in 2002–3) can quickly be transmitted around the world. To the extent that some security threats are global in nature (for example the control of nuclear weapons and the risks posed by dissident groups that seek to disrupt global economic and social systems), there is also a global level to defence policies. Finally, large international income inequalities, especially the extreme poverty of the 'bottom billion' of the global population (primarily in sub-Saharan Africa) constitute a global problem across many dimensions.[4] In addition to the ethical issues, it is in the self-interest of advanced economies to promote international development, in view of the interconnections between extreme poverty, political instability, mass migrations and public health.

Moreover, the globalisation of economic activity also makes national or regional policy actions less effective: for example, high tax rates or excessive regulation may prompt mobile factors to relocate to more business-friendly regimes. Conversely, national subsidies or tax breaks distort international location decisions, since a firm may opt to produce even in an inefficient location if it receives sufficiently high compensation from the host government. For these reasons, co-ordinating international policies can potentially restore the ability of governments to tax mobile factors and avoid undesirable 'subsidy auctions' in competing for footloose firms.

That said, the difficulty with international policy co-ordination is that there is not always consensus on the correct policy. Preferences may legitimately differ across countries on important issues such as: the appropriate level of taxation; the ideal level of social protection; and the optimal degree of risk aversion in food regulation. Accordingly, global governance arrangements are more easily achieved on technocratic issues such as elements of world trade and financial systems, with less progress on social issues. For this reason, it is sometimes argued that the development of global governance has been unbalanced: much progress has been made on co-operation in economic policy but there has been less effective co-ordination of labour or environmental regulations. However, in the absence of a directly elected 'world government', it is unlikely that much progress can be made on controversial issues that are the subject of much disagreement both within and across countries.[5]

Moreover, cross-country distributional issues also limit the scope for global co-operation. While there is a strong intellectual consensus (reinforced by the global financial crisis from 2007 onwards) that the largest global financial institutions require a common global regulatory approach, progress in designing a common set of rules has been relatively weak, with each country seeking rules that suit their own financial institutions.

These factors mean that global levels of governance are likely to remain quite circumscribed in the absence of sufficient consensus on various issues across sovereign nations. In terms of new initiatives, a primary area where global action may occur is in relation to climate change, in view of the emerging consensus on the nature and urgency of the problem. Even in that domain, the capacity to forge a global agreement that tackles global warming in an efficient yet equitable manner is open to question. One basic problem is that a fair global solution plausibly involves a significant transfer of funds from the advanced economies to the developing world, to compensate for the fact that the accumulated stock of carbon emissions has been primarily generated by high-income countries over many decades of industrial activity: achieving agreement on the scale of such redistribution will be difficult. A second problem is that it is difficult and costly to impose sanctions on non-compliant nations, so that any global initiative must rely on softer methods of promoting compliance – for example, peer pressure across member governments, plus monitoring by national and international 'civic society' groups such as Save the Earth, Greenpeace and other activist organisations.

EU Governance

EU membership is the most important international commitment of the Irish government. Although the scale of inter-governmental co-operation at the EU level faces many of the difficulties encountered at global levels of governance, the scope for establishing common policies is much greater at the EU level. This reflects the very close economic and social ties across the member countries, plus the elaborate institutional structure that has been developed (European Commission, Council of Ministers, European Parliament) to promote and sustain policy-making at the EU level. Moreover, since member states bargain over many issues, decision-making is facilitated by the multi-dimensional nature of political relations among the member states: for instance, some undesirable regulation in one area may be accepted in exchange for a concession on another issue. In other cases, the level of disagreement may be so strong that co-ordination is not possible, with countries retaining independent national policies. Although a national veto still remains on some policy issues (e.g. taxation), majority voting now applies in many areas.

Four Freedoms

In order to create a single market, EU law guarantees the 'four freedoms': the free movement of goods; the free movement of services and freedom of establishment; the free movement of persons (and citizenship), including free movement of workers; and the free movement of capital. In addition, EU competition law also now sharply restricts national autonomy in industrial policy. For instance, EU governments can now only invest in state-owned enterprises on a commercial basis: rescuing loss-making firms for non-economic reasons is no longer permitted. In addition, large public contracts must be advertised at EU-wide level, rather than directly allocated to domestic firms. In these ways, the EU can be interpreted as an international 'agency of restraint' that promotes more efficient allocations and depoliticises many economic decisions.

That said, the difficulty with international policy co-ordination is that there is not always consensus on the correct policy. Preferences may legitimately differ across countries on important issues such as: the appropriate level of taxation; the ideal level of social protection; and the optimal degree of risk aversion in food regulation. Since member nations bargain over many issues, some undesirable regulations may be accepted in exchange for concessions on other issues. In other cases, the level of disagreement may be so strong that co-ordination is not possible, with countries retaining independent national policies.

Democratic Accountability

A common criticism of international policy co-ordination is that it leads to a 'democratic deficit', with decisions made at a level that is too far removed from ordinary voters. The EU has traditionally suffered from this objection, since policy decisions have been made at inter-governmental Council of Ministers meetings that are held in private with no review by national parliaments.

The 2008 Treaty of Lisbon seeks to redress this imbalance in several ways. First, the design of the Treaty was extensively debated in a highly participatory Constitutional Convention before the final articles were agreed. In Ireland, this debate was further widened through the activities of the National Forum on Europe, which held a large number of public meetings to improve awareness and permit debate on European policy issues. Second, the Treaty improves democratic accountability. For instance, major EU policy decisions are supposed to be reviewed by national parliaments, in addition to the European Parliament. In addition, the European Council of Ministers conducts more of its business in public session and has a 'public face' in that the President of the European Council is appointed for a term of two and a half years and cannot hold any national mandate. Democratic accountability is further improved by the closer alignment of national population sizes and relative voting power in the Council of Ministers under the new Treaty.

Taxation

As indicated, many decisions concerning government spending and taxation remain at the national level, providing scope for significant variation in the level and nature of government intervention across member countries. Following the earlier discussion, harmonisation of tax rates on mobile capital is advocated by some member countries. However, there is little agreement on the appropriate tax rate: a high capital tax rate may be progressive and reduce pressure on other parts of the tax base but at the cost of a negative effect on growth performance, with countries having different preferences as to the optimal trade-off across these dimensions.

Ireland has opted for a low tax strategy and currently resists pressure to harmonise rates at a higher level. However, there is also a current proposal to design a common consolidated tax base, such that a multinational firm need only produce a single set of European financial accounts, with capital income taxed according to a formula that reflects its economic activities (such as sales revenues) in each country. To the extent that this is a voluntary code, the impact on Ireland may be relatively minor, but widespread adoption of a common tax base would limit the level of corporate income that is taxable in Ireland, in view of the export orientation of most multinational firms operating in Ireland.

Euro Zone and Financial Crisis

In 1999, a subset of eleven EU members adopted the euro as a single currency. By 2011, seventeen EU members had joined the euro area, with further members expected to join over the next decade. A monetary union offers microeconomic efficiency gains and facilitates the development of a deep, liquid capital market. Moreover, a large bloc is plausibly insulated from destabilising speculative attacks on its currency, permitting lower average interest rates. A core feature of European monetary union is that the member governments have delegated the operation of monetary policy to an independent agency – the European Central Bank (ECB). Perhaps the most important advantage is that a supranational central bank may be more effectively insulated from political pressures than are national monetary authorities.

The delegation of technocratic forms of government intervention, such as the conduct of monetary policy, to semi-autonomous institutions can be interpreted as a useful agency of restraint that ties the hands of political leaders who face enormous short-term pressures to adopt populist policies that may damage the economy in the long term. Democratic accountability is ensured through several mechanisms: the mandate of the ECB is fixed by treaty; the President of the ECB testifies before the European Parliament on a regular basis; and the ECB is in regular dialogue with the European Commission and the Euro Group of finance ministers.

However, a 'one size fits all' monetary policy may itself be a source of instability for member countries with business cycles that are not highly correlated with the core of the euro zone. In the early years of European Monetary Union (EMU), Ireland fell into this category: in view of our high growth rates, interest rates were inappropriately low and excessive inflation was the result. In the other direction, countries such as Germany, Portugal and Italy may have preferred a looser monetary policy at various times, in view of poor domestic performance in these economies.

Since the onset of the financial crisis in 2007, EMU has been subject to a severe test. In one direction, a common currency has provided a lot of insulation during the crisis. The ECB cut interest rates sharply in late 2008 and early 2009 from 3.75 per cent to 1 per cent and maintained this low rate until spring 2011. This cut in interest rates provided substantial relief for indebted households and firms throughout the crisis. In addition, the ECB has provided general liquidity to the European banking system, substituting for the breakdown of the inter-bank wholesale market in 2008 and 2009. In addition, the liquidity operations of the ECB have provided extraordinary support to the troubled banking systems in the euro periphery, with an outflow of private capital from these countries partly replaced by an inflow of official funding from the ECB.

However, the European periphery had accumulated a lot of debt during the pre-crisis years, with the global credit boom during 2003–7 allowing the private and public sectors in these countries to borrow large amounts (with the relative contributions of the private and public sector differing across the individual countries). In early 2010, debt markets became sceptical about the capacity of the new Greek government to meet its debt obligations (which had been partly concealed by the previous government), with the EU and IMF eventually combining to provide a bailout package for Greece. Ireland also received a bailout in November 2010, with Portugal following in April 2011.

These bailouts are intended to provide bridge financing for a temporary period during which the recipient countries reduce their dependence on external debt, by cutting fiscal deficits and deleveraging banking systems. Such fiscal austerity is more costly under a monetary union, since the negative output effects of a fiscal contraction cannot be offset by a monetary expansion or currency devaluation. The alternative is to conduct a debt restructuring, by which part of the debt is written off, inflicting losses on the creditor countries. In turn, such a major event may trigger significant disruption in the European financial system, such that the current priority among European policy-makers is to follow a twin-track process by which bridge financing is offered to the debtor countries and the capacity of the European financial system to absorb loan losses is improved.

Over the longer term, it is recognised that an extensive reform programme is required in order to avoid such a crisis in the future. On the debtor side, banking systems need to be more tightly regulated in order to avoid excessive debt. Similarly, fiscal policy has to be more prudent in order to avoid vulnerability to a sovereign debt crisis – we return to this topic later in the chapter. On the creditor side, financial institutions need to hold larger reserves in order to improve capacity to withstand loan losses. To these ends, the design of the European Stabilisation Mechanism (ESM) that will begin operations in 2013 is intended to provide the incentives for debtors and creditors to adopt more prudent policies.

At a deeper level, the crisis has underlined that a common currency area will be more robust if there is a common financial regulatory system (and a shared approach to resolving banking crises) and if common oversight of fiscal policy not only avoids excessive deficits but also ensures sufficiently large surpluses are accumulated during good years in order to reduce fiscal vulnerability during bad years.

Local Government

At the other end, some policy issues are being devolved from national to local and regional levels of government. Local government plausibly has an information advantage in designing and implementing policies that better reflect the preferences and needs of local residents. A closer relationship with the electorate may also improve the responsiveness and accountability of government.

However, decentralisation also brings risks, especially if fiscal and functional responsibilities are not clearly allocated between the centre and periphery. In Ireland, local government has traditionally played a very limited role. However, with the switch towards greater local financing and autonomy in the provision of services (e.g. waste collection, water services), the trend is towards greater diversity in local government in Ireland. The application of the subsidiarity principle is also more evident at the EU level: there is greater recognition that the EU should focus its energies on those policy areas where co-operation is most effective, with the return of some policy issues to national governments. For instance, with the move to direct payments in subsidising the agricultural sector, it is predicted that responsibility for the agricultural sector will be shifted from Brussels to national levels of government (see Chapter 11).

Finally, in light of the improved political climate since the 1988 Good Friday Agreement, progress has been made for better policy co-operation between the Republic of Ireland and Northern Ireland, with considerable scope for yet further integration. Significant scale economies can be achieved in areas such as tourism (e.g. with the creation of the all-island Tourism Ireland marketing organisation) and network externalities can be better exploited by more efficiently integrating the transport and energy networks between the two jurisdictions. Moreover, the economic success of the Republic of Ireland has led to some reorientation of activity in Northern Ireland, with a greater focus on pursuing cross-border business opportunities. Under the Good Friday Agreement, a number of inter-governmental agencies have been established to facilitate enhanced policy co-operation in areas such as the environment, agriculture, education, health, tourism and transport.

4 PUBLIC EXPENDITURE AND TAXATION

There are three types of government spending: public consumption; transfers; and public investment. The first category incorporates the provision of government services such as the civil service, education, health, the justice system and defence. The second includes social welfare payments, payments to the EU central budget and debt interest payments. The third relates to spending on infrastructure (e.g. the road network) and on the buildings and equipment associated with the provision of government services.

Public Consumption
Education and healthcare are the major items of public consumption. We only briefly review these sectors, since they are covered in more detail in Chapters 12 and 13. Spending on education and healthcare is in part motivated by redistributive considerations, to ensure access for all to at least a minimal level of services. At an efficiency level, private financing of education is plagued by credit problems and the healthcare sector suffers from myriad asymmetric information

problems. Finally, promoting education arguably confers positive externalities and is necessary to a healthy democracy, since political participation is positively related to education levels. Although these arguments justify public financing of the education and healthcare sectors, this need not involve monopoly public provision of these services: for instance, the state could provide vouchers to parents that could be used to pay fees at private schools or pay the insurance premia to private healthcare companies.

Transfers

The welfare budget is the largest component of transfer spending. Some transfers can be justified by imperfections in insurance markets. For example, private insurance schemes are unlikely to provide fairly priced protection against the risk of unemployment. However, the stronger motivation behind transfers is redistribution: voters are unwilling to allow the incomes of the unemployed, the sick or the old to fall below a minimum level. In designing a welfare system, there is a clear trade-off between the level of benefits and the need to provide incentives to seek employment (in the case of unemployment benefit) or to save privately for retirement (in the case of pensions).

Producer subsidies are another kind of transfer. Although these have been declining in recent years, subsidies are still used to attract multinational corporations and support local start-ups. One problem with producer subsidies is that behaviour is distorted: rather than focusing on innovation and maximising profitability, entrepreneurs may divert resources to lobbying the government for subsidies. However, the worst excesses of this kind of behaviour have been sharply circumscribed by stricter EU regulations on the allocation of state aids to industry. Most notably, the European airline industry has historically been a major recipient of state subsidies, but the European Commission now regularly prohibits the protection of 'national champions'. A second problem with producer subsidies is that Ireland competes with other EU countries for footloose firms: this bidding war may result in the successful country suffering a 'winner's curse', having to offer a subsidy larger than any potential benefits. With the rapid decline in unemployment, the structure of Irish producer subsidies has shifted from targeting job creation to encouraging strategic sectors with the potential for high growth.

Public Investment

Public investment has two economic functions: the provision of (a) public inputs that directly raise the productivity of the economy; and (b) public amenities that improve the quality of life and are valued by the community (see Chapter 10). Of course, the same project may contribute to both objectives. For example, an improved road network not only improves economic performance but the elimination of traffic jams is to be welcomed for its own sake in terms of reducing stress levels. Conversely, cultural projects and sports facilities not only improve the quality of leisure time but may indirectly improve economic performance by making Ireland a more attractive location for internationally mobile workers.[6]

The state plays a central role in ensuring the provision of infrastructure, such as the transport network or the planning framework for housing and urban development. Infrastructure is fundamentally characterised by external effects: the value of a network is greater than the sum of its parts. For this reason, the state plays a leading role in the planning and design of networks in transport, utilities, housing and urban development.

In addition to its planning role, the state also directly provides much infrastructure. For instance, although privately funded toll roads and bridges can make a contribution to the overall transport network, public good and equity considerations mean that much infrastructural investment is financed by the state. Direct provision also solves severe co-ordination problems: for instance, a laissez-faire system may see wasteful duplication in those areas likely to generate the highest toll revenues.

In the decade prior to the crisis, infrastructural investment was very high in Ireland, in a bid to redress the severe infrastructural deficit that emerged from a combination of low investment during the 1980s and early 1990s and rapid economic and population growth (see Chapter 10). The National Development Plan 2007–2013 set out an ambitious programme, with the objective of both improving the physical infrastructure (new roads; Luas extension; capital projects in the health and education sectors; new social housing) and the 'knowledge' infrastructure (government investment in human capital and scientific research).

However, it may have been more effective to adopt a more gradual rate of increase in public investment. The pro-cyclical timing of the acceleration in public investment can lead to high inflation in the construction sector, especially if it is already under pressure due to rising private investment activity. The scale of the increase in public investment may also run into administrative, planning and legal bottlenecks that further reduce returns. Over the medium term, it is certainly the case that a stable level of public investment is far preferable to the 'stop-go' cycle that has historically characterised Irish public investment dynamics.

The healthy state of the public finances up to 2007 meant that much of the investment was met by tax revenues. However, some of the investment took the form of public–private partnerships (PPPs), while tolls have partially financed some road and bridge projects (see Chapter 10). Although private sources of finance during normal times are typically more expensive (since a highly rated government can borrow at lower rates than private firms), this does enable the use of scarce private managerial talent to achieve social goals. Moreover, the PPP contract typically includes appropriate penalty clauses, such that the risk of cost overruns or time delays is potentially transferred to the private operator. There have been only a few PPP projects in Ireland, and the UK experience has been that the transfer of risk to the private operator has not always been successfully executed.

An important element in efficient provision of public infrastructure is that all projects are subjected to a comprehensive cost-benefit analysis. Economic analysis has a large part to play in such evaluations. However, especially with respect to the provision of public amenities, variation in individual preferences between private goods and public amenities means that evaluation of such projects also has to take into account social and political factors in addition to the economic dimension. In Ireland, full cost-benefit analyses have not been applied to all projects in a transparent manner, such that the rationale for some investment decisions is not always clear.

Furthermore, with the major downward shift in the projected growth of the Irish economy, the appropriate level of public capital is also smaller than previously estimated. Many projects that could be justified under optimistic growth scenarios are no longer sustainable, in view of the smaller population, lower activity levels and higher level of public debt.

Taxation
Chapter 4 will focus on taxation and the public finances, so we will only briefly discuss the role of taxation as a policy instrument. At one level, the main impetus for taxation is to finance public expenditure and the design of the taxation system is accordingly targeted at collecting revenues in a manner that least distorts economic decisions. However, there is a secondary role for tax policies in order to correct market distortions – such tax interventions can be 'revenue neutral' by rebating the revenues collected through a reduction in other taxes.

In relation to environmental protection, the role of taxation as a method to alter behaviour is widely recognised. For instance, Ireland has been a pioneer in reducing usage of plastic shopping bags, through the introduction of a small levy in 2002 that quickly converted most of the population to the use of re-usable bags. Similarly, bin charges have induced households to recycle more and avoid unnecessary packaging. At a wider level, it is widely recognised that a carbon tax has a key role to play in reducing carbon emissions, both domestically and internationally (see Chapters 4 and 10).

Along another dimension, user charges may be required to ensure efficient use of congested networks. In Ireland, there has been traditional resistance to charges for utilities such as the water network or waste collection. However, it is likely that such charges will have to be extended over time to include even traffic taxes to relieve pressure on limited road networks, especially in the Dublin area. Designing a scheme that retains access for low-income households is a difficult challenge.

Another form of tax intervention is the deployment of tax breaks to encourage certain types of activity. Tax breaks are also termed 'tax expenditures' to capture the idea that a tax break is often a substitute for a direct subsidy payment. In Ireland, tax breaks have been widely used to promote construction in certain areas and industries. In addition, tax breaks have also been used to promote the arts (income from artistic activity is tax free up to a generous threshold limit), the film industry and the bloodstock industry. In general, it is difficult to make the case for tax breaks – if an activity is evaluated as deserving of a subsidy it is more transparent to offer a direct subsidy than to provide indirect support through the tax system. Moreover, tax breaks are of most value to high-income households, such that the exploitation of tax breaks can lead to a regressive element in the tax system in relation to the highest earners. For such reasons, there is considerable political momentum to restrict the use of tax breaks.

5 OTHER POLICY INSTRUMENTS

State-Owned Enterprises

State-owned enterprises, ranging from Aer Lingus to the ESB, have historically played a major role in the Irish economy. Government ownership in the commercial sector may be explained by a number of factors. First, under-developed capital markets prevented private entrepreneurs from raising the finance required to build profitable firms in capital-intensive sectors such as transport. Second, rather than implement regulation of monopolies (as in the United States), European countries tended to favour government ownership of utilities such as electricity production and telecommunications. Third, state ownership was seen as facilitating the pursuit of social goals such as access to cheap services and regionalisation. Fourth, the investment policies of state-owned firms might be viewed as a substitute for official public investment, such that the investment programmes of these firms might be politically directed rather than determined on efficiency grounds. Finally, in many countries state-owned enterprises have facilitated political patronage, with decisions concerning employment and investment being manipulated for electoral purposes.

In recent years, there has been a global shift towards the privatisation of such state-owned firms (see Chapters 5 and 10). The development of sophisticated capital markets now allows private entrepreneurs to finance efficiently even large-scale ventures. Market liberalisation, sometimes mandated by EU law, has reduced fears of monopoly power in many sectors. Moreover, as indicated earlier in the chapter, the EU prohibition on state aid to rescue non-viable firms means that such firms can no longer be protected for political reasons. Finally, technological innovations such as in the telecommunications sector now make it more feasible to have multiple competitors even in 'network' industries (see Chapter 10).

Where monopoly power is likely to persist, governments typically now prefer to regulate private firms as an alternative to direct state ownership (see Chapter 10). Similarly, social goals (such as the provision of cheap postal services to remote areas) can be achieved by a combination of subsidies and regulation, without requiring actual government ownership. Finally, with accumulating evidence on the performance of privatised industries in other countries, ideological resistance to private ownership has weakened over time.

Another reason for the shift towards privatisation is that government ownership may actually be detrimental to performance. Managers and workers in a state-owned enterprise know that they need not seek to maximise profits, since there is no threat of loss of control to outside investors, and hence have a weak incentive to behave efficiently or control costs.

In addition, as indicated earlier, the government may direct state-owned enterprises to pursue non-commercial objectives, such as providing employment for supporters of the government or locating in disadvantaged or politically favoured areas.[7] A decline in clientelism and an improvement in the transparency of the political system have weakened the incentive of the government to manipulate the semi-state sector to achieve such non-economic goals. Even in the absence of privatisation, there are benefits to de-politicisation of these enterprises. Commercialisation of many Irish state-owned enterprises occurred in the 1980s, with significant improvements in performance. More recently, the privatisation process gained pace, with the disposal of the government interest in firms such as Eircom, Aer Lingus, ICC and ACC. The privatisation process may also extend to health insurance (sale of VHI) and parts of the public transport system.

In designing a privatisation process, the government faces several conflicts. To maximise revenues, the government should seek the highest issue price or permit a concentration of ownership among large shareholders, but this may conflict with a social goal to broaden the shareholder base. To secure the co-operation of powerful unions, the government may feel compelled to offer sharply discounted shares to incumbent workers in the state-owned firms and insert worker protection clauses into the privatisation contract, even if this reduces the value of the firm. Of course, the privatisation process should be fully transparent, to prevent state assets being sold at artificially low prices to politically connected business interests.

Privatisation generates a one-time cash windfall for the government. However, it is important to understand that the net impact on the government's balance sheet is much smaller: by transferring ownership, the government no longer receives dividends from the firm, reducing future government revenues. That said, to the extent that the firm is worth more in private hands and the buyout of incumbent workers is not too costly, the net financial gain of privatisation to the government will be positive.

Accordingly, the 2011 report of the Review Group on State Assets and State Liabilities recognises that there are considerable gains to improved commercialisation of state-owned firms and that some level of privatisation proceeds may be helpful in reducing the high level of public debt, while recognising the limitations laid out in the above discussion.[8]

Regulation and Competition Policy

The privatisation of firms with considerable monopoly power (such as Eircom), together with the principle of operating the remaining state-owned firms (such as the ESB and Bord Gáis) on a commercial basis means that the role of regulatory agencies has taken on new prominence in recent years (see Chapter 5). Ireland has a large number of sectoral regulators (such as the Commission on Energy

Regulation, the Commission on Communications Regulation and the Commission on Aviation Regulation) that seek to prevent abuses of monopoly power by monitoring market conduct and retaining powers of approval over the prices charged by firms in these industries. While regulators rely heavily on economic theory to identify instances of market abuse or excessive price mark-ups, it is not always straightforward to establish the scope for greater competition in certain sectors or the best methods to encourage the entry of new firms. Moreover, especially in network industries, incumbent firms may frustrate efforts to reduce barriers to entry, especially by making it difficult for new entrants to obtain access to key distribution channels.

An important problem in the Irish context is that regulatory decisions are subject to judicial review, such that much regulatory energy is diverted to legal battles with regulated firms that seek to overturn decisions through submissions to the courts. The considerable resources of highly profitable firms are also deployed to public relations campaigns that may have the intent of placing pressure on regulators to favour the interests of producers over consumers.

Even in sectors with many suppliers, market inefficiencies may arise if mergers and acquisitions lead to a reduction in the number of firms or if incumbent firms collude (explicitly or implicitly) to raise prices or erect barriers to entry. Accordingly, the Competition Authority has an important role to play in ensuring open competition is preserved. In recent years, the Competition Authority has received more powers to enforce competition, and the rate and intensity of investigations into anti-competitive practices has increased.

Moreover, the Competition Authority has been proactive in researching and analysing the level of competition in many important services sectors (Ireland scores poorly in international comparisons in relation to the level of competition in sheltered services sectors). A high priority under the EU/IMF bailout programme is to liberalise these sheltered sectors, with a reduction in mark-ups in these sectors having the potential to raise medium-term income levels in Ireland.

In addition to preventing abuses of monopoly power, the government also regulates many spheres of economic activity in order to redress other perceived failures of a laissez-faire system (see Chapter 5). Informational asymmetries justify safety regulations, since individual consumers are ill-equipped to evaluate products that potentially carry high risks (air travel, processed foods and machinery, to name just three examples) – accordingly, the markets for such goods can only operate effectively under the assurance of government-approved safety regulations (see Chapter 5). Of course, the trade-off faced in such regulatory systems is ensuring that such standards are not distorted in order to discourage innovation, restrict entry by new firms or act as a barrier to international trade. Regulation is also employed in pursuit of social goals, to ensure that businesses do not operate in ways that are prohibited under the relevant social legislation.

Finally, regulation plays an important part in environmental policy. For asymmetric information reasons, a market system may not be able to ensure that all firms produce using environmentally responsible techniques – accordingly, firms are monitored to ensure that production does not violate environmental standards. In relation to managing climate change, the allocation of carbon quotas is widely used as an alternative or a complement to a carbon tax. The relative merits of 'quantity' regulation (quotas) versus 'price' regulation (taxes) depend on the precise scenario, but a hybrid system that employs both tools may be the prudent choice when faced with a very uncertain economic environment, which is surely the case in relation to the climate change phenomenon (see Chapter 5).

Social Partnership

The role played by the social partnership process in contributing to the success of the Irish economy has been widely debated.[9] While there were various forms of national agreement during the 1970s, these were unstable and had fallen into abeyance by the early 1980s, with the depressed economy characterised by poor industrial relations and a high incidence of employer–worker disputes, in both the private and public sectors. By the mid-1980s, the severe economic crisis had generated a widespread desire for radical reform. One possible route was to adopt the UK reform model (a decentralisation of pay-setting, accompanied by a reduction in the power of trade unions). However, using the foundations of the National Economic and Social Council (NESC) *Strategy for Development 1986–1990* report, a consensual approach to reform was adopted.

During the period 1987–2007, there was a succession of national agreements that were negotiated between the government, trade unions, employer federations and a host of other representative groups. Although this approach was criticised for diminishing the role of elected politicians in formulating policies, the counter argument is that it simply acknowledged the reality that many policies are likely to be ineffective without the co-operation of employers and trade unions; moreover, ultimate decisions remain the responsibility of the elected government. Social partnership in Ireland is related to the 'corporatist' tradition of collective bargaining between unions and employer federations in a number of Continental European countries, but the scale of government involvement and the range of topics covered under the social partnership agreements is unusually extensive. While the main focus of these agreements has been on establishing national guidelines on wage increases, the remit of social partnership has also extended to the negotiation of labour protection regulations and a range of social policy initiatives.

In relation to the core pay agreement, the social partnership process is clearly important in determining public sector pay – although the baseline pay increases are further adjusted via two mechanisms that are exclusive to the public sector (the benchmarking process and the Review Body on Higher Remuneration in the Public Sector). It is not so clear that the national pay agreements are very important in determining pay in the private sector, since firms and workers deviate from the national agreements in line with sectoral requirements: in a market-based economy, pay and conditions in the private sector are ultimately determined at the level of the firm.

Especially in the context of EMU, there may be occasions on which a collective approach to pay determination may be helpful in dealing with macroeconomic problems. In particular, there are scenarios in which workers may accept that a loss of competitiveness requires a collective fall in wages: it is less disruptive to achieve this via a co-ordinated agreement than through decentralised pay negotiations. For this reason, there may be considerable value in a social partnership framework, even beyond its role in the determination of social policies, labour market regulations and public sector pay.

The scope of the social partnership approach has narrowed quite substantially during the crisis. Widespread consensus across the social partners was not possible in view of the differing views as to the source of the crisis or the optimal path to resolve the crisis. Accordingly, the government simply opted to impose many fiscal measures, while the wide variation in conditions in the private sector meant that employers withdrew from a common approach to wage determination in favour of firm-by-firm settlements.

However, a core element of social partnership has survived in that there is a common approach to public sector reform that has been agreed between the government and the many different unions representing public sector workers. In return for preserving pay at 2010 levels and avoiding compulsory redundancies, the Croke Park Agreement specifies an extensive programme of reforms across the public sector. Such a reform programme may not have been feasible without the social partnership framework. However, the level of progress in the implementation of the programme is not yet clear at the time of writing.

State Financial Policies

In addition to direct public spending on goods, services and transfers, a government may acquire financial assets and financial liabilities.

One motivation is to build a reserve fund that can help finance anticipated future increases in public spending. For instance, the National Pensions Reserve Fund (NPRF) was established in 2001 in order to finance future state pension liabilities. Rather than exclusively using budget surpluses to pay down the public debt, the plan was to allocate one per cent of GNP each year to the NPRF, which invests in a portfolio of financial assets. The dividend income and capital gains on these assets can then be employed to finance pension expenditures, as a partial alternative to raising future taxation.

However, the precise design of such a fund is critically important for its success and political acceptability. A major concern is the politicisation of investment decisions. At the extreme, this might involve discriminating between domestic projects on the basis of the political connections of entrepreneurs. Less obviously, it may induce the allocation of an excessive portfolio share to domestic over foreign assets, with lobby groups pressing the state fund to support domestic firms and workers.

This is a very difficult problem. On the one side, it is desirable to minimise political interference in the operation of the fund. On the other, in a democratic society the operators of a state fund must be politically accountable. Much of the international debate concerning the delegation of public tasks to independent agencies, such as central banks and industry regulators, is relevant here. An important principle is that the government defines the objectives of the agency but that the agency is given wide scope in the pursuit of these objectives, subject to the issuing of regular public reports justifying any deviations from targeted outcomes.

It should be clear that the correct investment approach for a state pension fund is to overwhelmingly hold overseas assets. First, this strategy minimises the politicisation problem. Second, it is a sensible hedge. Imagine if the state pension fund held domestic assets: in the event of a domestic downturn, the public finances would be hit not only by a decline in tax revenues but also by a contraction in investment income. By holding foreign assets, in contrast, 'tax base risk' is offset. Third, the state pension fund would be large relative to the domestic market but tiny in global terms, such that investing overseas improves flexibility and liquidity in portfolio management.

The initial investment strategy of the NPRF has largely respected these principles. Its equity and bond holdings were overwhelmingly international, with only modest holdings of domestic securities. However, it also had some involvement in funding domestic infrastructural projects, which increased the risk that the fund's strategy might be subject to political pressure.

However, it turned out that the NPRF has since late 2008 been essentially converted into a bank rescue fund. In order to relieve pressure on the government's direct balance sheet, the NPRF has been directed to sell most of its assets in order to purchase equity claims in the main Irish banks. While these assets may provide a return to the NPRF in the coming years, such a crisis-related role was not in the original design of the fund. Rather, it became a 'rainy day' fund that could be rapidly deployed to assist in meeting the large fiscal costs of rescuing the banking system.

The government also created a second major financial vehicle to help resolve the banking crisis. The National Asset Management Agency (NAMA) was created in 2009 in order to relieve the banking system of the development-related property loans that were the main source of bank losses. NAMA purchased these loans at steep discounts from the banks and now holds a huge portfolio of property loans. In cases where the debtor cannot repay the loan, NAMA can sell the underlying property assets in order to maximise recovery of funds.

The vast bulk of NAMA financing takes the form of government-guaranteed bonds. However, there is a minor role for private-sector financing, such that NAMA is not counted as part of the main public balance sheet. Accordingly, NAMA provides an important example of the way in which government can engage in 'financial engineering' to meet its policy goals. However, such measures are opaque and require extensive public monitoring in order to avoid the temptation to excessively use 'off balance sheet' devices to understate the true level of government intervention in the economy.

6 SIZE OF GOVERNMENT: ECONOMIC AND POLITICAL FACTORS

In evaluating tax and expenditure policies, a fundamental question is the optimal size of government. If the government is too large, it makes sense to prune expenditure and cut taxation: conversely, increases in spending and taxation are required if the government is too small to achieve desired policy outcomes. Of course, determining the optimal size of government is a difficult challenge and involves both economic and political dimensions.

Trends and International Comparisons

Although the government can also exert much influence through legislation, regulation, social partnership, moral suasion and financial engineering, measures of public expenditure and taxation are most widely employed as imperfect proxies for the size of government. However, there has been much interest in recent years in measuring other dimensions of government intervention in the economy. For instance, the World Bank's *Doing Business* survey ranks countries on many dimensions of government regulation and bureaucracy, while the OECD maintains a comprehensive database on regulation in its member countries. As is shown in Table 3.1, Ireland scores quite well along some dimensions of these indices, but its rank is quite low in areas such as the regulations concerning the ease of enforcing contracts.

Table 3.1

Business Environment[1]: Ranking of Selected Countries

	Doing business	Starting a business	Protecting investors	Enforcing contracts
Singapore	1	4	2	13
Hong Kong	2	6	3	2
New Zealand	3	1	1	9
UK	4	17	10	23
USA	5	9	5	8
Denmark	6	27	28	30
Canada	7	3	5	58
Norway	8	33	20	4
Ireland	*9*	*11*	*5*	*37*
Australia	10	2	59	16

Source: World Bank, *Doing Business Survey* 2011, www.doingbusiness.org.
[1] In terms of government regulation and bureaucracy.

In relation to levels of public expenditure, Table 3.2 shows that the share of total government spending relative to GDP in Ireland declined dramatically between its peak in the mid-1980s and 2000. This initially reflected the fiscal austerity programme in the late 1980s. However, the rapid pace of output growth during the late 1990s meant that the relative size of the public sector declined.

In terms of the composition of public expenditure, a dramatic decline in debt interest payments as a share of GDP was a major driver of the shrinkage in government size. Other factors also contributed to a decline in the size of government spending. First, Ireland's relatively young population meant that public expenditure on pensions is naturally lower, which is reinforced by the relatively greater role played by the private sector in financing pensions in Ireland. Second, lower unemployment in Ireland meant that social benefit payments were a smaller burden. Third, Ireland has fewer defence commitments than the major countries, such that military expenditures are lower.

However, there was a significant increase in the ratio of public spending to GDP during 2000–7, with public spending growing more quickly than output. In part, this reflected an ambitious public capital programme to redress the infrastructural deficit that had accumulated in the 1980s and 1990s. However, current spending also grew, with the employment and pay levels in the public sector both growing rapidly.

The 20 per cent decline in nominal GDP between 2007 and 2011, the increase in spending on unemployment benefits and debt interest payments and the relative stability of other types of public spending (relative to private sector output) meant that the ratio of public spending to GDP has climbed during the crisis period (see Chapter 4). This has been the case despite a reduction in public investment, significant reductions in public sector pay and restrictions on public sector recruitment.

Table 3.2

Composition of Public Expenditure[1] (as a Proportion of GDP)

	Total	Consumption	Investment	Interest	Social security
1985	53.2	18.3	3.8	9.8	14.3
1990	42.8	16.8	2.1	7.8	11.7
1995	41.1	15.7	2.4	5.3	11.8
2000	31.3	14.6	4.3	1.5	8.3
2007	36.8	16.3	4.7	1.0	10.4
2011	45.2	18.0	3.5	3.5	15.6

Source: European Commission, *AMECO Online* database.
[1] The category 'other' is not included in the table.

Causes of Variations in Size of Government
Wagner's Law
Many factors contribute to variation across countries and over time in government spending. First, across countries and over time there is a clear positive correlation between the level of income per capita and the share of public expenditure in national income: this tendency is known as Wagner's Law. One reason is that public subsidies to health care, education and pensions may be interpreted as luxury items, with an income elasticity of demand greater than unity.

As incomes grow, voters demand more of these services, placing upward pressure on public spending. However, the damaging costs of excessive taxation place an upper bound on the sustainable level of spending on these items. The fiscal reforms attempted by many countries in recent years may in part be a result of having approached this upper bound. The increasing mobility of capital and skilled labour also places limits on the feasible size of government, by placing a cap on sustainable tax rates.

Baumol's Disease

Another driving force behind upward pressure on public spending is the so-called Baumol's disease, named after the American economist who proposed the hypothesis.[10] Baumol's hypothesis is that an economy can be divided into progressive and non-progressive sectors. Productivity gains in the progressive sector drive up wages, which must be matched by the non-progressive sector if it is to attract labour.

Provision of education and healthcare services plausibly falls into the non-progressive sector, on the basis that productivity growth in such labour-intensive sectors is limited. It follows that the implicit relative price of these services must rise, as wages increase without a compensating improvement in productivity. If the income elasticity of demand for these services exceeds the price elasticity of demand, the ratio of public spending to national income will increase, even if the volume of services provided is unchanged. For this reason, the rapid increase in education and healthcare spending in Ireland during the boom period was mainly absorbed by rising wages, with a much smaller improvement in the level of services (see Chapters 12 and 13).

It is wrong to assume, however, that productivity growth in publicly financed sectors is impossible, as another factor behind slow improvement is the lack of competitive pressure to produce efficiently. Improved management, stronger cost controls and the outsourcing of some services may help in forcing more rapid productivity growth in these sectors. Moreover, recent technological change may enable new productivity gains. For example, Internet-based courses and learning aids may be feasible in many education sectors, while the electronic transmission of X-rays and other medical information permits the remote provision of medical expertise. An important challenge for policy-makers is to ensure that such new technologies are exploited, even in the face of resistance from traditional suppliers, such as public sector unions. In 2011, a new Department of Public Expenditure and Reform was established in Ireland, with a mandate to drive productivity growth in the public sector.

Demographic Factors

Demographic factors are also important in determining the level of public spending. In the 1970s and 1980s, Ireland had an unusually large cohort of children, placing pressure on the education budget. At the other end of the life cycle, many countries now face an increase in the proportion of old people in the population, with attendant growth in healthcare and pension expenditures. Currently, Ireland enjoys an unusually favourable demographic profile, with the vast bulk of the population in the working age bracket, which allows either a decline in government spending or an improvement in the quality of services and pension levels. However, the problems associated with the greying of the population will progressively place upward pressure on public expenditure levels in Ireland over the next fifteen years (see also Chapter 6).

Automatic Stabilisers
Welfare spending fluctuates over the economic cycle, as the number of people unemployed falls during expansions and rises during recessions. Such 'automatic stabilisers' induce a natural counter-cyclical pattern in government spending: however, this may be attenuated by pro-cyclical shifts in the level of benefits: during booms, the level of benefits tends to improve.

Political Economy of Public Spending
The preceding analysis generally assumes that the government acts to maximise social welfare. While the bulk of public expenditure may be usefully interpreted in this way, a substantial component is influenced by a more overtly political process, in which public expenditure allocations are the outcome of a struggle between interest groups, public sector workers and politicians. This process may produce outcomes that are contrary to social welfare: government failure may be as important as market failure in deviating from optimal outcomes.

Public Choice Theory
One reason why social welfare is not maximised is voter ignorance of the true costs of public expenditure. The Downs paradox (individual votes have no influence over the result of an election) suggests that it is not individually worthwhile for the electorate to learn much about the costs of different public spending programmes. In contrast, some groups have vested interests in specific areas of public expenditure (e.g. farmers and agricultural subsidies) and will act collectively to promote these specific public expenditures. In a famous book, the late Mancur Olson pointed out that such interest groups are easier to organise in a rich society and hence this problem will increase over time.[11]

The characteristics of the civil service bureaucracy can also contribute to government failure. Civil servants act as agents for the government in evaluating and monitoring the effectiveness of public spending. An influential hypothesis is that bureaucrats like to maximise the size of their departmental budgets, as this is associated with power and status. With each department seeking to promote its own expenditure programmes, the net result is to place upward pressure on the level of public spending. Similarly, the political influence of a cabinet minister may increase according to the size of her departmental budget.

An exception is the Department of Finance: arguably, its focus is on holding back the overall level of spending. For this reason, fiscal sustainability may be better achieved if the Department of Finance has significant control over expenditure levels across the public sector.

Design of the Political System

Much current research is devoted to analysing the impact of the structure of the political system on public expenditure decisions. For instance, it is suggested that governments that are coalitions of parties with significantly different political philosophies and short tenures in office are less able to control public expenditure. Each party in a coalition has a veto on reductions in its favoured areas so that a prisoners' dilemma results – it is in the collective interest to control spending but no single party has the incentive to accept unilateral spending reductions. Short tenures make it unfeasible to implement spending controls as it will not have the time to enjoy the benefits before the next election.

In such circumstances, it seems that fiscal control can only occur under 'crisis' conditions, with the public debt so high that there is no alternative to reform. Often, this requires suspension of normal political rivalries and the formation of a government of national unity. Elements of this story ring true for the Irish experience during 1977–87. Once fiscal control is established, fear of a return to instability may restrain expenditure for a long period. However, memories eventually fade and the pressure for a relaxation on public spending may resume. During the 2000–8 period in Ireland this dynamic played out, with rapid increases in public spending.

Another manifestation of politically driven fluctuations in public spending is the impact of the electoral cycle on public spending: in the run-up to elections, there is a tendency for public spending to increase (especially on visible projects) and taxes are reduced. The timing of these fluctuations suggests that such spending has little basis in terms of social welfare but rather is directed at winning favour for the incumbent government.

Formal Fiscal Framework

International evidence suggests that fiscal sustainability is facilitated by a formal fiscal framework that places a set of restrictions on the conduct of fiscal policy. A fiscal framework has several elements. First, it may formalise the political process determining budgetary decisions, with fiscal control best achieved by a transparent system that places ultimate responsibility for fiscal policy on the finance minister rather than by a collegial and secretive system in which lines of responsibility are not clearly designated.[12] Second, it may provide a multi-year horizon for planning public spending, in order to avoid annual volatility in public spending levels.

Third, it may specify a set of numerical fiscal rules to guide the medium-term behaviour of fiscal policy. The set of fiscal rules typically sets some medium-term budgetary objectives, such as keeping the level of public debt below a ceiling value and a target for the structural budget balance over the cycle. In turn, each annual budget must be set within the confines of these rules.

Finally, it may include a watchdog role for an independent fiscal council, with the remit to monitor the quality of budgetary decisions. Such a council can improve the public debate about fiscal policy by providing a non-governmental source of objective analysis of the public finances. This role can be especially important during boom periods, since it is politically difficult to run large surpluses in anticipation of future rainy days. Having an independent fiscal council may provide some support for politically difficult but economically desirable fiscal decisions.

The EU Growth and Stability Pact provided a limited type of fiscal framework (see also Chapter 4). It specified a debt ceiling of 60 per cent and a budget deficit ceiling of 3 per cent, and also required governments to make an annual report regarding the state of the public finances. However, the Pact did not require governments to run sufficiently large surpluses during boom periods, nor was the level of external surveillance sufficiently robust to avoid the accumulation of fiscal vulnerabilities in some peripheral countries.

At EU level, there is a wave of reforms to strengthen the Pact. Under the new procedures, there is greater co-ordination in budget setting across Europe under the 'European semester' fiscal process. In addition, there will be closer monitoring of each country's macroeconomic and fiscal risk profiles, so as to draw attention to emerging problems.

Moreover, it is envisaged that each member country should develop a strong national fiscal framework, especially since fiscal policy remains primarily a national competence. In Ireland, a Fiscal Responsibility Law is planned for 2011 which will specify a set of numerical fiscal rules and formalise a multi-year budgetary process. In addition, an independent Budgetary Advisory Council will be established in 2011.

7 CONCLUSION

The central theme of this chapter is that the state is a major economic actor. A well-functioning and effective government is necessary to achieve economic efficiency and redistributional objectives. The maximisation of social welfare requires that the government choose the optimal mix of policy instruments to attain its desired policy objectives.

The analysis in this chapter gives some clues as to the likely evolution of the government's role in the economy in the coming decades. One global trend is a shift from the government as provider to a greater use of private inputs to achieve social goals. Another trend is towards ever greater internationalisation of the policy-making process, as trade and financial linkages bind countries closer together. In the opposite direction, further decentralisation of some government functions to local levels of government is also likely to occur.

Public expenditure policies remain the primary method by which the state intervenes in the economy. During the boom period, the decline in the public debt and an extremely favourable demographic structure meant that the government had considerable freedom in making spending decisions. However, the crisis has resulted in a very high level of public debt and a dependence on external official financing. Accordingly, public spending will be very constrained for the foreseeable future, such that it has never been more important that rigorous evaluation procedures are employed to ensure that the state obtains value for money and delivers public services in an efficient and equitable manner.

Endnotes

1   See A. Shleifer and R. Vishny, *The Grabbing Hand: Government Pathologies and their Cures*, MIT Press, Cambridge MA 1998.
2   See R. Barro and X. Sala-i-Martin, *Economic Growth*, MIT Press, Cambridge MA 1995.
3   See J. Sachs, *Common Wealth: Economics for a Crowded Planet*, Penguin Press, New York 2008.
4   See P. Collier, *The Bottom Billion,* Oxford University Press, Oxford 2007.
5   See D. Rodrik, 'How far will international integration go?', *Journal of Economic Perspectives*, Winter 2000.
6   E. Glaeser, J. Kolo and E. Saez, 'Consumer city', *Journal of Economic Geography*, 1, 2005.
7   See Shleifer and Vishny, *op. cit.*
8   See *Report of the Review Group on State Assets and Liabilities*, April 2011, at www.finance.gov.ie/viewdoc.asp?DocID=6805.
9   See P. Sweeney, *Ireland's Economic Success: Reasons and Lessons*, New Island Press, Dublin 2008.
10 W. Baumol, 'Macroeconomics of unbalanced growth: the anatomy of urban crisis', *American Economic Review*, June 1967.
11 M. Olson, *The Logic of Collective Action: Public Goods and the Theory of Groups*, Harvard University Press, Cambridge MA 1965.
12 See P. Lane, 'A new fiscal framework for Ireland', *Journal of Statistical and Social Inquiry Society of Ireland,* 39, 2010.

CHAPTER 4

Taxation

Micheál Collins

1 INTRODUCTION

Taxation is a method for government to raise revenue by means of charges on persons or firms and taxes can be collected nationally or locally. Governments collect taxes for two broad reasons. First, it provides revenue to run the state, as outlined in Chapter 3, and pay for the provision of public services, infrastructure and the funding of redistributive policies. Second, taxation is used by governments as a corrective device to alter the behaviour of individuals, firms or the economy as a whole. In such cases, governments can use taxation to, for example, discourage certain consumption choices, encourage investment in certain sectors, or reduce citizens' disposable income in an attempt to dampen the demand side of the economy.

In Ireland, the government, via the Budget and Finance Act, alters its taxation policies on an annual basis. However, the government's ability freely to choose these policies is limited by competitive forces, EU rules and historical factors. In the case of the first, a small open economy such as Ireland cannot easily alter its company taxation structures without having consideration of the taxation regimes in competing economies. Similarly, the government is limited by EU rules that require it to adhere to certain fiscal targets and it is restricted by EU single market rules from altering many of its consumption taxes. Past economic policies funded through government borrowing also reduce taxation choices as this debt must be serviced and repaid from current taxation revenues.

The plan of this chapter is as follows. In Section 2 we consider the principles of a good taxation system. Section 3 considers the operation and features of the taxation system in Ireland and reviews that structure in both historical and international contexts. In Sections 4 and 5 we evaluate the Irish taxation system, first looking at taxes on income and then examining indirect, corporation and property taxes. Section 6 discusses the issue of deferred taxation, namely borrowing, building on the discussion of this topic in Chapter 3. Section 7 concludes the chapter.

2 PRINCIPLES OF A GOOD TAX SYSTEM

In *An Inquiry into the Nature and Causes of the Wealth of Nations*, Adam Smith set out a series of principles for the operation of a good taxation system.[1] Smith identified four maxims with regard to taxation in general, stating that:

(i) The subjects of every state ought to contribute towards the support of the government, as nearly as possible, in proportion to their respective abilities; that is in proportion to the revenue which they respectively enjoy under the protection of the state; (ii) The tax which each individual is bound to pay ought to be certain and not arbitrary. The time of payment, the manner of payment, the quantity to be paid, ought all to be clear and plain to the contributor and to every other person; (iii) Every tax ought to be levied at the time, or in the manner, in which it is most likely to be convenient for the contributor to pay it; (iv) Every tax ought to be so contrived as both to take out and to keep out of the pockets of the people as little as possible, over and above that which it brings into the public treasury of the state.

Known as the *canons of taxation*, these principles are generally summarised under the headings of equity, efficiency and simplicity and they have changed little since 1776. We explore each of these principles in turn below.

In the context of taxation, *equity* can usefully be explained via the concept of *ability to pay*, which relates the quantum of taxes levied to an individual's or household's economic resources. In general, an individual's economic resources are taken to be the flow of resources to them (their income) rather than their stock of resources (their wealth). What is known as *horizontal equity* implies that individuals with identical incomes should pay the same level of taxation, while *vertical equity* implies that individuals with different incomes should pay difference amounts. In practice this produces a *progressive* taxation system where as income increases an individual pays a higher *proportion* of income in taxes. The precise nature of that progressivity will depend on government choices regarding the structure of a taxation system. The opposite of a progressive taxation system is a *regressive* one, where as income increases the average rate of tax experienced by an individual decreases. When examining a taxation system over time we can also consider *intergenerational equity*. Ideally, each generation's taxes should cover its own expenses. Where a generation's expenditure exceeds spending, and unpaid public borrowing remains, one generation passes a burden of taxation on to another, violating the principle of intergenerational equity.

The issue of *efficiency* in a taxation system arises because, in general, the imposition of a tax distorts what would have been the market outcome. It does so by imposing a wedge between the price received by the seller and the price paid by the buyer. The fact is that this *tax wedge* alters the behaviour of these participants in the market. For example, say a farmer is willing to sell 50 apples at a price of 50 cent each and consumers are willing to purchase all his output at this price. If a 10 per cent tax is imposed on all fruit sales by government, this creates a wedge between the consumer demand price and the producer supply price. Consequently, both the consumer and the producer find themselves away from the optimal levels of demand and supply they would have chosen without the existence of the tax. (See later examples in relation to labour and other taxes.)

The flow of resources from consumers to government as a result of the imposition of the tax causes an *income effect*, whereby the purchasing power of consumers is reduced. Simultaneously, a *substitution effect* occurs as a result of consumers' response to the change in relative prices caused by the tax. An efficient tax is one where this substitution affect, also known as the *deadweight burden* of the tax, is minimised subject to raising the revenue target required by government. While different taxes will give rise to different sized substitution effects, in general efficient taxes are set with a negative relationship to goods price elasticity – low taxes where elasticity is high and higher taxes where price elasticity is low. Such an approach minimises the deadweight loss. A further alternative are *lump-sum taxes* which are levied at the same amount on all taxpayers, thereby implying no substitution effect. Such taxes can be difficult to implement and tend to be accompanied by undesirable outcomes when judged from the perspective of equity. Of course, these complications and deadweight losses could be completely avoided if the tax was not imposed in the first place. However, governments need to source revenue from somewhere and the challenge, from an efficiency perspective, is to do so with minimal distortion.

A simple taxation system is one where the compliance and administrative costs of the taxpayer and tax authority are minimised, given the requirement to raise sufficient revenue for the exchequer. Taxpayers face costs in understanding, completing and returning the appropriate tax payment given their resources. Tax authorities face costs in administering and policing the system. In general, these costs are positively correlated with the complexity of the taxation system. Therefore, a simple and understandable taxation system is likely to reduce costs for both government and citizens. It should also minimise the incentives for taxpayers to pursue various routes to minimise their taxation bill either legally (*tax avoidance*) or illegally (*tax evasion*).

For a policy-maker, the design of a 'good' taxation system which adheres to the above principles is challenging. In general, a balance has to be struck between the competing objectives of equity and efficiency while adhering to the desire to minimise complexity and raise sufficient revenue. Below, we outline the Irish taxation system and subsequently evaluate it relative to these principles.

3 THE IRISH TAXATION SYSTEM

Throughout this section and the remainder of the chapter various concepts and features of a taxation system are discussed. At the outset, some clarity on the meaning of these phrases is appropriate.

Governments can impose taxes *directly*, through the reduction of an individual's real income and the transfer of that revenue to government, or *indirectly* through the imposition of consumption taxes or user charges on goods and services. Therefore, direct taxes allow government greater ability to target taxation measures towards particular groups of specified earners and to pursue the aforementioned objective of progressivity. The *tax base* comprises that which is to be taxed and can include income, consumption, property, profits and wealth. A *narrow tax base* will concentrate tax collection across a limited number of these areas while a *broad tax base* will include many if not all of them.

The *incidence of taxation* measures on whom a tax falls. This can be on producers or consumers, on those at particular income levels or situated in particular industries or regions. In this regard a distinction needs to be made between the legal and effective incidence; for example, brewers may legally have to pay the excise duty on alcohol but in practice it may be fully paid for by the consumer. The *tax rate* captures the scale of the charge imposed by government relative to a goods/services price or income level. Within income tax, we consider *average tax rates*, also known as *effective tax rates*, which summarise the overall proportion of an individual's income that is paid in taxation. This differs from the *marginal tax rate*, which captures the proportion of the last euro in income that is paid in taxes. As such, marginal rates are always higher than average rates.

Tax Revenue: Historical and International Trends

The overall level of tax revenue in Ireland compared to the rest of the OECD and EU member states within the OECD is examined in Table 4.1. As taxation can be levied on all economic activity within a country, GDP is the international benchmark against which to assess the overall taxation burden. Irish data are compared against both GDP and GNP as these national income measures can diverge by as much as 17 per cent, and given some historical precedents to assess the tax burden against GNP. However, to do so only in relation to GNP would exclude some of the national tax base, specifically the profits of multinational corporations, and consequently overstate the comparable scale of the national taxation burden.[2]

The table shows that over the period from 1975 to 2005 there was an international trend towards higher overall taxation levels within the Organisation for Economic Co-operation and Development (OECD) and its European Union (EU) member states. During that period in Ireland, taxation climbed and then fell, driven by growth and the fiscal policies of the 1970s and 1980s and the economic expansion and taxation reductions post-1990. By 2005 Ireland's tax ratio was below average levels in the OECD and EU. A comparison between the 2005 and 2009 data reveal the impact of the global recession (from 2008) in the OECD, EU and Ireland. Taxation ratios fell over the period, driven by reductions in taxation revenue which outpaced simultaneous declines in economic activity.

Table 4.1

General Government Tax Revenue as a Percentage of GDP/GNP

	1975	1985	1995	2005	2009[1]
Ireland (% GDP)	28.7	34.6	32.5	30.6	27.8
Ireland (% GNP)	28.8	38.7	36.7	35.9	33.8
OECD EU[2]	32.2	37.6	38.9	38.7	37.8
OECD average	30.0	33.7	35.7	36.0	33.1

Source: OECD, *Revenue Statistics 1965–2006*, OECD, Paris 2010.
[1] Estimates.
[2] OECD EU represents EU member states that are also OECD members.

Table 4.2 shows the composition of tax revenue in Ireland and the OECD from 1985 to 2008. The major trends across that period have been a shift away from specific consumption taxes such as excise duties, reductions in the proportion of taxes collected from personal incomes and an increase in the contribution to taxation revenue from corporate profits. In Ireland, the increase in the relative importance of corporate taxes as a revenue source is notable and is reflective of the increasing role of that sector in the economy. Property taxes also increased over the period in Ireland and by 2005 accounted for 8 per cent of total revenues; this rapidly decreased as the number and value of property transactions declined in the latter half of that decade.

Table 4.2

Composition of Tax Revenue (Percentage of Total)

	1985		2000		2008	
	Ireland	OECD	Ireland	OECD	Ireland	OECD
Personal income tax	31	30	30	25	28	25
Corporate income tax	3	8	12	10	10	10
Social security and payroll taxes	17	23	16	25	18	26
Property taxes (including stamp duty)	4	5	5	6	6	5
General consumption taxes	21	16	22	19	24	20
Specific consumption taxes	22	16	14	12	11	10
Other taxes	2	2	1	3	3	3

Source: OECD, *Revenue Statistics, 1965–2009*, OECD, Paris 2010.

Using budget data on the expected flow of taxation revenue to the exchequer in 2011, Table 4.3 shows that the main sources of taxation revenue in Ireland are those related to personal income (including social insurance contributions by employees and employers), consumption taxes (VAT and excise duties) and corporate taxes. We examine each of these areas and consider the role of capital taxes, property taxes and other smaller sources of taxation revenue throughout the remainder of this section.

Table 4.3

Estimated Taxation Revenue, Ireland 2011

	€m
Income tax	14,125
Value added tax	10,230
Social insurance (employee and employer)	7,550
Excise duties	4,675
Corporation tax	4,020
Local government taxes and charges (including motor tax)	2,750
Stamp duties	955
Capital gains tax	410
Capital acquisitions tax	250
Customs	235
Total	45,200

Sources: calculated from data in Department of Finance, *Budget 2011*, Stationery Office, Dublin 2010; and annual reports of the Department of Social Protection and the Department of Environment, Heritage and Local Government.

Personal Income Taxes

In the current Irish income taxation system, an individual's gross pay from working is reduced by three taxation payments: income tax, the universal social charge (USC), and employees' pay-related social insurance (PRSI). To illustrate the operation of the system, take a single private sector worker aged 32 who is on the pay as you earn (PAYE) system and working throughout the year to earn a gross income of €50,000. We base our review throughout the remainder of this section on the structure of the taxation system in 2011; a structure that is likely to change annually as a result of decisions in the Budget and Finance Act.

Income tax is charged at the standard rate of 20 per cent on earnings up to €32,800 and above this income is subject to tax at the higher tax rate of 41 per cent. The USC is structured so that income up to €10,037 is charged at 2 per cent; between €10,037 and €16,016 it is subject to a 4 per cent rate; and all income above this level is charged at a rate of 7 per cent.[3] PRSI is charged at a rate of 4 per cent on all income once earnings exceed €352 per week (€18,304 per annum) with the first €127 of weekly earnings (€6,604 per annum) being exempt from the charge. Collectively, these three charges sum to the worker's gross taxation level. From this we deduct the employee's income tax credits to establish taxable income. Employees in the PAYE system are entitled to two tax credits which reduce their income tax liability: a personal credit and a PAYE credit, which have a value of €1,650 each. These can only be used against the employee's income taxation liability and cannot be used against the USC or PRSI. Table 4.4 summarises these calculations and shows that this employee's after-tax take-home pay is €35,133. The employee's effective tax rate is 29.73 per cent and the marginal tax rate is 52 per cent. The latter is calculated on the basis that an additional euro of income would be subject to income tax at 41 per cent, the USC at 7 per cent and PRSI at 4 per cent.

Table 4.4

Private Sector Worker: Calculation of Tax Liability (2011 Basis)

Gross Income		€50,000.00
Income taxation		
€32,800 at 20%	€6,560.00	
balance at 41%	€7,052.00	
Total income taxation (a)	€13,612.00	
Universal Social Charge		
€0–€10,037 at 2%	€200.74	
€10,037–€16,016 at 4%	€239.16	
balance above €16,016 at 7%	€2,378.88	
Total USC (b)	€2,818.78	
Employee PRSI		
4% on all income above €6,604 (c)	€1,735.84	
Gross taxes (a + b + c)		€18,166.62
Tax credits		
Personal tax credit	€1,650.00	
PAYE tax credit	€1,650.00	
Total tax credits		€3,300.00
Tax liability (gross taxes – tax credits)		€14,866.62
Take-home pay (gross income – tax liability)		€35,133.38
Effective tax rate (tax liability as % gross income)		29.73%
Marginal tax rate		52%

Entitlements to additional tax credits associated with family circumstances and certain tax breaks can reduce an individual's tax liability below the headline rates in Table 4.4. Similarly, non-PAYE workers, such as the self-employed and company directors, will record higher rates as they are only entitled to claim the personal tax credit.

The Social Insurance Fund receives pay-related contributions from employees, the self-employed and employers. These contributions are used to fund the provision of social welfare payments to those in society who may need them – jobseeker's allowance, illness benefit, maternity benefit, etc. Where the fund is unable to meet the cost of these payments it is subvented by the exchequer. As we have seen, employees contribute 4 per cent of their earnings to this fund once their income exceeds €352 per week (€18,304 per annum). Those who are self-employed pay 4 per cent of their profits (income) as PRSI once profits exceed €5,000 per annum. However, there is another tax charged: employers also pay to support the provision of this social insurance for their employees. Employers' PRSI is charged at a rate of 8.5 per cent of gross pay up to €356 per week and 10.75 per cent of gross pay above this, meaning that the net cost of an employee to an employer is €108.50 or €110.75 for every €100 of gross income.

Consumption Taxes
Value added tax (VAT) serves as the primary source of consumption taxes in Ireland. Most goods and services are subject to VAT at one of three rates. The standard rate is 21 per cent and this applies to most goods and services. A reduced rate of 13.5 per cent applies to a number of labour-intensive services and broadly consumed goods including heating fuel, electricity, restaurant services, newspapers and hotel/B&B lettings. A third zero per cent rate applies to many foods, medicines, books and children's clothing/footwear. In addition, some goods are deemed to be exempt from VAT and these include many services supplied in the public interest in areas such as health, childcare and education. There is a technical distinction between goods and services which are exempt and those that are charged at zero per cent. This relates to the ability of companies and the self-employed to claim VAT paid against VAT collected on these goods and services.[4]

Excise duties are a further source of consumption tax revenue for the Irish government. These duties, which are strictly regulated in the context of EU free trade rules, are charged in addition to VAT and apply to mineral oils (petrol, diesel, home heating oil), alcohol and tobacco. In the case of each of these goods, the combined charge of VAT and excise duties represents a large proportion of the retail price paid by the consumer. The inelastic nature of their demand has also made them attractive sources for additional exchequer revenue at Budget time. Excise duties are also charged on certain business premises and activities including betting, alcohol sales, restaurants, auctioneers and bookmakers.

Environmental taxes represent a recent and growing area of consumption-related taxation in Ireland. In general these taxes are intended to illicit some behavioural change among consumers by encouraging them to reduce or modify their consumption patterns. A carbon tax was introduced in 2010 at a rate of €15 per tonne of CO_2 equivalent. This means that the rate at which the carbon tax is levied is linked to how much pollution a good produces. For example, the carbon tax upon its introduction increased petrol prices by 3.5 per cent, natural gas prices by 7 per cent, peat briquette prices by 10.1 per cent and coal prices by 11.8 per cent. Over time, the government has signalled that it will increase the rate per tonne of CO_2 equivalent, which will drive up prices and revenue from this taxation source. Carbon taxes are charged alongside VAT and, where appropriate, excise duties.

Corporation, Capital and Property Taxes
Corporation Tax
The tax rate for most company profits in Ireland is 12.5 per cent. Companies operating in specified natural resource sectors (minerals and petroleum) alongside those who deal in development land are subject to a higher corporate tax rate of 25 per cent. Companies can reduce their tax liability below these levels through the use of various tax breaks and exemptions (see later).

Capital Taxes
Capital taxes are levied on the value of assets, or the increase in the value of assets. In Ireland there are two main forms of these taxes: capital gains tax (CGT); and capital acquisitions tax (CAT). CGT is charged on the capital gain (profit after associated transaction costs) made on the disposal of any asset and is levied on the person making the disposal. These gains are subject to tax at a rate of 25 per cent and the first €1,270 of annual gains is exempt from the tax.

CAT is levied on the increase in a person's or company's wealth and arises through either gifts or inheritance. The tax is charged at a rate of 25 per cent of the market value of the gain over and above certain specified thresholds. These thresholds depend on the relationship between the person giving the benefit and the beneficiary. Transfers between spouses are exempt from CAT, while there are generous thresholds for gifts/inheritances to children, with a CAT liability only arising above a figure of €332,084. These thresholds reduce to €32,208 for transfers among closely related people (near relatives and siblings) and to €16,604 where wealth increases come from any other person. Gifts below €3,000 per annum are exempt from CAT. Special provisions also exist for business owners and farmers who wish to transfer assets to family members. CAT does not arise on increases in wealth associated with transfers of the family home, payments for damages or compensation, most redundancy payments or lottery wins.

Property Taxes
Ireland remains an exception in the developed world in that it does not have any form of recurring residential property tax for all dwellings. However, there are three other forms of property tax, which are charged on property transactions: stamp duty; businesses, via local authority rates; and owners of second homes. Stamp duties arise on the sale of any residential property and are payable by the purchaser. Stamp duty is charged at a rate of 1 per cent on the purchase price up to €1 million and 2 per cent on the excess of the price above this threshold. Notionally, the 'stamp duty' is a fee associated with the state's need to record and register these transactions; but it is predominantly a revenue-raising source for the exchequer, although much less so than in the past.

Local authorities levy businesses that occupy commercial property in their area with an annual rates bill which is based on the value of that property as established by a central government agency, the Valuation Office. Within each local authority the level of the rate (known as the Annual Rate on Valuation or ARV) is determined on an annual basis by the elected council as part of its budgetary process. The annual rates bill for commercial premises is calculated by applying this ARV to the valuation of the property concerned and it is levied on the occupier of the building. There are exemptions available for unoccupied units and some educational and charitable institutions. These charges provide almost 30 per cent of the funding for Ireland's local authorities.

In 2009, an annual charge on non-principal private residences, payable by the owners to the local authority in whose area the property concerned is located, was introduced. This 'second homes tax' is at present structured as a flat fee of €200 per annum and is unrelated to the location of the property or the amount of public services it, or its owners/occupiers, can avail of. The Act establishing the charge provides that the Minister for the Environment and Local Government may increase the charge from time to time, having regard to changes in the consumer price index.

Other Taxes

A series of other taxes also provide revenue to the exchequer. The government imposes small rates of stamp duties on bank cards, cheques, stock market share transfers and many insurance policies. Deposit interest retention tax (DIRT) is collected at a rate of 27 per cent on the interest paid or credited on deposits of Irish residents in financial institutions. It is collected at source, meaning that the financial institutions deduct the tax from the interest paid and pass these funds to the Revenue Commissioners.

Where a working individual receives some additional non-monetary benefit on top of their salary, they are liable for benefit in kind (BIK) tax. These benefits may include, among others, the private use of a company car, free or subsidised accommodation, preferential loans received from an employer, free meals and subsidised childcare. BIK is levied at a worker's marginal tax rate, thereby treating the benefit in the same way as additional income.

The purchase and annual registration of motor vehicles produces another source of tax revenue for government in the form of vehicle registration tax (VRT) and motor tax. VRT is imposed as a percentage charge on the initial purchase price of a vehicle and since 2008 the levy is based on its CO_2 emissions. Rates range from zero per cent, for electric cars, to 36 per cent for the highest-polluting vehicles. Motor tax is an annual charge on all vehicles and is similarly structured with low charges (less than €200) for low-polluting and electric vehicles and increasing tax levels associated with higher levels of CO_2 emissions. The payment is collected by local authorities and the Department of Transport and its revenues are allocated to fund the local authorities where the vehicles are registered. Motor tax is unrelated to the usage levels of the vehicle.

Since March 2002, a plastic bag environmental levy has been charged on plastic shopping bags at the point of sale. The rate of the levy is set by the Minister for the Environment, Heritage and Local Government and stood at 22 cent per bag in 2011. Revenue from this levy is *hypothecated*, or specifically allocated, to an environmental fund to support waste management, litter reduction and other environmental initiatives. It is one of the few sources of tax revenue in Ireland that is hypothecated rather than flowing to the exchequer and merged into the overall collection and allocation of state revenues.

Two further revenue sources are related to land rezoning and development. In 2010 a windfall gain tax was introduced on the profits derived by landowners whose lands are rezoned as approved for development by local authorities. These decisions, taken in the interest of appropriately planning further urban development, can result in significant increases in the value of land, particularly when it is reclassified from agricultural use to residential or commercial use. As society is making these decisions in the interest of its own development, the tax captures much of these windfall gains for the use of society rather than for the benefit of landowners or land speculators. The tax is charged at a rate of 80 per cent on the amount by which the land increased in value as a result of the rezoning decision and is payable on the disposal of the land.

Development levies are imposed on non-residential developments following a local authority's approval of a planning permission for that development. The levy is based on the public facilities, such as roads, water, sewerage and parks, from which the development will benefit. They are set by each local authority and additional levies can be imposed for developments near certain urban redevelopment and infrastructural projects which the state is funding and which by their existence will further increase the value and benefits derived from the development.

4 EVALUATION: TAXES ON INCOME

Over the past four decades, Ireland's income taxes climbed to high levels in the 1980s, then slowly dropped on foot of social partnership agreements and economic growth during the 1990s and early 2000s, before climbing once again as the recession and economic collapse unfolded from 2008 onwards. Focusing on the years from 1997 to 2011, Table 4.5 reports the effective tax rates faced by two household types at either end of that period and in 2008, the year when income taxation levels reached their lowest point. Overall, the table reflects significant reductions in income tax across the period, with all household types experiencing large income tax cuts up to 2008. Over the eleven years from 1997 to 2008 a single employee on €60,000 received almost €10,000 in income tax cuts with their disposable income rising from €33,660 in 1997 to €43,500 in 2008. Over the same period the post-tax income of a couple earning €60,000 increased by €14,640, almost 25 per cent. At the lower end of the income distribution, a policy commitment to remove all at or below the minimum wage from paying income tax saw rates reduce to zero per cent. A need to generate additional taxation revenue from Budget 2009 onwards (delivered two months early in October 2008), saw a series of reductions in tax bands, cuts to tax credits and the introduction of the USC.[5] Collectively, these rapidly raised effective rates once again, although the effective rates for all earners remained well below the levels experienced in 1997.

Table 4.5

Effective Taxation Rates on Gross Annual Earnings,
1997, 2008 and 2011 (%)[1]

Income Levels	Single person			Couple: two earners[2]		
	1997	2008	2011	1997	2008	2011
€15,000	23.0	0.0	2.7	11.1	0.0	2.0
€20,000	28.5	4.4	9.8	15.9	0.0	2.3
€25,000	33.7	8.3	14.0	20.3	0.0	2.5
€30,000	37.1	12.9	16.8	22.2	1.7	4.7
€40,000	40.6	18.6	24.2	28.5	3.6	9.2
€60,000	43.9	27.5	33.4	36.6	12.2	16.8
€100,000	46.5	33.8	40.9	42.6	23.8	29.7
€120,000	47.1	35.4	42.7	43.9	27.2	33.4

Source: Department of Finance, *Budget 2011*, Stationery Office, Dublin 2010.
[1] Total income taxation includes income tax, PRSI and health and income levies for 1997 and 2008. Levies were replaced by the USC for 2011.
[2] Couple assumes two children and 65%/35% income division.

Behind the overall trends in Table 4.5 are a series of issues related to the functioning and impact of the Irish income taxation system. We examine these throughout the remainder of this section.

Tax Base

The tax base defines what types and levels of income are to be considered as subject to taxation. Currently, each of the three tax charges on income has a differently defined tax base. This occurs as there are different tax exemptions and reliefs for income taxes, PRSI and the USC. Of these three bases, the USC is the broadest, including most forms of income and offering limited reliefs and exemptions. However, the simultaneous existence of three bases undermines the aforementioned desire for simplicity in the taxation system and policy-makers have signalled a desire to consolidate the tax base further, most likely by merging PRSI and the USC.[6]

The narrowness of the income taxation base has been a subject of increasing attention in recent years. To illustrate this, we can use data from the tax system as structured in 2011. Under that structure, the combined effect of income tax rates and tax credits implies that a PAYE employee only begins to incur an income tax liability once their income has exceeded €16,500 per annum. Up to that point, their income incurs a tax rate of 20 per cent, but this liability is cancelled out by their entitlement to tax credits totalling €3,300 per annum (see Table 4.4). They are, however, subject to a charge under the USC. Data from the Revenue Commissioners following Budget 2011 (December 2010) suggested that in that year 37.9 per cent of income earners were exempt from income tax, while 44 per cent paid at the standard rate and 18.1 per cent paid at the higher rate.[7] While these figures include those in receipt of all types of income, including pensions, they reflect both the narrowness of the income tax base and the fact that there are large proportions of the Irish population living on, and earning, low incomes.

The structure of the income taxation system is such that not all forms of income face the same marginal tax rates. In particular, income from savings and capital gains are treated differently from earned income. As outlined earlier, DIRT is charged at a rate of 27 per cent and capital gains incur taxation at a rate of 25 per cent. These rates reflect a long-standing policy approach by successive governments where investment-related income is favoured relative to income from other sources. The tax expenditure system (see later) also incorporates generous reliefs which complement these rates and allow investors to write off the capital costs of their investment over short periods of seven to ten years, even when the value of these investments is inflating.

Tax Wedge and Employment
The combined impact of taxation on the take-home pay of workers has impacts on their labour market participation decisions, both at the margin (working additional hours) and at the point of entry and exit. As an employee's income level increases, high marginal taxation rates emerge and form a widening wedge between their gross earnings and their take-home pay. Using data from the 2011 tax system, Table 4.6 shows that once income passes €32,800 the marginal tax rate reaches 52 per cent; meaning an employee takes home only €48 out of every additional €100 earned. The table also highlights the existence of a number of steps in the structure of marginal tax rates in the Irish system. These emerge given the structure of tax credits, tax bands, PRSI thresholds and USC. Self-employed earners with incomes above €100,000 are subject to an additional USC surcharge of 3 per cent on all income above this threshold, bringing their marginal tax rate to 55 per cent.

The presence of high marginal tax rates and the step-effect nature of their increases have knock-on implications for the wider economy. An employee on average earnings (€36,472 in 2010) may find it unattractive to take on additional work hours given these rates.[8] For others, particularly those earning near the marginal tax thresholds, there may be an incentive to reduce work hours or to leave the active labour market and become unemployed – becoming so-called 'discouraged workers'. To reduce the labour market participation disincentive effects experienced by individuals whose spouse/partner is already at work, most tax credits are *individualised*, i.e. they can only be claimed by the person who is entitled to them and they cannot be transferred to another person, even within the same household. Consequently, a woman returning to work after having children will start earning with her own PAYE tax credit intact, although she is likely to have shared her personal credit with her partner.

Table 4.6

Summary of the Composition of Marginal Tax Rates for Irish Workers (2011)[1]

Income Range	Income tax[2]	PRSI[3]	USC[4]	Marginal rate
€0–€4,004	0%	0%	0%	0%
€4,005–€10,036	0%	0%	2%	2%
€10,037–€16,016	0%	0%	4%	4%
€16,017–€16,500	0%	0%	7%	7%
€16,501–€18,304	20%	0%	7%	27%
€18,305–€32,800	20%	4%	7%	31%
€32,801+	41%	4%	7%	52%
>€100,000 self-employed[5]	41%	4%	10%	55%

[1] The table assumes a single PRSI employee with entitlements to the personal and PAYE tax credit only.
[2] The personal and PAYE tax credit eliminate any income tax liability up to €16,500.
[3] PRSI is charged at a rate of 4% on all income once earnings exceed €352 per week (€18,304 per annum) with a weekly PRSI-free allowance of €127 (€6,604 per annum).
[4] Employees who earn less than €4,004 are exempt from the USC; once earning above this level the USC applies to all income.
[5] Self-employed income above €100,000 is subject to an additional USC surcharge of 3%.

High marginal tax rates may also dampen the entrepreneurial enthusiasm of high-income workers, including the self-employed. They also tend to be associated with increasing activity in the shadow or black economy where workers are paid in cash and do not declare their income to the Revenue Commissioners. While the scale of this activity is difficult to measure, the incentive for its emergence and growth is positively related to the marginal tax rate.

For government, it is difficult to avoid many of these marginal tax rate problems in a progressive tax system. Consequently, the challenge for tax policy-making is to balance the necessity of collecting sufficient taxation revenue against the disincentives inherent in high marginal rates which may undermine economic activity and as a consequence undermine tax revenue.

Reliefs and Exemptions

An individual can decrease their effective and marginal tax rates below the levels in Tables 4.5 and 4.6 by availing of tax reliefs and exemptions. These mechanisms, formally known as tax expenditures, are incorporated by government into the taxation system as a means of incentivising certain activity or accommodating certain needs. Examples include tax relief on pension contributions; incentives to invest in film making, small business and property; a tax break for charitable donations; a tax credit for blind employees; and a tax credit for one-parent families. A study by Collins and Walsh identified a total of 131 reliefs in the Irish system costing in excess of €11.5 billion in *revenue forgone* each year – revenue forgone measures the tax forgone by the exchequer as a result of the tax break. They also highlighted a need to reduce the quantity and scale of these tax breaks and to adopt more formal accounting and economic evaluation methods in recording, reviewing and extending tax breaks.[9]

The largest tax relief is on employee pension contributions, costing €2.9 billion in revenue forgone each year. Employees avail of the relief by making contributions to their personal pension funds from their pre-tax income. Consequently, a higher rate of relief is available to employees on higher income tax levels than those on lower incomes. Overall, the ability to avail of tax breaks is directly linked to higher incomes. The more income a person has, the more tax they are liable for and therefore the more tax they have available to be written down against various tax breaks. In 2010 a minimum effective tax rate of 30 per cent of income was set for earners with incomes of more than €250,000 in an attempt to minimise their use of tax breaks to reduce their tax bills – a 30 per cent rate is equivalent to the tax level faced by a PAYE worker earning €55,000. While there is merit in the provision by government of certain tax breaks, the evidence for many is limited and in some cases it is clear that they lead to unnecessary and arbitrary market distortions.

Equity and Simplicity

As Tables 4.5 and 4.6 show, the Irish income taxation system has a progressive structure. But the equity principle is undermined at the top of the income scale by the quantity and generosity of many tax breaks. Similarly, there are questions at the other end of the income distribution regarding the point at which taxes should begin to be imposed on earners. Budget 2011 began to collect tax, via the USC, from all earners on all income once their annual income exceeded €4,004. This marked a significant alteration in the approach to income taxation in Ireland, which had previously exempted earners up to the annual value of the minimum wage. The appropriateness of this policy reform can be judged against competing desires to protect the living standards of low-income workers and the need for exchequer revenue collected from a broad tax base. Undoubtedly, the debate on both these issues is likely to continue for some time.

From a simplicity perspective, the compliance and administrative costs faced by most Irish taxpayers are low. As taxes are deducted from wages before they are paid, most employees have limited need for interaction with the Revenue Commissioners. For the self-employed, directors and other corporate taxpayers, sophisticated on-line tax return systems and electronic cash transfers have made tax returns and compliance considerably simpler than in the past. It is likely that over the next decade the entire administrative side of the tax system will move to exclusively electronic exchanges. However, as we have seen, the Irish income taxation system is far from simple and the existence of multiple bases, thresholds, exemptions and rates provides a complex system that most taxpayers would be challenged to comprehend.[10]

5 EVALUATION: INDIRECT TAXES, CORPORATION TAXES AND PROPERTY TAXES

While income and social security taxes comprise more than 45 per cent of the tax take (see Table 4.3), the rest of the exchequer's revenue is derived from taxes on consumption, company profits and property. The performance of each of these taxes in the Irish system is considered in this section.

Indirect Taxes
Value Added Tax (VAT)
As Figure 4.1 shows, VAT is a regressive tax that collects a higher proportion of income from poorer households. In Ireland, as in most countries where VAT or equivalent general sales taxes have been in existence for some time, there are multiple VAT rates. This contrasts with countries, including a number in Eastern Europe, who have over recent decades introduced VAT at a single rate. The Irish system is characterised by a large number of exemptions and goods and services charged VAT at zero per cent. A study found that one-sixth of the consumption of the average household was zero rated, a further one-sixth was exempt, and less than half was subject to VAT at the standard rate of 21 per cent.[11] As a result, the potential base for VAT in Ireland is narrower than it could be and consequently the standard and reduced rate (13.5 per cent) are higher than they could be given the revenue-raising constraints faced by government when setting these rates.

While the progression of VAT rates across categories of goods and services is for the most part negatively related to their necessity, the fact that the consumption of most goods and services increases as income rises results in higher-income households benefiting more in absolute terms from the exemptions, zero ratings and reduced rates. These benefits further undermine the equity of the tax, and the complexity associated with their implementation and administration reduces the efficiency and simplicity of VAT. In general, such inequities and inefficiencies would make the case for reform of the VAT structure, but the ability of government to do this is limited by strict EU rules which in effect only allow goods and services to be moved to the standard VAT rate irrespective of their current status.

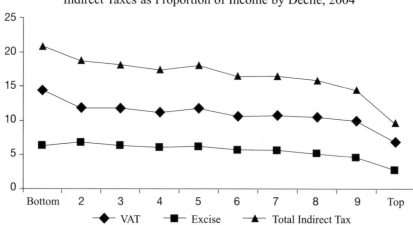

Figure 4.1

Indirect Taxes as Proportion of Income by Decile, 2004

Source: A. Barrett and C. Wall, *The Distributional Impact of Ireland's Indirect Tax System,* Combat Poverty Agency, Dublin 2005.

Excise Duties

Excise duties on fuel, alcohol and tobacco serve a dual function for government as both revenue generators and public policy tools to discourage consumption and reduce or minimise externalities such as pollution and health effects. The former is possible given that these goods are characterised by low price elasticities and consequently increases in excise levels produce limited demand effects and sizeable exchequer revenue effects. They are therefore a relatively efficient tax. Similarly, they are simple to operate, with the tax revenue collected from distributors, importers, and retailers. However, these taxes do raise a number of questions when considered in terms of equity.

The involuntary nature of some expenditure, such as on fuel to heat the home or because products are addictive, makes excise duties difficult, if not impossible, to avoid. Furthermore, data from the Household Budget Survey shows that households at the lower end of the income distribution spend a greater proportion of their disposable income on fuel, alcohol and tobacco – see Figure 4.1. Therefore, excise duties represent a greater burden to poorer households than better-off ones, implying that these taxes are regressive and violate the vertical equity principle. As the excise duty tax burden falls on households based on their consumption needs and addictions, households with similar incomes may pay significantly different amounts of total excise duties, violating the horizontal equity principle.

In terms of designing taxation policy, government needs to balance the problematic effects of these taxes against the objectives of revenue generation and discouraging certain consumption. The setting of excise duties is also influenced by levels in neighbouring jurisdictions because relatively high excise duties may result in a loss of the tax base as consumption shifts to purchases made outside the state. In recent years the government has avoided increasing the excise duties on tobacco and alcohol products as their levels in the Republic of Ireland were greater than those in Northern Ireland and the widening differential over previous years had shifted consumption and undermined the tax base.

Carbon taxes raise similar efficiency and equity issues when considered against the earlier principles, given that they are collected and imposed in a similar way to excise duties. Studies prior to the introduction of the carbon tax in 2010 suggested that the government should recycle some of the revenue from the tax to compensate low-income households whose consumption comprises a greater proportion of goods subject to the carbon tax than was the case for better-off households.[12] It was argued that such an approach would cushion the effect of the policy reform while still encouraging households to alter their carbon consumption patterns. However, a compensating mechanism was not introduced to accompany the policy as the exchequer was unable to afford it in 2010. Similar issues also arise for motor taxation and it can be argued that these taxes fall more heavily on rural households, large households and those living in areas with limited access to public transport.

Overall, reforms of indirect taxes have for the most part been driven by the desire for additional tax revenue rather than some other objective. Reflecting this, the National Recovery Plan 2011–2014 has signalled increases to both VAT and carbon taxes and earmarked certain revenues required by the exchequer on foot of these increases. Furthermore, from the perspective of the overall taxation system, the fact that it is difficult to avoid the regressive nature of indirect taxes, irrespective of their design and structure, challenges government to ensure that the other elements of the tax system are characterised by a high degree of progressivity.

Corporation Taxes
The corporate profits of both indigenous and foreign-owned firms in Ireland are taxed at a rate of 12.5 per cent. In international terms, Ireland's corporate tax rate is low, with only two other countries in the EU or OECD – Bulgaria and Cyprus, which both have a 10 per cent rate – possessing rates below this level. Data for 2010 suggest that the Irish rate is more than 10 per cent lower than the EU-27 average of 23.2 per cent and well below the top statutory rates on corporate income in Germany (29.8 per cent), France (34.4 per cent), Malta (the EU's highest rate of 35 per cent) and the United States (39 per cent).[13] The effective tax rate faced by companies in these countries is likely to be below these headline rates as they can avail of various tax breaks such as those for research and development, recruiting workers from disadvantaged groups or operating in regional or economically disadvantaged areas. In general, countries with higher headline corporate tax rates provide a greater array of corporate tax breaks. However, even taking account of tax breaks, the Irish corporate tax rate is low in international terms and this is regularly highlighted as a key incentive for new foreign direct investment.

In general, foreign-owned firms benefit from Ireland's low corporate tax rate by locating a subsidiary in Ireland whose profits are subject to tax in Ireland with no taxes payable in the corporation's home country until the profit is repatriated there. Upon repatriation, profits are taxed in the home country with a credit given for taxes already paid in Ireland. Companies are free to delay indefinitely the repatriation of these profits and as such benefit from an ability to use the portion of profit yet to be repatriated within their business. Shareholders also benefit from share price inflation associated with these higher profits and the benefits derived from the use of the additional funds. Irish subsidiaries also enjoy almost no restrictions on their ability to engage in *transfer pricing*. This allows multinational companies to artificially value sales between associated companies located in different countries and can be used to maximise the profit realised and taxable in lower tax jurisdictions such as Ireland.

The sustainability of Ireland's current corporate taxation model is under threat from a series of ongoing international reforms. The impact of the post-2008 recession on the fiscal balance sheets of countries such as the United States has focused attention on the need for governments to minimise tax leakages. As a result, incentives to repatriate profits have been introduced and a harder attitude is being taken to countries and territories that facilitate corporations not paying the tax they would be expected to pay. Simultaneously, within the EU proposals for the establishment of a common consolidated corporate tax base (CCCTB) have been made in 2011 by the European Commission after almost a decade of development of the proposal.[14] While the debate on CCCTB is likely to continue for some time, its emergence, if agreed, would require firms in all member states of the EU to calculate their profits in the same way, essentially imposing a uniform definition of how corporate income is defined and what can and cannot be discounted against it. The reform is also likely to require firms that operate in multiple countries to apportion their profits between those countries in accordance with a formula that weights the activities of the multinational in the different countries, rather than the company arranging its own internal balance sheet to maximise the profit it realises in the country with the lowest tax rate. While the CCCTB reforms seem logical, they would undermine the ability of firms to shift their profits and tax liabilities to Ireland and consequently reduce the flow of revenue from this sector to the exchequer.

A further international threat comes from reductions in headline corporate tax rates of other EU member states. While Ireland's low corporate taxation rate has been a competitive advantage for some time, an increasing number of EU member states are cutting their rates to compete with Ireland, and other states, for foreign direct investment. In the years ahead, it is unlikely that Ireland could fiscally afford to match these reductions. Finally, given the recent increases, outlined earlier, in income and indirect taxes and the proposals for recurring property taxes and additional user charges, it seems inevitable that attention will turn domestically to the feasibility of raising corporate taxes. Despite the importance accorded to corporate taxes, there is limited evidence to suggest that there are no deadweight exchequer losses associated with having the rate at 12.5 per cent rather than 15 per cent or 20 per cent. As one commentator put it, 'we know almost nothing about the fiscal price we are paying for investment'.[15]

Property Taxes

A study by the OECD in 2009 used time-series data from its member states to establish a hierarchy of taxes with regard to their negative effect on GDP per capita in the following order from the most to the least harmful for growth: (a) corporate income taxes; (b) personal income taxes; (c) consumption taxes; and (d) recurrent taxes on immovable property.[16] Notably, given the objective of economic growth, the Irish taxation system does not currently incorporate a recurring domestic property tax, despite this being the least harmful form of taxation.

Recommendations from the 2009 Commission on Taxation and commitments in the 2010/2011 EU/IMF Memorandum of Understanding suggest that a property tax generating between €0.5billion and €1 billion per annum will be introduced.[17] The form of property tax that government proposes to introduce is a site value tax (SVT). This lump-sum tax will levy an annual charge on the value of all developed and undeveloped zoned land including the site under every building in residential use. Land value derives from location and service access, meaning that, for instance, a site in an urban location with good transport and access to public services will incur more than a relatively isolated site. The tax base will exclude all unzoned land such as that used for agriculture and forestry. In time, the SVT may expand to replace commercial property rates and provide its total revenue to fund the local authorities in the area where it is collected. SVT differs from a residential property tax as it is based on the value of the underlying land and ignores the quality, scale or extent of development on that land.

A key attraction of an SVT, or any form of recurring property tax, is that it provides a stable annual flow of resources to the exchequer based on an immovable tax base. This contrasts with the volatile flow of funds from transaction-linked stamp duties which had served as the main source of state property tax revenue between the abolition of local authority domestic rates in 1977 and the housing market crash post-2007. SVTs also capture some of the welfare effects of state-funded local services and convert these benefits into a source of funding to support the state.

6 DEFERRED TAXATION: PUBLIC DEBT

Imposing taxation on incomes, consumption, profits and assets is not the only way in which government can access finance to pursue its spending and economic management objectives. It can also borrow money by selling bonds and using the proceeds to finance public spending. In doing so, governments are engaging in *deferred taxation* as implicit in the selling of a bond is a commitment to pay interest over its lifetime and repay its value upon maturity. To do this, governments will have to raise future taxation revenue from current and future taxpayers.

The appropriateness of governments borrowing today on the basis of taxpayers paying in the future is linked to how governments use these borrowings.

Where bond revenues are used to finance capital investments, such as hospitals, museums and transport infrastructure, the benefits derived from the provision of these facilities will flow to the future taxpayers who will service and repay the borrowing. As such, deferring taxation, so that beneficiaries finance the provision of government investments while they experience their benefits, has a logical basis.[18] Conversely, governments should finance day-to-day, or current, spending from current taxation revenue, thereby balancing the exchequer's current account. Current account deficits, where they occur, should only be associated with attempts to stabilise the economy in the short run and governments should cancel this effect out by running current account surpluses in other periods. Financing current account deficits from borrowing serves as an inappropriate transfer of avoided current taxation burdens to future taxpayers.

The scale of public debt is measured relative to a country's national income with the EU and European Central Bank regarding a debt/GDP ratio of below 60 per cent as being optimal. As Table 4.7 and Figure 4.2 show, over the past four decades Ireland has moved from marginally above this threshold in 1980, to well above it in 1987, to significantly below it in 2007 and back to well above it in 2011. Borrowing to fund the current account deficit drove national debt levels up in the 1980s while strong economic growth and budget surpluses decreased the debt burden to 2007. In 2000 Ireland ran a fiscal balance of 4.8 per cent of GDP, meaning that taxation revenues covered all current and capital spending and provided almost 5 per cent of GDP as an exchequer surplus. By 2007 Ireland's debt/GDP ratio reached a level of 25 per cent of GDP; a debt burden regarded as very low and suggesting that the nation's debt was small, manageable and of limited long-term economic significance. If anything, such a low debt level reduced the need for higher future taxes as its servicing and repayment would inflict limited fiscal strain and, given GDP growth, the debt burden would be further eroded.

Table 4.7

Government Debt and Financial Balances as % GDP

	General government gross public debt as % GDP				
Year	1980	1987	2000	2007	2011
Ireland	65.2	109.2	37.8	25.0	>110
Euro area			69.3	65.9	87.4
	Government financial balances as % GDP			
Year		2000	2007	2009	2010
Ireland		+4.8	0.0	-14.4	-31.9
Euro area		-1.9	-0.6	-6.3	-6.0

Sources: International Monetary Fund, *World Economic Outlook Database*, www.imf.org [accessed April 2011]; and OECD *Economic Outlook No. 88*, OECD, Paris 2010.

Figure 4.2

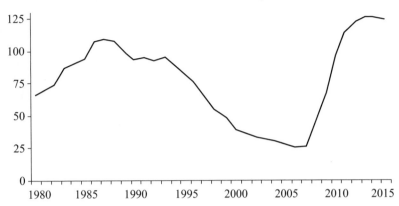

Ireland's National Debt as % GDP, 1980–2015

Source: International Monetary Fund, *World Economic Outlook Database*, www.imf.org [accessed April 2011].

The simultaneous collapse in the construction and banking industries from 2008 had significant knock-on effects for exchequer revenue and spending. Taxation revenue from employees' incomes and spending contracted rapidly, as did revenue from housing-related VAT and stamp duty. The concurrent international recession also decreased trade, corporate activity and corporation profits. Between 2007 and 2009 current taxation revenues fell by almost €15 billion or 31 per cent. Exchequer spending also increased to fund higher social welfare needs and to pay for capital injections into various banks. By 2010 Ireland's exchequer deficit reached record levels with the nation borrowing almost 32 per cent of GDP in one year. The uncertainty surrounding the final exchequer cost of rescuing and closing various financial institutions makes it difficult to accurately predict future debt/GDP ratios. However, the IMF expects that the national debt will exceed 110 per cent of GDP in 2011 and peak at 126 per cent in 2013.[19]

While Ireland's debt transformation is severe, debt/GDP ratios and exchequer deficits have also increased across the euro area as a response to the international recession. In 2009 and 2010 average euro zone budget deficits reached 6 per cent of GDP, twice the threshold laid down in the Stability and Growth Pact, which sets the acceptable parameters for fiscal policy among euro zone member countries.

This growth in debt carries a series of structural and policy implications for Europe and Ireland in the coming years. Proposals for independent fiscal councils to comment publicly on the appropriateness of government's taxation and spending decisions before and after they are announced are well advanced, with Ireland required to establish such a body under the terms of the EU/IMF Memorandum of Understanding (see Chapter 3 for a discussion of this). Similarly, the fact that Ireland's debt/GDP ratio has climbed to such a high level

(Figure 4.2) will necessitate ongoing higher taxation levels relative to those that existed over the decade since 2000. Questions have also been raised regarding the sustainability of servicing and reducing these debt levels over the next decade as opposed to restructuring them through debt write-offs and multi-decade loans.

The fact that future Irish taxpayers will pay for the fiscal and economic mistakes of the first decade of this century violates the logic of intergenerational deferred taxation discussed at the start of this section. The phenomenon of imposing this debt on future generations has also given rise to a consideration to create constitutional checks on governments' fiscal policy decisions.

7 CONCLUSION

This chapter has provided an overview of Ireland's taxation system, setting it in the context of economic theory, its features and operation and the nation's future liabilities. In a given year the taxation system, including tax expenditures, is a €55–65 billion system and it is clear that in the years ahead the system will face significant challenges and reforms.

Central to these will be the need to generate the additional revenue required to close Ireland's exchequer deficit and begin to repay the debt accumulated in the years since 2008. As part of doing this, the chapter highlighted the opportunities and needs for a broader tax base incorporating a recurring property tax, user charges, and reforms targeted at enhancing the simplicity, efficiency and equality of the tax system. These reforms will also need to address the backdrop of unemployment and tackle any tax-related disincentives to labour market participation and, where possible, use taxation policies to enhance growth, recovery and job creation. A further backdrop will be reforms at a European level relating to corporate taxation structures and the management of fiscal policy.

The cumulative effect of revenue needs, deferred taxation, international reforms and economic recovery in the years ahead will necessitate that taxation policy and taxation reform will be recurring public policy themes for the foreseeable future.

Endnotes

1   A. Smith, *An Inquiry into the Nature and Causes of the Wealth of Nations*, Strahan and Cadell, London 1776.

2   See M. Collins, 'Taxation in Ireland: an overview' in B. Reynolds and S. Healy (eds), *A Fairer Tax System for a Fairer Ireland*, CORI Justice Commission, Dublin 2004.

3   The USC does not apply to individuals with a gross annual market income of less than €4,004.

4   There are a total of six VAT rates in the Irish system. Additional rates of 4.3 per cent apply to agricultural livestock, horses and greyhounds; a rate of 5.2 per cent applies to certain agricultural outputs; and a rate of 13.5 per cent applies to residential properties constructed after 1993.

5   The USC was preceded by an income levy and health levy which were subsequently merged in Budget 2011 to create the USC.

6   See Department of Finance, *Budget 2010*, Stationery Office, Dublin 2009.

7   See Department of Finance, *Budget 2011*, Stationery Office, Dublin 2010.

8   Central Statistics Office, *Earnings and Labour Costs,* Stationery Office, Dublin 2011.

9   M. Collins and M. Walsh, *Ireland's Tax Expenditure System: International Comparisons and a Reform Agenda*, Policy Institute, Trinity College Dublin, Dublin 2010.

10 A comprehensive explanation is available on the websites of the Office of the Revenue Commissioners (www.revenue.ie) and the Irish Taxation Institute (www.taxireland.ie).

11 J. Bristow, *Taxation in Ireland: An Economist's Perspective*, Institute of Public Administration, Dublin 2004.

12 See S. Scott and J. Eakins, *Distributive Effects of Carbon Taxes*, ESRI, Dublin 2002.

13 Eurostat, *Taxation Trends in the European Union*, Eurostat, Luxembourg 2010.

14 See CCCTB proposal and background documents on the Commission website at http://ec.europa.eu/taxation_customs/taxation/company_tax/common_tax_base/index_en.htm.

15 Bristow, *op. cit*, p. 69.

16 OECD, *Going for Growth*, OECD, Paris 2009.

17 Commission on Taxation, *Report 2009*, Stationery Office, Dublin 2009; EU/IMF, *Ireland Memorandum of Understanding on Specific Economic Policy Conditionality*, Dublin 2010.

18 See A.L. Hillman, *Public Finance and Public Policy – Responsibilities and Limitations of Government* (2nd edn), Cambridge University Press, New York 2009.

19 International Monetary Fund, *World Economic Outlook*, IMF, Washington April 2011.

CHAPTER 5

Regulation and Competition Policy

Francis O'Toole*

1 INTRODUCTION

This chapter examines the general policy area of regulation and the associated specific area of competition policy, incorporating the regulation of natural monopolies (such as household waste collection in a specific locality) and various networks (such as the electricity transmission grid). The rapidly evolving research field of regulation, which now spans areas such as economics, ethics, law, public policy and sociology, requires the adoption of a rather broad definition of regulation, such as 'the intentional use of authority to affect behaviour of a different party according to set standards, involving instruments of information gathering and behaviour modification'.[1]

A set of formal rules, for example with respect to health and safety in the workplace, provides an example of regulation, as do, at a more macroeconomic level, the imposition of fiscal incentives such as taxes and subsidies (e.g. a carbon tax) that aim to alter behaviour and, at a consumer protection level, informational requirements with respect to whether or not the seller of a particular financial product is a tied agent. However, the recognised regulatory remit extends well beyond these standard economically based examples and into broader social policy-based areas such as: gay partnerships and marriage; the use of in vitro fertilisation; surrogacy; the rights and responsibilities (and even definition) of parents (and other relations such as grandparents); gene therapy; domestic and foreign adoption (including the rights and responsibilities of gay couples with respect to adoption); nuclear energy; genetically modified (GM) foods and food safety issues more generally; the (at least apparently) compulsory nature of Irish in Irish secondary schools; Internet gambling; and the markets for sexual services or illicit drugs, or even the market for votes and the associated policy debate in Ireland with respect to public funding of political parties and the appropriateness or otherwise of allowing corporate donations to political parties. In competition policy, recent high-profile examples include: Ryanair's attempted acquisition(s) of Aer Lingus; a proposed ban on the below-cost selling of alcohol products; the elimination of restrictions (e.g. on advertising) within certain professions; and the

possible removal of the cap on the size of retail premises. The latter two issues interested the International Monetary Fund (IMF) in the context of discussions related to Ireland's recently announced Programme for Support. In the specific context of natural monopolies and networks, recent prominent (and often very controversial) examples include: the appropriate regulation of the collection and disposal of Dublin's household waste; and the setting of appropriate retail prices for electricity and natural gas.

The importance of regulatory and competition policies is felt throughout the economy. For example, the EU Nitrates Directive, which imposes limits on the amount of nitrogen (from animal manure or fertiliser) that can be used in farming, highlights the specific importance of regulatory policies to the agricultural sector (see Chapter 11). In addition, and more recently, significant controversy has been caused by the imposition of a ban (resulting from EU conservation laws) on non-commercial turf-cutting on raised bogs. These two examples also demonstrate the importance of transnational regulatory policy and the need for co-ordination with respect to Irish and EU regulations. In the manufacturing sector, policies with respect to corporation taxes and grants have been responsible for the location of many foreign-owned manufacturing plants in Ireland, for example in the pharmaceutical sub-sector. The recent controversy surrounding Ireland's relatively low corporation tax rate again demonstrates the importance of transnational regulatory policy, but it also highlights the existence of tensions between the goals of national (i.e. Irish) and international (i.e. EU) regulations. In the services sector of the economy, the importance of regulatory policy, both domestic and transnational, has been more than aptly demonstrated by Ireland's banking crisis. The recent recapitalisation and restructuring of the Irish (as well as the UK) banking sector also demonstrates the importance of competition policy, both nationally and internationally.

This chapter will attempt to address many of the issues mentioned above. Section 2 provides an overview of regulation, addressing possible explanations and/or justifications for, and theories of, regulations and focuses specific attention on the risk-based approach to regulation. Section 3 reviews recent national and international policy approaches to regulation and regulatory reform at both a general level (e.g. the 'better regulation' movement) and a specific level (e.g. the use of regulatory impact assessments (RIA)). Section 4 explores Ireland's banking crisis from a regulatory policy perspective: the financial services sector has contributed significantly in recent years to the increased realisation of the importance of both domestic and transnational regulatory policy. Section 5 focuses attention on the specific regulatory policy example of competition policy and provides a number of examples of regulatory policies in action; while Section 6 addresses the specific policy area that intersects both regulation and competition, namely the regulation of natural monopolies and networks such as the electricity transmission and natural gas grids. Section 7 offers some concluding comments.

The above outline and the previous examples make it clear that a good understanding of regulation is essential background reading for an understanding of policy issues in both the Irish market and non-market sectors. As such, it should be no surprise to readers of the last four chapters in this book in particular to encounter many of the themes introduced in the rest of this chapter.

2 REGULATION: PRINCIPLES AND ISSUES

Reasons for Regulation
Information and Co-ordination
There are a number of possible reasons for the existence of regulations. At a very general level, informational and co-ordination problems could justify, or at least explain, the existence of many regulations. For example, basic fire safety standards are set so as to protect the vast majority of individual users of, say, cinemas, hotels and public transport as individually very few of these users would be in a position to assess the appropriateness, or otherwise, of the safety precautions taken by other individuals and businesses. A similar argument holds with respect to the existence of regulations regarding, say, maximum taxi fares. For example, a fare of €100 might well be acceptable to an individual (rich) tourist attempting to get from an airport to the city centre on a very cold evening, but it is generally regarded as inappropriate to take advantage of the tourist's initial informational deficiency. Indeed, many forms of regulation are responses to what are seen as informational problems, as it is argued that markets often under-provide relevant information. For example, what is the real price of an advertised one cent airfare, or how can one individual compare the costs of different loans? The latter question is addressed in the USA by the Truth in Lending Act (2001), which insists that all lenders must quote the annual percentage rate (APR) to potential borrowers; APRs can then be compared across different loan options.

Other regulations surrounding information requirements in at least some jurisdictions insist that car manufacturers provide fuel efficiency information, brewers of beer provide alcohol content information, cigarette packets carry health warnings, food products carry nutritional information and that league tables with respect to school performances are produced and published. In addition, various regulations insist upon what might be termed minimum standards, as opposed to just the provision of information, e.g. travel agencies and operators enter into various forms of travel bonds and retail banks must keep a certain proportion of their retail consumers' deposits in liquid assets.

Spill-over Effects
In addition, economists tend naturally to view the existence of (non-priced) spill-over effects or externalities as providing an explanation for the existence of many regulations (see Chapter 3). Technically, externalities imply the existence of a divergence between private costs and benefits and/or social costs and benefits and hence the presence of non-priced costs and/or benefits. Taking the standard

example of pollution – a negative production externality – a producer does not have to internalise the cost of the pollution that the production process imposes on others. A similar argument holds with respect to the placing of restrictions on the consumption of tobacco products, although of course reasonable readers can differ with respect to the appropriate limits of such regulations. For example, should an adult be allowed to smoke in a private car in the presence of children, or should adults be allowed to choose between a smoking and non-smoking pub? Of course, informational and spill-over explanations for regulations do not always separate out easily. For example, the requirement for drivers (and businesses more generally) to hold at least third party insurance is commonly justified by the belief that drivers (and society more generally) should be protected from the results of mistakes of another driver, even if each individual driver is allowed to rationally (or otherwise) decide not to protect himself or herself from his or her own actions. The existence of this regulation can be understood via the information explanation (how would one know which drivers are insured?) and/or by the spill-over explanation (why should you have to pay for my mistake?). Another possible example is provided by retail planning guidelines with respect to the location and scale of various types of retail development (e.g. shopping centres) at or near town centres, which set the rules by which business people make important (and often non-reversible) investment decisions.

Unequal Bargaining Power/Wider Social Policy
The reality of the existence of unequal bargaining power also underlies the existence of many regulations. For example, although at least some of the relatively small number of users of industrial saws or chainsaws may well be prepared to work without safety guards, many other users would prefer not to be put in a position where they had to actively request the installation of such (perhaps expensive) guards and hence perhaps not be employed in the first place (as a result of their rather conservative approach to safety matters). Arguably, the same applies with respect to the use of minimum wage legislation; at least some workers and employers would be prepared to transact at a lower wage but society in effect does not allow such voluntary transactions. However, at least some readers might regard the setting of some safety requirements and labour restrictions (e.g. some facets of the joint labour committee (JLC) agreements) as being excessively interventionist. Indeed, some might even feel the need for less regulation in the market for sexual services or the market for so-called recreational drugs, but most would probably feel uncomfortable if a non-interventionist position was used to justify the straightforward buying and selling of votes or vital organs (such as kidneys) or indeed people (e.g. babies).

More generally, it is clear that many regulations are explained on social policy grounds as opposed to what might be termed market failure grounds. For example, anti-discrimination legislation is difficult to explain on market failure grounds alone. The taxation of windfall profits (e.g. via a land development tax) or the existence of universal service obligations with respect to, say, the provision of a fixed-line telephone (at reasonable cost) or a basic daily postal delivery service (at, technically speaking, no direct cost to the recipient, no matter how isolated the home) can also be seen as addressing social policy objectives.

However, while information, co-ordination, spill-over effects and unequal bargaining power or, more generally, social policy grounds can be used to explain the existence of very many regulations at least after the event, it is not so easy to explain the existence of many other regulations, such as the requirement for bikers to wear safety helmets or for drivers and all passengers to wear safety belts or the ban on the publication of school league tables or the ban on private health insurers from offering discounts to non-smokers without stretching concepts of co-ordination failures, spill-over effects and social policy objectives beyond their usefulness. Indeed, the above-mentioned proposed explanations may also not be able to explain the general non-existence of arguably sensible regulations, for example with respect to informing any potential partner of at least some of your particular health and personality characteristics (or even defects) before the potential partner has made a potentially irreversible investment of one sort or another in you. As such, there is merit in examining plausible over-arching theories of regulation.

Theories of Regulation
There are a number of overlapping theories of regulation. From an economics perspective, it is tempting to focus particular attention upon the distinction between the public interest approach to regulation on the one hand and the interest group and private interest approaches to regulation on the other. The public interest approach to regulation highlights the claimed equivalence between the regulator's interests and the public interest. As such, the regulator may be said, in a somewhat paradoxical sense, to be disinterested; the public interest is somehow ascertained (say, with respect to food safety), and the regulator acts in a purely technical manner so as to achieve the desired end-state. In particular, there is no allowance made for any underlying power struggle between, say, the regulated parties (e.g. producers and sellers of food) and the parties for whose benefit the regulations are being put in place (e.g. consumers of food).

This approach may be appropriate in the context of basic food safety, but what about in the context of the appropriate regulation of genetically modified (GM) foods? In contrast, the interest group and private interest approaches highlight the private incentives of groups and individuals, respectively. In the interest group approach, attention is focused on the relationships between groups and the state. In the context of these evolving relationships a competition or battle is seen to take place between various different conceptualisations of what is the public interest. Corporatism, for example, can be seen as the process or as the result in this interest group approach; from an Irish perspective, the evolution of social partnership could be analysed from this perspective.

The private interest approach, also referred to as the economic theory of regulation or public choice, goes further, insisting that the individual incentives confronting each rational (economic) actor must be considered if regulation is to be understood. For example, it is claimed that regulatory capture, a process in which regulators over time appear to begin to represent the interests of the regulated, as opposed to society more generally, can only be understood if particular attention is paid to the incentives of the employees of regulatory agencies. It is these employees who interact with, and begin to depend upon, the regulated entities (e.g. with respect to the provision of data within a particular format by a certain date). From the public choice perspective, unless particular safeguards are put in place, it is hardly surprising that implicit understandings between these individuals and even their organisations begin to develop. For a possible example, see the later discussion on the Irish banking crisis.

In addition to the above interest approaches to regulation, there are other approaches which can be considered on their own merits or in conjunction with the interest approaches. For example, at particular times in history, it is clear that the force of ideas can drive regulatory developments. At a macroeconomic level the Keynesian revolution could be viewed as a prime example of a shift in ideas with significant policy implications, while at a more microeconomic level (albeit one with macroeconomic consequences), there was a shift towards privatisation in the UK and deregulation and market liberalisation in the USA during the early 1980s. Of course, all theories of regulation must be confronted with, and tested against, actual regulatory experiences. For example, the public interest perspective is hard to reconcile with the high prices that resulted from the air transport regulatory experience up until the late 1970s in the USA and later in Europe and elsewhere. In turn, however, the public choice perspective is itself difficult to reconcile with the actual deregulatory experiences of the 1980s and 1990s, which have reduced the power of at least some groups, unless, of course, recourse to the force of ideas approach is added to the mix.

Regulatory Strategies

Assuming the need for a regulatory response, various options exist with respect to the appropriate form of regulation, e.g. command and control (e.g. no smoking indoors in public places); production and/or consumption taxes (e.g. excise duties on motor fuels or, more generally, the imposition of a carbon tax); quotas (e.g. fishing or even pollution), perhaps supported by a system of tradeable permits; or simply naming and shaming (e.g. tax evaders or negative inspection reports for nursing homes or, albeit perhaps less likely, evaluation reports by students on individual teachers or lecturers). Even in the context of a standard externality, say insufficient take-up of the flu or, perhaps more controversially, the MMR vaccine, alternative and very different regulatory strategies can be followed, ranging from simple provision of information to subsidising consumption of the vaccine to compulsory vaccination; readers who are taken aback with respect to the latter suggestion might consider the example of water fluoridation. In contrast to these various measures, some market enthusiasts, in at least some contexts and referencing the Coase Theorem, simply highlight the need to specify property rights very clearly so as to facilitate negotiations and market-based transactions between affected parties. For example, if anglers have the right to clean water, anglers will be paid by the polluters for any pollution that the anglers choose to allow and if the polluters have the right to pollute the water, the anglers will pay the polluters so as to restrict the level of pollution to the appropriate level.[2]

Almost all regulatory strategies suffer from some disadvantages. For example, command and control tends to be inflexible in that, say, in the context of pollution reduction the adoption of a tradeable permit system would be more efficient in that those most able to reduce pollution could transfer (at an appropriate price) the right to pollute to those least able to reduce pollution. In addition, command and control, as well as other regulatory strategies, can suffer from what is termed creative compliance, e.g. the introduction of a maximum waiting period for hospital admission is often closely followed by the introduction of, in effect, a waiting list for the waiting list. More generally, there has been a move away from regulating by rule (which can be associated with a rather narrow understanding of regulation) and towards what might be termed market-based systems of regulation, e.g. where the regulator highlights the goals and allows maximum flexibility to the regulated with respect to attaining the goals. However, in the presence of serious or catastrophic risk (e.g. nuclear energy or some financial systems), it may not be appropriate to rely simply on the market system and the assumed rationality of all economic actors.

Risk-Based Regulation

The concept of risk has become an organising concept in regulatory matters, particularly with respect to allocating regulatory resources (in terms of the regulators) and perhaps even with respect to compliance efforts (in terms of the regulated). The adoption of a risk-based approach to regulation requires the estimation of both the probability of, in some sense, failure (to achieve the regulatory goal) and the impact of this failure in numerical or financial terms; and the appropriate ranking of the subsequent adjusted or weighted risks. The resulting risk ranking ranges from 'close to unacceptable' (e.g. nuclear energy) through 'as low as reasonably possible' (e.g. treatment of sex offenders within the community) to 'acceptable' (e.g. speeding). The appropriate regulatory strategy can then be assigned, for example command and control in the context of nuclear energy safety, through mandatory registration in the local police station in the context of sex offenders, to installation of speed cameras and/or speed bumps in the context of speeding.

While the risk-based approach to regulatory strategies has proved useful in dealing with certain types of risk, e.g. workplace accidents, the environment and retail financial services, the approach suffers from a number of implementation problems. First, there is the underlying fundamental problem of uncertainty versus risk, with the distinction being that only the latter can be estimated in any meaningful manner. As such, uncertainties (perhaps with huge potential impacts) often tend to be omitted from the analysis. Arguably GM foods might provide such an example, though the formal recognition of the existence of uncertainty in a particular context should not imply simple prohibition: for example, it is unlikely that physicists would be able to comprehensively prove that the Large Hadron Collider (LHC) in the European Organisation for Nuclear Research (CERN) is absolutely incapable of giving rise to a black hole sufficient in scale to swallow the collider itself, CERN and the earth. Second, the risk-based approach to regulatory strategies also arguably facilitates what might be termed the blame-shifting game. Take, for example, the mandatory registration of sex offenders at the local police station. In the event of recidivism, to what extent, if any, is the local police station responsible? This example also highlights the apparent lack of evidence with respect to the actual rate of recidivism in the first place. Indeed, given the more general absence of evidence, is it really possible to implement the risk-based approach to regulation to any degree of satisfaction in the first place? Third, and even when there is a significant degree of evidence available, it is evident that society, for good or bad, has not responded fully to the risk-based approach to regulation. For example, it is clear, at least from a risk-based approach to regulation, that an excessive amount of impact-adjusted risk is accepted by society with respect to road transport and an insufficient amount of impact-adjusted risk is accepted by society with respect to rail and air travel. Perhaps more controversially, it appears that the same could be said with respect to childhood obesity and radon gas (where society appears to accept too much impact-adjusted risk) and smoking and nuclear energy (where society appears to accept too little impact-adjusted risk, although the juries are still out with respect to the long-term effects of the Chernobyl and Fukushima nuclear accidents).

3 'BETTER' REGULATION

Criteria/Standards

There has in recent years been an international movement towards regulatory reform, or what has been more generally referred to as 'better regulation'. This movement has been spearheaded by the Organisation for Economic Co-operation and Development (OECD), embraced by the EU (EU Action Plan, 2002) and pursued by the UK (e.g. the Better Regulation Task Force), Ireland (see www.BetterRegulation.ie) and many other countries.[3] The following five general criteria or tenets of the better regulation movement are considered briefly below: legislative mandate; accountability and control; due process; expertise; and efficiency.

Legislative mandate refers to the need for the regime, agency or set of regulations to have a clear legislative mandate. Ideally it should be possible to judge the performance of regulations or agencies against expected results. However, it is also often both desirable and necessary to leave regulators some discretion, as technology, preferences and interpretations evolve over time.

Accountability and control refers to the agencies being under the control of some other democratic institution or at least being restrained by the exercise of some appropriate checks and balances, while *due process* refers to the need for the existence of fair and transparent procedures. For example, the decisions of many sectoral regulatory agencies in Ireland can be appealed to specially established tribunals or panels and, beyond that, to the courts. However, the existence of multiple forums for appeals can lead to somewhat wasteful duplication of expertise across different agencies, tribunals, panels and courts, as well as an increased level of uncertainty. *Expertise* refers to the need for the presence of the relevant expertise in the decision-making agency. *Efficiency* refers to the requirement that the regulatory regimes be operated or implemented in the most cost-efficient and proportionate manner and to the need for decisions to be taken in a timely manner.

In the Irish context of better regulation, these high-level criteria are implemented in the context of a proposed regulatory initiative as: necessity; effectiveness (i.e. is it well targeted?); proportionality (is there a better way of doing the same thing?); transparency; accountability; and consistency.

Proponents of improved regulation have in the past championed the increased use of international best practice and benchmarking exercises. A best practice approach to regulation aims to learn from the experiences of other jurisdictions but runs the risk of sample selection bias in that it may be very difficult if not impossible to pinpoint the exact reasons why some types of regulation perform very well in certain countries. For example, increasing the minimum legal drinking age (say from 18 to 21) may have worked well in some jurisdictions (e.g. in the USA in the late 1980s), but this does not necessarily mean that it would work well in Ireland at the present time. A benchmarking approach to regulation generally involves the setting of targets, perhaps in conjunction with associated rewards and penalties. However, a benchmarking exercise, when used in isolation, can be open to creative compliance. For example, and as mentioned previously in the context of the command and control regulatory approach, a commitment to reduce a waiting list for a specific operation by a certain date can be 'gamed' via the creation of a waiting list for a waiting list, with the length of the first waiting list being determined solely by the need to meet the formal commitment with respect to the length of the second (and benchmarked) waiting list.

Regulatory Impact Assessments
The better regulation policy approach also champions the use of evidence-based policy-making. In particular, better regulation highlights the need to assess fully all relevant costs, benefits and risks, and regulatory impact assessment (RIA) has become the desired toolkit of better regulation; indeed, economists could view RIA as being equivalent to a form of 'light' cost-benefit analysis (CBA). RIA comes in many formats, but it is possible to distinguish between an initial or partial RIA and a full RIA, with the former being conducted during the very early stage of the life of a proposed regulatory policy initiative and the latter only being

conducted on proposals that have made it past the initial RIA filtering stage. In keeping with the better regulation criteria, an RIA in general aims to: clarify objectives; consider appropriate alternatives, including that of doing nothing; achieve efficiency; and maximise future compliance.

RIA, by its very nature, focuses particular attention on those costs and benefits that can be quantified. It is argued that many of the RIAs conducted to date have tended to be weak with respect to: clear statement of the underlying policy objective; appropriate identification and analysis of the do-nothing alternative; and realistic consideration of the likely level of compliance. In particular, while it is tempting to equate the do-nothing alternative with the status quo or current situation, it would be inappropriate to do so in many situations. Imagine a proposal to introduce a new quantitative restriction on, say, the number of taxis in Cork. On the assumption that the current number of taxis in Cork is at present sufficient or even more than sufficient, it would be tempting to decide that such a restriction, if fixed at the current level, would not damage competition. However, a much more relevant alternative (i.e. counterfactual) would be the number of taxis that would likely have been present in Cork in, say, two years' time without the restriction, i.e. the restriction might well damage competition with respect to how the sector would likely have evolved in the absence of the restriction.[4]

This is not just some minor pedantic point as, albeit in a different context, all merger decisions must at least attempt to compare the world as it would likely evolve with the proposed merger (perhaps with conditions attached) against the world as it would likely evolve without the proposed merger, and the current world does not necessarily equate to the latter. Indeed, some have argued that the introduction of various types of seat belt law has given rise to such an increased incidence of dangerous driving that no net reduction in road deaths (compared to the relevant counterfactual) has been realised.[5] More generally, it is clear that some attempt must also be made to estimate and measure the likely reactions of the various interested parties to a proposed new regulation. In summary, the correct comparison when confronted with a proposed new regulation is the world as it would likely be without the proposed regulation and the world as it would likely be with the proposed regulation.

Notwithstanding these difficulties, it is clear that RIAs have at least two potentially very significant advantages. First, they can cajole policy-makers into revealing their perhaps previously unknown policy goals. Second, and perhaps most important in the context of initial or partial RIAs, they facilitate the early killing-off of really inappropriate regulatory initiatives. Finally, it should be noted that RIAs do not have to be restricted to the consideration of proposed new policy initiatives as RIAs could be carried out on the proposed retention (or non-retention) of current regulations.

Wider EU Regulatory Context

In many regulatory policy areas such as the environment, health and safety, competition and public utilities, the most important regulatory forum has moved from member states to the EU. As such, the discussion above is increasingly conducted at and relevant to an EU-level and even wider debate.

The growth of the European regulatory state has been facilitated by both demand and supply side factors. On the demand side, multinational firms increasingly sought out a one-stop regulatory shop, for example with respect to environment regulations; while on the supply side, national regulations required an international forum in order to address regulatory spill-over effects, for example with respect to environmental or tax competition. The EU Parliament's increasing powers with respect to the other two EU political institutions (the Commission and the Council of Ministers) appears to have increased the EU's legislative mandate. In addition, the existence and decisions of the European Court of Justice (ECJ) as well as the ongoing re-balancing of powers between the Parliament, Commission and Council of Ministers have increased accountability and control within the EU and have to at least some extent addressed past accusations with respect to there being a democratic deficit at the heart of the EU (see Chapter 3). There are now a significant number of European regulatory agencies, which in general deal with narrowly defined policy areas, similar in standing to the European Food Safety Authority (EFSA), which was established in 2002. The current highly Europeanised food safety regime has EFSA at the hub of the equivalent national organisations. EFSA champions food traceability and food science more generally and conducts prior risk analysis on behalf of the Commission, with the latter body being responsible for the formal making of decisions. For another example of Europeanised regulation, see the later discussion with respect to EU competition law.

4 REGULATION AND THE IRISH BANKING CRISIS

Although it is clear that the Irish banking crisis and the associated Irish fiscal crisis need to be put into their appropriate international context, it is also evident that the underlying Irish property bubble and the associated Irish regulatory failures were unique in their scale and impact (see Chapters 2 and 3).

Genesis of the Banking Crisis
The main players in the Irish banking crisis included: the (Irish and foreign-owned) banks (including building societies); the two main relevant regulators, namely the Central Bank (of Ireland) and the Financial Regulator, previously known as the Irish Financial Services Regulatory Authority (IFSRA); the auditors of the banks; a relatively small number of large property developers; and the public authorities such as the Department of Finance and various policy-makers. Other parties including the media and the collective public (e.g. multiple property owners) arguably also played their role. The role and influence of other internationally based (and hence less actively involved to begin with) players such as the IMF, the European Commission, the European Central Bank (ECB), the

OECD, and various purchasers of bonds in the relevant Irish banks (e.g. foreign banks) should, of course, also be acknowledged.

A significant number of banking practices, particularly with respect to the domestic mortgages market, had already elicited much negative commentary well before the Irish banking crisis formally broke. For example, loan to value thresholds in effect disappeared as first-time buyers were being offered mortgages of 100 per cent and above. In addition, loan to income thresholds were in effect replaced by the much more nebulous concept of 'affordability', with the latter term encompassing potential rental income as well as expected annual bonuses/commissions. To compound matters a large proportion of these mortgages were offered at fixed small margins above the ECB rate (tracker mortgages) and hence were very vulnerable (from the banks' perspective) to any future difficulties in the wholesale money markets. At the same time, the standard length of a mortgage increased rapidly from twenty years towards and beyond thirty years. Finally, a number of at best shoddy practices with respect to the keeping of appropriate records and documents in relation to domestic mortgages and commercial lending (e.g. property development) have since emerged. In summary, employees of at least some banking institutions appear to have been more concerned with the amount of lending (which would perhaps influence annual bonuses) as opposed to the quality of lending.

The focal point of the international financial crisis is generally dated as 15 September 2008, when Lehman Brothers filed for bankruptcy. However, other financial institutions in the USA and elsewhere had already been bailed out (e.g. Bear Stearns in the USA and Northern Rock in the UK) or would soon be bailed out (e.g. AIG, Citigroup and Bank of America in the USA and RBS and Halifax Bank of Scotland (HBOS) in the UK). The contagion effects of the international credit crunch were clear to see post the Lehman Brothers bankruptcy. For example, consider the repercussions associated with foreign deposits (e.g. residents and/or local authorities of the UK and the Netherlands) in the failed Icelandic banks. In addition, many financial institutions were left holding assets that consisted directly or indirectly of USA-based sub-prime mortgages or bonds in other vulnerable financial institutions and hence the wholesale money markets quickly dried up.

Although it was initially tempting to blame the developing Irish banking crisis on the developing international financial crisis, particularly against the backdrop of globalisation and hence the negative impact of the freezing of the wholesale money markets with respect to short-term loans to Irish banks, it eventually became clear to all that the Irish banking crisis was not simply a temporary liquidity crisis but a deep solvency crisis. However, by that stage, the Irish government (and hence the Irish state), in an initially very successful attempt to address the liquidity component of the Irish banking crisis, had already issued its comprehensive guarantee of 30 September 2008. The direct monetary cost of the Irish banking crisis is very difficult to estimate at this still relatively early stage.[6] The non-recoupable losses associated with Anglo-Irish Bank (approximately €30 billion) and Irish Nationwide Building Society (approximately €5 billion) likely amount to approximately €35 billion in total. Much of the state's capitalisations of AIB are unlikely to be recouped in a future sale, leaving an ultimate net loss of approximately €15 billion. A future sale of Bank of Ireland (or shares in same) would likely reduce the net loss associated with Bank of Ireland to approximately €4 billion, while net losses at EBS (approximately €2 billion) and Irish Life & Permanent (approximately €3 billion) brings the total estimated once-off losses to well over one-third of Irish GDP. At the time of writing, various different opinions exist with respect to the likelihood of Ireland being able to restructure its debt so as to facilitate the sharing of some of these losses with bond-holders or others. For example, Ireland could be somehow 'compensated', by various entities, either explicitly or implicitly, for not forcing senior unsecured bond-holders (e.g. other European banks and hence ultimately other EU member states) to share the burden. This 'compensation' could come in the form of a significant reduced interest rate on various components of Ireland's national debt.

Investigations, Reports and Possible Lessons
A number of investigations have been launched into various specific events associated with the Irish banking crisis. Three particular events appear to jump out, at least from a regulatory perspective. First, there was for a number of years a significant level of undisclosed directors' loans in Anglo-Irish Bank. It appears that this non-disclosure (involving in at least one year a total sum of well in excess of €100 million) was facilitated by repeated (and timely) transfers of loans to Irish Nationwide Building Society. Second, it appears that a significant short-term deposit (of over €7 billion) was made between Irish Life & Permanent and Anglo-Irish Bank in order to improve significantly the balance sheet of the latter. Third, it appears that significant loans were made by Anglo-Irish Bank to a small number of individual property developers so as to finance their purchase of a significant number of shares in Anglo-Irish Bank itself. These loans appear to have been made with the intention of reducing one individual's very significant exposure to Anglo-Irish Bank shares without flooding the market with Anglo-Irish shares.

It is important to note that no illegal action or inaction by any one individual, group or organisation is being alleged in the above paragraph. However, in each of these cases, it will be important from a regulatory perspective at least to examine the exact role of the various regulators and other players such as auditors, both passive (e.g. possession of knowledge) and active (e.g. facilitation and/or encouragement) and to examine the exact role of the existing regulations. Indeed, from a regulatory perspective, it would be particularly 'interesting' if, as is apparently claimed by the above players, no regulations were broken. Independently of whether or not regulations were broken it is clear that a fuller understanding of the Irish banking crisis (and hence Irish fiscal crisis) more generally will provide fertile territory for regulatory scholars for years to come. Indeed, at a minimum it seems clear that regulations will have to be introduced and/or clarified with respect to some of the previously mentioned measures such as loan to value, loan to income thresholds and disclosure of directors' loans.

Two substantial specific reports into the Irish banking crisis have already been published: *The Irish Banking Crisis: Regulatory and Financial Stability Policy 2003–2008*, A Report to the Minister for Finance by the Governor of the Central Bank, 31 May 2010 (generally referred to as the Honohan Report); and *Misjudging Risk: Causes of the Systematic Banking Crisis in Ireland*, Report of the Commission of Investigation into the Banking Sector in Ireland, March 2011 (generally referred to as the Nyberg Report). Although much public attention has, understandably and correctly, been focused on decisions related to the above-mentioned specific events and on the guarantee of September 2008 itself (which covered almost all existing liabilities, namely deposits, senior bondholders and dated subordinated bondholders as opposed to, say, just deposits and future bondholders), from a regulatory perspective, insufficient public attention has arguably been paid to one of the factors explaining the systemic failure of the Central Bank and the Financial Services Authority of Ireland, as outlined in the Honohan Report (p.9):

> 1.13 ... even if armed with the necessary information, to be effective there would have had to be a greater degree of intrusiveness and assertiveness on the part of regulators to challenging the banks. Although management of the FR [Financial Regulator] would not accept that their 'principles-based' approach ever implied 'light touch' regulation, the approach was characterised as being user-friendly in presentations aimed at expanding the export-oriented financial services sector.... Thus, it would have been known within the FR that intrusive demands from line staff could be and were set aside after direct representations were made to senior regulators. Also, attempts to formalise some of the principles (through Directors' Compliance Statements and a Corporate Governance Code) both came to naught following industry lobbying (and, for the first of these, in the face of concerns expressed by the Department of Finance).

A later reference (p.51) notes that the Minister for Finance also highlighted possible negative repercussions (of the implementation of the Directors' Compliance Statements) for Ireland's competitiveness. Indeed, the promotion of the Irish financial services sector was and remains one of the statutory objectives of the system of financial regulation in Ireland.

As such, at a general level, while it is important to compare and contrast the USA's overall rules-based approach to financial regulation with the Irish and UK's overall principles-based approach, it is more important to focus attention on the actual implementation and enforcement of the actual approach chosen as there will always be a need for both rules-based and principles-based regulations. In particular, in Ireland the principles-based approach was implemented and enforced in a rather 'light' manner, as evidenced by the following.

Whatever initiatives we take, the cost of regulation has to be reduced. As Finance Minster in Ireland, I saw what great entrepreneurial energies that a 'light touch' regulatory system can unleash. 25 years ago we [Ireland] were the sick man of Europe. Today we are among the richest countries in Europe. Ireland is indeed testimony to the fact that you don't need to be rich in natural resources to generate real wealth... Economic freedom through low taxes, open borders, good corporate governance, and light touch regulation have been absolutely indispensable to the scale of the success we have seen.[7]

5 COMPETITION POLICY

Competition policy provides one very important example of regulatory policy at both the domestic (Irish competition law) and international (EC competition law) level. Competition policy attempts to regulate competition between businesses by, for example, discouraging price-fixing or other types of anti-competitive agreements or actions by a dominant firm (e.g. refusal to deal or discriminatory pricing) and encouraging efficiency-enhancing agreements (e.g. product standardisation agreements).[8] Regulation and, more specifically, competition policy enthusiasts are not suggesting that unregulated competition (i.e. the pure market system) is a panacea for all of the economy's or society's issues of resource allocation. For example, visions of completely uncontrolled competition between, say, competing household waste collection trucks in a housing estate, competing buses racing towards the same bus stop and competing hospitals out hunting in ambulances for prospective clients highlight the need for a rational policy on, and specific regulatory framework for, competition, i.e. competition policy must be seen as a subset of regulatory policy, not vice versa. The most important concept in the area of competition policy is that of (significant) market power. From the perspective of an individual firm, the presence of market power indicates the ability of the firm to raise price significantly above the cost of production for a significant period of time. In contrast, the absence of significant market power indicates the presence of a competitive market. As such, the role of a suitably designed competition policy is to encourage the existence of competitive markets by discouraging the conditions that give rise to the presence of significant market power.

Perfect Competition, Monopoly and Contestable Markets
There are three market structures that are particularly important for an understanding of the economics of competition policy: perfect competition, monopoly and contestable markets. Perfectly competitive markets have the characteristic of being (allocatively) efficient, as firms are forced by the pursuit of their own self-interest to price at marginal cost (i.e. $P = MC$) and hence to produce the correct amount from society's perspective: price (P) represents the economic

125

value placed by society on the marginal or last unit of the product produced; while marginal cost (MC) represents the economic cost to society of producing that marginal unit. In contrast, the monopolist produces a level of output at which price is greater than marginal cost (P > MC), and hence produces too little when viewed from society's perspective. It is also argued that the monopolist's excess economic profits do not just represent a transfer from consumer to producer, as profit-seeking (or rent-seeking, as it is generally referred to) activities dissipate these profits over time. In particular, prior to the creation of the monopoly (e.g. markets for various mobile telephony services), firms will involve themselves in socially productive activities in order to increase their chances of being the chosen one, while once installed, the incumbent will involve itself in unproductive activities, when viewed from society's perspective, in order to sustain its monopoly position.[9]

Notwithstanding the strength of the above arguments against monopoly, there are also arguments in favour of monopoly. First, some economists and other social scientists view monopoly's excess profits as the short-term reward necessary for sustaining the competitive process in the long term. Second, it is argued that a monopolistic market structure may be more conducive to the pursuit of innovation and research and development which require significant levels of up-front and risky investments. Third, in the presence of significant economies of scale, it may be appropriate to place a limit on the number of firms allowed to enter a market. Indeed, in the extreme case of a natural monopoly, the appropriate number is one (see Section 6 for further details).[10]

More generally, the competitive process is facilitated by the presence of potential competition. Potential competition focuses attention on the ability of potential entrants to dissuade incumbent firms from attempting to take advantage of, or abuse, their market position. In the extreme case of a perfectly contestable market, potential competition can simulate perfect competition, even in a monopoly situation. The incumbent firm is forced to price at marginal cost, as any divergence between marginal cost and price would allow an equally efficient entrant to enter with a price below the incumbent's price but above marginal cost and to exit if/when the incumbent reduces its price sufficiently. It is sometimes claimed that competing on a specific airline route provides such an example, as the entrant's plane and other investments can be withdrawn and used elsewhere at little additional cost. In contrast, it would be difficult for an entrant to withdraw, without incurring substantial sunk costs, after attempting to compete with respect to the provision of a rail network or an electricity grid, for example. As such, the latter examples represent natural monopolies as opposed to contestable markets.

Indicators of Market Power
Price Elasticities and Definition of Market
There is no generally agreed-upon measure of significant market power. A firm's own-price elasticity of demand measures the percentage decrease (increase) in demand that would follow from a percentage increase (decrease) in the price of

the firm's product. However, a high own-price elasticity of demand (in absolute terms) does not necessarily imply the absence of significant market power as such a situation would only imply that the firm is not able to profitably increase price beyond its current level. It would not, however, prove that the firm has not already increased price significantly above the cost of production.

In practice, economists and, more important, the courts have to proceed on a case-by-case basis. In particular, market power can only exist in the context of a previously well-defined market. The relevant market, for competition policy purposes, is thought of as representing the minimum set of products over which a (hypothetical) firm would have to have monopoly control before it could be sure of exercising a given degree of market power. In practice, this 'given degree of market power' is perceived of as the ability to profitably raise prices by 5 or 10 per cent above competitive levels for a significant period of time (say, a year). For example, a proposed banana market might be rejected under this test if it can be shown or at least successfully argued that a sufficient proportion of banana consumers would switch to other fruits if banana prices increased significantly. In contrast, perhaps a proposed fruit market would be accepted under this test. Significant market power, in turn, is thought of as a position of economic strength enjoyed by a firm that enables it to hinder the maintenance of effective competition on the relevant market by allowing it to behave to an appreciable extent independently of competitors and ultimately of consumers.

Market Concentration and Barriers to Entry
Competition authorities have adopted the Herfindahl Hirschman Index (HHI) for the purpose of measuring market concentration. The HHI is defined as the sum of the squared percentage shares of all firms of the relevant variable (e.g. volume or value of sales) in the market. As such, the HHI varies between 0 (corresponding to a market with an infinite number of infinitesimally small firms) and 10,000 (corresponding to a market with a single firm, i.e. a pure monopoly). For example, a market consisting of only two equal-sized firms would have an HHI of 5,000 (= $50^2 + 50^2$). A market with an HHI below 1,000 is generally regarded as a non-concentrated market and, as such, as a market in which market power or competition policy issues are unlikely to arise. In contrast, a market with an HHI above a level of approximately 2,000 is generally regarded as a concentrated market and, as such, as a market in which market power issues could arise.[11]

Without entry barriers, any attempt by an incumbent firm to abuse an apparent position of significant market power would simply attract entry by other firms. The so-called *Chicago School* views entry barriers as being restricted to 'costs that must be borne by an entrant that were not incurred by established firms'. In the extreme, Chicago economists only accept restrictive licensing schemes as being valid examples of entry barriers. In contrast, the so-called *Harvard School* has a much broader definition of entry barriers in mind: 'factors that enable established firms to earn supra-competitive profits without threat of entry'. Economies of scale, excess capacity, lower average costs as a result of experience (i.e. learning by doing), brand proliferation, restrictive distributional agreements and product differentiation (perhaps as a result of excessive advertising) represent some of the major examples of entry barriers as justified by this broader definition. In practice, competition authorities and courts appear to feel most comfortable with the approach of the so-called Chicago School towards the formal definition of a barrier to entry, but with the approach of the so-called Harvard School in terms of actually deciding whether or not a specific market feature represents a barrier to entry.

General Competitive Environment
The existence, or otherwise, of a competitive environment within a market must also be considered. In this regard, economists distinguish between unilateral price effects concerns, which arise particularly in differentiated product markets, perhaps in the context of a proposed merger, and co-ordinated price effects concerns, which arise particularly in homogeneous product markets. Unilateral price effects arise where it is in the joint interests of two merging firms to increase their prices, even if their competitors' prices remained constant, i.e. the firms produce relatively close substitutes. A proposed merger of Bank of Ireland and Allied Irish Bank provides a useful hypothetical example. Co-ordinated price effects arise where conditions exist that tend to dampen price competition between all competitors. When reviewing the issue of co-ordinated price effects within a market, the relevant competition authority examines the market for the presence, or absence, of the following features (whose presence would tend to be supportive of tacit collusion): symmetry in market shares; stability in market shares; homogeneity of product and/or firm structure; transparency with respect to trading conditions (and, in particular, transparency with respect to prices); low price elasticity of demand (signalling the absence of a strong temptation to 'cheat'); the non-existence of maverick firms; the non-existence of strong buyers (and hence countervailing buyer power); and the non-existence of excess capacity (again, signalling the absence of a strong temptation to cheat).

Competition Law
Competition law addresses a number of specific concerns. First, and most important, anti-competitive agreements between firms (e.g. price-fixing or market-sharing agreements) are prohibited. In this regard, the courts generally distinguish between horizontal agreements (i.e. agreements between firms at the same level of the production and distribution chain) and vertical agreements (i.e. agreements between firms at different levels of the production and distribution chain). Horizontal agreements are generally discouraged, as the effect of such agreements is to dampen competition, at the almost inevitable expense of final consumers; allowance is made for considering certain classes of potentially beneficial, or pro-competitive, agreements (e.g. research and development joint ventures). In contrast, vertical agreements are treated on a case-by-case basis, as an agreement between, say, a manufacturer and a retailer that enhances the

efficiency of their relationship does not necessarily come at the expense of final consumers. Indeed, it may benefit final consumers. Second, the anti-competitive creation of a position of market power, or what is formally referred to as a dominant position, as well as the abuse of any existing market power, is also prohibited via abuse of market power or dominance legislation. Third, competition law also contains a pro-active approach to proposed mergers, acquisitions or takeovers, as a reactive approach would at times require the equivalent of unscrambling eggs.

EU and National Competition Law
EU competition law takes precedence over national competition law, provided that there is a significant effect on inter-state trade. This can be of huge practical and political significance as EU competition law arguably has not one but two policy goals: competition; and the pursuit of the single market. EU competition law limits the freedom of member states to intervene in the process of competition, through the actions of public undertakings (e.g. state-owned bodies) or private undertakings granted exclusive rights by member states. The state has limited exemptions from the application of EU competition law, but only with respect to 'services of general economic interest'; the provision of the traditional postal service (i.e. daily delivery to all addresses) and the standard state pension system offer generally accepted examples of the application of this exemption. Under the Treaty on the Functioning of the EU (TFEU), member states are also prohibited from granting state aid that would distort competition.

Two prominent examples provide proof of the importance of the rules on state aid. First, the continued existence of a special low rate of corporation tax for manufacturing and internationally traded services in Ireland would have fallen foul of these rules on state aids and hence the relatively low rate of 12.5 per cent is applied across all sectors. Second, the various recapitalisations and forced mergers of Irish (and other) banks and financial institutions has had to be approved case by case by the European Commission as otherwise state-supported financial institutions would arguably have been unfairly advantaged, for example by being able to offer superior deposit rates.

The European Commission enforces EU competition rules, the Court of First Instance hears appeals against Commission competition decisions, and the Court of Justice hears further appeals on points of law. However, in the pursuit of a policy of increased subsidiarity national courts and/or member states' competition authorities have been allowed and encouraged to directly enforce EU competition rules since May 2004; the increased similarity between national competition laws and Community competition law facilitated this shift.

Regulation and Competition Policy Examples
Below-Cost Selling
Perhaps the most controversial provision of the Restrictive Practices (Groceries) Order 1987 was the prohibition on retailers selling many grocery products (e.g.

bread and milk, but also alcohol) below the relevant suppliers' net invoice price. Fears of predatory pricing by the large retail multiples, where price wars which would eliminate the smaller competitors would be followed by the charging of excessive prices, were used to defend this provision. However, and crucially, off-invoice discounts (e.g. end-of-year rebates) were not taken into account when defining the net invoice benchmark, i.e. retailers were 'forced' to impose a mark-up that was at least equal in size to off-invoice discounts. Under the Order, the Office of the Director of Consumer Affairs, who was charged with prosecuting breaches of the Groceries Order, in 2004 fined Dunnes Stores and Tesco over €2,000 for selling baby food products below cost. The Groceries Order was eventually rescinded in 2006, but only after much debate and recrimination. The rescinding of the Groceries Order remains topical as one of the policy instruments currently being championed by certain parties in the battle against excessive alcohol consumption is a ban on below-cost selling of alcohol, particularly by the multiples.

Pharmacy Sector
The pharmacy sector and in particular the retail pharmacy sector is highly regulated in Ireland, although probably much less so than in many other countries. Indeed, a number of apparently excessive restrictions, from a public interest perspective, have been relaxed in recent years. Barriers to entry in terms of access to the relevant profession have been relaxed recently with the setting up of some new degree programmes. In January 2002, and following a High Court challenge, rather severe pharmacy location restrictions were also revoked. Among the location restrictions was a requirement that any new pharmacy had to locate at least 250 metres (5km in rural areas) from the nearest competitor and demonstrate that the proposed setting up would not have an adverse effect on the viability of competitors. Given that the state is by far the largest purchaser of medicines, it is not surprising that the state is involved in a process that fixes certain prices in retail pharmacies. However, the extent of the mark-ups agreed (e.g. with respect to the Drug Payment Scheme or with respect to wholesaling margins) between the state and various representatives within the pharmaceutical sector (i.e. manufacturers, wholesalers and retailers) has created much tension, particularly between the state, via the HSE, and the retailers. There remains in place an arguably justifiable comprehensive ban on mail order and Internet sales with respect to pharmaceuticals. However, sitting rather uneasily with this ban and more generally with the EU's single market policy is the large divergences in the retail price of medicines across the EU, e.g. between Spain and Ireland.

Office Supply Stores
Notwithstanding the previously mentioned general shortage of suitable data for the purpose of ascertaining directly whether or not significant market power exists, competition authorities have recently encouraged the appropriate interrogation of what data may be available in case useful inferences, either

positive or negative, can be drawn with respect to the appropriate market definition and the presence, or absence, of significant market power. The most cited case in this regard is the proposed merger of Staples and Office Depot (USA, 1997), where the crucial issue was whether or not, from a competition policy perspective, the three largest office supplies superstores (Staples, Office Depot and OfficeMax) were in a separate product market from the very many other, relatively small, office supplies stores.[12] On the basis of a detailed examination of prices and other data across different geographical locations in which different numbers of office supplies stores were present, the USA Federal Trade Commission was satisfied, as ultimately was the relevant Court, that the three office supplies superstores were in an office supplies (superstores) market as distinct from the wider sector that contained the much smaller office supplies stores. Crucially, using a large volume of retailer scanner data across both geography and time, the Federal Trade Commission demonstrated that product prices were significantly higher (all other factors, e.g. wages, land prices and local incomes, held constant) in geographical locations in which fewer than the three largest office supplies stores were present, but were not influenced by the presence, or absence, of the much smaller office supplies stores. As such, econometric interrogation of the data facilitated the drawing of two strong conclusions: (a) the appropriate product market consisted of various services provided by office supplies superstores; and (b) a decrease in the number of superstores from three to two would be expected to significantly increase prices.

6 REGULATION OF NATURAL MONOPOLIES AND NETWORKS

Specific sectoral regulation is required in the case of natural monopolies as the latter represents an extreme form of market failure, in that the relevant market cannot function efficiently or at all without a significant level of direct and ongoing regulation. A market is said to be a natural monopoly if its total output can be produced more cheaply by a single firm than by two or more firms. The provision of a national electricity transmission, or natural gas, grid, the provision of a railway network, the provision of a national daily delivery postal service and perhaps the provision of a national broadband (or even fibre-optic) network represent some of the standard examples of natural monopolies, many of which have in the past been referred to as public utilities. Other possible examples include the provision of a local, regional or national bus service or the provision of a local household waste collection service. A natural monopoly exists if there are very significant economies of scale. In such a case, an individual firm's marginal cost (MC) and average cost (AC) curves decline continuously and the firm's marginal cost (MC) curve will be below its average cost (AC) curve. As the number of firms increased, the average cost of production would also increase, dramatically.

CPI-X Pricing

Regulators can apparently achieve allocative efficiency by insisting that the natural monopolist produces a level of output at which price is equal to marginal cost. There are, however, at least two problems with this proposed solution. First, the regulator may not have enough information to be able to determine the output level at which price would be equal to marginal cost and it would not be in the natural monopolist's interest to provide the regulator with the appropriate information. Second, if the natural monopolist produces the allocatively efficient level of output, it will sustain losses, since pricing at marginal cost implies pricing below average cost as the marginal cost curve lies below the average cost curve in a natural monopoly. One possible solution to this latter problem is for the regulator to provide the natural monopolist with a subsidy to offset the losses associated with achieving allocative efficiency. However, these subsidies must be financed by increased taxation elsewhere, which, in turn, causes inefficiencies. It may also be difficult politically to be seen to provide a monopolist with a subsidy. Setting price at average cost, where the natural monopolist makes neither excess profits nor losses, avoids the problem of having to subsidise the natural monopolist, but at the expense of sacrificing allocative efficiency. Average-cost pricing regulation also suffers from the problem of dampening cost-reducing incentives. In practice, average-cost pricing is often adapted so as to encourage cost-reducing innovations by allowing scope for some 'excess' profits. This type of regulation, adjusted average-cost pricing, is referred to as rate of return regulation. More recently, regulators have adopted the so-called CPI-X approach, where CPI represents the inflation rate as measured by the consumer price index and X represents the required decrease in real prices within the relevant market. For example, if X was 3 per cent and inflation was also 3 per cent, there would be no change in nominal prices but a 3 per cent decrease in real prices.

Competitive Tendering

Rather than attempting to regulate the natural monopolist on an ongoing basis, it may be preferable to auction the right to be the natural monopolist. The auction can be done on the basis of bidders committing to charging a certain price and providing a particular service to customers in the future. The results of this process are likely to be close to the results obtained by average cost pricing regulation, as bidders would find themselves forced to offer lower and lower (quality-adjusted) prices until almost no net excess profits could be expected. A further possibility is for the auction to be done on the basis of a relatively large number of criteria; bidders would then compete on the basis of quality as well as price and other considerations. This latter possibility is referred to as a 'beauty contest'.

Public Ownership, Privatisation and Market Liberalisation

Rather than the state attempting to regulate the natural monopolist, many governments, particularly in Europe, in the past simply elected to be the (natural) monopolist. In an Irish context, airport management, airline ownership, electricity, natural gas and transportation provide examples of state ownership of enterprise. The distinctive feature (and advantage or disadvantage, depending on one's political perspective) of this approach is that the objective of the natural monopolist is no longer necessarily the maximisation of profits. Opponents of state ownership of enterprises generally point to the so-called soft budget constraint, with management and workers, it is claimed, being united in their efforts to extract public funds for 'their' enterprises (see Chapter 3). However, EU restrictions on state aids to public-owned enterprises have removed at least some of the force of this argument.

A movement away from public ownership and towards privatisation began in the early 1980s. The complementary experience in the USA in the late 1970s and early 1980s was one of market liberalisation or deregulation, e.g. aviation, telecommunications and inter-state trucking. In a European context, the UK government led by Margaret Thatcher was at the forefront of the privatisation movement, e.g. British Telecom (1984) and British Gas (1986). However, many of the large privatisations within the UK were subsequently followed up by the setting up of specialist independent regulatory agencies (e.g. Oftel, now Ofcom), as the process of competition failed to take off in industries that were still characterised by at least some elements of natural monopolies. The lesson from the UK privatisation experience appears to be that the creation of market conditions conducive to competition is at least as important as the formal owner-ship structure.

In an Irish context, the various regulatory agencies have ongoing important decisions to make with respect to pricing and investment decisions within the particular elements of markets that are naturally monopolistic, e.g. Commission for Energy Regulation (CER) and Commission for Aviation Regulation (CAR). In the context of a downstream natural monopoly (e.g. fixed-line telecommunica-tions), the level of the resulting consumer price is highly visible, while in the context of an upstream natural monopoly (e.g. transportation of natural gas or electricity transmission), the level of the access price charged to downstream firms may be less politically sensitive, but still of crucial importance, particularly so if the upstream firm itself also operates in various downstream markets.

After successfully selling its stake in Irish Life, the Irish state privatised Telecom Éireann (later Eircom). Initially, the privatisation proved to be a political success as Eircom's share price increased by over 20 per cent above its flotation price. However, Eircom's share price then fell, and remained, for the rest of its relatively brief (initial) existence as a public limited company, considerably below its flotation price. From a narrow economics perspective, the success, or otherwi·e, of the privatisation of Eircom should be judged primarily by the effect of the privatisation on the process of competition within the Irish telecommunications market(s). However, from a political perspective, the evolution of Eircom's share price, combined with Ryanair's attempted acquisition of Aer Lingus only days after Aer Lingus's part-privatisation, have arguably had significant repercussions for future possible privatisations in Ireland, e.g. Voluntary Health Insurance (VHI). More recently, the issue of privatisation has become linked to attempts to reduce Ireland's growing national debt, as witnessed by the recent publication of, and initial reaction to, the *Report of the Review Group on State Assets and Liabilities*, April 2011. This report, which focused attention on both commercial state bodies (e.g. ESB) and intangible state assets (e.g. the radio spectrum and carbon emissions permits), recommended a number of asset sales but crucially also recommended that, even if these assets were not sold, they should be restructured so as to facilitate the economy's competitiveness (see Chapter 3).

7 CONCLUDING COMMENTS

The purpose of this chapter has been to provide a broad overview of Irish and EU regulatory policy. In particular, it has attempted to address various explanations for regulations, theories of regulation and regulatory strategies while at the same time discussing a number of specific types or examples of regulations in Ireland and the EU, including competition policy and the regulation of networks.

From the author's perspective, there are at least three general lessons to be taken from Ireland's recent regulatory experiences and in particular the Irish banking and fiscal crises. First, while interesting debates can be held between followers of a rules-based approach to regulation and a principles-based approach to regulation, it is crucial that such a debate be informed by specific details of the proposed implementation of either such general approach. For example, given that a principles-based approach confers a significant level of discretion on the regulators and on the regulated entities, it is imperative that issues such as regulatory capture be considered. Of course, the adoption of a rules-based approach does not avoid the need to consider important issues such as creative compliance. Unfortunately, it appears clear from recent experience that in the absence of certain minimum at least implicitly agreed ethical standards, very few assumptions of the 'public interest' kind can be made with respect to how interested parties may behave. Second, and on a related issue, the appropriate link between regulators and other public authorities needs to be considered carefully. In this regard, it seems noteworthy that the relatively recent *Government Statement on Regulatory Reform* (October 2009) appears to be proposing a significant reduction in regulators' independence, as opposed to improving the currently available mechanisms with respect to accountability and transparency. This does not seem advisable with respect to either the current set of regulators (e.g. CER) or future possible regulatory or advisory bodies (e.g. a possible Fiscal Council with respect to the conduct of Irish fiscal policy). Third, the exact nature of the roles played by various EU institutions, such as the Commission and the ECB, in the response to Ireland's evolving banking and fiscal crises are likely to have significant long-term repercussions for Ireland's approach to the growth of the European regulatory state and perhaps even to further EU integration.

Endnotes

* The author acknowledges very helpful comments and suggestions by Carol Newman and John O'Hagan. Any remaining errors and all views expressed remain the sole responsibility of the author.
1 J. Black, quoted in R. Baldwin, M. Cave and M. Lodge, *The Oxford Handbook of Regulation*, Oxford University Press, Oxford 2010, p. 12. For an earlier review of regulation, see R. Baldwin and M. Cave, *Understanding Regulation: Theory, Strategy and Practice*, Oxford University Press, Oxford 1999.
2 R. Coase, 'The problem of social cost', *Journal of Law and Economics*, Vol. 60, 1960.
3 OECD: *The OECD Report on Regulatory Reform: Synthesis*, 1997; *Regulatory Reform in Ireland*, 2001; *OECD Guiding Principles for Regulatory Quality and Performance*, 2005; *Better Regulation in Europe: Ireland*, 2010.
4 For an extended discussion on this point, albeit in a slightly different context, see S. Lyons and F. O'Toole, 'Conceptual and applied problems with the UK competition filter', *Journal of Competition Law and Economics*, Vol. 2, 2006.
5 S. Peltzman, 'The effects of automobile safety regulations', *Journal of Political Economy*, Vol. 83, 1975; and S. Peltzman, *Regulation and the Natural Progress of Opulence*, AEI-Brookings Joint Centre for Regulatory Studies, Washington DC 2005.
6 The following estimates draw upon the author's reading of R. Curran, 'The burning issue: How many of our billions will we ever see again?', *Sunday Business Post*, 3 April 2011; and various other sources such as P. Lane, 'The Irish crisis', IIIS Discussion Paper No. 356, February 2011. In addition, the reader is directed towards some of the more sensible and informative blogs about the Irish banking crisis available at www.irisheconomy.ie.
7 From a speech by Charlie McCreevy, European Commissioner for Internal Market and Services, on 'The integration of Europe's financial markets and international cooperation', New York, 20 April 2005.
8 For a comprehensive review of the economics of competition policy (also known as antitrust economics), see S. Bishop and M. Walker, *The Economics of EC Competition Law: Concepts, Application and Measurement* (3rd edn), Sweet & Maxwell, London 2010. For a case study-based approach to the subject matter, see J. Kwoka and L. White (eds), *The Antitrust Revolution: Economics, Competition and Policy* (5th edn), Oxford University Press, Oxford 2009.
9 The earliest reference to the issue of rent seeking appears to be G. Tullock, 'The welfare cost of tariffs, monopolies and theft', *Western Economic Journal*, Vol. 5, 1967. In addition, a monopolist's costs may be higher than the equivalent competitive firm's costs, simply because the monopolist (as opposed to the competitive firm) can afford to be at least somewhat cost inefficient.
10 In response to these arguments, it is noteworthy that competitions policy and law in practice seldom (if ever) attempt to penalise a monopoly for being a monopoly (e.g. charging monopoly prices) but do attempt to penalise any economic behaviour that

unfairly attempts to create and/or maintain a monopoly (e.g. refusal to deal with suppliers and/or customers).

11 See the Competition Authority's 'Notice in respect of guidelines for merger analysis', N/02/004, 2002 (www.tca.ie), for further details of the practical application of the HHI. The Authority has recently begun a process of revising these guidelines.

12 See S. Dalkir and F. Warren-Boulton, 'Prices, market definition and the effects of merger: Staples–Office Depot', in J. Kwoka and L. White (eds), *The Antitrust Revolution: Economics, Competition and Policy* (5th edn), Oxford University Press, Oxford 2010, Case 7.

POLICY ISSUES AT A NATIONAL LEVEL

CHAPTER 6

Population, Employment and Unemployment

John O'Hagan and Tara McIndoe-Calder

1 INTRODUCTION

The experience with regard to employment and unemployment has been the truly remarkable 'story' of the Irish economy in the last twenty years or so. Table 6.1 illustrates clearly the dramatic changes that have taken place since 1993. Who could have predicted the scale of the change in the time between then and 2008? Employment in 1993 was just 130,000 higher than in 1961; the only period in which there was a significant increase in employment until then was during the 1970s, when over 100,000 net new jobs were created. Between 1993 and early 2000, however, over 475,000 net new jobs were created, quite a phenomenal increase in employment in such a short period. It did not stop there, though: a further 429,000 jobs were created between 2000 and 2008, bringing the total number of net new jobs created between 1993 and 2008 to almost one million. The decrease in unemployment during the same period, as seen in Table 6.1, was equally remarkable.

However, equally dramatic was the decline in employment between 2008 and 2011. Almost 280,000 jobs are likely to have been lost in this short period, with the unemployment rate rising from 5.7 per cent in 2008 to 14.3 per cent by the end of 2010. However, the level of employment in 2011 was way above that in 1993 and similar to that in 2004: as such the huge gains between 1993 and 2004 have not been lost.

The increase in employment was the main force behind the extraordinary increase in output in the economy in the 1993 to 2008 period. Definitionally:

(1) $Q = (Q/E) \cdot E$

That is, the output of an economy (Q) can be expressed as the product of the average productivity of those in employment (Q/E) and the level of employment (E). As we will see later, the level of employment in Ireland in some years increased by over 6 per cent; this alone would have pushed up Q by 6 per cent assuming no change in productivity. Thus, increases in E were the main factor explaining the exceptional growth in Q in the period 1993–2008. Productivity, though, was also increasing during this period, hence ensuring a much faster increase in Q than in E; the causes of this growth in productivity are the subject matter of Chapter 7. The growth in productivity in the 1990s and 2000s, however, was lower than that in the 1960s and not much higher than that in the 1970s and 1980s. The remarkable thing is that the huge increase in employment was not accompanied by any decrease in the growth of productivity.

Table 6.1

Employment and Unemployment: Ireland's Changing Fortunes

	Employment (millions)	Unemployment rate (%)
1961	1.053	5.0
1971	1.049	5.5
1980	1.156	7.3
1986	1.095	17.1
1990	1.160	12.9
1993	1.183	15.7
2000	1.684	4.5
2006	2.035	4.6
2008	2.113	5.7
2010	1.859	13.6
2011[1]	1.826	14.5
2012[1]	1.831	13.3

Sources: CSO, *Quarterly National Household Survey (QNHS)*, Stationery Office, Dublin (various issues); ESRI, *Quarterly Economic Commentary, Winter 2010*, ESRI, Dublin 2011; IMF, *World Economic Outlook*, Washington DC, April 2011.
[1]Forecast.

Just as employment increases drove the increase in output in the boom years, decreases in employment have driven the huge decline in output between 2008 and 2011. Thus swings in employment, and not productivity, are the driving force behind the huge swings in output in Ireland over the last 20 years.

Sections 2 and 3 examine the issues of population and labour supply and emphasise the critical role that migration plays in this regard, a factor that marks Ireland apart from other Organisation of Economic Co-operation and Development (OECD) countries. Section 4 looks at the issue of employment, its growth and composition, and compares Ireland's performance to that of a number of other countries. The huge reliance on employment growth in the construction sector in the 2000s is highlighted. Section 5 does likewise in relation to unemployment. The rest of the chapter examines the various factors that may influence the level of employment, and hence the level of unemployment, in a small open economy such as that of Ireland. Section 6 examines three factors that impinge on job creation, arising from the Single European Market and globalisation: namely increased competition for goods; increased mobility, and migration of labour across national boundaries; and technological change. As the section highlights, the adaptability and skill levels of the labour force are the key issues in responding to these global pressures.

A major reason perhaps for the different responses in different countries to the phenomena of migration, technological change and the globalisation of trade relates to the *flexibility* of the labour market, and this is the subject matter of Section 7. Issues such as the wage-setting process and the effects of employment legislation on employment creation are discussed in some detail. The effects of prolonged payment of unemployment and related benefits and the effectiveness or otherwise of active labour market policies in dealing with unemployment will also be examined in Section 7. Section 8 concludes the chapter.

2 POPULATION

Population Change and its Components

The size of the population has major emotive significance in Ireland, not surprisingly given the huge reduction in population in Ireland following the Famine (see Chapter 1). As a result, the size of the population has in a sense become an objective of policy in itself (for a discussion of this see Chapter 2). Table 6.2 outlines the trends in population dating back to 1841. The population of the Republic of Ireland in pre-Famine days was over 6.5 million. The decline in this population size in the post-Famine period is all too obvious: a fall of over two million in twenty years despite a high birth rate. Population continued to decline

Table 6.2

Population of the Republic of Ireland, 1841–2011 (millions)

Years	Population	Years	Population
1841	6.529	1961	2.818
1851	5.112	1971	2.978
1861	4.402	1981	3.443
1871	4.053	1991	3.526
1881	3.870	2002	3.917
1891	3.469	2006	4.240
1901	3.222	2008[1]	4.429
1911	3.140	2010[1]	4.478
1926	2.972	2011[2]	4.500
1951	2.961		

Sources: CSO, *Statistical Yearbook 2010,* Stationery Office, Dublin 2010, Table 1.1; CSO, *Population and Migration Estimates,* Stationery Office, Dublin 2010, Table 1; *Regional Population Projections 2011–2026*, Stationery Office, Dublin 2008, Table 5.

[1] Preliminary.

[2] Forecast. Census 2011 results not available for certain months.

up to 1926; almost fifty years later there was no increase on the 1926 level, when the population in 1971 still stood at only 2.978 million. Since then population size has increased by almost 1.5 million with most of this increase occurring between 1991 and 2010; the population in 2008 in fact exceeded its 1861 level for the first time. This for many is seen as a very positive development and reflects a reversal of a demoralising decline that had persisted for almost a century and a half. The fear now, of course, is that a trend of declining population could become established again in years to come.

The total population of a country depends on three factors: the number of births, the number of deaths and the level of net migration. The difference between the number of births and deaths is known as the natural increase and in most countries the natural increase translates directly into a population increase. This has not been the case in Ireland, where in the past the change in population has 'tracked' much more closely the trend in migration than that of the natural increase.

As seen in Table 6.3, the number of births per annum reached a peak in the 1970s and declined significantly after that; it increased again in the 2002–6 period, and reached a new peak in the period 2006–11, but this was more a reflection of the increase in the size of the child-bearing female population than of any large increase in the birth rate. This means that the natural increase in the population is averaging around 40,000+ per annum.

Table 6.3

Components of Population Change, Selected Intervals
(annual average in thousands)

	Total births	Total deaths	Natural increase	Population change	Estimated net migration
1926–36	58	42	16	0	-17
1951–56	63	36	27	-12	-39
1956–61	61	34	26	-16	-42
1961–66	63	33	29	13	-16
1966–71	63	33	30	19	-11
1971–79	69	33	35	49	14
1981–86	67	33	34	19	-14
1986–91	56	32	24	-3	-27
1991–96	50	31	18	20	2
1996–2002	54	31	23	49	26
2002–6	61	28	33	81	48
2006–11	70[1]	28[1]	42[1]	56	13[2]

Sources: CSO, *Statistical Yearbook 2010*, Stationery Office, Dublin 2010, Table 1.2; CSO, *Population and Migration Estimates*, Stationery Office, Dublin 2010.
[1] Total births and deaths based on actual/preliminary 2006–10 figures.
[2] Forecast for 2011.

Migration

While there have been significant changes in the natural increase, they are slight compared to the huge swings in net migration that can occur: 40,000 per annum in some years in the 1980s, to net immigration of 2,000 in the early 1990s, around 25,000 in the late 1990s and almost 48,000 in the 2000s, with net out-migration again in recent years of 30,000 per annum or more.[1]

The *net* immigration figure is the balance between two flows – *gross* outflows and gross inflows – of people. Looking first at gross inflows, immigration increased steadily, up from 40,000 in 1996 to over 105,000 per annum between 2006 and 2008. This figure fell to 30,000 in 2010 and may fall further in 2011 and beyond. Initially the increase was due primarily to returning Irish nationals, who accounted for around half of total gross immigration between 1996 and 2000. In absolute terms the immigration of Irish nationals continued after 2000 at the levels of the period 1996 to 2000, but there was also a large inflow of non-Irish nationals, initially from 'Rest of the World' (mainly Africa, Nigeria in particular) and, since the enlargement of the EU in 2004, a further huge increase of non-Irish nationals from 'Rest of EU', mainly Poland. This was the most obvious change in Irish society in this period, i.e. the increasing number of non-Irish nationals who to this day make up a significant share of the country's population and labour force. The evidence for this is clear to see, not only in Dublin but across the country, including many small rural towns. Even in 2010 there were 15,000 people from outside Ireland and the UK who immigrated into Ireland (Table 6.4).

Table 6.4
Estimated Migration Classified by Nationality, 2006–10 (thousands)

	Irish % of total	UK	Rest of EU	Rest of world	Total
		Immigration			
2006	18.9 17.5%	9.9	62.6	16.4	107.8
2008[1]	16.2 19.3%	7.0	42.3	18.3	83.8
2010[1]	13.3 43.2%	2.4	10.1	4.9	30.8
		Emigration			
2006	15.3 42.5%	2.2	12.3	6.2	36.0
2008[1]	13.4 29.6%	2.4	23.0	6.4	45.3
2010[1]	27.8 42.4%	2.6	27.0	8.2	65.5

Source: CSO, *Population and Migration Estimates*, Stationery Office, Dublin 2010, Tables 2 and 3.
[1] Preliminary.

There was also substantial out-migration over the entire period. It was of course until recently less than gross in-migration and substantially so in some years, but nonetheless the persistence of out-migration during the boom years is noteworthy. For example, even in 2006 there was out-migration of 36,000 people, over 15,000 of them Irish nationals (Table 6.4). Between 2006 and 2010 the level of out-migration nearly doubled and could increase further in 2011 and 2012. Out-migration by Irish nationals rose to almost 28,000 in 2010, but as mentioned there was in-migration of Irish nationals of over 13,000 in the same period, meaning that there was *net* immigration of less than 15,000, much less than the 50,000 figure popular in the media in early 2011.

Table 6.5 provides an age breakdown of migrants over the period 2002 to 2010, which is of relevance to the later discussion. The most remarkable feature up to 2008 was the huge proportion of total immigrants in the active age groups of 15 to 24 and in particular 25 to 44. This means that the vast bulk of the immigrants came here for work, with few young dependents. Most of the dependents were probably attached to Irish nationals returning home, with tiny numbers associated with the immigration of non-Irish nationals. This means that, unless they had children since they arrived in Ireland, many immigrant workers have no family ties to Ireland and hence are still highly mobile, reinforcing the point made earlier that many of the immigrants could go elsewhere if and when employment prospects turn down, something that is borne out by Tables 6.4 and 6.5. It is apparent that well over half of the out-migration between 2008 and late 2010 was accounted for by non-nationals, mostly from 'Rest of EU', and that the vast bulk of this occurred in the active age groups of 15 to 24 and 25 to 44. It is interesting to note, in fact, that even in 2006 around 30,000 people in these age groups emigrated, but of course there were around 90,000 immigrants, reflecting a very fluid migration situation in these age groups.

Table 6.5

Estimated Migration Classified by Age Group, 2002–10 (thousands)

	0–14	15–24	25–44	45–64	65 and over
			Immigration		
2002	7.0	19.8	35.2	4.2	0.8
2004	6.1	18.7	28.8	4.2	0.7
2006	11.5	31.6	57.2	6.1	1.4
2008[1]	13.6	23.7	39.2	5.8	1.5
2010[1]	3.6	8.2	14.6	3.0	1.4
			Emigration		
2002	2.5	18.7	3.1	0.1	1.2
2004	1.5	14.1	9.2	1.3	0.4
2006	2.2	15.9	14.2	2.0	1.6
2008[1]	1.5	18.2	20.3	2.6	2.8
2010[1]	1.2	28.2	29.9	3.5	2.5

Source: CSO, *Population and Migration Estimates*, Stationery Office, Dublin 2010, Tables 2 and 3.

[1] Preliminary.

3 LABOUR SUPPLY

Labour supply in any country depends on three factors: the total size of the population; the proportion of that population of working age; and the proportion of the working-age population seeking or in work. This is illustrated by the identity:

(2) $$L = (P) . (Pa /P) . (L/Pa)$$

where L is the size of the labour force, P the size of the population, and Pa the size of the population of working age. The labour force, in turn, consists of those in employment (E) and those unemployed (UE). Hence:

(3) $$L = E + UE$$

Two further identities of interest to this discussion are the following:

(4) $$Q/P = (Q/E) . (E/P)$$

(5) $$\text{where } E/P = (E/L) . (L/Pa) . (Pa/P)$$

Equation (4) links the demographic factors back to (1). It states that output per person employed and the proportion of the population employed determine output per head of population. We saw in Equation (1) that increases in E were the most important factor accounting for record increases in Q in Ireland in the ten years after 1993; E/P also increased at a record rate in this decade, thereby pushing up Q/P (our measure of living standards, as seen in Chapter 2) to record levels. E/P (the proportion of the population in employment), as can be seen from Equation (5), is influenced by three factors, all of which increased in the fifteen years up to 2007 (see Chapter 7): E/L (the proportion of the labour force in employment) increased as unemployment decreased; Pa/P (the proportion of the population of working age), as shall be seen later, increased because of demographic factors; and L/Pa (the proportion of the working population in the labour force) increased, principally because of increased participation by married females in the labour force. These very favourable demographic trends, in terms of their impact on living standards, became known as Ireland's 'demographic dividend' in the 1990s and early 2000s. Since 2008, though, there has been a decline in E/P, although the extent of this is not fully known yet (see below).

Working-Age Population

As a result of the fall in the birth rate in the 1980s and 1990s, there was a later fall in the population aged 15 and under. However, because of the high birth rate prior to this, and more important the trends in migration observed above, there was a large increase in the population aged 15 to 64, and especially in the prime working-age population, 25–64. As seen, a large proportion of the immigrants were of prime working age, thereby disproportionately pushing up the population in this age group. The number of people aged 25 to 64 rose from 2.18 million in 1991 to over 2.91 million by the year 2006; this is a very large increase in such a short period and had a marked effect on Ireland's age dependency ratios.

Table 6.6

Percentage Age Dependency Ratios,[1] 1981 to 2011

Year	Young	Old	Total
1981	51.4	18.2	69.6
1991	43.4	18.5	61.9
1996	36.5	17.6	54.1
2002	29.3	16.4	45.7
2006	29.8	15.9	45.7
2011[2]	30.0	16.8	46.8

Sources: CSO, *Census 2006 – Principal Demographic Results*, Stationery Office, Dublin (various issues); CSO, *Regional Population Projections 2011–2026*, Stationery Office, Dublin 2008, Table 5.

[1] The ratios in the first two columns are obtained by dividing the population aged 0–14 and 65 years and over by the population aged 15–64. The final column is the sum of these two.

[2] Forecasts based on assumptions about migration made in 2008, which would perhaps be hard to sustain in 2011.

Table 6.6 highlights these changes in the composition of the population. In 1981, the number of people aged under 15 years amounted to 51.4 per cent of those aged 15 to 64, but in just over 20 years this had dropped by almost 21 percentage points. At the same time, the population aged 65 and over, expressed as a proportion of the 15–64 population, also declined, albeit slightly. As Table 6.6 illustrates, these favourable demographic trends have now run their course; importantly, though, there will be no worsening of the demographic situation until after 2021, when the percentage classified as 'old' will begin to rise significantly. These projections, however, depend very much on what happens with regard to migration over the next decade or so. The return to significant out-migration since 2008 could alter these projections; but the experience of the last ten years should, if anything, have brought home the difficulty of projecting future migration trends.

Participation in the Labour Force

An important factor when examining the employment situation in any country is the proportion of the working population that actually seeks work. This is known as the labour force participation rate.

Table 6.7 provides data for Ireland, a number of other small EU countries, two countries of particular interest to Ireland (namely the UK and the USA) and the

OECD group; where possible these will also be used as the comparator countries in the other tables in this chapter. As can be seen in Table 6.7, the labour force participation rate for males in Ireland in 2009 was about average for most other countries listed; but for females was less. The figure for females for Ireland was 62.9 per cent, compared to a figure of 56.5 per cent in Greece (the lowest rate), 70.2 per cent in the UK, and 77.3 per cent in Denmark (the highest rate).

Table 6.7

Percentage Labour Force Participation Rates[1] in
Selected OECD Countries, 1994 and 2009

	Males		Females	
	1994	2009	1994	2009
Belgium	72.0	72.8	51.2	60.9
Denmark	83.7	84.0	73.8	77.3
Greece	77.0	79.0	43.2	56.5
Ireland	*76.2*	*79.6*	*45.8*	*62.9*
Netherlands	79.6	84.1	57.3	73.5
Norway	81.6	81.4	70.9	76.5
OECD	81.4	80.2	57.8	61.3
UK	85.1	83.2	67.1	70.2
USA	84.3	80.4	69.4	69.0

Source: OECD, *Employment Outlook*, OECD, Paris 2010, Table B.

[1] Ratios refer to persons aged 15 to 64 years who are in the labour force, divided by the total population aged 15 to 64.

A noteworthy feature is that female participation rates are increasing in most countries, Ireland being no exception. Following a substantial increase up to 1994, the rate increased further in Ireland, up from 45.8 per cent to 62.9 per cent, a large rise in such a short period. By 2009 the rate for Ireland, as can be seen, exceeded the OECD average but, as discussed above, was still well below some key comparator countries, in particular the UK. It is difficult to predict how much further this participation rate will grow in Ireland, but with the lower birth rate, and if employment prospects improve in the 2010s, it could increase to UK levels, if not to those in Denmark and Norway. If this happened, it would lead to a large increase in the labour force arising from this factor alone.

The increase in the female participation rate is due primarily to the increase in the participation rate of married females. The dramatic changes in this regard can be seen in Table 6.8. There have been huge changes in the participation rate for all of the age groups shown and these increases could continue for the next decade, bringing Ireland into line with other EU countries in this regard. The really striking increases are in the age groups over 35, with a large increase also in the 25–34 age group: up from 31.7 per cent in 1986 to 73.1 per cent in 2010.

The participation rate for married females in the 45–54 age group increased from just 18.7 per cent in 1986 to 66.1 per cent in 2010, reflecting a quite dramatic economic and social change.

Table 6.8

Percentage Labour Force Participation Rates, Married
Females by Age Group, 1986–2010

Age group	1986	1996	2002	2006	2010
25–34	31.7	62.6	64.7	70.1	73.1
35–44	19.5	52.1	61.9	63.9	67.3
45–54	18.7	37.2	55.7	62.0	66.1
55–59	13.1	25.1	35.3	47.0	55.4
Total	20.9	40.6	48.1	52.3	54.8

Sources: CSO, *Labour Force Survey* (various issues), Stationery Office, Dublin 1987–97, Table 8B; CSO, *Quarterly National Household Survey (QNHS), Quarter 4 2010*, Table S2.

Conclusion

A consideration of migration trends is central to any discussion of labour supply in Ireland. It, more than any other factor, determines changes in the size of the population and the growth of the labour force. As seen from Table 6.3, more than half of those added to the Irish population on an annual average basis between 1996 and 2008 were as a result of net inward migration. Between 2008 and 2011 the trend of net outward migration began to exert marked downward pressure on population growth and for the years ahead it will be what happens on the migration front that will largely determine labour supply for the next decade. The increases in the labour force participation rates of females aged 25 to 64 may be dwarfed by the changes in net migration, but in themselves they are very significant changes which, after the effects of net migration are removed, will also have a marked bearing on the growth of the labour force in years to come.

4 EMPLOYMENT: GROWTH AND COMPOSITION

Overall Employment

The first point worth noting from Table 6.9 is the tiny size of the workforce in Ireland: around 1.9 million in 2009, as opposed to 8.6 million in the Netherlands, 28.8 million in the UK and 141.2 million in the USA. Given that there is an effective common labour market between Ireland and the UK, it is very important for labour policy purposes to bear in mind the relative sizes of these two labour markets in particular.

Table 6.9

Employment and Employment Growth in Selected OECD Countries

	Employed (millions)		E/Pa (%)	
	2009	1999	2008	2009
Belgium	4.454	58.9	62.4	61.6
Denmark	2.746	76.5	78.1	75.7
Greece	4.532	55.4	61.9	61.2
Ireland	*1.939*	*63.0*	*68.1*	*62.5*
Netherlands	8.634	70.8	76.1	75.8
Norway	2.509	78.0	78.1	76.5
OECD	530.537	65.2	66.5	64.8
UK	28.832	71.5	72.7	70.6
USA	141.189	73.9	70.9	67.6

Sources: OECD, *Labour Force Statistics 1989–2009*, OECD, Paris 2010, Part 1; OECD Directorate for Employment, Labour and Social Affairs, Online Database, 2011.

The most striking fact in relation to employment in Ireland up to 2008 had been its growth relative to other countries. In the ten years to 2004, employment grew on average by 4.1 per cent per annum in Ireland compared to less than 1 per cent growth in many countries; only the Netherlands, at 1.6 per cent had a comparable rate of growth to that in Ireland. This is remarkable given that employment in Ireland had actually declined in the 1980–86 period and had not managed to rise significantly over the entire period 1980–90 (see Table 6.1).

The growth of employment continued to outpace all of the countries listed in Table 6.9 up to 2008. This means that for fifteen years Ireland had managed to outperform the smaller European countries as well as the UK and the USA in the employment growth stakes. Since then, though, there has, as we have seen, been a decline of over 12 per cent in employment, thereby reversing the employment gains for the years 2004 to 2008.

Up to 2004, Ireland of course had a much greater increase in potential labour supply than any of the other countries, hence unemployment would have remained at a very high level and the position of net immigration might have been translated into substantial net emigration without this growth in employment. Much of the early immigration was after all due to the return of people who had emigrated in the depressed labour market conditions of the 1980s. Much of the immigration in the 2000s, though, as seen earlier, was due to immigration of non-Irish nationals.

The last three columns in Table 6.9 show the ratio of total employment to population size aged 15–64 years for each of the countries listed. Despite the rapid growth of employment in Ireland up to 2009, just 62.5 per cent of the population aged 15–64 were in employment in 2009, lower than that experienced by the OECD in the same year; the figure for the USA was 67.6 per cent, the UK 67.6

per cent and those for Denmark and Norway as high as 75.7 and 76.5 per cent respectively. These figures reflect what was seen in Table 6.7: the near average labour participation rate for men and the low figure for females (albeit increasing rapidly, as seen earlier) compared to these countries.

It could be argued, therefore, that the employment increase in Ireland in the ten years up to 2004 was strongly associated with a huge increase in the labour force, an increase that was simply bringing Ireland up to the international norm in terms of the proportion of the total working-age population in employment.

Part-Time and Temporary Employment
An important issue relating to employment in some countries, including Ireland, is the extent to which it consists of part-time employment and/or temporary employment. The available data suggest (Table 6.10) that the level of part-time employment as a proportion of total employment is low throughout the countries examined. In this regard Ireland is not out of line with its OECD counterparts. Similarly, there appears to have been no significant increase in part-time employment, especially amongst males, in the period up to 2009.

Table 6.10

Incidence and Composition of Part-time Employment
in Selected OECD Countries,[1] 2009

	Part-time employment (% of total employment)			Temporary employment (% of dependent employment)
	Men	Women	Total	Total
Belgium	6.6	31.8	18.2	8.2
Denmark	13.6	24.8	18.9	8.9
Greece	4.5	14.4	8.4	12.1
Ireland	*10.7*	*37.4*	*23.7*	*8.5*
Netherlands	17.0	59.9	36.7	18.3
Norway	11.3	30.4	20.4	9.2
OECD	8.4	26.1	16.2	11.6
UK	10.9	38.8	23.9	5.7
USA	9.2	19.2	14.1	–

Sources: OECD, *Employment Outlook*, OECD, Paris 2010, Table E; OECD Directorate for Employment, Labour and Social Affairs, Online Database, 2011.
[1] Part-time is usual hours of work of less than 30 per week.

There is a marked gender difference in relation to part-time employment, as may be seen in Table 6.10. Only 10.7 per cent of total male employment in Ireland in 2009 was part-time, whereas 37.4 per cent of female employment was part-time. These percentages vary considerably from country to country, but on balance the position in Ireland was not unusual, although there are very marked variations across countries, as can be seen in the table.

What is more important perhaps is the extent to which part-time employment is involuntary, i.e. chosen by the individual only because they could not get full-time work. The evidence suggests that most part-time employment is in fact voluntary, reflecting therefore a desire for such employment; largely it seems from female employees entering the labour force and with a preference for part-time work as it fits better with family and other commitments.

A different but related issue is the extent to which employment is in temporary work.[2] This is a much debated topic in labour market economics as some economists believe that an increasing proportion of jobs will have to be temporary if labour markets, especially in Europe, are to be sufficiently flexible to cope with an employment crisis, a topic that will be returned to later.

As seen in Table 6.10, temporary employment in Ireland in 2009 accounted for 8.5 per cent of dependent employment. This compares to figures of 8.9 per cent in Denmark, 18.3 per cent in the Netherlands, 5.7 per cent in the UK, and a weighted OECD average of 11.6 per cent. As such there is no evidence that employment here was overly based on part-time employment.

Although experiences across the OECD vary, it does appear that younger and less educated workers disproportionately fill temporary jobs. On the other hand, temporary workers are a diverse group who work in a wide range of occupations and sectors. Other characteristics of temporary employment include the tendency for temporary jobs to pay less than permanent ones, as well as sometimes offering less access to paid vacations, sick leave, unemployment insurance and other fringe benefits, including access to training. Temporary workers are generally less satisfied with their jobs and more often report inflexible work schedules and monotonous work tasks than their permanent employment counterparts.[3] There is no evidence, though, as mentioned, that this is a particularly acute problem in the Irish context, and this may be due to the weakness of employment protection laws in Ireland, which gives employers sufficient flexibility not to need to resort to temporary contracts (see below).

Sectoral Composition of Employment

Table 6.11 outlines the composition of employment in Ireland from 1994 to 2010; while the data are not strictly comparable the table shows some broad trends in this composition in the period.

The once central position of the agriculture sector has truly diminished (see Chapter 1) and now accounts for just 4.6 per cent of total employment (down from over 12.0 per cent only seventeen years ago). There are now more people employed in hotels and restaurants than in the total agricultural sector, reflecting the increased importance of tourism to the Irish economy and the marked trend towards eating out by Irish people. The numbers employed in the health sector are almost the same as in total manufacturing and the numbers employed in education are more than 70 per cent higher than in agriculture.

Table 6.11

Employment by Sector: Ireland

	1994	(000s) 2004	2010	2010/1994
Agriculture, Forestry and Fishing	*147.0*	*113.8*	*84.9*	*0.58*
Industry of which:	*343.3*	*492.0*	*365.4*	*1.06*
Other production services	251.8	294.3	240.1	0.95
Construction	91.5	197.7	125.3	1.37
Services of which:	*730.2*	*1,394.4*	*1,573.2*	*2.15*
Wholesale and retail trade	169.2	259.5	269.1	1.59
Accommodation and food services	68.4	107.2	119.8	1.75
Transport, storage and communication	55.9	152.1	163.8	2.93
Financial and other business services	114.3	148.0	164.5	1.44
Public administration and defence	66.4	90.1	107.8	1.62
Education	80.5	121.4	149.8	1.86
Health	101.0	177.4	234.9	2.33
Other	74.5	190.7	199.0	2.67
Total	*1,220.6*	*1,902.3*	*1,851.5*	*1.52*

Source: CSO, *Quarterly National Household Survey (QNHS),* Quarter 4 2010.

The services sector as a whole is now almost four times the size of the industrial sector and six times that of the manufacturing sector (other production services). As can be seen in the final column in Table 6.11, employment in all of the services sub-sectors grew between 1994 and 2010, but in particular in transport, storage and communication, and health. The figures in relation to employment in construction, though, tell the story of the overall economy: 91.5 thousand in 1994, 197.7 thousand in 2004, and back to 125.3 thousand (and still falling) in 2010.

Despite the continuing decline in the share of total employment accounted for by agriculture in Ireland, this proportion is still six times higher than in the UK and more than double that in Denmark. In contrast, Ireland has a higher share of total employment in industry than these countries.

Turning now to services, the share of total employment in Ireland accounted for by services was around the EU average in 2005 but was still well below the rates applying in Belgium, Denmark and the UK. Services, though, accounted for almost two-thirds of all employment and it is instructive to look at the breakdown of this total by sub-sector. Ireland had a higher share of total employment than the EU average in hotels and restaurants and financial and other business services. The UK, though, as one would expect, had a considerably higher proportion than Ireland of total employment in the financial and business services sector. Ireland had a lower percentage of employment than the EU average in education and a considerably lower proportion than in Belgium and Denmark. The same applies in relation to the health sector. The sector, however, with the lowest relative percentage of employment in Ireland was public administration and defence (5.1 per cent in Ireland compared to an EU average of 7.3 per cent).

5 UNEMPLOYMENT: EXTENT AND FEATURES

International Comparisons

Table 6.12 provides the key information on recorded unemployment rates in Ireland and selected OECD countries, including, as mentioned earlier, some small EU countries, since 1994. The unemployment rate is given by $E/(E + UE)$ and the picture is fairly clear.

Table 6.12
Standardised Unemployment Rates in Selected OECD Countries[1]

	As a percentage of the labour force			
	1994	2000	2005	2009
Belgium	9.8	6.9	8.4	7.9
Denmark	7.7	4.3	4.8	6.0
Greece	8.8	11.2	9.9	9.5
Ireland	*14.3*	*4.2*	*4.4*	*11.9*
Netherlands	6.8	2.8	4.7	3.4
Norway	6.0	3.2	4.5	3.1
OECD	7.6	6.2	6.8	8.3
UK	9.3	5.4	4.8	7.6
USA	6.1	4.0	5.1	9.3

Source: OECD, *Employment Outlook*, OECD, Paris 2010, Table A.
[1] All series are benchmarked to labour force survey-based estimates and have been adjusted to ensure comparability over time.

Between 1994 and 2005, all countries bar Greece experienced significant declines in unemployment, with the OECD average declining from 7.6 per cent in 1994 to 6.8 per cent in 2005. The most dramatic decline of course was for Ireland, down from 14.3 per cent to 4.4 per cent in the same period. Between 2005 and 2009, though, unemployment in the OECD area increased from 6.8 per cent to 8.3 per cent, with a much more dramatic increase in Ireland, up from 4.4 per cent to 11.9 per cent in 2009. In contrast, unemployment in Belgium, the Netherlands and Norway declined. This contrast will be probably more marked still in 2011, with unemployment in Ireland rising to over 14 per cent but with no major increase in these countries. The success story in terms of employment since 2009 has in fact been Germany (not included in tables), with large drops in unemployment experienced there, and unemployment standing in mid-2011 at just over 6 per cent.

Comparison/Measurement Problems
Standardised Unemployment Rates
The discussion above is based on the assumption that the data can be used for valid comparison both across countries and over time. Is this the case? There are three main issues of concern here. The first is whether or not all countries are using the same methods of defining and compiling data on unemployment; the second is whether or not over time there is a consistent series for Ireland; the last is whether or not there are certain categories of persons that are not, and perhaps cannot be, included by any country but which should be included in any discussion of labour market slack (i.e. where labour demand is less than labour supply) in an economy.

International comparison of unemployment rates is fraught with difficulty, despite the best efforts of the OECD and the EU. Nonetheless, there are reasonably reliable comparative data for the EU member states, if not for most of the OECD countries, and these are the data that inform comparative studies and international policy debate.

In relation to Ireland, there are two main sources of data on unemployment: the Quarterly National Household Survey (QNHS) and the Live Register. The QNHS gives two measures of unemployment: the International Labour Office (ILO) measure and the Principal Economic Status (PES) measure. The first of these is the internationally recognised measure of unemployment and defines somebody as 'unemployed' if their response in the survey makes it clear that: they did not work even for one hour for payments or profit in the previous week; they actively sought work in the previous four weeks; and they are available to start work within two weeks. This is a strict measure of unemployment and much more so than the Live Register measure. The latter counts each month all those in receipt of unemployment benefit or unemployment assistance (now called jobseeker's allowance, but referred to throughout this chapter by the more generic terms), plus those who, though entitled to no payment, wish to have social insurance contributions 'credited' to them; in addition, casual and part-time workers who work for not more than three days in the week may be entitled to register on account of the days they do not work. There is little doubt therefore that it gives an overstatement of the number unemployed in the normal sense of the term.

153

It is the ILO data, therefore, that are used for international comparison, as the methods used to arrive at these data are considered to give a more accurate indicator of the underlying level of unemployment in a country. These data are also used in this chapter, unless indicated otherwise. It is important to remember that the ILO definition is quite a restrictive measure of unemployment and perhaps gives the most favourable picture of the unemployment problem in a country. It excludes, for example, many who are in involuntary part-time work and also those described as discouraged and marginalised workers.

Invalidity/Disability Benefit Issue
There are also many people unable to work through invalidity or disability; the proportion of the working-age group in this category has grown significantly in some EU countries in recent years, with some commentators suggesting that some of the decrease in unemployment in the 2000s, in the Netherlands and the UK in particular, could be linked to this development. For example, in the UK in late 2007 there were more people aged under 35 on disability benefit than on unemployment benefit and a major programme has been put in place to get many of these people back to work, along the lines of the policies used to bring the long-term unemployed back into the labour force in the UK in earlier years.[4]

As the OECD states, too many workers leave the labour market permanently due to health problems and, indeed, expenditures on disability programmes in many OECD countries far exceed expenditures on other income-replacement programmes (such as unemployment benefits) for working-age persons.[5] A large number of OECD countries, they indicate, have seen substantial increases in the share of disability beneficiaries in the working-age population. It appears that vulnerable groups such as women, young individuals and the low-skilled are most affected by this trend.

Helping disabled people find and keep jobs is a major challenge for all OECD countries, including Ireland, especially given that the potential personal, social, and financial benefits are huge. Although it is costly to leave disabled people outside the labour force, no country has so far been successful in crafting policies that will help disabled people return to work. The OECD suggests various broad areas for improvement including: individual benefit packages with job search support, rehabilitation and vocational training; new obligations for disabled people including, for those who are capable, a requirement to look for work; involving employers and trade unions in reintegration efforts; and more flexible cash benefits, depending on job capabilities and changes in an individual's disability over time.[6]

Long-Term Unemployment
Apart from the level of unemployment, its composition is also of considerable interest to economists, for reasons already alluded to. The most important

consideration in this regard relates to whether it is short-term (less than 12 months) or long-term (12 months or more) unemployment.

Long-term unemployment (LTU) in Ireland rose significantly between 1980 and 1994. The long-term unemployment rate was only 2.8 per cent of the labour force in 1980, rising to 8.3 per cent in 1988 and rising again in the early 1990s to 9.0 per cent of the labour force. As Table 6.13 shows, a marked decline took place in LTU between 1994 and 2002. The reductions on all three counts were remarkable; the numbers in absolute terms were down to over a sixth of their level in 1994. The drop in the LTU rate is even more dramatic and the share of LTU in total unemployment dropped from over 60 per cent in 1994 to around 20 per cent by late 2002 (see Table 6.13). As a result, the LTU rate (1.1 per cent) in late 2002 was below the level pertaining in 1980.

Table 6.13

Long-Term Unemployment in Ireland, 1990–2010

	Number (000s)	Unemployment rate	Long-term unemployment rate
1990	110.2	12.9%	8.3%
1994	128.2	14.7%	9.0%
1998	49.4	6.1%	3.0%
2002	20.4	4.4%	1.1%
2006	29.2	4.6%	1.4%
2008	33.2	5.7%	1.5%
2010	127.0	13.9%	5.9%
2010 Q4	153.9	14.1%	7.3%

Source: CSO, *Quarterly National Household Survey (QNHS),* Quarter 4 2010.

This picture remained largely unchanged up to 2008, when the first rise in LTU on all counts was recorded. Between 2008 and late 2010 there was a dramatic worsening of the situation, with the LTU rate rising from 1.5 per cent to 7.3 per cent in two years and the numbers in LTU more than quadrupling. The LTU problem of the 1980s and early 1990s had returned to Ireland in less than two years. This in many ways could be the most worrying legacy of the economic crisis of the last three years.

Table 6.14 provides data on LTU for the countries shown. As may be seen, the share of LTU in total employment decreased between 1999 and 2008 in all countries bar the USA, but levels there were still way below European levels. The share of LTU in total employment rose again in the USA in 2009 and indeed rose also in Ireland, Norway and the UK. As seen already that figure rose dramatically again in Ireland in 2010, meaning that in 2011 Ireland had almost certainly the worst LTU rate for the countries listed, and probably three times that of the UK. This confirms that the LTU problem is very serious indeed in Ireland, both in an absolute and a relative sense.

Table 6.14

Long-Term Unemployment in the OECD
(Percentage of Total Employment)

	1999	2008	2009
Belgium	60.5	47.6	44.2
Denmark	20.5	13.6	9.1
Greece	55.3	47.5	40.8
Ireland	*55.3*	*27.1*	*29.0*
Netherlands	43.5	34.8	24.8
Norway	7.1	6.0	7.7
OECD	31.7	25.5	23.6
UK	29.6	24.1	24.6
USA	6.8	10.6	16.3

Source: OECD Directorate for Employment, Labour and Social Affairs, Online Database, 2011.

6 ADAPTING TO NEW TECHNOLOGY, AND INCREASED TRADE AND MIGRATION[7]

What causes employment levels to rise and fall in any country, including Ireland? First, there are arguments relating to global factors such as increased competition in international trade, technological change and greater freedom of movement of labour, especially in the EU, and hence a potentially large increase in migration. These are factors that would affect every country in Europe, but some to a greater extent than others. How each country fares depends largely on the skill level and adaptability of its labour forces in the new circumstances. These issues will be discussed in this section. Second, there are structural arguments relating to such issues as the role of unions and wage bargaining/setting, employment protection legislation and the taxation and social welfare systems. These issues will be discussed in Section 7.

The Single Market, Trade and Technological Change
Given the extent of Ireland's trade and factor and corporate links with the world economy, it is inevitable that the increasing globalisation of economic activity has, and will have, a major effect on economic activity and employment in Ireland (see later chapters). Added to this is the deepening of the Single European Market and the removal of barriers to free trade in services, mergers and acquisitions and capital flows with the consequential implications for economic activity, competition and employment in Ireland. Ireland's entry into the euro zone in the late 1990s was a further major commitment to the benefits and challenges of the single market. It appears in 2011 that these challenges were

156

never properly understood and that this was a key cause of the drop in employment since 2008.

It is generally believed by economists that an increasing intensity of trade and integration will lead to higher incomes, but that it will also lead to the displacement of labour in some activities and the expansion of labour in others.[8] The net impact on employment should be negligible as long as labour and product markets function well and wages are reasonably flexible. Thus, if decreased overall employment should result from increased trade intensity and competition it is not trade or competition *per se* that is causing the problem but the functioning of the labour and product markets, a topic that will be returned to in a later section. The evidence, according to the OECD, supports such an argument. This indeed is the reason why Ireland has adopted such a pro-trade liberalisation, pro-competition stance in the last forty years.

Increasing international trade and economic integration may also have an impact on innovation and the absorption of technological change. It is argued by some that labour-saving technologies are, at least in part, introduced in anticipation of and/or in response to the increased competition both on domestic and foreign markets that arises from the increased globalisation of trade and European integration. As such, the effect of increased international integration and technological change are difficult to separate in practice.

Technology is central to the process of growth (see Chapters 7 and 9): it allows increases in productivity and thereby real incomes. But does it destroy jobs and in the process create unemployment?

Fears about widespread job losses associated with the emergence of new technology are not new and are in the aggregate largely unfounded. They date back to at least the time of the Industrial Revolution in the early nineteenth century, when the Luddite movement in England destroyed new machinery for fear of job losses. It is true that technological change involves a process of job destruction in some older occupations, firms and industries, but it also involves a parallel process of job creation in new and emerging sectors and occupations. There are many historical examples of predictions of large-scale technological unemployment being followed in fact by large net expansions of jobs, the experience in the last two decades or so with regard to the IT sector in the USA being the most recent striking example.

Technology and trade, then, do not lead to a decrease in the level of employment, but they allow for a decrease in the annual hours of work per employee, thereby allowing for increased per capita incomes *and* increased voluntary leisure time. The average working year has declined steadily over the last hundred years and is continuing to fall, as seen in Table 6.15. For all countries listed, bar the Netherlands, average annual working time decreased between 1999 and 2009, and markedly so in Ireland. The other striking finding revealed in Table 6.15 is the significant variation across even developed countries in average annual working time. In particular, in 2009 it was 1,739 hours in the USA, more than 12 per cent higher than the figure for Ireland, and 26 per cent more than in the Netherlands.

This is an issue that is discussed in Chapter 7, in which comparative living standards are examined. From a labour supply point of view the question is to what extent the variation in hours is a reflection of work preferences or a slack labour demand. Those supporting the USA model argue for the latter, whereas Europeans tend to argue that the former applies.[9]

Table 6.15
Average Annual Working Time in the OECD
(Hours per Worker)

	1999	2008	2009
Belgium	1,581	1,568	1,550
Denmark	1,569	1,570	1,563
Greece	2,107	2,116	2,119
Ireland	*1,725*	*1,601*	1,549
Netherlands	1,361	1,389	1,378
Norway	1,473	1,423	1,407
OECD	1,820	1,764	1,739
UK	1,723	1,652	1,646
USA	1,847	1,796	1,739

Source: OECD Directorate for Employment, Labour and Social Affairs, Online Database, 2011.

While Ireland's adoption of new technology will be discussed in later chapters, particularly Chapter 9, it is worth noting here that there are four key technology areas that will influence the country's success in IT: infrastructure; competitive market conditions; education and training; and access for all. It has been, and will be, the country's ability to take appropriate action on all four fronts that will allow us to absorb and adapt to the new technology: our ability to do this in turn will be the key to employment, not only in manufacturing, but more important perhaps, given its scale, in the services sector as well (see Chapters 9 and 13).

Labour Market Integration

Labour market integration is a highly contentious aspect of economic integration in Europe. Popular opinion, especially in periods of high unemployment, holds immigrants responsible for high unemployment, abuse of social welfare programmes, street crime and the deterioration of neighbourhoods. Economic theory predicts that in a world of no unemployment there will be both winners and losers resulting from labour migration. Without migration, however, the worldwide allocation of productive factors is inefficient. Improving the overall efficiency of the world economy through migration then leads to a net gain which must be split between the home and foreign country.

In a situation where there is no unemployment and workers initially earn better wages in the domestic economy than in the foreign economy, migration will result in labour flowing from the foreign to the domestic economy. This may push down wages at home, harming domestic workers while benefiting domestic consumers. The opposite happens in the foreign economy. Wages there tend to rise as some foreign labour moves to the domestic economy; thus, remaining foreign workers are better off while foreign consumers are made worse off. The net outcome is positive for the efficiency reasons outlined above, but serious distributional issues can arise.

For most European economies labour is comprised of both highly skilled and low-skilled workers. Recognising this distinction allows a more nuanced understanding of the dynamics of labour market integration under net-inward or net-outward migration. It is in this context that one may view some immigrant labour as a complement or substitute for domestic labour. If immigrant labour is a complement to native workers, immigration will raise the demand for native workers, resulting in higher wages, higher employment, and an unambiguously favourable impact on unemployment.

The empirical evidence for Ireland suggests that although the skill make-up of immigrants was higher than that of the native population, immigrants tended to fill low-skilled jobs and thus acted as complements to the skilled Irish workforce, even if this meant that migrants achieved a low occupational attainment relative to their educational attainment.[10] It remains to be seen whether the favourable impact of migration on the Irish labour market will continue when the economy is contracting or growing much more slowly. Preliminary evidence suggests (see Table 6.5) that recent immigrants are still highly mobile and that many returned to their home countries as employment in construction collapsed. In this way the ease of movement between Ireland and the new European member states helped to ease the adverse unemployment impacts of the downturn in Ireland between 2008 and 2010.

Education, Training and Skills Adaptability

Over the last twenty years the structure of work in the industrialised world has, for the reasons mentioned above, been changing. There has been a shift in demand away from low-skilled, low-wage jobs towards high-skilled, high-wage jobs. The change in the nature of work arises not only from the transformation of jobs by technology and international trade but also from the 'natural' sectoral changes that have occurred with regard to employment (see Table 6.11). Allied to this, because of immigration, there was a marked transformation in labour supply in many sectors.

The skills required in services are different from those needed for industry; hence the declining industrial workforce cannot be automatically transplanted into services jobs. The new wave of employment creation leads, as mentioned earlier, to a transformation of the competencies required from the workforce. Not only do they need different qualifications and skills but the continuously changing nature of work also requires them to have a high degree of flexibility that was not necessary in the past when permanent, stable positions were the norm.

The skills of the labour force, then, have to be altered to take account of the changing environment and nature of work that accompany this. In the absence of this adjustment, mismatch can, and may have, become a serious problem in the labour market. Evidence for this is reflected in repeated statements of serious skills shortages in parts of the EU.

It is for these reasons that the EU has placed special emphasis on upgrading the skills and competencies of the labour force, as part of the search for a solution to maintaining and increasing employment. Not all persons have acquired adequate initial education and training before they enter the labour market and these are the people most likely to experience long-term unemployment in Ireland and elsewhere in Europe. The first priority, then, must be to reduce through preventive and remedial measures the number of young people who leave school without some qualification (see Chapter 13).

The next concern is to ensure that those who have acquired satisfactory initial qualifications make the transition to employment, and this may be assisted by a more employer-led approach to education, particularly vocational education. Last, and perhaps of most relevance in relation to the issues discussed in this section, is the need to emphasise continuing education and training (see Chapter 13), as individuals need the opportunity to upgrade their knowledge and competencies to prepare themselves for the changes brought about by increasing international trade, migration and technological change. For similar reasons the Irish government in the past slightly altered its policy on work permits and visas for immigrants seeking work, i.e. it was actively recruiting suitably qualified people intended for designated sectors where skills shortages were particularly acute. The challenges in 2011 are pressing: identifying the areas for employment growth and ensuring the skill levels of the Irish labour force match the resulting employment opportunities.[11]

7 FLEXIBILITY IN THE LABOUR MARKET

It has already been mentioned that structural rigidities in labour markets, especially in those of many countries in Europe, may largely explain why unemployment was and is at such high levels in these countries. Putting it more positively, it is argued that it is the countries with flexible labour markets that have experienced the lowest rates of unemployment in the 2010s. There are several dimensions to the structural rigidity and labour market flexibility arguments and some of the key ones are looked at here.

First, wage and price adjustments are examined, with attention devoted to industrial relations and product market competition. Second, quantity adjustments (which refer to barriers facing the movement of people in and out of jobs) are analysed. Policies to enhance quantity adjustment include reforms of employment protection legislation and active labour market policies. Last, the effect of the tax and social welfare systems on the working of the labour market will be examined briefly.

Wage Adjustments

Price formation in the labour market is, of necessity, different from that in other markets. This is because wages are not simply a price of one type of product among others, but determine to a large extent the well-being of the majority of people in modern society. Societies' concern about social justice and the distribution of income therefore becomes integrally linked to wage-setting. Because of this, distinct social arrangements and institutions intervene in every country in the market-clearing role of wage adjustments. However, even if the operation of the price system for labour is different from that for products, the effects of prices being too high are the same, i.e. wages above market-clearing levels will result in excess supply and therefore lower levels of employment than would otherwise be the case.

Industrial Relations

The response of wages to market conditions has to be seen against the background of the institutional arrangements, particularly those relating to industrial relations and the role of trade unions, in the labour market in each particular country. These arrangements have been partly designed to encourage stable employment relationships and to avert the income insecurity that can accompany rapid price adjustments in the market for labour, as happened in the USA in the 1980s. However, in so doing, these arrangements may encourage anti-competitive behaviour in the labour market and, as in all markets, this will result in lower demand because prices are not set at their clearing rate. This of course must be set against the advantages for employees of the protective industrial relations arrangements and the potential advantages for employers, in that these arrangements may strengthen co-operation by workers and prevent the harmful behaviour that may be inherent in a more atomistic wage-setting environment.

Given the above, it is generally recognised that income restraint by trade unions and individual workers is essential to employment creation in Ireland and that there *is* a trade-off between pay and employment. In the multinational high-tech sector of the economy, pay moderation can lead to more employment in the medium to longer term, through increased profitability and its effect on investment location decisions. In the more traditional labour-intensive parts of the traded sector there is likely to be a substantial trade-off between pay and employment, as in many cases pay moderation is essential in this sector, simply to retain existing jobs. In the sheltered private sector, pay moderation is necessary to underpin the competitiveness of the traded sector and also to generate increased employment in this sector. Last, in the public sector, given a fixed budget, there is a very direct and almost immediate trade-off between pay and employment.

While the unionisation rate in Ireland fell in the 1990s, in line with many other countries, the rate in Ireland was still above that in the UK and way above that in the USA, although well below the Scandinavian countries (see Table 6.16). It is noteworthy that the unionisation rate in low-unemployment Denmark was 69.1 per cent in 2007, 53.7 per cent in Norway, but only 19.8 per cent in the Netherlands. As such, it is almost impossible to draw any conclusions between the rate of unionisation and unemployment.

Table 6.16
Union Membership (Percentage of Employees)

	1997	2006	2007
Belgium	55.6	54.1	52.9
Denmark	75.6	69.4	69.1
Greece	30.4	n/a	n/a
Ireland	*42.7*	*32.6*	*31.7*
Netherlands	25.1	20.4	19.8
Norway	55.5	54.9	53.7
OECD	35.9	29.4	n/a
UK	30.7	28.2	28.0
USA	13.6	11.5	11.6

Source: OECD Directorate for Employment, Labour and Social Affairs, Online Database, 2011.

In relation to the wage bargaining process, there is a degree of corporatism in the Irish labour market, with a large proportion of wages having until recently been determined by national wage agreements (see Chapter 3). Ireland therefore appeared to have adopted the system of wage bargaining (i.e. centralised), preferable for such a small country where participants are more likely to take wider economic interests into account.[12] The OECD, though, has warned in general against too little differentiation of relative wages by skill, region or other dimensions. It also acknowledges that it might be best to accept the variation in national industrial relations and practices evident across member states and concentrate instead on 'identifying policies that increase wage flexibility in the presence of such structures ... and that greater allowance be made for the potential contribution of centrally co-ordinated bargaining to achieving aggregate wage restraint, at least in those countries whose histories and structures are compatible with such an approach'.[13]

In recent years, though, the position in Ireland has changed dramatically and many now question the desirability of centralised wage setting, at least if it does not recognise the reality of competition in product markets in a single currency area and thereby the limitations of passing on wage increases into prices. It has also, many argue, led to an unacceptable increase in pay in the public sector, arising from the powerful union base in this sector compared to that in the private sector.

Competition in Product Markets
Imperfect competition in the product market can also affect the wage level and thereby the level of employment and unemployment. If there is an absence of competition in the product market, firms have an option of choosing 'supranormal' profits ahead of increased employment. They also have the option of retaining the entire surplus for themselves or sharing it with existing employees. The latter will happen if the workers have bargaining strength, or the rents may be willingly shared with workers to encourage efficiency and to boost work motivation, i.e. the employers may be prepared to pay what are called 'efficiency wages'. Whatever the rationale for rent sharing with workers, such arrangements favour the 'insiders' at the expense of the 'outsiders' and create a united lobby between unions and employers to oppose the removal of the imperfect competition in the product market that is giving rise to the rent.

The solution to reducing the distortionary effects of imperfect product market competition on labour market outcomes is clearly to remove the opportunity for producers to earn rent, and this calls for a strict and tough competition regime, a topic that is covered at some length in Chapter 4. More important, the opening of the EU market to increased competition, internal and external, has greatly reduced the potential for such imperfect competition. Besides, entry into the euro zone has removed the exchange rate option for dealing with excessive wage rises: employers and employees must now 'live' with the euro exchange rate, which is in turn determined by market conditions. The potential benefits, of course, are reduced exchange rate risk, more transparency of prices, fewer transaction costs and increased employment levels overall.

The main concern now relates to the public sector, where for some time the tax price of its services can be shielded from any immediate effect on employment in the public sector. In time, though, the higher tax price for public services must be paid for out of taxation, thereby impacting on Irish competitiveness and ultimately therefore on Irish employment, tax revenue and public sector employment. Wage negotiations still take place at the level of the whole public sector and in recent years there has been a realisation that in return for this, much greater work flexibility and public sector reform will be required.[14]

Minimum Wage
A national minimum wage (NMW) was introduced in Ireland in 2000. Although the ESRI predicted that this would decrease employment and increase unemployment and inflation, 95 per cent of firms surveyed a year later viewed the NMW as having had no impact on the number of employees they had subsequently hired. Those paid less than the NMW are concentrated in sales and personal services, which reflects a wider concern that younger female and non-Irish national workers are most likely to experience low pay.

Many studies have shown that the adverse impact of minimum wages on employment is modest. This, however, depends on the level of the minimum wage and how it interacts with the tax system. The important thing in this regard is to ensure that work pays better than remaining on social welfare benefits and also that high rates of labour taxation do not apply at low income levels (see Chapter 4). An employer considering hiring a low-skilled or inexperienced worker is likely to compare the worker's expected productivity with the *sum* of the minimum wage and employer-paid social security contributions when deciding whether or not to hire. In the case of Ireland the evidence shows that the minimum cost of labour, as a percentage of labour costs for the average employee, is one of the lowest in the EU and hence the adverse labour effects of a minimum wage are likely to be small.[15] This, though, was in 2006. Besides, the minimum wage, relative to median income, is high in Ireland. As shown in Table 6.17, in 2008 this ratio was 0.53 for Ireland, compared to 0.46 in the UK (our main competitor market), and 0.34 in the USA. The unweighted OECD average was 0.46. The minimum wage was reduced in Ireland in 2010 but with a change of government this reduction was reversed in 2011. Given that the median wage has declined since 2008, the ratio of minimum wage to median wage in Ireland could become the highest in the OECD, even higher than in France.

Table 6.17

Ratio of Minimum to Median Wage and Unemployment
Benefit to Previous Earnings in the OECD

	Ratio of minimum to median wage		Unemployment benefit, % previous earnings	
	1999	2008	1997	2007
Belgium	0.54	0.51	39.7	40.0
Denmark	–	–	62.5	47.7
Greece	0.50	0.53	15.8	12.6
Ireland	–	*0.53*	29.0	37.2
Netherlands	0.47	0.43	52.2	33.9
Norway	–	–	38.6	33.6
OECD	0.41	0.46	30.2	24.7
UK	0.42	0.46	18.3	12.1
USA	0.38	0.34	13.9	13.6

Source: OECD Directorate for Employment, Labour and Social Affairs, Online Database, 2011.

Employment Protection Legislation

Employment protection relates to the 'firing' and 'hiring' rules governing unfair dismissal, lay-off for economic reasons, severance payments, minimum notice periods, administrative authorisation for dismissals and prior discussion with labour representatives. A number of benefits are alleged to justify employment protection legislation: encouraging increased investment in firm-specific capital; reducing contracting costs by setting general rules and standards; and early notification of job loss to allow job search prior to being laid off. As against this, employment protection legislation imposes constraints on firms' behaviour that can raise labour costs and adversely affect hiring decisions. It may also provide strong incentives for employers to use forms of employment (e.g. short-term contracts) that do not involve high firing costs. Labour security legislation does not only affect the actions of employers, it also influences the bargaining power and, hence, strategy of the insiders (see earlier). With the legislation in place, workers' fear of job loss will be greatly diminished and they will push for higher real wages. This will then have an impact on labour demand. Labour security legislation could therefore cause labour demand to be inflexible both directly (i.e. through employers' immediate decisions) and indirectly (i.e. through its promotion of higher real wages). In fact, employment protection laws are thought by many to be a key factor in generating labour market inflexibility.

It appears, though, that a certain level of employment protection is justified to protect workers from arbitrary or discriminatory dismissals. However, the OECD believes that dismissals that are required on economic grounds must be allowed and that the provision of more explicit, long-term commitments to job security should not be imposed on all firms but decided on a firm-by-firm basis. Whether and to what extent reform is required clearly depends on the country-specific circumstances. A related issue is that the emphasis is now increasingly on employment security rather than job security, that is on guaranteed employment rather than employment in a specific job. The best way to ensure this is to increase adaptability and employability, as discussed earlier. After all, labour reallocation is an important driver of productivity growth, in that less productive firms tend to destroy jobs and more productive ones create jobs and empirical evidence shows that the process of firm birth and death, as well as the reallocation of resources from declining to expanding firms, contribute significantly to productivity and output growth.[16]

Attempts have been made to construct various summary indicators to describe the 'strictness' of employment protection in each country, including Ireland. Given the complexity of constructing such indicators, they are inevitably somewhat arbitrary, but nonetheless are indicative. An OECD study ranking EU countries according to 'strictness' of protection in the areas of individual dismissals of regular workers, fixed-term contracts and employment through temporary employment agencies showed in 2008 that employment protection was ranked relatively low as a problem in Ireland (see Table 6.18). This applied in particular to temporary employment and less so to regular employment, as can be seen from the table.

Table 6.18
Employment Protection in the OECD, Strictness Indicators (0–6)

| | Regular employment | | Temporary employment | |
	1998	2008	1998	2007
Belgium	1.7	1.7	2.6	2.6
Denmark	1.6	1.6	1.4	1.4
Greece	2.3	2.3	4.8	3.1
Ireland	*1.6*	*1.6*	0.3	0.6
Netherlands	3.1	2.7	2.4	1.2
Norway	2.3	2.3	3.1	3.1
OECD	2.1	2.1	1.9	1.8
UK	1.0	1.1	0.3	0.4
USA	0.2	0.2	0.3	0.3

Source: OECD Directorate for Employment, Labour and Social Affairs, Online Database, 2011.

However, compared to the USA, Ireland, and indeed most of Europe, has much more strict employment protection, with scores of 0.2 for the USA in relation to regular employment in 2008 (0.3 for temporary employment), against figures of 1.7 and 2.6 in Belgium, 1.6 and 1.4 in Denmark, and 1.6 and 0.6 in Ireland. Indeed, the important data relate to regular employment, where the figure of 1.6 for Ireland is much higher than in the USA, but also Denmark, and most important, perhaps, the UK at 1.1.

Taxation
Payroll taxes, such as employers' social security contributions, raise the costs of employing labour over and above the wage paid. Income taxes and employees' social security contributions reduce the return to working. These taxes, therefore, are important because they directly affect the rate of return from decisions to enter the labour market and thereby affect the supply of labour. They may also influence the choice between working in the black economy and declared paid employment. These taxes may have an even greater impact on employment and unemployment through their influence on wage determination and therefore on the demand for labour. In a perfectly competitive labour market these effects would be minimal, but, as seen earlier, most labour markets are far from perfectly competitive. Hence, cuts in real wages through the imposition of increased personal income taxes or social security contributions may be resisted by workers and compensated for by higher nominal wages – but at the cost of higher unemployment. Likewise, an increase in employers' social security contributions can also result in unemployment when workers resist offsetting wage cuts. In the light of increased competition, both within the EU single market and globally, though, the scope for such resistance by trade unions and workers is significantly reduced, as discussed earlier.

Reductions in average tax rates at low levels of earnings are clearly an important way of increasing the income differential between being in and out of work, for the groups for which this is the most serious problem (see earlier). It appears that particular attention needs to be devoted to social security contributions in this regard, not just to the level of these contributions but also to their structure: employers' taxation not only influences the number of people who are employed but it may also influence the type of worker who is hired.

The rate at which social benefits are withdrawn, as seen in Chapter 4, is another important aspect of the problem. A feature of many tax and benefit systems, including that in Ireland, is that they can embody very high marginal tax rates for those on low incomes, especially those with large families, as benefits are reduced and earnings are taxed. There have been some successful attempts to address this problem in Ireland in the last decade. As OECD evidence shows, tax cuts on average incomes were particularly striking in Ireland in the period 1994 to 2004, with targeted reductions for low incomes very prominent.[17] As a result, by 2006 Ireland's tax wedge (i.e. the gap between what the employer pays and what the employee receives) was the lowest in the OECD. That situation would have changed significantly, though, between 2008 and 2010 and it will be a priority that it does not worsen further. This will be difficult to avoid, however, given that increases in taxation are inevitable in the years to come in dealing with the fiscal deficit crisis (see Chapter 4).

Unemployment Payments
The rationale for unemployment insurance payments is 'to relieve people who have lost a job through no fault of their own from immediate financial concerns, and thus allow efficient job search. Insurance benefits, therefore, have an economic efficiency as well as a social equity objective.'[18] In relation to unemployment assistance payments, which apply in Ireland after twelve months and effectively for an indefinite period, the social or equity role, in reducing poverty among unemployed people and cushioning the adverse effects of high and rising unemployment, becomes paramount. As a result of the above, there would be strong political objections to any cuts in unemployment benefits or assistance and this clearly 'flavours' any debate on the causal connection between unemployment benefit/assistance and unemployment. However, the possibility of such a causal connection, and its extent, must be addressed, as it has been recently in countries such as France, Germany and Italy, where unemployment persisted, at high levels, for more than a decade and led to a build-up of large-scale long-term unemployment and a 'handout' dependency. A similar problem is likely to have arisen in Ireland since 2008, an issue that the EU/IMF team overseeing Ireland's special loans is also acutely aware of, with a suggestion that they wish to see the rate of payment reduced the longer some people are out of work.

Few economists question the fact that there *is* a link between the benefit system and unemployment. At the simplest level, unemployment payments may create an option of leisure and low income, which some people might choose in preference to full-time work and a higher income. However, such payments could affect employment in many other ways. First, receipt of such payments may prolong intervals of job search, even for those who want to work. Second, because unemployment payments reduce the cost of becoming unemployed, employed people may take a tougher stance in industrial relations disputes or in collective bargaining over wages (see earlier), thereby exacerbating the high real wage problem. Last, payments may increase employment in high-turnover and seasonal industries, by subsidising these industries relative to those that provide long-term contract jobs.

As seen in Table 6.17, unemployment benefits as a percentage of previous earnings increased markedly in Ireland between 1997 and 2007. Even though unemployment benefit rates have since been reduced, so have pay rates; and if anything the ratio may have increased, especially for older workers. As can be seen, the figure for Ireland is much higher than for the USA and in particular for the UK. On the other hand it is lower than for Denmark, a low-unemployment country. So the evidence for the employment effects of unemployment payments is again mixed.

The adverse effects of unemployment payments may, however, result not so much from the existence and level of these payments, but more from the entitlement conditions, the administration of the system and other institutional background factors. For example, payment of unemployment benefits is conditional upon the claimant being available for, and willing to take, full-time work. If this condition is not effectively implemented, people *not* in the labour force (i.e. not available for or not seeking work) may register as unemployed simply to collect unemployment payments. If this condition is strictly enforced and payments stopped if it is not met, many of the distortionary effects of unemployment payments could be substantially reduced. A related issue is that the employment agency must not only enforce this condition but must also facilitate effective job search, the final topic to which we now turn.

Active Labour Market Policies[19]

Issues

The OECD as far back as 1994 was unequivocal concerning the changes that needed to be effected in benefit administration. They suggested, for example, much more in-depth verification of eligibility, much better matching of workers to job vacancies, and fieldwork investigation of concealed earnings and related fraud. A more fundamental problem, they claimed, was making unemployment payment, especially to the long-term unemployed, effectively conditional on availability for existing vacancies. In particular, they stressed that the long-term unemployed should be expected to take, and unemployment payments made conditional on taking, even low-status jobs. As the OECD noted, much may depend upon achieving a social, political and analytical consensus on this, rejecting the opposite idea that modern economies should be able to afford to make work optional. The real concern here is that if people are allowed to drift into long-term unemployment, as happened in Ireland in the 1980s and early 1990s, and again since 2008, the problem becomes more difficult to overcome. At an individual level long-term unemployment may lead to significant deskilling and demotivation. At a macroeconomic level, and partly as a result of this, the long-term unemployed may not be regarded as 'employable' and in a sense may cease to be part of the labour market.

A similar problem has arisen in recent years in relation to groups receiving *non-employment* benefits. As discussed earlier, the numbers on some non-employment benefits have grown. These benefit recipients represent a large share of the potential workforce and if their numbers are not reduced employment rates will remain low for years to come in many OECD countries. The pattern in relation to non-employment benefit recipients 'suggest that there could be a high pay-off to extending activation measures, currently available to the unemployed, to persons receiving these non-employment benefits'.[20] Recent experience demonstrates that there is considerable scope to apply activation strategies to persons receiving non-employment benefits, albeit with appropriate modifications for the specific characteristics of each group.

Solutions

What was suggested above was effectively a much more active approach to labour market policy on behalf of the employment service in each country. The purpose of active labour market policies is threefold: first, to mobilise labour supply; second, to improve the quality of the labour force; and third, to strengthen the search process in the labour market. They are particularly appropriate for those experiencing long-term unemployment (and many of those on long-term disability benefit), because as mentioned many of them are effectively not participating in the labour force. Because of the deskilling and demotivation that has taken place, they need assistance with education and training, and because of demotivation and the indefinite nature of unemployment and related payments the search for jobs may not be as active as might be desired.

Active labour market policies can be classified into four categories: first, there are state employment services (e.g. placement and counselling); second, there is labour market training (i.e. for unemployed and employed adults); third, there are youth measures (e.g. remedial education, training or work experience for disadvantaged young people); and last, subsidised employment (i.e. subsidies to increase employment in the private sector, support for the unemployed persons starting their own enterprises and direct job creation in either the public or non-profit sector).

In the last decade or so many countries increased both the number and variety of instruments used to activate jobseekers. Job placement efforts have been enhanced, there is a greater emphasis on testing and monitoring work availability, there is earlier intervention in the unemployment spell, and participation on programmes is compulsory; and there is more efficient administration of public employment services. There is considerable evidence that these measures have made a significant impact on the numbers in long-term unemployment in several countries, including Ireland in the past. However, such measures are costly, and ongoing evaluation of the cost-effectiveness of each programme needs to be undertaken.

The OECD carried out an evaluation of active labour market policies in 2009, before the current long-term unemployment crisis really emerged.[21] It found that the number of staff in FÁS Employment Services and Local Employment Services, relative to the number of wage and salary earners in the economy, appeared to have been relatively very low, about half the average level of staffing of similar institutions in Northern and Western Europe. As such, it called for a refocusing of existing resources and an increase in them.

A requirement to register with FÁS was introduced for LTU youth in 1996 and in 1998 the National Employment Action Plan (NEAP) was introduced. These initiatives, together with increased control activity by the Department of Social Welfare (now the Department of Social Protection), helped to reduce LTU in the 1990s. Interviews under NEAP continue, but their frequency is very low and enforcement by the Department of availability for work requirements, the report found, was only partly effective. This is mainly because its procedures are not a substitute for regular employment counselling, which whenever possible, the OECD says, should refer clients directly to job vacancies. The report also called for an external audit of FÁS, particularly in terms of its purchase of training from outside bodies. Later inquiries revealed major problems in the organisation and a total revamp is apparently under way in 2011.

Finally, the OECD report noted that several large groups – lone parents, adult dependents of benefit recipients, and people with disabilities who have remaining work capacity – received benefit without formal requirement to be available for work, an arrangement that is increasingly out of line with international practice. It also commented on the tendency for the implementation of administrative reforms to be slow. With the sudden rise in LTU in Ireland in the last three years, it seems that the employment service might not in any way be geared up to deal with the return of this most worrying of labour market problems.

8 CONCLUSION

The outstanding economic policy failure in the last forty years in Ireland was the inability to increase employment in the 1980s, despite the huge increase in the potential labour force in this period. The result of this failure was a dramatic increase in the unemployment rate and the emigration of almost 200,000 people. More seriously, perhaps, the sustained failure to increase employment meant not only that the high level of unemployment persisted into the mid-1990s, but also that an increasing proportion of that total drifted into long-term unemployment and, in many cases, therefore effectively left the labour market.

On the other hand, the outstanding policy success of the last forty years, indeed of the whole post-Independence era, was the increase in employment between 1993 and 2004, and the corresponding huge reductions in unemployment and the dramatic switch from large-scale emigration to significant immigration. In a very short period the disastrous failures of the 1980s had been turned around into one of the most remarkable success stories in terms of employment growth in the Western world. A variety of explanations for this have been looked at in this chapter, with further insights to follow in Chapter 7. There are no simple explanations, though. The policy of attracting foreign investment, much of it in the high-tech sectors, allowed Ireland to cope with the trade and technological effects of globalisation (see Chapter 9). The positive policy stance on trade in general, and the EU and the euro in particular, may have helped in this regard (see Chapters 1, 7, and 9). The advent of the 'borderless' economy meant that Ireland's peripheral location mattered much less than before (see Chapter 9). The increased emphasis on competition in the non-traded sector of the economy added to Ireland's competitiveness (Chapters 5 and 9), while the centralised wage bargaining process appears to have delivered on competitive wage setting and a good industrial relations climate (Chapter 3).

Past policies on education also appear to have been a factor (see Chapters 7 and 13) and the relatively flexible employment protection environment that was in place would have assisted in the huge employment increase that the above facilitated. Ireland also appears to have had a relatively 'entrepreneur-friendly' climate, as measured by relative cost, length of time and minimum charter capital required to form a private limited liability company (see Chapter 7). Finally, changes in taxation and the increased emphasis on active labour market policies made inroads into the most intractable unemployment problem that Ireland faced in the mid-1990s, namely that of long-term unemployment.

The employment growth between 2004 and 2008 appears now to have been illusory, based as it was on unsustainable increases in building activity. Between 2008 and end 2010 all of the employment increases of this period had been reversed. The credit-based building boom could not be maintained and a large drop in employment in construction and other activities was inevitable; it was the speed and scale of the decline that surprised commentators most. Besides, since the early 2000s, Ireland steadily lost competitiveness, especially in terms of wage costs. By 2008 this loss of competitiveness had become acute, especially in the context of Ireland being a member of the euro zone. Problems on this front, which had been disguised during the credit-fuelled boom between 2004 and 2008, came home to roost in 2009. Ireland has regained some of its competitiveness since then (see also Chapters 2 and 9): in May 2010 the real harmonised competitiveness indicator (HCI) had fallen 6.1 per cent below its January 2005 position and has probably fallen further since. It would need to, though, as Ireland's real HCI in May 2010 was still 16 per cent above its 2000 level, an unsustainable level if employment growth is to resume.[22]

The boom in employment in the 1993 to 2004 period of course followed decades of failure to provide jobs for Irish people, the result being large-scale emigration in the 1950s and again in the 1980s. This also resulted in extraordinarily high unemployment levels in the decade 1985 to 1995. Potential labour supply had been increasing rapidly in Ireland from 1980 and a large employment increase was required to absorb this growth in supply; without it there was initially, and would have continued to have been, large-scale emigration and high levels of unemployment. The country, in other words, for the first time in its history provided employment to those who needed it. This has been the norm for decades in other small European countries such as Denmark, the Netherlands and Norway. Indeed, the unemployment rate in Ireland was in 2007, and is still, higher than in these three countries and the proportion of those of working age in employment in Ireland lags well behind that for these countries. Much progress has been made, but more has to be achieved and the failures of the past on the employment front must not be repeated.

That is the challenge that lies ahead. The employment gains of the decade up to 2004 have not been reversed, but the gains between 2004 and 2008 have been totally wiped out. As unemployment, and particularly LTU, spiralled between 2008 and 2011, net emigration resumed and fears of a repeat of the decade of the 1980s have re-emerged. The spectre of emigration still haunts the Irish psyche, as it has done ever since Famine times. The costs of emigration now of course do not compare with then, or even the 1950s and 1980s, but yet the question remains: why can an independent state like Ireland not provide employment for its own nationals? It is true that emigration of Irish nationals continued during the period 1993 to 2004 and many returned with enhanced experience and skills. The scale of the out-migration of Irish nationals has increased substantially, though, since 2008 and the worry is that many of these people will not return unless there is a very significant upturn in employment.

Endnotes

1   Census 2011 was held on 10 April 2011, but its results will not be known for some time, particularly in relation to accurate estimates of migration flows between 2006 and 2011.

2   OECD, 'Taking the measure of temporary employment', *Employment Outlook*, OECD, Paris 2002.

3   *Ibid.*

4   See 'Sickness claims rise in stressed-out south', *Financial Times*, 22/23 March 2008.

5   OECD, *Employment Outlook*, OECD, Paris 2009.

6   OECD, *Annual Report 2004*, OECD, Paris 2004, p. 35.

7   The OECD does outstanding research work in relation to data on employment and related matters, and employment policies, both in general and by member country, and this chapter draws extensively on its work. Its key publication is the annual *Employment Outlook*, which comprises general chapters, detailed research reports and detailed statistical tables.

8   See OECD, 'Institutional and policy determinants of labour market flows',

Employment Outlook, Paris 2010, for a good discussion of this issue.

9   Not only has the working year declined but so has the working life, as the retirement age fell in most the developed world. This is likely to be reversed, though, everywhere, including in Ireland, as life expectancy and hence the fiscal cost of pensions increases.

10 A. Barrett and D. Duffy, 'Are Ireland's immigrants integrating into its labour market?', IZA Discussion Paper Series, No. 2838, Bonn 2007.

11 See *Programme for Recovery 2011–2014*, Department of Finance, Dublin 2010.

12 See OECD, *Employment Outlook*, OECD, Paris 2006, pp. 80–8, for a good review of wage-setting institutions and policies in OECD member states. Table 3.7 in this report illustrates the huge variation in practice in terms of the level of both centralisation and co-ordination.

13 *Ibid.*, p. 88.

14 See *Programme for Recovery 2011–2014*, op. cit., for a discussion of the so-called 'Croke Park Agreement' and other issues relating to this.

15 OECD 2006, *op. cit.*, pp. 86–8.

16 OECD 2010, *op. cit.*

17 OECD 2006, *op. cit.*, Table 3.11.

18 OECD, *Jobs Study: Part II*, OECD, Paris 1994, p.171.

19 A comprehensive review of these policies is contained in OECD, 'Activating the Unemployed: What Countries Do', *Employment Outlook*, Paris 2007.

20 OECD 2006, *op. cit.*, p. 75.

21 OECD, *Activation Policies in Ireland*, Social, Employment and Migration Working Papers, No. 75, OECD, Paris 2009.

22 National Competitiveness Council, *Annual Competitiveness Report 2010*, Dublin 2010.

CHAPTER 7

Growth in Output and Living Standards

Jonathan Haughton

1 THE CELTIC TIGER

Between 1986 and 2007 Irish gross domestic product (GDP) rose every year; over this period, real GDP increased by a total of 266 per cent, an average of 6.4 per cent per year. Then came three lean years: GDP declined in 2008, 2009 and 2010, pulling GDP down by a total of 11 per cent from its peak. The economy is set to expand again, by between one and two per cent – depending on whose forecasts one believes – in 2011.

The more remarkable story is not the recent recession, but the sustained and rapid growth that vaulted Ireland from a poor also-ran at the fringe of Europe to one of the world's wealthiest nations. As measured by GDP per capita (in purchasing power terms), Ireland was the eighth richest country in the world in 2009, counting only countries with populations of a million or more.[1]

How did Ireland become so rich? What were the keys to the rise of the Celtic Tiger? And can this affluence be sustained?

These are the questions that we address in this chapter, beginning with the numbers. To anticipate the argument: Ireland's economic growth in the late 1990s and 2000s was real and impressive and the country is indeed very rich, if not quite as affluent as the GDP per capita numbers imply. Taking a long view, most of Ireland's recent growth may be thought of as an overdue catch-up. The recession of 2008–10 represented a correction related to the housing bubble, and would have occurred even if the rest of the world had not gone through the worst global recession since the 1930s: 2009 was the first year in half a century when world real GDP actually declined. There were corrections of similar magnitudes in a number of other overheated economies, including Estonia, Latvia, Lithuania and Iceland.

Why is Ireland rich? And what underlies the growth that propelled Ireland to the ranks of the most affluent nations? It is helpful to address these questions in two steps. First, we use the Solow growth model to identify the proximate determinants of growth and living standards: how much is due to high levels of investment, long hours of work, or more technology. This then guides us in our search for the more fundamental explanations, which are likely rooted in policy decisions, demographic changes, and the evolution of the world context over the past generation – essentially since Ireland joined the European Economic Community in 1973. The narrative in this chapter thus picks up where the story in Chapter 1, on Irish economic history, leaves off.

It is argued that Ireland experienced two growth spurts – one in the late 1990s and early 2000s, and another from about 2002 to 2007 – which were driven by fundamentally different causes. The first growth spurt was due to a fortunate confluence of events – the opening of the economy and society to trade and the flow of ideas, the arrival of the EU single market that made Ireland an attractive platform for US investors, a boom in the US economy that provided a supply of investment, an improvement in the educational level of the Irish labour force, transfers from the EU, a highly credible macroeconomic stance, fiscal discipline, improved labour relations and relatively modest taxes. This created a virtuous circle: as jobs were created, well-educated and experienced workers immigrated (or did not leave); an entrepreneurial 'can do' attitude took root; financing remained available. The second growth spurt was driven internally, by a massive and unsustainable boom in investment in housing, the result of rising incomes (and hence demand for housing), and loose credit.

The recession has shaken Ireland out of its creeping complacency. Fiscal discipline had weakened; the minimum wage was one of the highest in the world; rising prices and wages led to an erosion in competitiveness, so foreign direct investment went elsewhere and exports flagged; the banking system became insolvent. Most of these problems are now being tackled, and the country's fundamental strengths, including a young, well-educated and relatively hard-working labour force, remain intact. We return to these themes below.

2 HOW AFFLUENT IS IRELAND?

Output and Income

Since 1995, Ireland has caught up economically with its peers in Western Europe. This is shown clearly in Figure 7.1, which compares the evolution of Irish per capita output since 1980 with that of the USA, Denmark and the UK. Denmark is included here because it is, like Ireland, a small open economy, and has often been held up as a role model for Ireland to emulate.

Two measures of Irish affluence are shown in Figure 7.1. The first is GDP per capita, which measures the money value of goods and services produced and marketed in the economy in a year; it represents the value added by economic activity within the geographic borders of a country, and is the most commonly used indicator of economic activity. There was a clear acceleration in the growth of Irish GDP/capita starting in about 1994, with slower but still robust increases after 2000, and a sharp turndown after 2007.

Figure 7.1

Irish GDP and GNP Per Capita Compared, 1980–2009

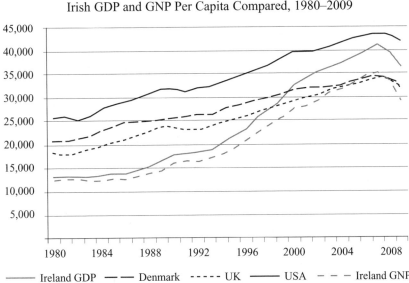

Source: World Bank, *World Development Indicators*, http://data.worldbank.org/data-catalog/world-development-indicators [accessed April 2011].

In order to compare output across countries, the measures of GDP/capita in Figure 7.1 are shown in 'international dollars' in the prices of 2005. A serious problem in cross-country comparisons of this sort is that prices differ substantially from one country to the next: a euro in Ireland barely buys a cup of coffee, but converted into rupees and spent in India, it would buy a whole meal. So if the exchange rate were used to convert India's GDP into euro, it would understate the true purchasing power of India's GDP. The standard solution is to re-compute every country's GDP using a common set of 'international' prices, giving a measure of purchasing power parity (PPP) GDP that is reasonably comparable across countries. By this measure, GDP per capita in Ireland in 2007 came close to the US level, and it remains well above the levels of the UK or Denmark.

However, in the Irish case, GDP is not a particularly good indicator of affluence. Not all of the goods and services produced in Ireland accrue to Irish citizens or residents; for instance, profit that is repatriated does not contribute to local incomes. A more satisfactory measure of the output that stays in Ireland is gross national product (GNP): it starts with GDP and adds net factor income from the rest of the world (NFIROW). In 2010 these amounts, in billions of euros, were as follows:

GNP	=	GDP	+	NFIROW
124.9	=	153.9	+	-29.1

The most striking feature of these numbers is the uncommonly large value of transfer payments out of Ireland, mainly the repatriation of profits by foreign firms operating in Ireland. An unknown, although no doubt significant, part of the factor income flows may be attributable to profit outflows that reflect transfer pricing, as some corporations overstate their exports and understate their imports in order to book their profits in low-tax Ireland – the corporation income tax is just 12.5 per cent, compared to 35 per cent in the USA. As a result of this measurement error, reported GDP may overstate 'true' GDP by as much as 10 per cent.

This makes a difference: in 2009, seventeen countries had levels of GDP per capita that were higher than Ireland's GNP per capita, making the Irish case look far less exceptional. Using GNP rather than GDP per capita, Ireland passed the UK level in 2006 and is very close to the Danish level, but still remains well below the level in the USA, as Figure 7.1 shows.

Other Measures of Living Standards
We have seen that Ireland has caught up with its European peers, as measured by GNP per capita. This is now true of most other measures of living standards, although in most of these cases the improvements lagged the rise in GNP per capita by a few years. The most striking feature of Table 7.1, which shows a selection of measures of living standards, is how similar Ireland now looks to the rest of the European Union.

Ireland's life expectancy continues to rise, and it has surpassed the EU average for both men and women. The infant mortality rate – defined as the number of deaths of infants up to six months old per 1,000 population – is very low by historical standards, and is now well below the EU average. These measures, considered to be good indicators of health outcomes in general, show that Ireland has now caught up with the standards that prevail in Western Europe (see also Chapter 12).

GNP represents an annual flow of final goods and services; even when GNP rises, it can take time to build up a good stock of assets – cars, houses, and fine roads. This helps explain why Irish visitors to France, for instance, are often struck by the high quality of the infrastructure, in a country whose consumption per capita is now appreciably lower than that of Ireland (see Chapter 10). However, Table 7.1 shows evidence of catch-up: car ownership per capita rose by an astonishing 141 per cent between 1990 and 2008, a measure that goes a long way towards explaining the increasingly high levels of congestion on Irish roads. House building rose above the long-term sustainable level after 2001; where Ireland had 330 houses per thousand people in 1990, this figure had risen to 440 by 2007, despite a 22 per cent increase in the population over the same period, bringing Ireland close to the EU average of 450 houses per thousand people.

Ireland is also connecting fast. The stock of telecommunications assets has risen remarkably, with a tripling in the number of mainline phones between 1980 and 2002; there is high mobile phone penetration – more than one such phone per person! – although home use of the Internet, at 67 per cent, is only marginally above the EU-27 average (65 per cent), and well below the 90 per cent rate seen in the Netherlands. There has also been an explosion in airline traffic.

Table 7.1

Indicators of the Quality of Life

	Ireland			EU-27	USA	EU-27 best
	1970	1990	2008	2008	2008	2008
Health						
Infant mortality rate	20	8	3.1	4.7	6.1	1.8
Life expectancy, F	74	77	82.1	81.5	80.4	84.8
Life expectancy, M	69	72	77.4	75.4	75.4	79.0
Crime						
Crimes/1,000	–	–	21	65	37	131
Prisoners/100,000	–	–	72	87	529	131
Homicides/millions	–	6	8	10	56	4
Environment						
CO_2/capita, t	6	9	10.6	7.9	23.2	24.8
Municipal waste, kg/cap	–	–	733	524	745	306
Particulate matter	–	–	12.6	28.1	–	12.6
Connectivity						
% hh, Internet	–		67	65	69	90
Airline pass, m	1.5	4.8	30.0	798	699	–
Fixed lines/1,000	–	281	390	480	518	670
Mobile phones/1,000	0	7	1,030	950	860	1,580
Human resources						
Third-level education			44.8	31.4	41.0	46.7
Total fertility rate			2.10	1.53	2.12	
Assets						
Houses/1,000	280	330	420	450	428	–
Cars/1,000	–	227	548	553	451	828

Sources: Central Bank of Ireland, *Bulletin*, Central Bank, Dublin (various issues); World Bank, *World Development Indicators*, www.worldbank.org [accessed April 2010]; CSO, *Measuring Ireland's Progress 2009*, Dublin 2010; US Census Bureau, *The 2011 Statistical Abstract*, www.census.gov [accessed May 2011].
Note: data for 2008 refer to 2008 or to the most recent available year.

By European and US standards, Ireland has a very low level of reported crime. The incarceration rate remains relatively modest, with an average of 3,881 prisoners in custody on any given day in 2009.

Tourism operators boast of Ireland's wild and open beauty – the woodlands were cleared by the sixteenth century – and its clean air and water. While water is relatively clean, and the levels of particulates in Irish urban areas are lower than in any other EU country, emissions of CO_2, the main 'greenhouse gas', now exceed the EU-27 average. Besides, Irish firms and households generate 733kg of municipal waste per person per year, the highest level in the EU, and close to the 750kg level of the United States.

There is another interesting way to evaluate Irish levels of affluence. The United Nations Development Programme annually constructs its *Human Development Index*, which combines measures of life expectancy, educational achievement (mean years of schooling of adults aged 25 and over; and expected years of schooling for those of school-going age), and the log of GDP per capita (in PPP terms) into a single index. The most recent figures refer to 2010, and rank Ireland fifth in the world with a score of 0.895 (out of a maximum possible 1.000). Ireland's Human Development Index has risen rapidly since 1980, as Table 7.2 shows.

Table 7.2

Human Development Index for Ireland

1980	1985	1990	1995	2000	2005	2010
0.720	0.739	0.768	0.799	0.855	0.886	0.895

Source: United Nations Development Programme, *Human Development Report 2010*, http://hdr.undp.org/en [accessed April 2011].

An unsurprising consequence of the increase in real incomes and consumption has been a drop in absolute poverty, particularly over the past decade and a half. Using a poverty line set at 60 per cent of average income in 1987, the proportion of the population in poverty was then 16 per cent, falling to 15 per cent by 1994, 8 per cent by 1998 and 5 per cent by 2001 (see Chapter 8). By then, those most likely to be poor were parents living alone (24 per cent), the unemployed (18 per cent) and children (7 per cent).

It appears that income inequality did not change substantially during the economic boom – incomes at the top of the distribution may have risen rapidly, but the increase in the labour force participation rate helped raise the incomes of those near the bottom of the distribution – although this conclusion is somewhat tentative given the difficulties inherent in comparing data from household surveys with different designs.[2] The most important implication is that the gains of rising incomes were spread widely, rather than accruing to any single group. Inequality in Ireland appears to be similar to that found in the UK and Italy, but is greater than in the Nordic countries and lower than in the United States (see Chapter 8).

Employment and Population
An economy's success could also be measured by its ability to provide employment for those who want it, and to sustain a larger population. Between 1960 and 1986 the rise in employment was negligible, from 1.05 to 1.09 million. Then came a remarkable, and historically unprecedented, burst of job creation, pushing employment up to 2.12 million by 2007, as shown in Figure 7.2 (see also

Chapter 6), before dropping sharply to 1.85 million as of the end of 2010. Between 1986 and 2007, employment rose from 31 per cent to 49 per cent of the total population, before declining to 41 per cent in 2010.

Migration flows have mirrored the changes in employment, albeit with a lag of a few years. There was immigration in the 1970s, when Irish economic growth was higher than elsewhere in Europe. Emigration resumed in the early 1980s, peaking at 44,000 (1.3 per cent of the population) in 1989. In due course the pendulum swung back, and about 150,000 people migrated into Ireland in the course of the 1990s, with a further 375,000 net arrivals between 2000 and 2008. The 2006 census showed that 21 per cent of the population was born outside the Republic, a number that is likely slightly larger now. This is substantially higher than in most other high-income countries, including the USA (12 per cent), and even Australia or Canada (19 per cent each). There was net out-migration of about 8,000 in 2009 and 25,000 in 2010, when employment in Ireland fell more sharply than in most other countries.

Figure 7.2

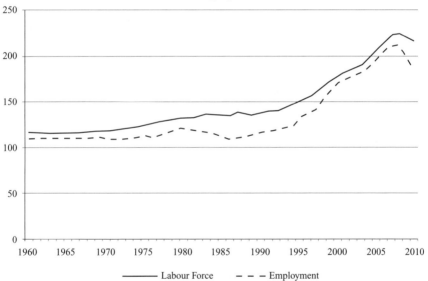

Labour Force and Employment, 1960–2010

Sources: World Bank, *World Development Indicators*, http://data.worldbank.org/data-catalog/world-development-indicators [accessed April 2011]; CSO, www.cso.ie [accessed April 2011].

The importance of the inflow of migrants can hardly be understated. Between 1997 and 2006 the total population rose by 609,000; during this same period a total of 575,000 people moved to Ireland. With out-migration essentially offsetting the natural increase of the population from births (minus deaths), recent population growth is essentially entirely due to the wave of in-migration. There were similar waves of immigration into France and Germany when they grew rapidly in the 1960s, but the welcome mat grew thin once employment growth faltered.

The unemployment rate, 5 per cent in 1960 and 7 per cent in 1980, surged to 17 per cent by 1986, remaining in double digits for a decade before falling very rapidly in the late 1990s to a low of 3.7 per cent in 2001, after which it edged up again slightly, reaching 6.0 per cent in 2008 and 13.6 per cent by 2010. The high unemployment rate of the 1980s was a consequence of slow economic growth, coming at a time of diminished employment opportunities abroad (particularly in the UK), a rapid increase in the working-age population, and a system of taxes and subsidies that made working un-remunerative for many low skilled workers. The recent surge in unemployment is a direct consequence of the recession.

One consequence of Ireland's poor track record in creating employment prior to the early 1990s was to keep many women out of the labour force completely. As recently as 1987 the labour force participation rate for women was 40 per cent, one of the lowest in the EU, although by 2006 it had risen to 64 per cent, somewhat above the EU average (see Chapter 6).

An Obsession with Output per Capita?
It is clear that most measures of living standards are correlated, if not perfectly, with GNP per capita. That is one of the reasons why economists and others tend to use GNP per capita as their primary measure of welfare.[3]

Is this an unhealthy obsession? In an oft-quoted speech (see also Chapter 2), Robert Kennedy in 1968 said, 'we will find neither national purpose nor personal satisfaction in an endless amassing of worldly goods ... the gross national product measures neither our wit nor our courage, neither our wisdom nor our learning, neither our compassion nor our devotion to country. It measures everything, in short, except that which makes life worthwhile.'

Perhaps the only way to respond to Kennedy's challenge is to ask people how satisfied they are with their lives, and then to determine whether these subjective evaluations are linked to GNP per capita. In a recent study in which a sample of adults were asked whether they felt excluded from society, 10 per cent of Irish respondents answered 'yes', slightly below the 12 per cent response for the EU-15 countries. Fully 92 per cent of Irish households reported that they were 'fairly' or 'very' satisfied with their lives, somewhat above the EU-15 average of 88 per cent; this lies below the level in Denmark (97 per cent) but well above the level in Greece (71 per cent). Commenting on the findings, Alber and Fahey write, 'the comparisons of countries across Europe [show that] ... the level of GDP per capita in the country in which the individual lives turns out to be the best predictor of individual life-satisfaction'.[4]

A more recent study ranked countries based on responses to surveys of (subjective) happiness that were administered to 80,000 people around the world. Ireland was ranked 11th, behind Denmark (first), Austria (third), Finland (sixth) and Sweden (seventh), but ahead of the UK (41st), the USA (43rd) and France (62nd). Interestingly, only one of the top ten countries in this study was poor (Bhutan), and it appears that individual happiness is strongly correlated with health, wealth and access to education (see also Chapter 2). A particularly strong (negative) correlation was found between happiness and unemployment; this is a likely channel by which the economic growth of the 1990s may have influenced well-being in Ireland.[5]

In short, Robert Kennedy overstates the case: GNP may not measure personal satisfaction, but it is closely correlated with it, in which case it is indeed a useful guide to happiness!

We are left with the conclusion that Ireland is indeed a rich country. The interesting question, then, to which we now turn, is: how did it get there?

3 DETERMINANTS OF IRISH AFFLUENCE

We have established that Ireland has closed the gap with Western Europe by almost all measures of affluence, and that most of the catch-up occurred since the mid-1990s. We now need to ask what explains this recent success, and why, by 2008, the episode of rapid growth had come to an end.

The immediate cause of the increase in the output of the Irish, or any other, economy is a rise in the inputs – the factors of production – used to generate output. The relationship between output (Q) and inputs of labour (L), capital services (K) and 'human capital' (H) may be summarised as a *production function* of the form

$$(1) \qquad\qquad Q = A(I).F(L,K,H)$$

where the function F(.) is increasing in its arguments. The term A(I) is usually taken to represent 'technology', but this should be interpreted broadly to include everything that enhances the productivity of inputs, including such things as better managerial techniques or regulatory changes that spur competition; the I refers to 'institutions', and reminds us that economic productivity is strongly influenced by the fundamental structure of economic organisations. Economic historian Douglas North won a Nobel Prize largely on the strength of his work emphasising the importance of institutional change – such as the development of private property rights, or patent law – in enhancing economic growth over time.

A first cut at the determinants of Irish growth may be obtained from Table 7.3, which summarises Irish economic performance since 1960, starting with the original 'golden age' of growth in the 1960s, the period of the first oil shock in the mid-1970s, the dismal period of the early 1980s (when per capita consumption declined), the early recovery that began in the late 1980s, the growth spurt of 1994–2000 when real GNP rose by 8.5 per cent per year, the echo of the boom, which maintained solid economic growth until 2007, and the recent recession.

Table 7.3

Measures of Recent Performance

	1960 –1973	1973 –1979	1979 –1986	1986 –1994	1994 –2000	2000 –2007	2007 –2010
				(annual growth rates, %)			
Output							
Real GDP	4.4	4.2	1.8	4.7	9.7	5.5	-3.7
Real GNP	4.2	4.2	1.1	4.6	8.5	5.5	-2.4
Inputs							
Employment	0.0	1.3	-0.7	1.3	5.8	3.2	-4.2
Capital services			-5.2[1]	1.1	6.2	6.1[2]	
Memo: capital stock			0.3[1]	0.2	2.4	6.0	3.1[3]
Output per capita							
Real GDP/capita	3.7	3.3	1.5	4.6	8.5	3.5	-4.7
Real GNP/capita	3.5	2.6	0.4	4.5	7.4	3.5	-3.4
Productivity measures							
Real GDP/worker	4.3	3.5	2.9	3.4	3.7	2.2	0.8
Real GNP/worker	4.2	2.8	1.8	3.2	2.6	2.2	2.2
Real GNP/capital services			6.1[1]	3.5	2.2	-1.2[2]	
Real GNP/capital stock			0.2[1]	4.4	6.0	-0.5	-6.4[3]
Consumption							
Real consumption/capita	3.2	2.7	-0.1	3.3	5.8	3.1	-3.7
				(levels in end year)			
Employment (millions)	1.06	1.15	1.09	1.20	1.69	2.12	1.85
Population (millions)	3.07	3.37	3.54	3.57	3.81	4.39	4.47
Unemployment rate	5.9	7.1	17.2	14.8	4.3	4.6	13.6

Sources: Central Bank of Ireland, *Bulletin*, Central Bank, Dublin (various issues); World Bank, *World Development Indicators*, www.worldbank.org [accessed April 2010]; CSO, *Measuring Ireland's Progress 2009*, Dublin 2010; US Census Bureau, *The 2011 Statistical Abstract*, www.census.gov [accessed May 2011]; M. Keeney, 'Measuring Irish capital', Central Bank of Ireland Research Technical Paper 13/RT/06, Dublin 2006.
[1] 1981–86. [2] 2000–4. [3] 2007–9.

The surge in economic growth in the late 1990s was associated with very rapid increases in the amount of labour used: employment rose by a remarkable 5.8 per cent per year. Employment growth slowed to an annual rate of 3.2 per cent between 2000 and 2007, still a high rate by any standard, but enough of a reduction to be reflected in sharply lower growth in output. Between 2007 and 2010, employment fell more rapidly than GDP; as discussed below, much of this was due to the collapse of the housing sector.

Properly measured, there was also a surge in capital services since 1994, so in some sense the growth spurt was also a marvel of capital. The capital stock of an economy changes over time as capital is added (investment) or subtracted (depreciation and scrappage). Prior to 1994, total additions to the capital stock

183

barely matched subtractions, which explains the very slow growth rate – for instance, the capital stock rose by just 0.2 per cent per year between 1986 and 1994.

There is a further wrinkle: not all investment is equally productive in the short run, so a thousand-euro investment in software should raise output by about €375 in the next year, while an equivalent investment in housing would raise output by perhaps €36 per year.[6] These reflect the flow of *capital services* that result from investment. In the 1994–2000 period, although the total capital stock rose by 2.4 per cent annually, capital services rose by 6.2 per cent per year; the explanation is that investment during that time was flowing disproportionately into capital with a quick pay-off. This is in contrast to the period 2000–7, when capital services rose less quickly than the capital stock, due mainly to the surge in investment in housing (which has a long slow payback) relative to other investment.

Between 1960 and 2000, GNP grew consistently faster than either inputs of labour ('employment') or capital, which means that, by any measure, productivity rose. This effect was particularly strong in the late 1990s, confirming, as seen earlier, that the growth spurt was also a marvel of productivity. To see this, it is helpful to work with a growth version of equation (1); using g to denote a growth rate, we have

$$(2) \qquad g_Q = \alpha_L.g_L + (1 - \alpha_L).g_K + g_A$$

which says that the growth of output (Q) may be decomposed into a weighted average of the growth of effective labour (L) and the growth of capital services (K) plus the growth of technology (A).[7] The weight α_L is typically taken as the share of labour income in national income. The last term is a residual that cannot be observed directly, but it measures that component of growth in Q that cannot be attributed either to growth in labour or growth in capital services, and so gives the *growth in total factor productivity*.

Some relatively recent figures on the growth of Irish total factor productivity (TFP) are displayed in Table 7.4. The pattern they show is quite remarkable, although somewhat exaggerated because they are based on GDP figures that are subject to measurement error. The figures indicate that between 1975 and 2001, Irish TFP rose by a total of 98 per cent (or 75 per cent if GNP is used rather than GDP), far outstripping the EU-15 mean of 39 per cent, and well above the total TFP growth of 32 per cent seen in the USA and Japan over the same period. There is nothing pre-ordained about TFP growth: since 1975 it also rose rapidly in Finland and Portugal, but hardly changed in Greece. The increase was particularly rapid during the last part of the 1990s.

Since 2000, the growth of TFP in Ireland has fallen almost to zero. Between 2000 and 2007, real GNP rose by 5.5 per cent annually; during the same period employment rose by 3.2 per cent and the capital stock by 6.0 per cent; these increases almost entirely 'explain' GNP growth; just 0.8 percentage points of growth are attributable to changes in TFP.

Table 7.4

Total Factor Productivity Growth, 1975–2001

	1975–85	1985–90	1990–95	1995–2001	1975–2001
		(annual growth rates, %)			(total % rise)
Ireland	*1.8*	*2.9*	*2.6*	*4.0*	*98*
EU-15	1.4	1.5	1.1	1.0	39
USA	1.0	0.9	0.9	1.5	32
Japan	1.4	2.8	-0.3	0.2	32
Finland	1.5	2.0	1.8	3.3	70
Portugal	1.9	3.6	1.3	1.8	71
Greece	-0.2	-0.1	0.1	1.9	10

Source: Spring Singapore, www.spring.gov.sg, July 2004.

In short, the nature of economic growth changed fundamentally between the late 1990s and the first years of the twenty-first century. We return to this point in more detail below.

During the recession – which we take to include the years 2008–10 – the capital stock rose by 3.1 per cent per year, while employment fell by 4.2 per cent annually and GNP shrank by 2.4 per cent per year. Technically, TFP fell by 2.0 per cent per year during this period, although a change like this is difficult to interpret.

4 FROM OUTPUT PER PERSON TO OUTPUT PER WORKER

Decomposing GNP per Person[8]

In one important respect, 1994–2000 stands out from the periods both before and after it: GNP per capita rose by 7.4 per cent annually, or about twice as quickly as at any other time. Yet GNP *per worker* did not grow especially quickly during this period. This apparent anomaly calls for an explanation.

The answer lies in the fact that about half of the rise in GNP per capita since 1994 is attributable to an increase in the share of the population that is working: even if these newcomers were no more productive than other workers (so GNP per worker remains unchanged), they would add to total output and, for a given population size, this would boost GNP per capita.

A more detailed decomposition is set out in Table 7.5. The identity shown there breaks down annual real GNP per capita *growth* into its component parts, and also shows the annual (log) percentage growth rate of each component for three time periods – the growth spurt of 1994–2000, the subsequent period of consolidation between 2000 and 2007, and the recent recession.[9]

Table 7.5

Decomposition of GNI/Capita Growth

$\dfrac{\text{GNI}}{\text{population}} =$	$\dfrac{\text{GNI}}{\text{hour}}$.	$\dfrac{\text{hour}}{\text{worker}}$.	$\dfrac{\text{worker}}{\text{labour force}}$.	$\dfrac{\text{labour force}}{\text{adults 15–64}}$.	$\dfrac{\text{adults 15–64}}{\text{population}}$
1994–2000					
7.1	3.1	-0.6	1.9	1.7	0.9
2000–7					
3.5	2.0	0.2	-0.1	1.3	0.4
2007–10					
-3.4	5.1	-2.7	-3.3	-1.4	-0.8

Sources: as for Table 7.1.
Note: totals may not add up due to rounding and approximation errors.

It is clear from Table 7.5 that in all periods, the single most important contributor to any rise in GNP per capita was increases in output per hour worked, which is the part of economic growth that the Solow model is designed to explain (see later).

This decomposition shows that an eighth of the growth in Irish GNP per capita up to 2007 was due to an increase in the proportion of working-age adults in the population (whose output was therefore not diluted as much by the presence of children or retirees). Even more important was the increase in the proportion of working-age adults in the labour force (the labour force participation rate). In the boom period of the late 1990s, but not since then, the rise in GNP per person was helped considerably by a rise in the proportion of the labour force that was actually working (which is the mirror image of the unemployment rate).

These factors, which were unusually favourable in the late 1990s, are sometimes referred to as the 'demographic dividend', although in earlier years the need to create jobs was seen as a demographic drag! Together they accounted for over half of the rise in GNP per capita during Ireland's growth spurt and for almost half of the (much slower) increase during 2000–7. The important point is that these factors are not expected to contribute much to growth in the years ahead, as the population ages, labour force participation reaches a plateau, employees reduce the hours they work per year, and the unemployment rate nudges back up (as it had already done by early 2008).

The numbers in the last row of Table 7.5 show that during the recent recession, people worked fewer hours, the unemployment rate rose, and some workers withdrew from the labour force. The surprising finding is that GNP per hour worked – a good measure of 'labour productivity' – rose sharply. There are a number of plausible explanations: the least productive workers may have lost their jobs; the least productive firms may have been the first to fail; job losses may have been concentrated in a low-productivity sector (housing); and workers may have put in more effort, lest they lose their jobs.

Explaining Output per Worker: the Solow Model

The demographic dividend has largely come and gone, which returns the focus to the determinants of changes in output per worker – one measure of labour productivity. To organise our ideas, it is helpful to return to the production function of equation (1). If inputs are doubled, it is reasonable to suppose that output would also double; more generally, this implies that equation (1) is linearly homogeneous in labour, physical capital and human capital. So we may write

(3)
$$\frac{Q}{L} = A(I).F\left(1, \frac{K}{L}, \frac{H}{L}\right)$$

or

(4)
$$q = A(I).f(k, h)$$

Used creatively, Equation (4) can be illuminating. It implies that output per worker (q) will rise if:

- the capital stock rises – via investment, mainly financed by savings – since this boosts k. (Note that by investment is meant the acquisition of more physical capital such as machinery, buildings, or infrastructure, and not financial 'investment' which merely amounts to a transfer of ownership of existing wealth);
- workers acquire education, training and experience, and enjoy good health, since this raises h;
- technical advance, innovation and institutional change occur, since these increase A(I).

These are useful, if rather obvious, conclusions. However, it is possible to make the analysis much more interesting.

Solow Growth Model
The 'workhorse' for understanding the role played by investment and other factors of production in economic growth is the model developed by MIT professor and Nobel laureate Robert Solow. Here we develop the model graphically and apply it to the Irish case.

The production function in Equation (4) may be graphed as the curve 0–q in Figure 7.3. It curves because of the 'law' of diminishing marginal returns: as the amount of capital per worker (k) rises, output per worker (q) also rises, but less and less quickly.

Now assume that a constant fraction, s, of output is invested. This gives the investment supply curve 0–s.q, which has the same shape as the production function but is only s per cent as high.

Figure 7.3

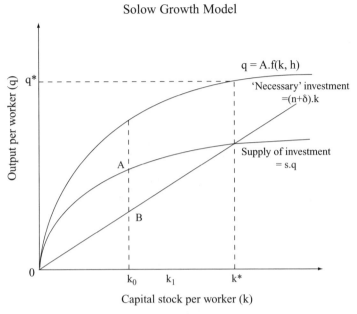

Solow Growth Model

To complete the story we may add a line that reflects the investment that would be necessary to prevent k (and therefore q) from falling. Simply to maintain the capital stock per worker, we need to:

- Invest enough to replace the wear and tear ('depreciation') of the capital stock; represented by δ; this is of the order of 5 per cent per annum in most economies.
- Invest enough to equip newcomers to the labour force; otherwise their arrival would dilute the capital stock and capital per worker (k) would fall. An n per cent rise in the labour force thus requires n per cent more capital for this purpose.

Taken together, 'necessary' investment per worker thus represents $(n+\delta).k$, and is shown by the straight line in Figure 7.3.

A poor country will have a low stock of capital per worker, such as k_0. At this point, the supply of investment (s.q) exceeds necessary investment $((n+\delta).k)$, leaving an investment surplus that will serve to deepen the stock of capital. Thus by the next year, the stock of capital will rise to k_1, and so on.

There is an important implication. Poor countries should be able to grow faster than rich ones, because their investment 'surpluses' are larger relative to Q/L.

Note that the process stops at k^*. In other words, investment alone can raise k to k^*, and therefore output per worker to q^*, but then growth stops – unless, of course, other influences can be brought to bear.

This has an immediate and interesting implication: economies should experience (conditional) convergence. For a given savings rate (s), technology (A.f(.)), employment growth rate (n) and depreciation rate (δ), all countries should converge on the same k* and hence the same level of output per worker.

Has Ireland Converged?

It is natural to ask whether recent Irish economic growth follows the predictions of the Solow model, in effect causing the Irish economy to converge to those of the rest of the EU.

This question may be addressed with the help of Figure 7.4, which shows GDP per worker in 1960 (in 2005 international PPP US dollars) on the horizontal axis and the annual percentage growth rate of GDP per worker from 1960 to 2009 on the vertical axis. In 1960 Ireland was relatively poor, grouped with Greece, Spain, Japan and Mexico. The Solow model predicts that poorer countries should grow faster than richer ones, until they have caught up: thus South Korea (initially poor) should grow faster than Switzerland (initially rich). It follows that we would expect the observations in Figure 7.4 to fall along a line that slopes downwards to the right, which is indeed what we see, with a correlation coefficient between the two series that comes to -0.55. Viewed this way, it would appear that Irish economic growth was no more than one would have expected. Taking the 1960–2009 period as a whole, then, it makes sense to use the Solow model to try to identify the proximate causes of Irish growth (in output per worker).

Figure 7.4

Initial Income and Subsequent Growth: OECD, 1960–2006

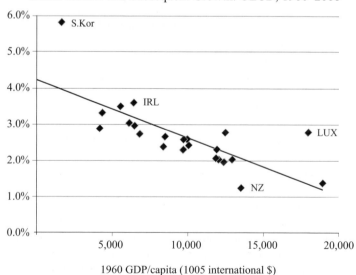

1960 GDP/capita (1005 international $)

Source: World Bank, *World Development Indicators*, http://data.worldbank.org/data-catalog/world-development-indicators [accessed April 2011].

Ireland is at the upper edge of these observations, suggesting that its economic growth (per worker) was somewhat higher than one would have expected, given the Solow framework. A case can therefore be made that Ireland has experienced a relatively rapid convergence. This calls for an explanation.

Applying the Solow Model

We now use the Solow model to help understand, in more detail, the factors that have influenced the growth of gross national income (GNI) (or GDP) per worker over the past decade and a half.

Investment

In the Solow model, a higher savings rate, by allowing more investment, would cause an acceleration of economic growth in the short run, and allow growth to continue longer *but not indefinitely*. In other words, even if Ireland were to invest a higher proportion of its GNP, it would not permanently grow faster than other countries.

Since 1997, Ireland's investment rate has been slightly higher than the EU-25 average of about 20 per cent of GDP. Table 7.6 shows that the Irish investment rate was particularly high in the 1970s and early 1980s, falling sharply for almost a decade before recovering somewhat after 1994.

Table 7.6

Gross Investment and Economic Performance, 1960–2007

	1973–79	1979–86	1986–94	1994–2000	2000–7	2007–10
	(average for period, as % of GDP)					
All investment	25.0	23.0	17.1	21.3	25.4	22.2[3]
Housing investment				5.5	10.7	6.5[3]
	(annual growth rates, %)					
Real GNP/ worker[1]	2.8	1.8	3.2	2.6	2.2	2.2
Capital services		-5.2[1]	1.1	6.2	6.1[2]	

Source: CSO, www.cso.ie/default.htm [Accessed April 2011].
[1] 1981–86. [2] 2000–4. [3] 2007–9.

All of the increment in the investment rate between 2000 and 2007 is attributable to a surge in investment in housing. The housing market is highly cyclical: this is clear from Figure 7.5, which graphs the number of new houses completed annually from 1970 to 2010. Given current population growth and other demographic changes such as the trend towards smaller households, there is a demand for about 50,000 new houses annually; in 2006, completions were almost double this level, clearly an unsustainable situation. It will take some time for the overhang of unoccupied houses to be put into use, especially if net emigration continues.

Figure 7.5

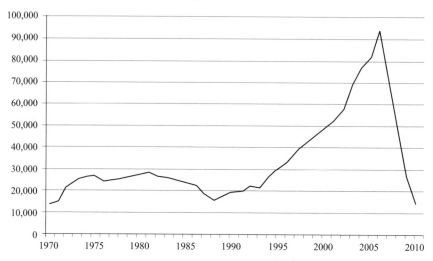

House Completions, 1970–2010

Source: Department of the Environment, Community and Local Government, *Housing Statistics*, April 2011.

It has been argued that the provision of capital services actually fell between 1980 and 1989, due in part to the accelerated obsolescence of equipment (especially for transport) that resulted from high oil prices. This situation is shown in Figure 7.6, where the broken line measures the evolution of the value of the capital stock, while the solid line tracks the evolution of capital services (i.e. the capital stock weighted by its annual productivity). In the early 1990s, as seen previously, investment went disproportionately to high-return activities (machinery, software, equipment); after 2000, investment was directed to long-lived assets, most notably housing.

With the end of the housing boom the investment rate has fallen. This need not be fatal: the United States has had an investment rate lower than the Irish rate for over half a century, but this has not prevented the USA maintaining its position of affluence. The trick is to use the investment productively, and this requires complementary inputs of skilled labour and technology – topics to which we now turn.

Labour Force Growth

The growth in total output (Q) consists of the growth in output per worker (Q/L) plus the growth of employment (n). Clearly, if employment grows more slowly, this will directly reduce the rise in output (for a given level of output/worker).

191

Figure 7.6

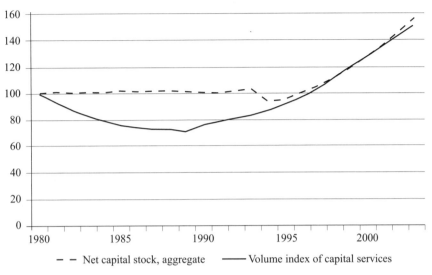

Capital Stock and Capital Services, 1980–2004

- - Net capital stock, aggregate ———Volume index of capital services

Source: Keeney, *op. cit.*

But there is an additional effect. The Solow model implies that slower growth in the labour force (n), by reducing the number of new workers who need to be equipped with capital, will delay, again not indefinitely, the time when economic growth *per worker* (i.e. Q/L) stops. Formally, when n falls the line 0-(n+d).k swivels down, and k* moves to the right (see Figure 7.3).

Between 1994 and 2000, the period of most rapid growth, employment in Ireland grew by a remarkable 5.8 per cent annually, significantly faster than the 1.1 per cent annual rise in the population over the same period (see Chapter 6). The rapid rise in employment was due to a large inflow of young people into the labour market, a resumption of immigration (of working-age men and women), and a substantial rise in the proportion of adults employed (with an associated dramatic fall in the unemployment rate). After 2000, employment grew only half as quickly, but still expanded by a fifth by 2007. By 2005, 67 per cent of the working-age population – defined as those aged from 15 to 64 – were employed, up from 52 per cent in 1994, and higher than the EU-27 mean of 63 per cent. '

The reversal since 2007 has been dramatic, with rising unemployment and falling labour force participation, especially for men, as Table 7.7 shows clearly.

During the boom years, the rapid growth in employment helped raise Ireland's total GNP, but the new workers had to be equipped with capital, which one would expect to restrain the growth of GNP per capita, for any given investment rate. Yet the growth of GNP per worker (q) continued to expand at its historical trend rate.

Table 7.7

Employment Rates, 1994–2005

	Ireland			EU-27	Netherlands[1]
	1994	2007	2010	2009	2005
% of population 15–64 employed	52.2	69.2	60.2	64.6	77.0
Male employment rate (%)	64.6	77.6	64.2	70.7	82.4
Female employment rate (%)	39.6	60.7	56.3	58.6	71.5

Source: CSO, *Measuring Ireland's Progress*, Stationery Office, Dublin 2010, Table 3.2.
[1] The Dutch figures are shown here because they were the highest in the EU-27.

This is a remarkable case of the dog that did not bark. Employment grew by 1.3 per cent annually between 1986 and 1994, and 5.8 per cent annually in the period 1994–2000. Simply equipping these additional workers to the standard of existing workers would typically require investment equivalent to about 14 per cent of output, or over a half of total investment.[10] Normally this would have halved the growth of GNP per capita, yet this did not happen.

In other words, the growth in GNP per worker was maintained in the late 1990s despite an unusually rapid increase in employment, a phenomenon that also characterised the Asian tigers, including Singapore and Taiwan, during the periods of their most rapid growth.

This requires an explanation. One possibility, still within the framework of the Solow model, is that the services of the capital stock expanded, and we saw above that this was indeed the case. Another possible explanation is that human capital improved, a point to which we turn below.

Human Capital
Education, training, experience and good health make workers more productive, and more employable. Thus increases in 'human capital' can boost economic growth. There are likely to be diminishing returns to additional human capital, which means that the effect, at the margin, on economic growth will eventually become negligible. Formally, an increase in human capital (h) will shift the curves 0-q and 0-s.q in Figure 7.3 upwards, pushing the steady state capital–labour ratio (k*) to the right.

Universal secondary education was only introduced in Ireland in 1968, and older workers are not particularly well educated by Western European standards (see Chapter 13). However, the recent expansion of higher education has created a well-educated cohort of young people; 45 per cent of those aged 25–34 had some third-level education in 2009, up from 27 per cent in 1999, and well above the EU-27 rate of 31 per cent. In passing it is worth noting that in Ireland women are substantially more likely than men to get tertiary education, as in all other countries of the EU, but the gap is especially wide in the Irish case, where 51 per cent of young women, but only 39 per cent of young men, have received higher education.

The improvement in the quantity of higher education does coincide substantially with the growth spurt of the late 1990s and 2000s, and undoubtedly played a significant role, although Ireland is by no means the European leader in this area. In 2007 Ireland produced locally 0.7 PhDs in mathematics, science and technology per thousand of population, in line with the EU-27 average, but well below the levels of Sweden (1.7), Portugal (1.4) and the UK (1.0).

On average, the Irish educational system provides a solid, if not spectacular, base (see Chapter 13). A standardised test administered to 15-year-olds in OECD countries in 2006 found that Irish students scored 517 in reading literacy (compared to an OECD average of 492), 501 in mathematics, and 508 in science (compared to OECD averages of 498 and 500 respectively). Only Finnish students performed consistently better at reading – perhaps Ireland is a literary society – but Irish students were in the middle of the pack when judged by their performance in mathematics and science (see Chapter 13 for more recent evidence, which suggests that performance was even less satisfactory).

Technological and Institutional Change
Logically, within the framework of the Solow model, the only potentially persistent source of growth is technological change, including institutional progress. Formally, this raises the A parameter year after year, which shifts upwards the 0–q curve (see Figure 7.3) and hence also the 0–s.q curve. That technological change is the only durable source of economic growth is not surprising; 'modern' economic growth, with its concomitant rise in popular living standards, only began with the Industrial Revolution in the late eighteenth century.[11]

Technology may be created or acquired. A narrow view of technology would focus on the creation and application of technology through spending on research and development (R&D). The numbers in Table 7.8 show that Irish spending on R&D, as a proportion of GDP, is low by EU standards: it is rising, but slowly.

Table 7.8

Research and Development Spending as a
Proportion of GDP, 1991–2008

	Ireland				EU-27	EU maximum: Sweden	EU minimum: Slovakia
	1991	1996	2001	2008	2008	2008	2008
R&D/GDP (%)	0.93	1.32	1.17	1.43	1.90	3.75	0.47

Source: CSO, *Measuring Ireland's Progress*, Stationery Office, Dublin December 2010, Table 2.4.

This level of spending is too low to explain much of Ireland's economic growth. But until recently, Ireland was a 'follower' country that, like China, could still acquire technology that had been created elsewhere.

The acquisition of technology is helped if a society and economy is highly open: to trade (making it easy to import goods, including investment goods, that incorporate improved technology); to ideas (so that managerial, organisational and institutional changes can be learned and copied); to foreign direct investment (so that international firms can bring best-practice technology and skills); to allowing labour market flexibility (so that resistance to technological change is low); and to competition (forcing firms to stay on their toes).

By such measures, Ireland has become a truly open society. Exports of goods and services in 2010 were equivalent to 102 per cent of GDP, similar to the situation found in most of the smaller economies of Eastern Europe. Irish exports rose by 125 per cent between 1995 and 2000, but increased by just 29 per cent in the following five years. Indeed, Ireland's share of world exports peaked in 2001–2 when it reached 1.35 per cent; two years later, its share of world services exports peaked, at 2.39 per cent of the global total. The real value of exports fell by 4 per cent in the recession year of 2009 – less than the drop in trade worldwide – and rebounded sharply in 2010 with a rise of 9.5 per cent (see Chapter 9).

Ireland is very receptive to foreign investment, which flowed in to the tune of 20 per cent of GDP as recently as 2002. By 2006 the flows had reversed, and Ireland had become an important source of investment abroad: in 2006, outflows of direct investment amounted to $22.1 billion, equivalent to 10.1 per cent of GDP; this was partly offset by $12.8 billion worth of inflows (5.9 per cent of GDP). Among EU countries, only Luxembourg, which is also an important financial centre, has flows of a comparable order of magnitude. However, there were modest net inflows of foreign direct investment in 2009 and 2010, perhaps reflecting an improvement in the country's competitiveness. Net inflows of portfolio investment were important in 2010; it is possible that Irish stock prices were low enough to appear attractive to outside investors.

Ireland's march towards openness is not new. It began in earnest in the 1960s with the Anglo-Irish Free Trade Agreement, and was boosted by EU membership (1973) and the advent of the European single market (1992). The Irish growth spurt of the late 1990s and 2000s may have required such openness, but Ireland was not unique among European countries – including those that grew far less quickly – in this respect.

5 GROWTH IN OUTPUT: A SYNTHESIS

Let us now return to the central puzzle of this chapter: what accounts for Ireland's growth spurt of the late 1990s, the continued strength of the economy after 2000, and the sharp slowdown by 2008? This is a puzzle that is all the greater because, as we have just seen, Ireland in the 1990s had almost no scope for changing fiscal, monetary or exchange rate policy.

The simple version of the story runs something like this: with relatively low taxes and macroeconomic stability, Ireland by the early 1990s was an attractive destination for US companies wishing to serve the European market. Investment flowed into export-oriented manufacturing, where it had a quick pay-off, raising output and employment very rapidly. As more households could count on steady earnings, the demand for consumer durables (especially cars) and housing increased, but with a lag.

This consumer demand was fuelled by cheap credit, made possible after Ireland switched to the euro in 1999 – the real interest rate essentially fell to zero, and consumers responded by taking out mortgages and expanding their use of credit (which rose by more than 15 per cent in both 2005 and 2006). The adoption of the euro also boosted Ireland's financial services sector. Over-exuberant developers built excessive numbers of houses, and the inevitable correction began in 2008 as the construction sector contracted; meanwhile, high wages, a strong euro and high prices cost Ireland its competitive edge in many export markets. The harmonised competitiveness indicator for Ireland, which tracks relative prices, rose from 93.7 at the end of 2000 to 122.1 by December 2007 – a sharp deterioration in competitiveness that made Ireland the second most expensive country in the EU at that time. The index has since dropped to 110.1 (by the end of 2010) as wages and house prices have fallen (see also Chapters 2 and 9). Nonetheless, having converged to European levels of output per worker (or per capita), Ireland is now converging to European levels of economic growth, much as the Solow model would lead one to expect.

Growth Environment
There are, however, four areas in which Ireland, wittingly or not, has espoused pro-growth strategies, or has been just lucky: the role of the state; attitudinal changes; social protections; and the US factor.

Role of the State
Like the USA, UK and Japan, but unlike most of the richer EU countries, the government sector in Ireland is relatively small (see Chapter 3) – if the recent bailouts of the banking system are not included. The low tax burden helps limit distortions to the choices that households make about work, consumption and investment (see Chapter 4). More specifically, Ireland's regime of low tax rates on corporate income makes the country attractive to foreign investors: the effective marginal tax rate on the profits generated by foreign investments in Ireland is estimated at 13 per cent, well below the OECD mean of 21 per cent;[12] formally, the corporation tax rate is just 12.5 per cent, compared with an EU average of 31 per cent and a US rate of 35 per cent – although these overstate the difference, because other countries tend to provide more tax breaks of one kind or another. Ireland also has the lowest restrictions on inflows of foreign direct investment of any OECD country.[13]

The relatively light weight of the state sector is possible in part because of low military costs, and health and educational systems that are inexpensive relative to their outputs (see Chapter 3). But one might point to 1987 as the turning point: in national discussions, the government promised to lower taxes if wages were restrained and labour peace restored. Thus began a dynamic that differs sharply from the European norm where governments typically promised more welfare payments, rather than lower taxes, in return for wage restraint. This is reflected in the structure of personal income taxes: an 'average' production worker who is married with two children would have disposable income equal to 103 per cent of gross pay in Ireland, compared to 96 per cent in the USA and 83 per cent in the EU (see Chapters 3 and 4). The comparatively modest size of the public sector – civil servants are not numerous (and class sizes are large), but they are comparatively well paid – has also kept in check the proportion of the public with a vested interest in raising taxes.

Some argue that much of the credit for the rise in employment in the 1990s and 2000s should go to national wage agreements that kept labour costs low and bought labour peace; they point to a reduction in strikes since 1987 – there were only six industrial disputes in 2007 – as evidence of the success of these efforts. However, this argument is not entirely compelling: labour unrest abated in most of Western Europe at the same time, without a corresponding rise in employment; and in practice, actual wage increases bore little relation to the rates negotiated in national agreements – hardly surprising given that Ireland's labour market is integrated with that of the UK and, increasingly, the rest of the EU.

One can also measure the weight of government by the extent of rules and regulations. Like the UK and USA, but in contrast with most of continental Europe, Irish rules protecting employment and product markets are relatively light, again a feature that endears the country to investors (see Chapters 3 and 4). The 1990s also saw a new government commitment to fostering competition (see Chapters 3 and 9), with changes that were particularly successful in the airline industry but have yet to affect some expensive and cosseted groups, such as lawyers.

Every year the World Bank publishes an 'Ease of Doing Business' ranking: in the 2011 version, Ireland was ranked ninth out of 183 countries, behind Denmark (sixth) and the UK (fourth), but ahead of Germany (22nd), France (26th), China (79th) and Greece (109th). The average rank for the EU countries was 37. Although Ireland was among the top twenty countries in five of the nine dimensions that are used to compute this ranking, it scored relatively poorly in its rules for property registration and, to a lesser extent, its procedures for enforcing contracts and dealing with construction permits.

Attitudes
Although it is hard to quantify, there appears to have been a change in attitudes over the past three decades, a change that favours economic growth. In the 1970s, college students tended to aspire to jobs in the Foreign Service, or as employees in well-established firms. Now they are more likely to want to be entrepreneurs. In 2007, 8.2 per cent of Irish adults were either thinking of setting up a business or had just started one; this was lower than the rate in the USA (9.6 per cent), but

substantially higher than in France (3.2 per cent), Japan (4.3 per cent) or the UK (5.5 per cent).[14]

There is no better metaphor for the transformation than the relative decline of staid, state-owned Aer Lingus and the rise of tough, profitable, private and entrepreneurial Ryanair, although this story has a twist because Aer Lingus has responded by re-inventing itself as a budget carrier.

By the 1990s Ireland's fertility rate, once the highest in Western Europe, had fallen close to that of a number of other EU countries, a symptom of changing attitudes, including an increasing disregard for some of the teachings of the Catholic Church. In the 1970s, over 90 per cent of Roman Catholics went to mass every Sunday; by 2005 this number had been halved. Curiously, the fertility rate rose during the recent recession.

It is difficult to account for the change in attitudes, but a case can be made that high unemployment in the UK and the USA made emigration less attractive in the early 1990s; forced to stay at home, but unable to find wage-paying work, many young, increasingly well-educated people started to improvise, learned to like the change, and began to succeed. With greater opportunities for success, attitudinal change was strengthened. At the same time Ireland became better informed about, and more closely attuned to, attitudes prevalent in continental Europe.

Social Protection

The comparatively small government sector has a price too – less social protection, including relatively modest spending on health, education and pensions, and fewer national cultural institutions. Government pensions and transfers (such as unemployment assistance) do reduce income disparities in Ireland, but less markedly than in almost any other EU country.

On the other hand, this relatively hard-nosed attitude towards social protection has probably helped economic growth. A decade ago, the structure of taxes and subsidies was such that, for low-skilled workers, it did not pay to go to work. This structure has now been rationalised, unblocking a serious barrier to employment; equivalent changes have been much slower to arrive in countries such as France and Germany.

US Factor

If the USA did not exist, Ireland would not have experienced a growth spurt in the 1990s, although since 2000 most of the economic growth has been home-grown. In the 1990s, four-fifths of foreign direct investment originated in the USA, and US firms now account for a quarter of manufacturing employment and about a half of manufacturing output and exports (see Chapter 9). The high-tech wave that lifted the US economy in the 1990s and 2000s washed over Ireland too, but not over most of the rest of Europe. The point is not that US investors raised the Irish investment rate, but rather that the investments they made, and the associated learning and external economies of scale, had a large and immediate effect on output, and employment.

It may now be more realistic to think of the Irish economy not as a region of Europe, but as an outpost of the USA attached to the edge of the EU.

We still need to ask why US investors steered so much of their investment to Ireland rather than, say, Scotland or Greece or Portugal or India. In part the answer is because Ireland made them welcome, with low taxes and other benefits. But Ireland has historically had close links with the USA; there are strong cultural similarities between the two countries; and they share a common language.

By 2006, foreign investors owned assets in Ireland equivalent to $41,700 per capita, four times the level in the EU countries ($10,980). Irish companies have begun to return the favour, and in the same year they held assets internationally to the tune of $29,110 per capita, well above the EU mean of $12,990 and higher than the US level of $7,960 (see Chapter 9).[15]

The Combination

In a nutshell, the Irish growth spurt occurred because all the economic planets came into alignment at the same time. The key elements: a booming US economy providing firms there with the profits to invest abroad; a 10 per cent tax on manufacturing profits to attract them to Ireland, coupled with relatively light regulation of labour and product markets; the lure of a pool of well-educated and English-speaking workers; the creation of a Single European Market that could be served efficiently from Ireland; a credible and conservative macroeconomic stance; wage restraint due to the inertia built into early rounds of national agreements; and a new-found attitude favourable to entrepreneurial activity (see also Chapter 6, in which a similar conclusion is reached).

Once the boom began, it led to a virtuous circle, raising the demand for housing and other construction, as well as for a wide array of services such as restaurants, banks and accountants. Although manufacturing employment peaked (at 318,000) in 2001, over 400,000 jobs were created between 2000 and 2007; perhaps surprisingly, given the attention that the sector has received, only a quarter of these new jobs were in construction (whose share of jobs rose from 8 to 13 per cent between 1998 and 2007). Large numbers of jobs have also been created in recent years in finance, health care and public administration.

A 1999 book on spatial economics presents a model of 'punctuated equilibria' that matches the Irish case rather well.[16] Consider a region that exports some good. Part of the export earnings are spent and re-spent locally; the computer exporter pays local workers, who buy restaurant meals from chefs, who spend their money buying haircuts, and so on. Now suppose that as the region grows, the proportion of export spending that goes into local purchases rises, which is plausible. Then it can be shown that as exports rise, local income will rise too, at first fairly slowly, then increasingly quickly, and then it will suddenly jump from one equilibrium path to another, before resuming a slower and steadier rise. Ireland has just jumped.

The Recession of 2008–10

This chapter is fundamentally about long-term growth, but a few further comments are in order about the sharp and painful recession of 2008–10. This exacerbated the slowdown that would have been inevitable in response to the end of the housing bubble, first by reducing demand for exports, and second by reducing inflows of foreign direct investment.

Two serious imbalances emerged very quickly. The first is the turnaround in public finances, from a general government balance of 0.2 per cent of GDP in 2007 to a general government deficit of 7.3 per cent in 2008 (compared to the EU-27 average deficit of 2.3 per cent of GDP), 14.4 per cent in 2009, and a truly stunning 31.9 per cent in 2010. A corollary has been a rapid rise in government debt, from 25 per cent of GDP in 2007 to 44 per cent by the end of 2008, and 94 per cent by the end of 2010. In retrospect, it is clear that part of this unravelling of government finances was due to an excessive reliance on taxes with a volatile base – such as on corporate profits, and stamp duty, which melted away in recession – and inadequate spending restraint in boom years. Although it was not obvious at the time, the government has been running a structural deficit for several years; the words of billionaire investor Warren Buffet certainly apply: 'you only find out who is swimming naked when the tide goes out'.

The second major imbalance is in the banking sector, which is effectively bankrupt. Over the past decade the major banks were too aggressive in lending, particularly for property; for instance, the average new housing loan rose from €75,000 in 1998 to €266,000 by 2007. The most dramatic case was that of Anglo Irish Bank, which grew particularly rapidly, but manipulated loans to directors and had close links with property developers (see Chapter 5); when its loans turned sour, it was nationalised in January 2009 and delisted on the Irish and London stock exchanges, at which point its shares were valued at just 2 per cent of their peak price. But the two largest banks are not in much better shape: government injections of €3.5 billion into the Bank of Ireland (March 2009) and AIB (May 2009) had little effect on their share prices, implying that the market considered them to be insolvent (see Chapters 2, 3 and 5). Private credit grew by 20.0 per cent annually during the 'go-go' years of 2000 to 2007; it fell by 5.5 per cent per year in 2009–10 when the banks' ability to lend was far less (and demand for credit low).

The problem is that the banks are carrying large quantities of non-performing loans ('toxic assets'). As long as these remain on the banks' balance sheets, the banks will be restricted in the amounts they will be able to lend safely, even for legitimate business needs – although after the excesses of earlier in the decade, perhaps a modicum of restraint would be appropriate. The government has established a National Asset Management Agency (NAMA) to buy the toxic assets from the banks. In principle, this would leave the banks in private hands while providing them with enough capital to lend. Meanwhile, the taxpayer would be stuck with the non-performing loans; with luck and a speedy return to economic growth, these assets might turn out to be valuable, but there is also a risk that they might end up being nearly worthless. The rapid projected rise in government debt is due in part to the anticipated need to borrow in order to acquire the banks' toxic assets. The situation is complicated by the fact that the banks will only be recapitalised adequately if the government over-pays for the toxic assets (or nationalises the banks, which would also amount to paying too much (i.e. €0) for institutions with negative net worth).

Other countries have weathered financial and economic crises comparable to that now faced by Ireland. Sweden saw a surge in private lending in the late 1980s, and asset prices rose by over 125 per cent in the second half of that decade, eroding competitiveness and weakening exports. Between mid-1990 and mid-1993, GDP fell by 6 per cent, unemployment rose from 3 per cent to 12 per cent, the public sector deficit ballooned to 12 per cent of GDP, and there was a 'tidal wave' of bank bankruptcies. In 1992 the government provided a guarantee to bank depositors, but forced the banks to write down valuations quickly and to liquidate bad debts, and required bank shareholders to accept losses ('take a haircut'), before injecting capital equivalent to about 4 per cent of GDP. The cost, up front at least, to the Irish government will be far larger than it was in Sweden, but the point here is that even difficult financial crises do have solutions. The IMF argues that Ireland is on the right track with its commitment to NAMA and to budget restraint, but that it will need patience and that 'the task ahead is formidable'.

The cost of the banking crisis is sufficiently high that it seriously eroded confidence in the country's financial institutions, and by late 2010 there were large withdrawals of bank deposits. To prevent a collapse of the banking system, the government was effectively forced to agree to an €85 billion 'rescue package' from the IMF, EU, UK, Denmark and Sweden. Of the total, €35 billion is said to be for bank recapitalisation and 'banking contingencies', while the rest is to finance the budget – in practice, the part that requires the capitalisation of NAMA. The interest rate on the rescue package funds is about 5.8 per cent; although higher than, say, interest on German bonds, it is lower than the interest rate on Irish government securities in the marketplace.

By absorbing the bank losses, the government has taken on an enormous risk: if economic growth falters, and the state finds itself with insufficient revenues, there would be a sovereign debt crisis.

6 WILL GROWTH CONTINUE?

The period of rapid economic growth is now over. The relevant question for the future is whether Ireland will be able to maintain its position as one of the most productive and affluent countries in the world. Sweden, once one of the most affluent countries in Europe, has in recent years slipped in the rankings. So has Japan, still struggling for an encore after its spectacular growth prior to 1989. Can Ireland expect the same?

'Forecasting is difficult' wrote Nobelist Niels Bohr, 'especially about the future.' Even so, some things are clear.

On the positive side, an interesting feature of the 'punctuated equilibria' model is that if exports fall, the economy will not decline as quickly as it grew. Having reached a higher plateau, the economy will be able to remain there relatively easily. This helps explain why most observers expect Irish economic growth to be in the range of 1–2 per cent in 2011, and higher than that in 2012. Moreover, corporate income tax rates remain low, entrepreneurialism is alive and well, and anticipated improvements in infrastructure and the regulatory environment are likely to help sustain growth.

Against this, the decomposition of Section 4 indicates that the 'demographic dividend' is essentially over, although in the short run there is a pool of unemployed (yet experienced) labour that is available to be employed.

Second, the Solow framework predicts that the *growth* in GNP per worker will eventually fall, although continued external economies and ongoing improvements in human capital and technology could postpone this somewhat. Such a fall has already occurred: labour productivity grew by 3.1 per cent annually from 1994 to 2000, but since then has risen by just 2.2 per cent per year (including during the recession).

Third, some of the economic planets discussed in Section 5 are going out of alignment: perhaps the most important is the rise of the EU members of Eastern Europe, which have quite explicitly tried to emulate the 'Irish model' and now provide cheap entry points to the EU market, much as Ireland did a decade and a half ago.

And fourth, Ireland became a victim of its own success. By 2007 it was a high-cost destination for investors, as the boom ran its course.

Even staying near the top of the GNP per capita ranking will be challenging. Irish education is good, not extraordinary; the investment rate is solid, but is no longer delivering the expected increases in labour productivity growth; government regulatory policies are fairly light, but the public sector is not universally honest, transparent or efficient (as the OECD points out in a recent report).[17] The World Economic Forum ranked Ireland twenty-ninth worldwide in 2010 in its 'global competitiveness index', and the *World Competitiveness Yearbook* ranks it twenty-first; whatever one may think of rankings of this nature (see Chapters 2 and 10), these do not point to overwhelming international confidence in the growth prospects of the Irish economy.[18]

Moreover, if investment and jobs can flow rapidly into Ireland, they can leave quickly too. In 2007, there were 292,000 jobs in industry; yet since 1970 an estimated 274,000 industrial jobs have been lost.[19] Given the rapidity of turnover of industrial jobs, the sector could shrink rapidly.

For now, the danger of complacency has receded, and it is useful to remember that Ireland has resilience. People are not afraid of working: the average retirement age is 64.1, compared to an EU-27 average of 61.2. More young people (aged 25–34) have acquired a higher education than in any other EU country except Cyprus. The air and water continue to become cleaner. GDP/capita is still well above the EU-27 average (in purchasing power terms). Labour markets are open, and workers will continue to flow into and out of the country with ease. Export competitiveness has already improved sharply.

Endnotes

1 World Bank, *World Development Indicators*, www.worldbank.org [accessed April 2011].

2 See B. Nolan, *Trends in Income Inequality in Ireland*, ESRI, March 2006 (Combat Poverty Agency Research Seminar).

3 In measuring living standards, it might make more sense to use gross national product (GNP) rather than gross domestic product (GDP). However, for most countries, GNP and GDP are very similar; and GDP data are published more quickly than GNP figures (which require measures of international flows of factor payments and transfers).

4 J. Alber and T. Fahey, *Perceptions of Living Conditions in an Enlarged Europe*, European Foundation for the Improvement of Living and Working Conditions, and European Commission, Luxembourg 2004, p. 51.

5 A. Oswald, 'Happiness and economic performance', University of Warwick, April 1997.

6 These measures of the rental cost of capital are the averages, over the period 1980 to 2004, as estimated by M. Keeney, 'Measuring Irish capital', Central Bank of Ireland, Research Technical Paper 13/RT/06, Dublin 2006.

7 For a derivation of equation (2), see D. Perkins, S. Radelet and D. Lindauer, *Economics of Development* (6th edn), Norton, New York 2006.

8 As discussed earlier, GNP relates to income and GDP to output. It was argued that in most countries both of these are approximately the same. This is not the case in Ireland, with the earlier statistics indicating that GDP exceeded GNP in some years by 16 per cent or more. It is also likely, though, that much of this discrepancy is due to the fact that GDP is not an accurate measure of output either, due to the transfer-pricing practices of multinational companies. While the true measure of output for Ireland is likely to lie between the GNP and GDP measures, we believe that it may lie closer to the GNP measure and as such GNP and not GDP will be used in this subsection.

9 This table shows logarithmic growth rates, which is why they may differ slightly from those given in Table 7.3.

10 This assumes a capital/output ratio of three.

11 The term 'modern economic growth' was coined by Nobel Laureate Simon Kuznets, whose *magnum opus* traced the growth of the UK and USA over the past two centuries.

12 K. Yoo, *Corporate Taxation of Foreign Direct Investment Income 1991–2001*, OECD Working Paper UnECO/WKP(2003)19, Paris 2003.

13 S. Golub, *Measures of Restrictions on Inward Foreign Direct Investment for OECD Countries*, OECD Working Paper ECO/WKP(2003)11, Paris 2003.

14 N. Bosma, K. Jones, E. Autio and J. Levie, *Global Entrepreneurship Monitor: 2007 Executive Report*, Babson College and London Business School, London 2008.

15 UNCTAD, *World Investment Report 2007*, www.unctad.org/wir [accessed April 2008].

16 M. Fujita, P. Krugman and A. Venables, *The Spatial Economy*, MIT Press, Cambridge MA 1999.

17 OECD, *Economic Surveys*: *Ireland*, OECD, Paris 2003.

18 World Economic Forum, www.weforum.org [accessed April 2011], *World Competitiveness Yearbook*, Lausanne, Switzerland 2010.

19 Based on information from the Department of Enterprise, Trade, and Employment, as reported in Department of Finance, *Budgetary and Economic Statistics*, Dublin March 2004. The lost jobs refer to notified redundancies.

CHAPTER 8

Social Justice: Distribution, Poverty and Policy Responses

Michael King

1 INTRODUCTION

Reducing inequality and eradicating poverty are key policy objectives for a small open economy like Ireland, both from a competitiveness angle and a quality of life perspective. Greater levels of equity and lower incidences of poverty afford more Irish citizens the opportunity to participate in the modern economy, reduce costly social problems and foster trust, co-operation and a greater sense of community.

Yet Ireland is characterised by significant inequalities and deep-rooted poverty. Despite the economic expansion of the last twenty years, in 2009 14 per cent of Irish adults earned less than 60 per cent of the median income, the amount deemed necessary to participate fully in society. When we consider the most vulnerable groups, we find that Ireland experiences one of the highest rates of child poverty in Europe, and significant poverty among the elderly. In terms of inequality, while Ireland is not exceptional by international standards, significant inequalities exist not just in income and wealth but in education and health status.

The extent of inequality within countries varies significantly. Data from the United Nations (UN) illustrates that the ratio of income of the top 10 per cent of earners to the bottom 10 per cent of earners ranges between over 60 in Bolivia and Colombia, countries with extreme income inequality and weak welfare systems, to less than 10 in many developed countries. In Ireland, the ratio of income of the top 10 per cent of earners to the bottom 10 per cent of earners is around 8, but in the absence of taxation and transfers the ratio would be 160.

Research suggests that there is greater income inequality between countries than within countries. Estimates from the IMF in 2008 suggest that the gross national income (GNI) per person is 205 times higher in Luxembourg, the world's richest economy, and 115 times higher in Ireland than in Liberia. The contrasts in income inequality are mirrored in areas such as health and education. Women are expected to live to the age of 84 in euro zone countries compared with 44 in Afghanistan and Zimbabwe. Literacy rates for people aged over 15 range from very close to 100 per cent for most developed countries to 33 per cent and 36 per cent for Chad and Ethiopia respectively.

A child born in rural Chad is likely to live to the age of 50 without the opportunity to become truly literate and will survive on lifetime earnings of $40,000, whereas a European child born into a middle- to high-income family will most likely enjoy third-level education of some kind, have an opportunity to live into their 80s and enjoy life earnings of approximately €3,000,000. While the contrasts may be less extreme, statistics show that children born on the same day in different parts of the same Irish city will enjoy different life expectancies, education opportunities and future income possibilities. This brings us to the question of 'what is fairness'? To help answer this question we start with the concept of social justice.

Social justice can be seen as the extension of the legal concepts of equality and fairness into the wider aspects of society and the economy. Recognising the dignity of every human being, social justice seeks greater levels of equality and solidarity in society. But how exactly do we define fairness? This, of course, is open to interpretation. At the core there are two approaches in thinking about social justice; equality of outcome and equality of opportunity. Achieving equality of outcome would mean the equalisation of income or wealth, and while the absolute equality of outcomes was tried in communist regimes in the twentieth century, all rich countries move somewhat in this direction through redistributive policies. We can turn to the American philosopher John Rawls (1921–2002) for the rationale for seeking equality of outcome. He argued that to maximise social justice the welfare of the worst-off person in society should be increased. Rawls specifically argued that in calculating total societal welfare we are solely concerned with the outcome for the poorest individual or family. Designing policy from this perspective would lead to very radical policy conclusions aimed at equalising income.

The second concept is the idea of equality of opportunity. Equality of opportunity is attained when all citizens enjoy an agreed norm of education and healthcare that opens up the opportunity for all citizens to participate and succeed in society. When accompanied with a basic level of income support for the poorest in society, achieving equality of opportunity is often the centrepiece of government policy. The focus on equality of opportunity with modest income supports was endorsed by the World Bank's 2006 *World Development Report*. The report defined fairness (equity) as a situation where individuals should have equal opportunities to pursue a life of their choosing, where a person's life achievements should be determined primarily by his or her talents and efforts, rather than by pre-determined circumstances such as race, gender, social or family background and be spared from extreme deprivation in outcomes, particularly in health, education and consumption levels.

This chapter is structured as follows. Section 2 explores the historical reasons for the development of inequality and poverty. Section 3 outlines the case for and against pursuing greater equality and poverty reduction, illustrating the trade-offs that can be present. Section 4 discusses the nature and trajectory of inequality and poverty in Ireland and Section 5 describes the political economy of redistribution, placing the Irish welfare system in an international context. Section 7 describes Ireland's policies that are aimed at reducing inequality and poverty, focusing on some practical examples. Section 7 concludes the chapter.

2 CAUSES OF INEQUALITY AND POVERTY

The obvious question for many is why is there so much poverty in the world? Why are some countries forty times richer than others? A better way of asking these questions is perhaps to ask why some countries are rich. The reality of human history is that for approximately 200,000 years humans survived day to day initially by hunting and gathering plants and berries, before progressing to small-scale farming in some regions of the world around 10,000 years ago. While some regions enjoyed concentrated but ultimately modest increases in economic well-being in the last 3,000 to 4,000 years (Egypt, Greece, the Roman empire and the Italian city states) due to innovations in finance, the development of trade routes and the concentration of political power, significant increases in income levels only began around 200 years ago. Modern economic growth began in the 1800s when the Industrial Revolution facilitated the division and specialisation of labour and began the process of urbanisation. Initially, only a small number of European countries, North America and other European colonies enjoyed the higher living standards that accompanied the Industrial Revolution.

Hence, the birth of significant global inequalities was not the result of some regions doing so badly, but others doing so extraordinarily well. During the last fifty years, some regions of the world have followed the path to modernity and high incomes, most notably significant parts of Asia; others, particularly Africa, have failed to join the transformation due to a combination of geographic isolation, poor government institutions and local conflicts.

Does this historical process tell us anything about inequality and poverty in countries such as Ireland? The answer is yes. The free market capitalism that drove the Industrial Revolution led to wage differentials within countries, between people of different levels of education, experience and skills. As a result, significant income inequality can occur in a developed country when there are differences in skill levels, health outcomes, or indeed any characteristic that is highly rewarded in modern economies, such as motivation, dependability and consciousness. For example, research in the USA attributed the rise in inequality since 1970 to the increase in wages for skilled workers which came about due to technological change, increasing trade and the decline of manufacturing.

Inequality from wage differentials can be deepened by unequal ownership of capital (wealth) in the form of financial or physical assets. Income inequalities in the past can cement current inequalities through the enjoyment of significant income from investments. The evidence suggests that the importance of labour and non-labour income in inequality differs by region. In Western Europe, non-labour income is the most important factor driving inequality, whereas in North America labour income is a more important driver.

Does the nature of economic growth mean that inequality will continue to rise? In a seminal paper, the Russian-American economist Simon Kuznets argued that economic inequality increases over time while a country is developing, and then after a certain average income is attained, inequality begins to decrease.[1] The prediction of changes in inequality as a country develops is depicted in what is known as the Kuznets curve (see Figure 8.1). Among many suggestions as to why this might be the case is the idea that owners of capital and workers in sectors with rising productivity benefit disproportionately in the early stages of development. As the capabilities of the state increase, however, improving education and health opportunities for all citizens and the emergence of redistributive policies gradually reduce the inequality.

Figure 8.1

The Kuznets Curve

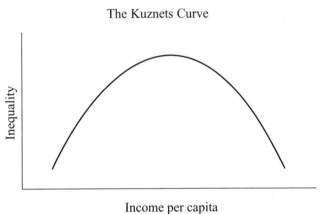

Income per capita

Evidence for the Kuznets curve is mixed as the structure of economic growth can be very different between countries. In the USA, inequality rose in the second half of the nineteenth century and declined over the twentieth until the 1970s, when it started increasing again. In the UK inequality also rose after 1977, after almost a century of declines following the initial rise during the Industrial Revolution. In Scandinavia, a region known for higher equality, inequality followed the Kuznets curve more closely, rising slowly between 1850 and 1900 before declining steadily thereafter. As the story of these countries attests, the relationship between income and inequality is not straightforward.

Irrespective of an aggregate relationship between per capita income and inequality, why do some high-income countries have higher levels of inequality than others? Research suggests that the greater the ethnic diversity in society the less focused are national policies on reducing inequalities. In the USA, research suggests that the percentage of the African-American population predicts less generous welfare systems. In addition, in cross-country studies, ethnic fractionalisation strongly predicts less redistribution and higher inequality.[2]

Policy can also play an important role in determining the level of inequality. Right-of-centre governments in the UK and the USA in the 1980s and early 1990s deliberately pursued policies of lower taxation and lower redistribution that increased inequality. However, the low level of inequality in Scandinavia is not the result of recent reforms because since the 1850s inequality in Scandinavia was always about half that in the UK and USA.[3] Rather than relying on the existence of an aggregate relationship between per capita income and inequality, it is better to focus directly on policies, or a combination of policies, which will generate economic growth without adverse distributional effects.[4]

3 BENEFITS AND COSTS OF REDUCING INEQUALITY AND POVERTY

Benefits

If everyone has a basic standard of living, is inequality something to worry about? While some level of inequality is unavoidable in society, people have always recognised the corrosive nature of high levels of inequality. Lessons that can be learned from inequalities in social relations at the level of the family or peer group can be reflected in national and international politics. As humans we suffer from innate feelings of insecurity and shame when compared unfavourably, and the opposite feelings of superiority and over-confidence when compared favourably. Adam Smith in his 1776 book, *An Inquiry into the Nature and the Causes of the Wealth of Nations*, pointed to the natural consequences of high levels of inequality when he wrote, 'The affluence of the rich excites the indignation of the poor, who are often both driven by want, and prompted by envy, to invade his possessions.'[5]

Intuitively, it is easy to understand how the quality of social relations can deteriorate in a more unequal society. Inequality affects our ability to identify with and empathise with other people. The literature suggests that in developed countries health and social problems are closely related to levels of inequality, not average income levels, while rates of mental illness are five times higher in the most unequal societies.[6] Similarly, in more unequal societies people are five times as likely to be imprisoned and six times as likely to be clinically obese. In addition, levels of societal trust and sense of community are demonstrably higher in more equal societies. While the evidence cannot be strictly considered as causation, the data is suggestive of an important link.

Inequality can also have important effects on people's expectations. Research published in 2004 outlined the outcome of a social experiment conducted with 321 high-caste and 321 low-caste 11–12-year-old boys from rural villages in India.[7] (The Indian caste system is a type of social structure which divides people on the basis of inherited social status.) The experiment was undertaken in two stages. Initially, the boys were asked to complete a set of puzzles without knowledge of each other's caste. In this scenario, the low-caste boys did slightly better with the puzzles than the high-caste boys. In the second scenario, each boy's name, village, father's name and caste, and grandfathers' names and castes were announced before the puzzle commenced. The researchers recorded a significant drop in the performance of the low-caste boys. Similar results have appeared in studies of whites and African-Americans in the USA. This research points to the reinforcing nature of inequality when expectation levels of different groups are affected by class or economic distinctions.

Inequalities can transcend generations. Intergenerational inequality begins with the handing down of accumulated wealth and personal expectations about life. When social mobility is low, inequalities are perpetuated endlessly into future generations, creating extreme inequalities. In addition, at the bottom end of the income distribution, some communities and families can be condemned to poverty for generations if equality of opportunity has not been successfully achieved. Over time, segmentation and ghettoisation can emerge as differences in wealth can enshrine differences in culture, education norms, sense of self and other indications of class identity.

Strong economic arguments also exist for reducing inequality and poverty in Ireland. As a small open economy, Ireland must remain competitive and succeed in export markets. First, as Ireland competes internationally on the quality of our labour force, a meritocratic society with full equality of opportunity reduces the losses from poverty when individuals do not reach their true potential. Second, Ireland needs to continue to attract the best international talent from around Europe. While high incomes undoubtedly attract some non-Irish nationals to Ireland, the quality of life, including, for example, low levels of crime and good social cohesion are also important. Third, the long-term costs of high levels of inequality are high. Higher levels of poverty and inequality are associated with higher levels of crime, lower levels of health, higher unemployment, and lower educational outcomes, all of which involve significant long-term costs to the taxpayer.

Costs

When the benefits of poverty reduction and greater equality are documented, one might wonder why high levels of inequality prevail in many countries. Indeed, there is research from the UK to suggest that a greater understanding of the effects of inequality can have a significant influence on people's attitudes to it.

However, the benefits of inequality cannot be considered without reference to the costs associated with policies designed to reduce inequality. There are costs to society incurred in the pursuit of greater equality, and concern over these costs go a long way to explaining why we do not see concerted political efforts to reduce inequality. Indeed, the history of the twentieth century is littered with examples of poorly designed policies pursued in the name of equality of outcomes that seriously harmed economic growth prospects by ignoring the costs of taxation and redistribution. Economists call these costs the *excess burden of taxation*, *diminishing returns to high tax rates* and *disincentive effects* (see Chapter 4).

The excess burden of taxation, also known as the distortionary cost of taxation, is the economic loss that society suffers as a result of a tax. First discussed by Adam Smith in the eighteenth century, the excess burden of taxation occurs because individuals or firms change their behaviour when a tax is imposed. An income tax, for example, reduces the return to working an additional hour, and thereby makes it more likely that the worker will choose to enjoy leisure instead of working for some part of the week. In business, the taxation of company profits reduces the return to investment, making it less likely that the firm will undertake a project. A sales tax such as value added tax (VAT) is perhaps an even more intuitive example. A sales tax on goods and services will increase the cost of the goods at the point of purchase, and thus, by the basic laws of supply and demand, will reduce the number of units purchased. These are hidden losses to taxation: hence the term 'excess burden of taxation'.

The level of excess burden for a given tax will differ between countries. For example, if citizens have high levels of work ethic, a tax on labour income will lead to a smaller reduction in the number of hours worked. High levels of work ethic have been cited as a reason why some countries, such as the Scandinavian countries, can prosper with high levels of income tax without significant losses in economic efficiency.

At very high levels of taxation, the excess burden of taxation can lead to diminishing returns to tax authorities. If the government increases tax rates beyond a certain point the tax base will begin to disappear. At very high rates of income taxation, people will simply choose not to work, will work in the informal economy, or will fail to declare their income to the authorities. The stories of the economic inefficiencies in the Soviet Union in the last century are testimony to the impact effective 100 per cent income tax rates have on individual motivation and private sector innovation. In a globalised world, where capital can move freely between countries, taxation on capital or company profits is perhaps the most obvious example of diminishing returns to high tax rates. If taxes on capital or company profits are increased to a high level, the capital can simply move jurisdictions. As a result, the presence of the excess burden of taxation and diminishing returns to high tax rates limits the ability of governments to tax.

An additional cost to high levels of redistribution can occur when transfers to the unemployed cause a proportion of welfare recipients to reduce their efforts to be self-reliant. Such transfers can in some cases act as a disincentive to finding paid employment. There is little disagreement that welfare payments are warranted for people who suffer from bad luck such as job loss or illness. However, welfare programmes need to be careful not to discourage the pursuit of paid employment among recipients. Any change in behaviour due to this disincentive effect is an economic loss to society.

211

4 INEQUALITY AND POVERTY IN IRELAND

In this section we explore the different dimensions of inequality and poverty, discuss different approaches to their measurement, and provide a full picture of the nature and extent of economic inequality and poverty in Ireland. We focus specifically on the concepts of equality of outcome and equality of opportunity defined in Section 1. For an alternative approach, we discuss the capabilities approach developed by the Indian economist Amartya Sen. Throughout our analysis, an attempt is made to highlight the life cycle approach to poverty and urban and rural differences that exist in Ireland.

Dimensions of Inequality and Poverty

Poverty and inequality can exist across four dimensions: economic, political, social, and affective (see Table 8.1). The economic sphere encompasses income, wealth and access to services; the political sphere is associated with the distribution of influence in the political process; the social sphere is concerned with the distribution of recognition and respect in the community; and, finally, the affective sphere concerns the distribution of love, care and solidarity. There is a tendency for social scientists to focus on the economic and political dimensions, and this is due in part to the availability of data on these aspects, but also due to the intangible nature of the social and affective spheres.

Table 8.1

The Dimensions of Inequality and Poverty

Economic	Income, wealth and access to services
Political	Representation and power relations
Social	Recognition and respect
Affective	Love, care and solidarity

Before focusing on the economic dimension, it is worth making a few important observations about the interconnections between the dimensions. Even in modern democracies, with the established principle of 'one person one vote', economic inequalities can lead to imbalances in access to political influence. This is particularly the case when private donations to political parties are not sufficiently regulated. The relationship between income level and enjoyment of love, care and solidarity is less straightforward. Low-income communities can be characterised by high levels of community spirit and strong family relationships. Conversely, we know wealth does not necessarily lead to personal happiness. Finally, the distribution of respect and recognition in society differs between cultures and ultimately depends on what is valued in society. In modern consumer societies, traditional reasons for respect, such as integrity and community involvement, can be overtaken by displays of wealth and exclusive memberships.

Inequality of Outcomes

Measurement

When we consider equality of outcomes, we typically think of income. In Section 1, a measure of income inequality was mentioned, namely the ratio of the income share of the top 10 per cent of earners to the income share of the bottom 10 per cent of earners. While this represents a good starting point, the measurement of inequality can be taken a step further with the development of a Lorenz curve. Developed by the American economist Max Lorenz in 1905, the Lorenz curve is drawn with the cumulative percentage of wealth measured along the y-axis and the cumulative percentage of households measured along the x-axis (see Figure 8.2). To draw the Lorenz curve, the proportion of income earned by the poorest 10 per cent of the population is calculated, followed by each additional 10 per cent of the population until the point is reached where 100 per cent of wealth is owned by 100 per cent of the population. The Lorenz curve simply joins the points on the graph that represent how much income is earned by each additional 10 per cent of the population. If income is equally distributed, each additional 10 per cent of the population will earn an additional 10 per cent of income and, since we are looking at cumulative percentages, the Lorenz curve would be a straight line emanating from the origin. This is known as the line of absolute equality and will have a slope of 45°. When we plot the data for a particular country, the Lorenz curve will bow away from the line of absolute equality down to the right. The more unequal a society is, the further it will deviate away from the line of absolute equality. Changes in the Lorenz curve over time illustrate the evolution of inequality in a country.

Figure 8.2

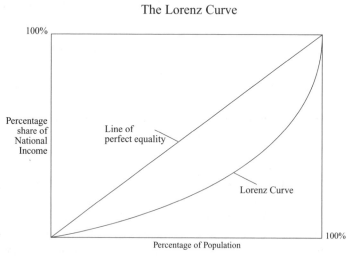

The Lorenz Curve

A related measure of inequality is the Gini coefficient. It is calculated as the ratio of the area between the Lorenz curve and the line of absolute equality (numerator) and the whole area under the line of absolute equality (denominator). The extreme values of the Gini coefficient are 0 and 1, although they are often presented as percentages, between 0 and 100 per cent respectively. A low Gini coefficient indicates greater equality in society, with absolute equality represented by a Gini of zero. Conversely, a Gini of 100 per cent means that the top 10 per cent of income earners enjoy 100 per cent of all income in society. The Lorenz curve is most often used to depict the distribution of income; if data are available it can also be used to illustrate the distribution of wealth.

Ireland's Income Distribution
How does Ireland perform using these different measures of inequality? Table 8.2 provides the data necessary to draw Lorenz curves for Ireland for different years. The table shows the distribution of disposable income after taxation and transfers in Ireland between 1980 and 2009. Overall, there is a remarkable degree of consistency, with the percentage of disposable income earned by each decile of the population remaining broadly constant over the thirty-year period. When the income shares of the top 20 per cent to the bottom 20 per cent are compared over time a number of points are worth noting. The ratio fell during the economically depressed 1980s but rose through the economic expansion of the 1990s. This can be attributed to an increase in the share of income enjoyed by the top 20 per cent of earners. After 2004, however, the income share of the bottom 20 per cent increased as the welfare state expanded, and as a result the ratio fell. The ratio fell further between 2007 and 2009, but this time because of a fall in the share of income enjoyed by the top 20 per cent of earners. Given the relationship between the Lorenz curve and the Gini coefficient, it is unsurprising that these

Table 8.2

Distribution of Disposable Income

	1980	1987	1994/5	1999/2000	2004	2007	2009
Bottom	1.7	2.28	2.23	1.93	2.1	2.2	2.4
2nd	3.5	3.74	3.49	3.16	3.04	3.5	3.6
3rd	5.1	5.11	4.75	4.52	4.27	4.9	5.0
4th	6.6	6.41	6.16	6.02	5.69	6.2	6.3
5th	7.9	7.71	7.63	7.67	7.43	7.7	7.7
6th	9.3	9.24	9.37	9.35	9.18	9.4	9.1
7th	11	11.16	11.41	11.2	11.11	11.5	11.0
8th	13	13.39	13.64	13.48	13.56	13.8	12.9
9th	16.2	16.48	16.67	16.78	16.47	16.9	16.2
Top	25.7	24.48	24.67	25.9	27.15	28.3	25.8
Ratio of top 20% to bottom 20%	8.06	6.80	7.23	8.39	8.49	7.9	7.0

Sources: CSO, *Household Budget Survey* (various issues); EU, *Survey on Living Conditions (EU-SILC)*, 2005.

214

changes are also reflected in changes in the Gini coefficient. Ireland's Gini coefficient fell from 32.4 in 2005 to 28.8 in 2009. Based on these measures, there is reason to believe that inequality behaved in a counter-cyclical manner in Ireland since 1980.

Table 8.3 places Ireland's performance in an international context, comparing Gini coefficients (after taxes and transfers) for twenty-three European countries, ranked by the 2009 Gini coefficient. The period was characterised by significant economic volatility, rising unemployment and destruction of wealth in many European countries. For most of the last two decades, Ireland experienced higher levels of inequality than many central European and Scandinavian countries. This seems to have moderated to some degree as the decline in Ireland's Gini between 2005 and 2009 has meant that Ireland has fallen from eighth place to thirteenth place in the group of twenty-three countries considered.

Table 8.3

European Comparison of Gini Coefficients
(After Taxes and Transfers)

	2005	2009	Change 2005–2009		2005	2009	Change 2005–2009
Latvia	36.1	37.4	1.3	*Ireland*	*36.1*	*37.4*	*1.3*
Portugal	38.1	35.4	-2.7	Netherlands	38.1	35.4	-2.7
Romania	31	34.9	3.9	Denmark	31	34.9	3.9
Greece	33.2	33.1	-0.1	Belgium	33.2	33.1	-0.1
UK	34.6	32.4	-2.2	Finland	34.6	32.4	-2.2
Spain	31.8	32.3	0.5	Austria	31.8	32.3	0.5
Italy	32.8	31.5	-1.3	Sweden	32.8	31.5	-1.3
France	27.7	29.8	2.1	Norway	27.7	29.8	2.1
Germany	26.1	29.1	3	EU-15	26.1	29.1	3

Source: Eurostat online database, http://epp.eurostat.ec.europa.eu.

Regional and Life Cycle Inequalities

Regional inequalities exist within Ireland, although these have fallen since 2000. According to Central Statistics Office data for 2008, residents of Dublin enjoy disposable income (after taxes and transfers) that is 12 per cent higher than the national average, while residents of the southern and eastern regions enjoy disposable income that is 3 per cent higher than the national average. This is balanced by 8.5 per cent lower than average disposable income in the border, western and midland regions. At county level, Donegal and Offaly are the counties with the lowest levels of average disposable income, whereas Dublin, Kildare, Meath and Limerick are the only four counties with disposable income above the national average. Differences in standards of living are likely to be smaller when differences in the cost of living between the counties are taken into consideration. There is also a rural/urban dimension to inequality, and extensive rural development policies are in place to deal not only with this but also to avoid the decline of rural areas due to migration

Inequalities can emerge at different points in the life cycle. For children, students in full-time education and the elderly, opportunities to earn money are limited and consumption is financed by parental support or the drawing down of accumulated financial wealth such as pensions. It has been shown that in Ireland and around the world, low-income households tend to have more children. This can lead to the situation where a small number of children have access to significant resources when growing up, while more modest resources are spread more thinly over a larger number of children. Such inequality is likely to lead to very real differences between socio-economic groups in education and health status. A second inequality related to the life cycle occurs when households fail to save adequately for their retirement. This can occur as people prioritise immediate consumption while working or fail to adequately anticipate their retirement needs. This latter issue has been exacerbated by the sizeable losses incurred by private pension funds during the recent financial crisis.

Ireland's Distribution of Wealth

Unlike many OECD countries, Ireland does not have a reliable survey of household wealth, although this may change if Ireland participates in the EU survey initiative on household finance and consumption. We do know that the explosion in asset prices up to the end of 2007 resulted in significant increases in household wealth for those with financial assets and those who owned property. Estimates from 2007 suggest that Ireland ranked second only to Japan in terms of personal wealth in 2006.[8] Estimates also suggest that the top 1 per cent of the Irish population held 20 per cent of the wealth, the top 2 per cent controlled 30 per cent, and the top 5 per cent disposed of 40 per cent of private assets. When the value of housing is excluded, the distribution of financial wealth is more unequal, with the top 1 per cent controlling 34 per cent of all wealth. These numbers suggest that wealth is more unevenly distributed than income in Ireland and this conclusion is consistent with international experience; even in countries with relatively equal income distributions such as Germany and Sweden, the distribution of wealth is very unequal.

Despite the fact that some older people in Ireland tend to suffer from relative poverty, a second group of older people enjoy significant personal wealth, where such divergence reflects the outcome of a lifetime of divergent income paths and investment decisions. This divergence occurred during Ireland's economic expansion between 1994 and 2007 as significant returns to employment occurred in some professions and at management level in the private sector, while stock market and property investments early in the period produced very high returns. As property prices and the stock market have fallen significantly since 2007, inequality in wealth will have reduced somewhat in Ireland.

Poverty of Outcomes

Absolute Poverty

Poverty can be described as the state of not having enough money to take care of basic needs such as food, clothing and shelter. At a broad level, poverty can be measured in either absolute or relative terms and is generally calculated as a head count indicator; the fraction of the population falling below a minimum standard of income. Absolute poverty is defined as the fraction of the population below some threshold of income. The simplicity of absolute poverty, and its specified income level, is undermined by the need to change the threshold income level as countries grow and the cost of living rises. For example, a measure of absolute poverty in 1960s Ireland would be out of date in the twenty-first century.

The theoretical distinction between inequality and poverty is worth noting. In our measures of inequality, some households (exactly 10 per cent) must by definition be located in the bottom 10 per cent of the income distribution. As a result, stagnant inequality is consistent with falling absolute poverty, where the poorer members of society are able to enjoy a superior standard of living.

The most famous examples of absolute poverty lines are the US$1 a day and US$2 a day used as part of the Millennium Development Goals (MDGs). Each year, the UN estimates the proportion of people living under these thresholds across the globe and it has been estimated that in 2008, 1.4 billion people lived on US$1 a day and 2.7 billion lived on less than US$2 a day. After 2015, the international community may decide that the US$2 a day poverty line is a more appropriate target. Moves in this direction have already begun. In 2008, the World Bank proposed a revised income threshold of US$1.25 to replace the US$1 a day threshold.

As the absolute income thresholds of the MDGs hold little relevance for high-income countries, nationally income thresholds are established that appropriately reflect expectations about the minimum standard of living. In the USA, the Census Bureau adjusts the absolute poverty threshold each year. In 2011, an income threshold of approximately $22,000 for a family of two adults and two children under the age of 18 was used.

Relative Poverty

The alternative approach, relative poverty, occurs when people fall behind, by more than a certain degree, from the average income and lifestyle enjoyed by the rest of the society. An advantage of a relative measure of poverty is that it does not need to be adjusted as average earnings change. Ireland's first official poverty measure, the 'at risk of poverty rate' is a measure of relative poverty and refers to all individuals who earn less than the threshold of 60 per cent of the median income. This measure is used by the National Action Plan for Social Inclusion and by the EU.

Each of these poverty measures focuses on income and such an approach can be criticised in a number of ways. First, there are limitations to income as a single identifier of poverty. Focusing on income alone fails to take into consideration

THE ECONOMY OF IRELAND

household characteristics such as savings or outstanding debts.[9] First, monthly income may fluctuate from year to year and so it poorly represents long-term income. For example, savings accumulated in the past adds to the capacity to consume now, while servicing accumulated debt reduces it. Second, the level of past investment in consumer durables and household assets influences the extent to which current income is available for immediate needs.[10] Third, households may be in receipt of non-cash benefits and services from the state or non-state organisations which would not be reflected in a measure of poverty based on income alone. Fourth, the non-consideration of work-related expenses such as transport and childcare may also affect the net income actually available to support living standards and avoid deprivation. Finally, regional differences are also important. Where prices are considerably higher in one part of the country than another, deprivation in high-cost regions might not be captured by a simple income-based indicator.

Reflecting these concerns, social scientists developed an approach to poverty measurement based on access to basic necessities. Basic necessities include food, heating, clothes, shelter and furniture as well as an ability to engage in family and social life. Ireland's second official poverty measure, known as 'consistent poverty', is a hybrid of this approach and the at risk of poverty rate described above. Households and individuals who are at risk of poverty (earn less than the threshold of 60 per cent of the median), and experience an enforced absence of at least two items from the official deprivation list of eleven items, are deemed to be in 'consistent poverty'. The list of eleven essential items is presented in Table 8.4.

Table 8.4

Eleven-Item Basic Deprivation Scale

Two pairs of strong shoes
A warm waterproof overcoat
New rather than second-hand clothes
A meal with meat, chicken or fish (or vegetarian equivalent) every second day
A roast joint (or equivalent) once a week
Had to go without heating during the last 12 months*
Keep the home adequately warm
Replace any worn-out furniture
Buy presents for friends or family once a year
Have family or friends for a drink or meal once a month
Have a morning, afternoon or evening out in the past fortnight for entertainment

* Presence rather than absence constitutes deprivation.

The absolute and relative measures of poverty discussed so far simply measure the proportion of the population falling below a minimum standard of income. They are, however, insensitive to the depth of poverty in the sense that transfers from the least poor to the most poor do not reduce poverty, but transfers from the most poor to the least poor may bring some households out of poverty. In this latter scenario, poverty may have been reduced but we cannot claim that social welfare has increased. This is known as a violation of Dalton's Principle of Transfers.[11] An alternative measure, which takes into consideration the depth of poverty, is the poverty gap measure. It weights the head count measure by how far a given household is below the poverty line and has the advantage of not violating Dalton's Principle of Transfers.

Evidence

How has Ireland performed by these various measures of poverty in recent years? Ireland experienced a decline in the 'at risk of poverty' rate (threshold of 60 per cent of median income) from 20 per cent in 2003 to 14 per cent in 2009 (see Table 8.5). A similar trend was found for consistent poverty, which fell from 8.8 per cent in 2003 to 5.5 per cent in 2009. The data suggest that the recent financial crisis and the increases in unemployment have led to an increase in the level of poverty before transfers are included and the level of consistent poverty for the first time in a over a decade.

Table 8.5

Key National Indicators of Poverty and Social Exclusion

	2003	2004	2005	2006	2007	2008	2009
At risk of poverty rate: [1]							
Including transfers	19.7	19.4	18.5	17.0	16.5	14.4	14.1
Excluding transfers	39.8	39.8	40.1	40.3	41.0	43.0	46.2
Consistent poverty	8.8	6.8	7.0	6.5	5.1	4.2	5.5
Poverty gap (EU definition)	22.4	19.6	20.3	16.6	17.6	17.7	16.2

Source: CSO, *EU Survey of Income and Living Conditions,* 2003–9, www.statecentral.ie.
[1] At risk of poverty rate refers to the 60 per cent threshold.

Research on the socio-demographic characteristics of households in poverty found that similar types of household suffered from 'consistent poverty' and were 'at risk of poverty'. The importance of education as a buffer against poverty is evident, as those without formal educational qualifications accounted for half of income-poor households in 2007. Families headed by a person ill or disabled formed an increasing share of consistently poor households over the decade.

When we consider poverty over the life cycle, important results are revealed. The period of economic growth up to 2007 was characterised by falls in poverty among children, the working-age population and the elderly. However, child poverty remains a serious problem in Ireland. By EU standards Ireland has amongst the highest rates of child poverty, with 6.5 per cent of children (66,000) experiencing consistent poverty and 23.4 per cent (237,000) in income poverty. While the association between lone parenthood and poverty is stronger in Ireland than in other similarly sized EU countries, consistent poverty levels for children

219

in lone-parent families declined between 2004 and 2007 from 24 per cent to 16 per cent, with a similar fall in the at risk of poverty rate.[12] While the progress was undeniable, poverty in lone-parent households remains an acute issue.

Inequality and Poverty of Opportunity

Because the data are so readily available, the analysis of economic outcomes can dominate consideration of issues of inequality; however, equality of opportunity is arguably a more reasonable policy goal. A focus on equality of opportunity is consistent with the natural dispersion of talent and motivation in society, and with a philosophy where economic outcomes should not reflect predetermined circumstances such as gender, race, place of birth, family endowments of wealth or ethnic group.

We can assess equality of opportunity with a measure of intergenerational socio-economic mobility, which captures how people fare in life relative to their parents. Equality of opportunity in education, healthcare and access to employment would mean that young people's outcomes, such as income or education, are not determined by their parents' outcomes. If this were the case we would say there is high economic mobility between generations. We measure economic mobility with an elasticity measure, where 0 represents the desirable scenario of complete economic mobility between generations and 1 represents a complete absence of economic mobility, a situation where a child is destined for the same outcomes as their parents.

Research in Brazil, one of the most unequal societies in the world with a Gini coefficient just below 0.6, has illuminated our understanding of the persistence of inequality and poverty between generations. It is estimated that more than a fifth of the total earnings inequality in Brazil can be attributed to predetermined factors such as parental schooling, father's occupation, race and region of birth. However, the role of predetermined factors is likely to be higher as important issues such as parental wealth, quality of schooling and gender were not reflected in this estimate.[13]

Studies of the relationship between the income levels of fathers and sons in high-income countries suggest significant differences. Elasticity estimates for the Scandinavian countries and Canada range from 0.13 to 0.28, depending on the methodology used, suggesting significant levels of economic mobility between generations. In contrast, elasticity estimates for the UK and the USA range between 0.4 and 0.6. It is no surprise that countries with more generous welfare systems and superior state services in health and education enjoy greater levels of socio-economic mobility.

The story of social mobility in Ireland is unique. In some respects, as Ireland has urbanised and developed into a modern economy since the 1960s, the absence of a long-standing class structure, at least within the Catholic majority, provided an opportunity for workers from all backgrounds to prosper. However, as norms of education and consumption diverged between those who prospered and those who did not, social mobility was destined to decline, but the economic boom of the last twenty years provided a golden age of opportunity for most. This assertion is backed by recent evidence that found that the era of high economic growth was associated with increased levels of social mobility.[14]

Nevertheless, one might expect that with low levels of redistribution and a return to modest growth rates, social mobility will decline towards levels in comparable countries such as the UK.

Capability Approach to Poverty and Inequality

So far our measures of poverty and inequality have been based on access to resources. Amartya Sen's 1979 essay 'Equality of what?' challenged the focus on economic outcomes and access to resources.[15] Sen argues that these approaches do not consider a range of important aspects of deprivation such as natural/social environment characteristics (pollution and crime levels, for example), personal characteristics (for example illness, which can reduce the ability to participate in society and enjoy material wealth), and freedoms in the political and social sphere. Instead, Sen suggests that poverty be considered as the absence of capabilities or states of being such as being nourished, being loved, being able to work, having an ability to participate in democratic decision-making or an ability to pursue one's dreams (see earlier discussion of various dimensions of inequality and poverty). We can consider a number of examples that vindicate Sen's approach, such as an elderly person with considerable material wealth, who is not properly looked after, reducing unnecessarily her range of capabilities; or a malnourished child with a parasitic infection who may have access to sufficient levels of food but remains malnourished. The merits of the capability approach are undermined by the challenges faced in adhering to Sen's ideas in a practical sense. However, it is worth keeping in mind that it remains an important critique of the more orthodox approaches discussed in this chapter.

5 POLITICAL ECONOMY OF POVERTY AND INEQUALITY REDUCTION

Political Preferences and Systems

Political preferences for methods of wealth redistribution and poverty reduction vary both across and within countries. Political theory suggests that as democracies emerge, there will be an increasing constituency favourably disposed to redistribution. This occurs because the small number of people who enjoy very high incomes will be out-voted by the majority of voters who earn less than the average income. An alternative theory points to an opposing force, where the initially wealthy use their disproportionate economic resources to influence political outcomes, preventing efforts towards redistribution. Cultural norms of solidarity and work ethic will also play an important role. As discussed in Section 3, political preferences for redistribution will depend not only on an understanding of the benefits of equality but also on sensitivities to the disincentive effects of high taxation and social transfers. All of these forces combine to define a country's unique set of preferences for redistribution.

Perceptions of inequality can be garnered from globally comparable surveys such as the World Values Survey. This survey is conducted across a range of countries and asks respondents in fifty-six countries whether they believe that incomes should be made more or less equal. The results are striking: in only eight countries the mean preference was in favour of greater income equality, with forty-six of the remaining forty-eight countries characterised by a greater preference for larger income differences as an incentive for individual effort. The countries that favour more equal incomes include Switzerland, Iran, Germany, Chile, Slovenia, Romania and India. These countries have Gini coefficients which range from 0.28 in Germany to 0.52 in Chile, suggesting that a preference for greater income inequality is not necessarily related to current levels of income inequality. A number of developing countries and Eastern European countries, such as Ghana, Mali, Peru, Indonesia, Thailand, Russia and Ukraine, report significant preferences for larger income differences as an incentive for individual effort.

In many societies, people have a strong preference for equality of opportunity over equality of outcome. When presented with the statement, 'It's fair if people have more money or wealth, but only if there are equal opportunities', the majority of respondents agree. In Britain, the USA and Germany, over 70 per cent more people agree than disagree with that statement.[16]

It is possible to observe the outcome of two hundred years of political preferences for redistribution in the welfare states across Europe. We distinguish between four different models. First, the Scandinavian or 'social democratic' model has a strong focus on social rights, a high degree of universality and is financed through general taxation and social insurance contributions. The Scandinavian model is considered the most generous welfare state and is associated with high levels of taxation. Second, the 'continental' or 'social capitalism' model is also characterised by generous welfare benefits, the difference being that benefit rights are often enjoyed by those who contribute through work-based social insurance schemes. Third, the Anglo-Saxon/UK model is primarily needs-based and combines modest universal schemes and extensive means-tested assistance. The fourth model, known as the southern European model, involves a more basic system of income redistribution, where the primary source of welfare is often a combination of the family, private charity and the Church, rather than the state. This type of model is in operation in Portugal, Spain, and Greece. The USA would be characterised as being at the less generous end, similar to the southern European model.

We can place these four welfare systems into a simplified left–right political spectrum. Ignoring for our purposes consideration of personal freedoms, we define the political right as a low tax and low redistribution platform and the political left as a high tax and generous redistribution platform. Referring to our approach taken in Section 3, the political right are more sensitive to moral hazard and welfare dependency, whereas the political left are more sensitive to those who are genuinely in need of state support. The Scandinavian and continental models could be characterised as more left of centre welfare models, while the Anglo-Saxon and southern European models, with their more modest levels of taxation, could be considered to be to the right of the political spectrum.

Evidence and Position of Ireland

Data from the OECD on Gini coefficients, before and after taxation and transfers, can provide a solid basis for the comparison of the depth of welfare systems and the level of personal taxation. Table 8.6 ranks OECD countries by the change in the Gini coefficient before and after taxes and transfers. Along with the Netherlands and Switzerland, the Nordic countries Norway, Finland, Sweden and Denmark have the lowest inequality after taxation and transfers. However, they are not necessarily the countries with the highest levels of redistribution. When measured as the change in the Gini coefficient before and after government taxes and transfers, Belgium, Italy, Germany, France and Poland, along with Sweden, have the most generous welfare systems. The data reveal that Ireland has a low level of initial income inequality but that our redistributive policy is very modest by international standards.

Table 8.6

Redistribution Effect of Government Policy

	Gini coefficient (before taxes and transfers)	Gini coefficient (after taxes and transfers)	Redistribution policy	% change
Belgium	0.49	0.27	0.22	44.90
Italy	0.56	0.35	0.21	37.50
Germany	0.51	0.30	0.21	41.18
Sweden	0.43	0.23	0.20	46.51
France	0.48	0.28	0.20	41.67
Denmark	0.42	0.23	0.19	45.24
Netherlands	0.42	0.27	0.15	35.71
Norway	0.43	0.28	0.15	34.88
OECD total	0.45	0.31	0.14	31.11
Finland	0.39	0.27	0.12	30.77
UK	0.46	0.34	0.12	26.09
Ireland	*0.42*	*0.33*	*0.09*	*21.43*
USA	0.46	0.38	0.08	17.39
Switzerland	0.35	0.28	0.07	20.00

Source: OECD Online Database (see www.oecd.org).

Categorising the Irish welfare model within the four models is less than straightforward. During the economic expansion in the 2000s, Ireland was able to pursue the joint objectives of increases in welfare benefits and a reduction in taxes. Conversely, with the economic downturn of 2008 and the ensuing budget deficits, Ireland was faced with the prospect of tax increases and welfare cuts. In normal economic circumstances, governments operate under a resource constraint and the typical policy choice is between low taxation and low welfare or high taxation and generous welfare. In terms of the four European models, Ireland is best described as a hybrid between the Anglo-Saxon model and the southern European model. Using indicators of service effort (benefits in kind as a proportion of GDP) and transfer effort (cash benefits as a proportion of GDP), Ireland, along with Greece, Spain and Portugal, can be characterised as having a low service and transfer effort. Within each category a distinction can be made between transfers which are means tested and those which are not. Ireland fits most comfortably with the Anglo-Saxon model insofar as it aims to provide universal minimum protection with an emphasis on means testing and flat-rate rather than earnings-related provision. Ireland and the UK are both exceptional in the EU for the high proportion of means testing. In Ireland in 2002, 24.5 per cent of all social expenditure was means tested.

Preferences Over Time

When we compare welfare systems internationally a striking stylised fact emerges. Most countries' chosen balance between taxation and redistribution endures over time. Preferences seem to emanate from deeply held convictions that change very slowly over time. Through survey data we can gain an understanding of the convictions of voters in different countries.[17] In the USA only 29 per cent of respondents surveyed believe that the poor are trapped in poverty. This contrasts with 60 per cent of Europeans who share this belief. In addition, 60 per cent of Americans believe the poor are lazy, while only 26 per cent of Europeans share this belief. In fact there is no reason to believe that this is the case.[18] It was found that 60 per cent of the members of the bottom quintile of the income distribution in the USA in 1984 remained in that quintile in 1993, while only 46 per cent of Germans in the bottom quintile of their income distribution remained in that bottom quintile nine years later. Besides, there is reason to believe that those in the bottom quintile of the American income distribution work far more hours than their counterparts in many European countries.[19]

Despite the consistency in preferences for the welfare system, changes can occur. The deepening of the welfare state has historically been associated with the sweeping to power of left-of-centre governments, often during times of great economic and political challenge such as the Great Depression or emerging from World War II. In the USA, one component of the policies pursued by Franklin Delano Roosevelt between 1933 and 1936, collectively known as the New Deal, comprised the Social Security Act of 1935. The act enshrined in USA law for the first time the right to benefits for retirees and the unemployed. In the UK, following World War II, Clement Attlee's Labour government not only established the universal public health care system, the

National Health Service, but introduced significant welfare benefits such as flat-rate pensions, sickness benefit, unemployment benefit, child benefit and funeral benefit.

Reverses to the welfare system are also possible. As noted in Section 2, the emergence of centre right governments in the early 1980s in the USA and the UK led to an increase in inequality as welfare states were weakened and taxes reduced.

In Ireland, the domination of centrist populist political parties since the foundation of the state has meant the slow evolution of the welfare state and the absence of revolutionary reform. The current crisis may have provided the opportunity for a radical revision of the Irish welfare state, either a strengthening of its reach or its reduction to lessen the excess burden of taxation and disincentive effects. In the watershed general election of 2011, Ireland elected a centrist coalition, and with a high likelihood of both increased taxes and reductions in state benefits due to fiscal tightening, it seems unlikely that significant reform in either direction will be possible in the foreseeable future. Nevertheless, the 2011 election has seen a historical peak in first preferences for left-wing parties and independents.

As Ireland emerges from the current downturn, a very serious underlying political economy issue will take centre stage in Irish politics and that is the issue of an ageing population that will make up an even bigger proportion of the voting public. The ageing population who have paid taxes right through their working lives will expect that, even in challenging times for the public finances, old age pensions are maintained at reasonable levels. As the Irish population ages and people live longer, the influence of pensioners in the Irish political system will increase over time.

6 POLICY EFFORTS AND CHALLENGES

In the pursuit of social justice a number of alternative approaches can be taken by governments. The legislative framework provides the rules that underpin equal opportunity. However, the achievement of equal opportunity takes considerably more effort than the existence of legal rights. The provision of public minimum levels of education and health care needs to be supplemented by a minimum standard of living for all citizens to ensure that social mobility between generations is possible and that people are fully rewarded for their talents and efforts irrespective of social background. This section describes Ireland's policies aimed at reducing inequality and poverty and focuses on Ireland's policy responses, social transfers in particular, towards vulnerable groups. It is worth noting that the public provision of education and healthcare remain essential to the pursuit of equality of opportunity and this aspect of education and health policies is covered in detail in Chapters 12 and 13.

Equality Legislation

The starting point for pursuing equality of opportunity is legislation. There have been several important policy and legislative changes to progress equality in Ireland over the last number of years. These include the adoption of equality legislation – the Employment Equality Act 1998 and the Equal Status Act 2000 – and the establishment of equality institutions – the Equality Authority and the Office of the Director of Equality Investigations. The Employment Equality Act outlaws discrimination in employment on nine distinct grounds: gender, family status, marital status, age, disability, sexual orientation, religion, race and membership of the Traveller community. The Equal Status Act goes a step further, providing comprehensive legal protection against discrimination in the delivery of goods and services, whether provided by the state or the private sector. Further, the establishment of the Disability Authority and the Human Rights Commission are also developments with potential to contribute to reducing poverty, inequality and discrimination.

Social Transfers

Social transfers represent the foundation of the modern welfare state (see Chapter 3) and they come in various guises, each with different effects on incentives and social justice. Transfers can differ in coverage levels, either universal or targeted, and form taken, money or in-kind transfers.

Universal payments are paid regardless of a person's income or social insurance record. Universal cash entitlements can be simple to administer, but fail to discriminate between deserving and non-deserving cases. An excellent example of a universal entitlement is child benefit, which was introduced in 1944.

Effective targeting of entitlements can be considered more socially just, particularly when the savings from targeting outweighs the administrative costs of means testing. Examples of targeted benefits provided to citizens once a means test is satisfied include the family income supplement for the low paid and the one-parent family payment. The jobseeker's allowance involves a different form of conditionality. To receive the jobseeker's allowance one must be unemployed but available for and genuinely seeking work. The weekly benefit is €188. In Budget 2010 this was reduced for those under the age of 25 to encourage engagement in training and further education (see also Chapter 6).

Economic theory suggests that cash transfers are preferred by recipients because it allows them to choose their preferred basket of goods. In contrast, in-kind transfers allow a paternalistic state to tilt recipients' expenditure patterns towards goods and services deemed in their interest to consume, such as fuel and education. Examples in Ireland of in-kind entitlements include the fuel allowance given to the elderly as well as the public provision of healthcare and education (see Chapters 12 and 13). If the recipient does not derive satisfaction from the in-kind transfer provided, they would have been better off receiving the transfer in cash to spend on goods of their choosing.

Table 8.7 outlines the multi-faceted nature of the Irish welfare system. Social transfers exist for a variety of groups who have experienced adverse outcomes, such as the unemployed, the low paid, individuals who experience illness or disability and bereaved partners. Groups at risk of poverty such as the elderly and lone parents are also provided for. A number of transfer schemes are subject to a means test on income or wealth, including the family income supplement, the carer's allowance and the fuel allowance as well as the non-contributory pension. Another set of benefits are provided conditional on a record of Pay Related Social Insurance (PRSI) contributions made while in previous paid employment. This chapter now delves into policies focused on two of the most vulnerable groups at risk of poverty: children and the elderly.

Table 8.7

Summary of the Irish Welfare System

Group served	Government intervention (type)	Complementary policies
Unemployed	Unemployment insurance, known as jobseeker's allowance (targeted) Back to work programmes (targeted)	Rent supplement Mortgage interest supplement Fuel allowance (means tested)
Low paid	Family income supplement (targeted and means tested)	Minimum wage laws Fuel allowance (means tested)
Children	Child benefit (universal) Early childhood care and education (both universal and targeted) Back to school clothing and footwear allowance (targeted and means tested)	Child protection laws
Lone parents	One-parent family payment (targeted and means tested)	Fuel allowance (means tested)
Elderly	Contributory pensions (conditional on PRSI contributions) Non-contributory pensions (means tested)	Free travel (universal) Fuel allowance (means tested)
Widow, widower or surviving civil partner (WWSCP)	WWSCP contributory pensions (conditional on PRSI contributions) WWSCP non-contributory pensions (means tested)	Bereavement grant (conditional on PRSI contributions)
Illness	Illness benefit (targeted) Blind and invalidity pension (targeted, means tested) Back to work programmes (targeted)	Fuel allowance (means tested)
Special groups	Disability insurance Carer's allowance (targeted, means tested)	Affirmative action for minorities Fuel allowance (means tested)

Children

As children represent the future of Ireland, government intervention is essential to reduce the high poverty rates among the young. Table 8.7 details four different policies aimed at increasing equality of opportunity and reducing child poverty in Ireland, two of which will now be discussed (the others relate to education policy).

Child Benefit

As a universal entitlement, child benefit is paid to all parents in the state towards the cost of rearing a child and it was increased significantly during the 2000s. The cost of child benefit to the state rose from 6 per cent of all social welfare spending to 15 per cent over the ten years from 1993 to 2003. In 2011, the rate is €140 per month for the first and second child, €167 for the third child and €177 for the fourth and subsequent children. With the need to reduce government expenditure a key priority, many have advocated that child benefit become a means-tested payment. From the perspective of social justice, this would seem to be an appropriate course of action, yet the administrative challenges of doing so have so far prevented such a change.

Lone Parents

In 2006, the government published a discussion paper on proposals for reforming the way the welfare system supports lone parents.[20] The report pointed to the fact that children of lone parents have a high probability of experiencing poverty. According to the EU's Survey of Living Conditions (EU-SILC) in Ireland in 2004, almost 50 per cent of individuals in single-parent families are at risk of poverty, while 30 per cent experience consistent poverty. This is much higher than the national figure and compares unfavourably to rates of poverty in two-parent families. To address this phenomenon, in 1997 the government introduced the one-parent family payment (OPFP), which provides a payment for men and women who are bringing up children without the support of a partner. To qualify for the one-parent payment one must be a parent or legal guardian, not living with a spouse, civil partner or cohabitee, have an income of less than €450 per week and satisfy a means test. In 2011, the OPFP provided a weekly payment of €188 for those unemployed or earning less than €146.50 per week, and €29.80 for each dependent child. If a parent or guardian is in receipt of the OPFP, they cannot also be in receipt of the jobseeker's allowance. There are two main differences between the OPFP and the jobseeker's allowance: OPFP recipients receive additional payments for each child; and they do not have to prove they are looking for work or engage in back to work training.

The 2006 Discussion Paper recommended that reform was required to reorient the incentives to encourage lone parents to enter the workforce. The report argued that passive income supports alone were not sufficient to comprehensively address poverty. There were perhaps good reasons for arguing that encouraging lone parents into the workplace would lead to an increase in household income and act as a good example to children and their peer group. However, one might also take the alternative view that because lone parents experience significant parenting pressures and provide an important caring role they should not be pushed into the workplace. As many of the recommendations of the 2006 report have not yet been implemented, the subtle debate over whether the current OPFP involves disincentive effects that ultimately condemn many one-parent families to unemployment will continue.

Elderly Population
Pensions Provision
As the Irish population becomes older in the next fifty years, issues of intergenerational equity will take centre stage in policy debates. At present a significant part of the Irish pension system is paid for by present-day taxpayers, whereby taxes paid by the working generation finance the consumption of retired generations. This is known as a pay-as-you-go system, which aptly describes the public component or first pillar of the Irish pension system as well as the generous pension scheme for public sector workers involving a commitment of a monthly pension of 50 per cent of final salary (adjusted over time). From the perspective of poverty reduction, the non-contributory pension provides a minimum standard of living for elderly people in the state.

The second pillar of the Irish pension system comprises private voluntary pensions and while just over 50 per cent of the workforce have enrolled in private pensions, their financial depth, even before the recent financial crisis, was insufficient. It has been estimated that middle-income earners would have to save an additional 10 per cent of income per year to provide a pension of 50 per cent of pre-retirement income. The third pillar typically refers to non-pension wealth such as other financial assets or property assets that can be wound down in retirement to fund consumption.

Part of the reason for the unsustainable public pension costs and insufficient private saving for retirement involves underlying demographic changes and each raises important issues of intergenerational equity. The OECD predicts that old-age dependency rates – the ratio of old-age dependents to working-age population – will increase in Ireland from an average of 20 per cent in 1990 to 45 per cent by 2050. This means that where the taxes of five workers were available to pay the cost of each elderly person in 1990, by 2050 OECD countries will have to rely on the taxes of two workers for each elderly person. Ireland will reach an old-age dependency ratio of 45 per cent about twenty years after the majority of western European countries, because of our high birth rates in the 1980s and significant immigration between 1993 and 2008.

In addition, the cost of healthcare has been rising faster than the overall cost of living (see Chapter 12): between 1996 and 2002, healthcare costs rose over twice as fast as the rate of inflation. As medical treatments become increasingly sophisticated, this trend is likely to continue, putting further pressure on the standard of living of the elderly population.

Intra-generational and Intergenerational Inequity

The unsustainable public pension costs, the insufficient private savings, and the high personal wealth of a small number of elderly people will lead to significant issues of intra-generational and intergenerational equity in future years. Public sector workers enjoy a guaranteed pension of 50 per cent of final salary, compared with significantly lower pension provision for the vast majority of workers with private pensions. In addition, the recent financial crisis has devastated many private pension funds, reducing further the monthly payments, while public sector pension funds have been unaffected. For private sector workers without private pensions, the contributory pension will only offer 20 per cent of final income if the final salary is twice the average income.

In essence, the taxpayers of today are paying taxes today for the currently retired, but the pension benefits are unequally split between retired public and private sector workers. In the medium term, as the old-age dependency rate rises to EU levels, Ireland will be faced with a significant transfer of resources from a shrinking working population to a growing elderly population. If public sector pensions are maintained at current levels, and the non-contributory pension remains at 34 per cent of gross annual industrial earnings (GAIE), significantly higher taxation, and associated costs, will be required to keep the promises made to the burgeoning elderly population.

Looming Pensions Crisis

A number of policy options exist to help Ireland deal with the looming pensions crisis and associated inequities, each with implications for social justice. These include: increasing the pension age; encouraging private saving for retirement; and reducing pension entitlements. First, increasing the pension age helps reduce the old-age dependency rate by increasing the number of people in paid employment. For those looking forward to retirement this may not be a welcome prospect, but efforts in this direction have already begun. In the National Pensions Framework published in 2010, plans to increase to 66 the eligibility age for the state pension were announced. A commitment to gradually increase the state pension age to 68 by 2028 was also given. If you are currently under the age of 25, it would be prudent to assume that you will not receive the state pension until 70 years of age. Second, the government can use tax policy to encourage people to save for their own retirement through private voluntary pensions. At present, taxpayers can avail of tax relief at their personal marginal rate of tax when they divert a proportion of the earnings into a private pension scheme. The current system discriminates against low earners. High earners can enjoy tax relief on pension contributions at the higher rate of tax, whereas low earners who pay tax at the lower rate can only avail of tax relief of 20 per cent.

To deal with this inequity, the National Pensions Framework has proposed that the current tax relief scheme be replaced by a state contribution equal to 33 per cent tax relief for all private pension contributions, but as of 2011 this has not been introduced. A complementary policy, introduced in recent years, is the mandatory offering of private pension schemes to all private sector workers over a certain minimum age. The third approach, the reduction in state pension levels, is perhaps the most controversial from the perspective of social justice, but is nevertheless a real possibility. With an estimated 10.1 per cent of GNP diverted to state pensions in 2056, if the 34 per cent of GAIE is honoured, the likelihood exists, however painful, that the state pension will have to fall. Increasing the pension age will reduce this cost to some degree, but the cost may still prove too great. The fourth option is to renege on promises to public servants and reduce public sector pension entitlement. While this is a challenging reform from a political and legal perspective, it should be considered a viable approach. The political obstacles to reforming the public sector pension system have meant that most changes are only relevant for new entrants to the public sector. The final policy option involves a deliberate attempt to increase the size of the working-age population in paid employment through immigration or an increase in the fertility rate. Such policies will help reduce the old-age dependency rate and provide much-needed revenue to pay for pension costs, but their usefulness is dependent on the availability of paid employment. The long-term solution to the looming pension crisis will likely be some combination of all four policies.

7 CONCLUSIONS

In most developed countries a broad political consensus prevails: policy should seek to ensure equality of opportunity accompanied by a minimum standard of living for all. As a result, political competition and debate generally focuses on modest proposals aimed at either deepening the welfare system in the pursuit of greater equality or strengthening individual incentives through tax reductions and smaller state benefits. Today's consensus is based on both notions of social justice that inspire redistribution and provision of public services, and lessons about the distortionary effects of high levels of taxation laid bare by the failed communist political experiments of the twentieth century.

Behind the consensus, the level of redistribution varies across countries, and these differences can be observed in the depth of the welfare state and the associated level of taxation preferred by voters. When we compared Ireland with other countries in Section 5, we noted that Ireland is characterised by low taxation and modest levels of redistribution by European standards.

However, it is worth noting that the policy of modest social transfers and the public provision of basic services is unlikely to lead to dramatic reductions in inequality and relative poverty within countries, for two reasons. First, even when high-quality education and healthcare are provided to all citizens, modest social transfers fail to provide a level playing field for children in the face of significant inequalities in income and especially wealth. The cross-country evidence suggests that higher levels of redistribution are an essential ingredient, along with the provision of public services, to achieve high levels of social mobility between generations. Second, as it is possible for some members of society to reject government provision of education and healthcare, opting instead for often higher-quality alternatives in private markets, the option to reject undermines attempts at achieving inequality of opportunity.

In the lead-up to the economic crisis, Ireland was in the fortunate and unique position of having sufficient resources to increase social transfers while reducing taxation. While this was unlikely to continue indefinitely, the speed of Ireland's downturn after 2007 and the depth of the subsequent fiscal crisis has cast doubt on Ireland's ability to afford the current welfare system. The need to reduce Ireland's fiscal deficit is likely to overshadow concerns of inequality and poverty in the short to medium term.

Nevertheless, while trying to balance the books Ireland should tread carefully. Lower inequality and poverty is an important cornerstone for Ireland's competitiveness, while reducing the long-term fiscal burden of challenging social problems. Of course, the primary objective of government is not to help build a high-income and successful economy as an end in itself, but as a means to supporting a trusting, co-operative and self-actualised society. Section 2 noted how more equal societies are specifically characterised by higher levels of trust and co-operation. It could be argued that now that Ireland has become one of the richest countries in the world, government policy should shift to building a more equal society with more meaningful levels of equality of opportunity. Voters will ultimately decide if this is a priority objective for Ireland in the coming years.

Once Ireland emerges from its current fiscal crisis, in election after election the Irish people will be asked to adjudicate on proposed changes to taxation and redistribution levels that will affect the degree of inequality and poverty experienced in society. On each occasion, a full understanding of the benefits of lower inequality and poverty as well as the costs to economic efficiency from higher taxation will be the starting point for debate as we ponder our future direction.

Endnotes

1   S. Kuznets, 'Economic growth and income inequality', *American Economic Review*, Vol. 45, No. 1, 1955.

2   A. Alesina and E. Glaeser, *Fighting Poverty in the U.S. and Europe: A World of Difference*, Oxford University Press, Oxford 2004.

3   F. Bourguignon and C. Morrison, 'Inequality among world citizens: 1820–1992', *American Economic Review*, Vol. 92, No. 4, 2002.

4   R. Kanbur, 'Income distribution and development', in A. Atkinson and F. Bourguignon, (eds), *Handbook of Income Distribution,* North Holland, Amsterdam 2000.

5   A. Smith, *An Inquiry into the Nature and the Causes of the Wealth of Nations*, Volume II, V, Part II, University of Chicago Press, Chicago 1976 (first published 1776).

6   R. Wilkinson and K. Pickett, *The Spirit Level: How More Equal Societies Almost Always Do Better*, Allen Lane, London 2009.

7   K. Hoff and P. Pandey, 'Belief systems and durable inequalities', Wold Bank Policy Research Working Paper, No. 3351, Washington 2004.

8   Bank of Ireland Private Banking Ltd, *The Wealth of the Nation 2007*, BOIPBL, Dublin 2007.

9   H. Russell, B. Maître and B. Nolan, 'Monitoring poverty trends in Ireland 2004–2007: key issues for children, people of working age and older people', ESRI Research Series No. 17, Dublin 2010.

10 C. Whelan, B. Maître and B Nolan, 'Multiple deprivation and multiple disadvantage in Ireland: an analysis of EU-SILC', ESRI Policy Research Series No. 61, Dublin 2007.

11 H. Dalton, 'The measurement of the inequality of incomes', *Economic Journal*, Vol. 30, 1920.

12 C. Whelan and B. Maître, 'Europeanization of inequality and European reference groups', *Journal of European Social Policy*, Vol. 19, No. 2, 2009.

13 F. Bourguignon, F. Ferreira and M. Menendez, *Inequality of Opportunity in Brazil,* World Bank, Washington DC 2005.

14 C. Whelan and R. Layte, 'Economic boom and social mobility: the Irish experience', ESRI Working Paper No. 154, Dublin 2004.

15 A. Sen, 'Equality of what?', Tanner Lecture on Human Values, Stanford University, 22 May 1979.

16 G. Marshall, A. Swift and S. Roberts, *Against the Odds? Social Class and Social Justice in Industrial Societies*, Oxford University Press, London 1999.

17 Alesina and Glaeser, *op. cit.*

18 E. Glaeser, 'Inequality', NBER Working Paper 11511, Boston 2005.

19 P. Gottschalk and E. Spolaore, 'On the evaluation of income mobility', *Review of Economic Studies*, Vol. 69, 2002.

20 Government of Ireland, *Proposals for Supporting Lone Parents*, Department of Social Protection, Dublin 2006.

SECTION IV

POLICY ISSUES IN THE MARKET SECTOR

CHAPTER 9

Manufacturing and Internationally Traded Services

Carol Newman*

1 INTRODUCTION

As history demonstrates, economic development brings a gradual process of structural change whereby a dependence on the agricultural sector in the early stages of development is replaced by a process of industrialisation creating a strong and vibrant manufacturing sector. Recent history has also taught us that a dramatic economic boom, such as that experienced in Ireland in the 1990s, can accelerate the pace of structural change, while harsh landings and economic bust can have profound short-term impacts on employment and output. In recent years, most developed economies have experienced a decline in the share of output and employment attributable to the manufacturing sector and a corresponding increase in the role and importance of services. Ireland is no exception, with the contribution of manufacturing to output declining from 34 per cent in the late 1990s to 27 per cent in recent years, a large proportion of which consists of outflows of profits of multinational firms. Rising costs have led to many manufacturing firms, including Irish-owned firms, seeking alternative production locations. This has happened to such an extent that recently Ireland has become a net investor abroad. As a result emphasis has shifted away from traditional manufacturing sectors towards high value-added activities such as high-skilled manufacturing and internationally traded services. This structural change will have consequences for Irish economic growth given the historical importance of the manufacturing sector in terms of its contribution to employment, internationally traded activities and aggregate productivity growth.

This chapter focuses on the key features of the manufacturing and internationally traded services sectors in Ireland. Both sectors contribute significantly to output, employment and exports, but both are dependent on the world economy, which makes them particularly vulnerable to world market conditions and unfavourable changes in domestic competitiveness. Increasingly the boundaries between what is classed as manufacturing industry and what is classed as services are blurred, making it difficult to discuss one sector without making significant reference to the other. In this chapter, a clear distinction is made between the modern and traditional manufacturing sectors with the former covering all high-technology enterprises, most of which are multinational corporations (MNCs), and the latter including all other sectors, the vast majority of which are indigenous. Non-traded and traded services are also differentiated. Non-traded services are those which must be consumed at the point of purchase (such as retail trade or hospitality), while traded services are those that can transcend borders, relying to a large extent on sophisticated technology and telecommunications networks. In this chapter we focus on the latter; the former are covered elsewhere in the book (see Chapters 5, 11, 12 and 13).

While the focus of this chapter is on long-run trends in manufacturing and internationally traded services, the consequences of the current economic crisis for these sectors, although transient in nature, cannot be ignored. During a recession, depressed world markets will reduce the demand for all goods and services, including Irish exports, and given the outward focus of the manufacturing and traded services sectors in Ireland this is likely to have significant short-term implications for their performance. Ireland's export performance is discussed in this chapter with evidence suggesting that Ireland has weathered this particular storm well, for the most part due to the strong performance of the internationally traded services sector. The collapse of the banking sector also has the potential to have at least short-term effects on enterprise development in general in Ireland by severely limiting the availability of credit to small and medium-sized enterprises, thus stifling entrepreneurship and the growth of indigenous firms. This is expected to be a short-term consequence of the crisis, however, given that the banking sector is currently undergoing significant restructuring and a change in governance so that it will be, for the most part, state run. This will allow credit for productive purposes to flow once again. These issues are addressed in Chapters 3 and 5.

The most significant, potentially long-term, consequence of the current crisis for the manufacturing and internationally traded services sectors is the complete deterioration of the public finances, leading to rising taxes on employment, and potentially profits, and limited funding available for providing the types of service enterprises need to grow and prosper. For example, essential public infrastructure projects may be put on hold, making it more difficult for firms in Ireland to do business and reducing Ireland's attractiveness for investors. Ireland's physical infrastructure deficits and other bottlenecks are discussed in detail in Chapter 10. A further concern in relation to the public finances is the extent to which government support for education, technology, innovation and research can continue into the future. The collapse in employment levels in the last three years, particularly in the construction sector, will have consequences for the manufacturing and internationally traded sectors if the displaced workers do not have the skills demanded (see Chapters 6 and 13). Moreover, Ireland's ability to innovate and engage in research and development (R&D) activities will be crucial if new opportunities in the high value-added technology and services sectors are to be exploited. It appears, at least for now, that these parts of government expenditure have been ring-fenced and are an important component of the government's recovery strategy, but the sustainability of high levels of investment is in question. There have also been some positive aspects to the current crisis for manufacturing and internationally traded services sectors that are worth mentioning. Ireland's performance in relation to cost competitiveness has improved, leading to falling costs of production for the first time in over a decade. Furthermore, with excess labour supply there are real opportunities for improvements in labour productivity at a new lower equilibrium wage.

While it is clear that the impact of the crisis cannot be ignored, this chapter is more concerned with the nature and importance of the manufacturing and internationally traded sectors and the broader issues of relevance to their growth and development. The remainder of this chapter is structured as follows. Section 2 begins by discussing the rationale for government supports for the manufacturing and internationally traded services sectors and discusses the role that direct interventions in the form of fiscal incentives and grants have played in Irish industrial policy over the last few decades. A brief discussion of the role of regional policy initiatives and the future policy agenda for Irish government is also provided. Section 3 looks at the nature and importance of the manufacturing sector by analysing trends in output, employment, productivity and exports. Section 4 describes the nature and importance of the internationally traded services sector and concludes with a case study illustrating the process of structural change from manufacturing to services that has occurred over the last number of years. In Section 5, the role of foreign direct investment (FDI) is explored, with emphasis on the importance of productivity spill-overs for economic growth. The increasing levels of outward direct investment (ODI) are also given some attention. Section 6 concludes the chapter with a discussion of some emerging issues relating to the strategic development of manufacturing and internationally traded services in Ireland.

2 ROLE AND EVOLUTION OF INDUSTRIAL POLICY IN IRELAND

Rationale for Government Intervention
Industrial policy covers all government interventions that affect the activities of firms operating in the industrial sector. The types of policy aimed at supporting industry are wide reaching, ranging from policies that affect the ability of firms to trade and compete on world markets to the direct provision of financial assistance to firms in the form of grants or tax incentives. The primary aim of industrial policy is to promote economic growth through creating jobs and facilitating productivity improvements. Modern industrial policy is increasingly of relevance to firms operating in the traded services sector who behave very much like modern manufacturing firms in terms of their ability to trade internationally, innovate and experience productivity improvements. This is reflected in the recent change in terminology used in Ireland from *industrial* policy to *enterprise* policy.

Regional industrial policy, as shall be discussed later, also plays a role in fulfilling equity objectives through redistributing resources to disadvantaged areas. In particular, promoting economic activity in rural locations affected by the decline in the importance of the agricultural sector has been a key feature of Irish and EU industrial policy objectives.

Aside from equity considerations, the rationale for state intervention in the manufacturing and internationally traded services sectors is justifiable where market failure occurs. Thus, the role for government in the provision of infrastructure, the education and training of the labour force and the promotion of R&D activities, all of which improve competitiveness and thus the productivity of firms and their ability to compete, is clear and economically justifiable. Infrastructural investments can be justified on public good grounds and this is covered in detail in Chapter 10. R&D expenditures confer positive external effects in the form of productivity spill-overs; as such the social return exceeds the private return, making private investment alone sub-optimal, thus justifying public R&D investments. Investment in education and training are covered by a number of justifications including public good and equity arguments but also information and credit market failures (see Chapter 13).

Direct financial supports to specific firms and industries are more difficult to justify on economic grounds. For example, providing supports to sectors that are in decline as a result of an inability to compete on world markets is not justifiable as no market failure has occurred. In contrast, government intervention to support a particular activity that is not taking place due to information failures is economically justifiable, for example the promotion of environmental awareness. Moreover, the productivity spill-overs associated with high-technology activities forms the key rationale for financial supports aimed at promoting R&D investments by the private sector and in attracting technology-intensive MNCs.

In fulfilling economic growth objectives, industrial policy increasingly focuses on creating favourable economic conditions so that firms can operate efficiently and compete effectively. Both the theoretical and empirical economics literature propose that a key determinant of growth is the extent of openness of economies in terms of both trade and capital markets. The past two decades have seen an increasingly integrated world economy, primarily through the expansion of the World Trade Organisation, both in terms of scope and membership. The role of industrial policy has thus moved away from providing direct financial assistance, towards: removing constraints to competition; facilitating productivity improvements through creating a low-cost environment, good physical infrastructure and encouraging R&D investments and productivity spill-overs; and promoting trade and foreign investment.

Key Features of Industrial Policy in Ireland
Ireland's approach to industrial policy has involved a combination of direct interventions in the form of capital grants and tax incentives for industry, and policies aimed at creating the right conditions for these sectors to evolve,

including labour market policies, policies aimed at encouraging exports and inward investment, and regional development policies. In fact, the most often-cited contributing factor to Ireland's growth performance over the last two decades was the change in policy emphasis, dating back to the 1960s, towards an outward-looking focus, particularly in the manufacturing sector (see Chapters 1 and 7). The key development that changed the nature of industrial policy in Ireland was Ireland's entry into the European Union (EU) (then the European Economic Community) in 1973 and subsequent commitment to free trade within the EU internal market. Not only did this add to the attractiveness of Ireland as a location for foreign investors, but it also expanded the size of the market for domestic firms. Ireland also benefited from the macroeconomic policy discipline imposed by signing up to the Maastricht Treaty in 1992 and by Structural and Cohesion Funds which were invested in the public infrastructure system and rural development initiatives.

These measures were important in improving Ireland's competitiveness and making it an attractive place to do business. The evolution of industrial policy in Ireland is discussed in detail in Chapter 1 and policy issues relating to labour markets, human capital investments and regulation, all of which fall under the umbrella of industrial policy, are covered elsewhere in the book (see Chapters 6, 7 and 13). Here we focus on two direct policy intervention tools which, despite the lack of a clear economic rationale for their use, have proved instrumental to the success of the manufacturing sector, and to a lesser extent internationally traded services. They are fiscal incentives in the form of corporation profits tax and direct capital grants to firms. We also briefly look at the regional dimension to industrial policy in Ireland and in particular the role of the EU in this regard.

Corporation Taxes
The importance of corporation taxes in attracting FDI is well documented in the literature and is one of the key factors contributing to Ireland's attractiveness as a place to invest.[1] In the early stages of EU membership, in an effort to promote inward foreign investment and indigenous exports, full corporate tax relief on profits generated through export sales was introduced by the Irish government. Coupled with the other favourable conditions for investment, including free access to the large EU market, an English-speaking, relatively low-cost labour supply and strong cultural connections with the USA, Ireland became one of the most FDI-intensive countries in Europe. A strategy of low rates of profit taxes has since been an important feature of Irish industrial policy. However, pressure from the European Commission to harmonise taxes across all EU countries since the late 1970s has continually threatened to eliminate Ireland's competitive advantage in this regard. In response to changes in EU legislation, in 1978 Export Profit Tax Relief was phased out and replaced by a 10 per cent rate for all manufacturing and some internationally traded services. Subsequent pressures to harmonise taxes across sectors led to Ireland introducing a 12.5 per cent rate in

2003 for all sectors. This rate, however, still remains substantially below the average for Western Europe but pressures to increase the rate as part of the EU bail-out package have been met with considerable concern and objection from Ireland (see Chapter 4).

Capital Grants

Capital grants have played an important role in the support and evolution of the manufacturing sector in Ireland.[2] Since the 1950s grants have been made available to firms in the manufacturing sector for capital investments. These grants were for all companies producing manufactured goods for export. In the early stages of EU membership financial assistance was also given to domestic companies prepared to restructure following the introduction to free trade. The Industrial Development Authority (IDA), established in 1949, was responsible for the provision of grants and was later split into IDA Ireland, which became responsible for grant provision to foreign companies, and Enterprise Ireland (formerly Forbairt), which became responsible for supports to Irish companies.

Over time, the awarding of grants became more aligned with strategic priorities for the sector and grants were extended to cover a range of activities including training and R&D as well as loan guarantees. In the 1970s, for example, priority was given to the development of high value-added sectors including electronics, chemicals, pharmaceuticals and healthcare through the process of attracting foreign multinational market leaders in these sectors. These policies were considered a success, particularly given the agglomeration effects observed in these sectors in subsequent years when competition for investment intensified. Ireland was a tried-and-tested location for high value-added sectors that an increasing number of firms wanted to be a part of.

A number of developments over the course of the 1980s and 1990s further changed the way in which grants were awarded. The publication of the Telesis Report in 1984 called for a change in emphasis toward developing domestic industry, while the Culliton Report in 1992 called for a reduction in the use of grants and a shift in focus towards policies aimed at improving competitiveness more generally. Furthermore, from 1994, EU state aid rules determined the permissible size of grants awarded. As a result, grants are now awarded on the basis of geographical location, the skill levels of the people employed, and the nature of the activities being carried out. Emphasis is placed on activities in the high-tech sector, which increasingly covers service-type activities.

Overall, the role of grant supports has been important to the evolution of the industrial sector in Ireland and there is strong empirical evidence to support their association with employment generation. However, since 2006, changes to EU limits have further restricted the extent to which state aid can be provided. Consequently, the government must look to other means of maintaining Ireland's competitive position in terms of attracting FDI and promoting sectors of strategic importance.

Regional Industrial Policy

The decline in the importance of the agricultural sector will generally lead to a gradual outward migration from rural areas to urban centres. The earliest forms of industrial grants in Ireland were given to companies, both foreign and Irish-owned, to establish in peripheral locations that were disadvantaged in resources as a result of this process of structural change. An important dimension of the IDA's development strategy has been focused on achieving an even redistribution of manufacturing employment throughout Ireland. Regional industrial policy objectives have also been facilitated to a large extent by EU Structural Funds created to help underdeveloped regions in the EU in a number of different ways aimed at promoting regional industrial development. There is some evidence that these policies were successful, given that the levels of migration from rural to urban areas observed in most developing countries did not materialise in Ireland. However, the most successful regional locations are those located around urban centres where industrial clusters, and the benefits that go with them, such as increasing returns to scale and productivity spill-overs, for example, were already well developed.

While the regional flavour to industrial policy has diminished considerably, due particularly to the widespread acknowledgement of the benefits of agglomeration, most direct financial supports provided to firms are decided on a case-by-case basis and as such a certain regional dimension still remains in Irish industrial policy. The spatial dimension of economic development is now explicitly incorporated into the National Development Plans 2000–2006, and more recently 2007–2013, under the Rural Social and Economic Development Programme and covers a range of Irish- and EU-funded initiatives such as LEADER, CLÁR, and INTERREG.

Future Policy Agenda

The most significant industrial policy developments at EU level in recent times are set out in the Lisbon Agenda, which was established by the European Council in 2000 with the aim of making the EU 'the most dynamic and competitive knowledge-based economy in the world capable of sustainable economic growth with more and better jobs and greater social cohesion, and respect for the environment by 2010'. In 2005, the mid-term review of the Agenda highlighted sustainable growth and employment as the most pressing goals of the EU. In October 2007, the National Reform Programme (NRP) 2008–2010 was produced with the aim of bringing together a broad range of policies and initiatives focused on sustaining Ireland's strong economic growth and employment position. The report established twenty-four guidelines for achieving these aims, covering macroeconomic policy objectives, structural market reforms and employment guidelines, all aimed at ensuring the future of the traded sector as it transforms into a knowledge-driven, high value-added entity with less emphasis on manufacturing and an increasing role for internationally traded services. The economic crisis since 2008 has limited the extent to which many of the guidelines implemented can have a real effect, although it is clear that the government remains committed to following the framework provided by the NRP to promote economic growth and job creation. Of particular note is their commitment to the Smart Economy Framework and policies aimed at promoting research and innovation.[3]

The government's strategy for developing the smart economy is to prioritise innovation-driven enterprise and high-quality employment. Opportunities have been identified in a number of sectors, including: key services sectors, such as health informatics, financial analytics and digital lifestyle management; tourism; the food sector; life sciences; software; the creative arts; next generation network-enabled sectors; the internationalisation of domestic construction expertise; and developing technologies to support the lifestyles of an ageing population.[4] Future policy will attempt to achieve economic recovery through growth in these sectors. The core mechanism is internationalisation, in terms of internationalisation of enterprises, but also improving Ireland's international networks and profile.

Of critical importance to the internationalisation process is the creation of a more competitive business environment. This is particularly the case given the increasing levels of competition for investment from China and Central and East European countries and the challenge of sustaining high levels of investment in education, R&D and infrastructure amidst a public finance crisis. The government's Strategy for Science, Technology and Innovation 2006–2013 sets out to transform Ireland into a knowledge economy through substantial increases in R&D investments through third-level education as well as a range of initiatives aimed at promoting enterprise R&D. One example of this is the substantial investment that has been made into developing Ireland's nanotechnology infrastructure. The industry-led research initiatives that have been established will link leading companies in this sector to leading researchers in the major higher educational institutions (see also Chapter 13).[5]

3 NATURE AND IMPORTANCE OF THE MANUFACTURING SECTOR IN IRELAND

This section reviews the trends in output and employment in the manufacturing sector over the last two decades. An important indicator of performance is productivity and, given that the manufacturing sector is the main productive sector of the economy, understanding the constraints to productivity growth within the sector is crucial in any evaluation of the contribution and prospects of the sector. This section also examines the contribution of international trade in manufactured goods to the economy.

Output and Employment
As discussed in the introduction, a distinction is made between the modern and the traditional manufacturing sectors. The modern manufacturing sector covers all

243

high-technology multinational enterprises (chemicals; computers and instrument engineering; electrical machinery and equipment; and the reproduction of recorded media) while the traditional manufacturing sector encompasses all other sectors. In 2008, the year for which the most recent disaggregated statistics are available, modern manufacturing accounted for 59 per cent of gross value added of the sector and 37 per cent of employment. Table 9.1 presents net output and employment levels in the manufacturing sector in Ireland for selected years between 1995 and 2007. Net output of the manufacturing sector in Ireland amounted to almost €70 billion in 2007 (2010 prices) and the sector employed approximately 223,000 people. Output has continually grown since 1995 although the pace of growth has slowed considerably: between 1995 and 2000 output almost doubled, while between 2000 and 2007 output grew by a much more moderate 16 per cent. Up to 2000, the increase in output was primarily accounted for by the modern sector, which experienced a very high growth rate in output in the late 1990s, but which has slowed in recent years. Growth in output of the traditional manufacturing sector was also strong up to 2000 but since then it has also stagnated. It should be noted, however, that output figures, particularly in the modern manufacturing sector where foreign-owned firms dominate (see later), may be distorted by foreign MNCs switching profits from subsidiaries located in other countries to avail of lower corporation profit taxes in Ireland.

The trend in industrial output growth beyond 2007 is captured by the industrial output indices presented in the lower panel of the table. These indices are based on a monthly survey of manufacturing firms with more than twenty employees and so are not directly comparable with the value of output figures presented. The impact of the financial crisis and subsequent recession in Ireland is evident in the trend presented. By 2009 manufacturing output had fallen to 2005 levels, with a marked deterioration evident in the traditional sector. In 2010, however, there is some evidence of recovery, particularly in the modern manufacturing sector.

Over the course of the 1990s the sector grew by 27 per cent in terms of employment but since 2000 it has experienced a decline in employment of over 32,000 people. This loss in employment can be partly attributed to productivity growth (evidenced by the fact that output has simultaneously increased over this period, particularly in the modern manufacturing sector) but also to the off-shoring of manufacturing production to more competitive locations, leading to plant closures and job losses. The decline in employment in traditional sectors such as textiles is common across all OECD countries with low-cost non-OECD countries attracting this kind of investment to their shores. This trend is likely to continue into the future as more and more developing countries sign up to the World Trade Organisation, making them increasingly attractive as locations for labour-intensive manufacturing activities. In contrast, however, Ireland maintains a comparative advantage in certain high-skilled manufacturing activities that are unlikely to be off-shored, particularly if productivity improvements are sustainable.

Table 9.1

Net Output and Employment in the Manufacturing Sector
in Ireland, 1995, 2000, 2005 and 2007; and Industrial
Output Indices 1995–2010

	Net output (€ billion)				Employment (000s)			
	1995	2000	2005	2007	1995	2000	2005	2007
Manufacturing	21.6	59.9	65.8	69.7	221	255	218	223
Modern[1]	10.7	36.8	38.7	38.0	78	107	89	90
Traditional	10.9	21.1	27.1	31.7	142	148	129	133
	Industrial output indices (base 2005=100)[2]							
	1995	2000	2005	2006	2007	2008	2009	2010
Manufacturing	35.9	74.3	100.0	103.3	109.0	105.8	101.7	110.1
Modern[1]	24.3	67.3	100.0	104.1	111.2	109.8	112.7	124.8
Traditional	78.1	94.5	100.0	101.6	104.7	100.4	86.2	87.8

Sources: CSO, *Census of Industrial Production* (local units), Database Direct (various years); and *Industrial Production and Turnover*, CSO, 2011. See www.cso.ie.

Note: value figures are in 2010 prices adjusted using Industrial Price Index (CSO).

[1] Disaggregated statistics by three-digit NACE code are not available, so figures for value of output and employment in modern manufacturing exclude net output and employment for the reproduction of recorded media sector. The industrial output indices, however, cover all modern manufacturing firms.

[2] Note that the NACE system of classification was revised in 2008 with many manufacturing activities reclassified as services activities. Differences in values pre- and post-2008 should therefore be treated with some caution as they may reflect the change in classification as opposed to actual changes in values.

As highlighted in the introduction to this chapter, manufacturing's share of total employment and output of the economy has declined sharply since 1999. An increasing share of economic activity is now attributable to the services sector. The favourable profile of the manufacturing sector in terms of growth prospects implies that this structural change may have implications for future economic growth. First, manufacturing is a high-productivity sector and aggregate productivity growth in Ireland over the last decades has largely been attributable to the manufacturing sector. Second, manufacturing, up to recently, has been the main internationally traded activity and as such a weakening of the sector will have implications for exports, a key driver of economic growth, unless alternative export opportunities are found.

Productivity and Cost Competitiveness[6]
Productivity
A vibrant manufacturing sector is an important source of productivity growth given that productivity improvements are generally harder to achieve in more labour-intensive sectors such as the services sector. Productivity is one component

of competitiveness and refers generally to the efficiency with which factors of production are converted into outputs. Productivity gains can be attained through a wide variety of means, ranging from decisions made by individual firms in relation to management practices, R&D and technology adoption, to government policies which support investment, entrepreneurship, competition and innovation. Productivity is a relative concept and performance should be gauged relative to our main competitors.

At near full employment during the late 1990s and early 2000s, productivity growth was a key driver of the Irish economy. Between 1995 and 2005 labour productivity, measured as annual growth in output per hour worked, grew by an average of 7.4 per cent per annum for the manufacturing sector as a whole with productivity growth in the modern sector of 9.4 per cent per annum and in the traditional sector of 4.3 per cent per annum. In fact, the strong performance of the modern manufacturing sector was a key driver of productivity growth for the economy as a whole during this period, with the highest productivity growth rates recorded in technology-intensive manufacturing and services sectors. This trend mirrors the performance of most OECD countries, which have experienced declining levels of employment in manufacturing over the last two decades, which can in part be attributed to productivity improvements. Since 2005, productivity growth has slowed considerably to a rate of less than one per cent per annum. While this rate is comparable to the UK and France, it is lower than the OECD average and lags far behind that of some emerging economies such as South Korea, Poland and Hungary.

The declining trend in productivity growth is also borne out by the data presented in Table 9.1. By taking a simple comparison of the value of output to the numbers employed it is clear that the highest productivity levels are achieved in the modern manufacturing sector. It should be noted, however, that this will include the returns to R&D and improved management practices conducted by MNCs in other countries, and so these rates may overestimate the actual productivity growth of the sector. With appropriate adjustments, productivity growth may be as little as half of the reported figures. Also of concern is the fact that Ireland's productivity lags behind EU and US levels in traditional manufacturing sectors, suggesting that productivity improvements in the 'home-grown' manufacturing sector are still lagging.

With the decline in the relative importance of manufacturing compared with other sectors of the economy, it is unlikely that the same scale of aggregate productivity growth will be attainable in the future, given that manufacturing makes up the productive part of the economy. Productivity gains are much more difficult in the more labour-intensive services sectors, particularly given the high cost of doing business in Ireland. An important mechanism for achieving productivity growth is innovation, where firms adopt and adapt tried and tested technologies from other firms and industries to improve the efficiency of production. Ireland performs well by European standards on innovative activity, ranking fifth out of the Euro-16 on a summary innovation index including 29 different measures including R&D and information technology (IT) expenditure. Unlike other countries, however, Ireland's innovation ranking has not improved in the last number of years and domestic firms, in particular, are less likely to engage in innovative activity or achieve significant returns from innovation. The importance of innovation is discussed further in Section 5.

Cost Competitiveness
An important indicator of the potential performance of the manufacturing sector is cost competitiveness. Cost competitiveness refers to the general environment within which the sector operates rather than the behaviour or performance of the firm specifically. Like productivity, it is a relative concept in that it measures the extent to which the cost of doing business in Ireland is more or less expensive than our main trading partners. Cost competitiveness is measured using the Harmonised Competitiveness Indicator (HCI), which takes into account prices and business costs, both pay and non-pay related.

One silver lining to the current economic crisis is that for the first time in a decade Ireland's cost competitiveness is improving. Between 2005 and 2008 Ireland experienced a 7.7 per cent loss in cost competitiveness, but since then real cost competitiveness improvements have been realised, with the HCI falling to 6.1 per cent below the 2005 level in May 2010. This is due to both favourable movements in the exchange rate and falling prices. Labour costs have also declined: between 2004 and 2007 the growth rate of Ireland's labour costs exceeded that of the Euro area but in 2008 and 2009 the rate of growth was lower than the EU-27 and euro area averages. Declines in non-pay costs have also contributed, with declines observed in areas such as rental of commercial property and the cost of utilities. The cost of some business services has also declined, although Ireland still remains expensive relative to many other countries. The ease with which firms can do business is also affected by other factors in an economy, such as the efficiency of infrastructure, the availability of skilled labour, and the availability of capital, either internationally or through credit markets. These issues are dealt with elsewhere in the book (see Chapters 6, 10 and 13). It should be noted, however, that the real HCI is still 19 per cent above its January 2000 level, suggesting that Ireland so far has endured only part of the adjustment process to a lower cost base, with much more required if Ireland is once more to become a competitive place to do business.

International Trade
The link between economic growth and export expansion has long been established. Exports fuel economic growth directly by bringing additional income into the economy, which increases domestic demand, and indirectly through the productivity improvements that result from exposure to competitive pressures. The latter may occur through more efficient allocations of resources or the adoption of new technologies required to compete on world markets, for example. While there is much debate in the literature on the direction of causality (are

exporting firms more productive *a priori* or do they become more efficient once exposed to world markets?), there is no doubt that firms that export are more productive than those that do not.

Ireland has a long tradition of export-led growth, which can explain much of Ireland's phenomenal growth rate in the 1990s (see Chapters 1 and 7). In recent years, however, Ireland's share of the world market for merchandise goods has slipped: Ireland fell from being ranked twenty-second in the world for goods exports in 2000 to thirty-first in 2009.[7] Table 9.2 illustrates the proportion of total gross output of the manufacturing sector attributable to exports. The most recent year for which such a disaggregation is available is 2007, so where possible the analysis is supplemented with more up-to-date statistics.[8] It should be noted that the figures presented in the table do not illustrate the decline in exports between 2007 and 2009 due to the global economic crisis. According to the latest CSO figures, however, exports have recovered in 2010 and early 2011.

Table 9.2

Percentage Contribution of Manufacturing to Exports and
Export Destinations for Ireland, 2000 and 2007

	Firms	Output	UK	Other EU	USA	Elsewhere
			2000			
Manufacturing	62.7	79.0	19.0	50.4	13.9	16.7
Modern[1]	75.6	93.9	15.6	49.5	17.2	17.7
Traditional	60.0	59.2	27.8	52.2	5.6	14.2
			2007			
Manufacturing	49.8	86.2	17.1	52.5	16.8	13.6
Modern[1]	68.9	95.2	12.4	52.3	21.7	13.6
Traditional	45.4	73.2	25.8	53.0	7.6	13.6

Source: CSO, Census of Industrial Production (local units), Database Direct (various years).
[1] Excludes NACE 224, for which this disaggregation was not available.

In 2007, 86 per cent of output in the manufacturing sector was exported, up from 79 per cent in 2000. Of particular note is the fact that for the modern manufacturing sector almost all output is exported (95 per cent). The most important sectors by far are chemicals and related products (Standard International Trade Classification (SITC) 5), which accounted for 62 per cent of all commodity exports in 2011. In terms of the destination of exports, the share going to the UK has declined in all sectors since 2000. This is consistent with the general trend observed throughout the 1990s. The UK still remains an important destination for exports, however, particularly for the traditional manufacturing sector, with one quarter of all exports going to the UK market in 2007. For all sectors, other EU countries (excluding the UK) remain the most important export destinations with their share increasing over time. The share of exports going to the USA also increased between 2000 and 2007, while the share of exports going to the rest of the world declined. Recent figures for 2011 suggest that the overall picture may have changed: while the EU remains an important destination for exports, the proportion of exports to the USA increased to 22 per cent and the proportion going to the rest of the world to 17 per cent. The figures for 2011, however, include both goods and services, which may explain some of this discrepancy.

The contribution of the Irish manufacturing sector to Ireland's export base is paramount in understanding its economic success story of the last two decades. However, the dependence of the manufacturing sector on export markets leaves it vulnerable to world market conditions. Any international developments that depress demand will have consequences for the Irish manufacturing sector. Furthermore, the declining role of the sector is of concern if the sectors that replace it do not generate significant export activity. Thus a key challenge of Irish policy-makers is the promotion of alternative export-based sectors. A sector presenting significant development opportunities in this regard is the internationally traded services sector, to which we now turn our attention.

4 INTERNATIONALLY TRADED SERVICES

For most developed economies, the last number of years have seen a significant structural shift away from agricultural and manufacturing production towards service activities. Ireland is no exception, with services accounting for almost 70 per cent of gross value added in 2009. A number of factors have contributed to the growth of the sector over the last two decades. First, the rapid pace of advancement in information and communications technology (ICT) has made it significantly easier for services companies to trade internationally. Second, the fragmentation of the production process means that an increasing number of services (for example logistics, IT, etc.) are required to monitor and control the production process in corporations. Third, firms increasingly find it more efficient to outsource many of their service activities, leading to these activities being reclassified from manufacturing to services. Finally, the distinction between manufacturing and services is increasingly blurred, with manufacturing firms often providing services with the products that they sell (for example, products are often sold with training and support services or financial packages provided through the manufacturers themselves). In this section we focus on internationally traded services, with other services sectors, such as retail, hospitality, health and education, covered elsewhere (see Chapters 11, 12 and 13). This section first addresses how trade in services is defined before moving on to analyse the contribution of internationally traded services to the economy. Following this, an Irish case study is presented that highlights the changing nature of manufacturing production and its evolving link with the services sector.

Definition and Governance

The growing importance of trade in services worldwide has prompted national governments to come together to negotiate the rules that will govern the internationally traded services sector in the future. The two most notable reforms to emerge from this process have been the EU 2006 Directive on Services in the Internal Market at a regional level; and the General Agreement on Trade in Services (GATS) at an international level. GATS is the services counterpart to the well-known General Agreement on Tariffs and Trade negotiated in Uruguay in 1986. GATS defines trade in services to encompass four different modes of service delivery.[9] Mode 1 refers to *cross-border trade*, which covers service flows across countries, for example an Irish university providing online courses that can be taken by students around the world. Mode 2 refers to *consumption abroad*, which covers situations where the consumer of a service physically travels to another country to avail of that service, for example an Irish tourist holidaying in Spain or an Irish patient travelling to the USA to avail of medical treatment. Mode 3 requires a *commercial presence* and refers to situations where the supplier of the service establishes a commercial presence in the country where the service is being provided, for example subsidiaries of an Irish insurance company setting up a branch in the UK. Mode 4 refers to the *presence of natural persons* and covers situations where an individual must travel to another country to supply a service, for example an Irish engineer building a hotel in Dubai. The sectors classed as internationally traded are described in Table 9.3.

Table 9.3

Sectoral Classification of Internationally Traded Services

Business services and professional services	*Construction and related services*
Accountancy services	Distribution services
Advertising services	Education services
Architectural and engineering services	Energy services
Computer and related services	Environmental services
Legal services	Health and social services
	Tourism services
Communication services	Transport services
Audiovisual services	Movement of natural persons
Postal and courier, express mail services	
Telecommunications	

Source: World Trade Organisation, *General Agreement on Trade in Services*, Services sectoral classification list, available at www.wto.org.

The generation of an internal EU market for services and further liberalisation of services internationally through GATS negotiations are expected to have positive benefits for Ireland. Forfás predict that the services sector will grow in response to the new liberalisation measures, in terms of output, exports and employment. These benefits, however, are contingent on labour supply matching the skill set required (see Chapters 6 and 13). Indirect benefits are also expected.

For example, by providing easier access to the international market, the internationally traded services sector will be exposed to greater competition, leading to lower prices. This will benefit final consumers, including Irish consumers, of services but will also improve cost competitiveness for other firms, such as those in the manufacturing sector, that use these services.

Contribution of Internationally Traded Services

Table 9.4 presents the value of Irish services exports for the period 2003 to 2009. In 2009 exports of services amounted to almost €67 billion in real terms, corresponding to a 14 percentage point increase, on average, each year between 2003 and 2009. Despite the small decline in 2009, Ireland ranks ninth in the world in terms of services exports.[10] What makes the fast pace of growth of services exports even more remarkable is when it is interpreted against the backdrop of the financial crisis and worldwide recession which has led to depressed demand conditions, and the fact that the value of merchandise exports fell during this time. The total value of services exports amounts to approximately one-third of total sales in the services sector in Ireland. Table 9.4 also illustrates the proportion of exports by destination. The EU is the most important destination for our services exports, with the UK and Germany being of particular importance. Over time the importance of the USA as a destination has declined, which could be due in part to the global financial crisis. Services exports to the rest of the world are also growing in importance.

Table 9.4

Value of Internationally Traded Services

	2003	2004	2005	2006	2007	2008	2009
Services exports (€ billion)	35.3	41.1	45.0	55.5	65.3	68.4	66.6
% UK	25.2	25.3	25.3	22.5	22.0	22.5	20.2
% Germany	9.4	9.7	12.1	10.1	9.9	9.8	9.8
% Rest of EU	27.8	27.5	29.6	29.1	30.9	32.7	33.3
% USA	13.5	11.8	7.9	9.7	6.4	6.9	6.3
% Rest of world	24.1	25.6	25.0	28.7	30.8	28.0	30.5

Source: CSO, *Service Exports and Imports* (various years), available at www.cso.ie.

A disaggregation of the sectors that are important for services exports is presented in Table 9.5. It should be noted that in almost all sectors the value of exports increased between 2003 and 2008. The figures presented here reflect the relative importance of different sectors. The most important contributing sectors to services exports are computer services and other business services, which together account for over 55 per cent of total services exports. While insurance and financial services are also of importance, both have declined in importance as export sectors, particularly in recent years: hardly surprising, given the impact that the financial crisis had on these sectors. Tourism has also declined in importance.

A large share of global trade consists of intra-firm trade, in other words the transfer of goods and services within MNCs across borders, usually for the purpose of avoiding taxes. As already mentioned, this practice can significantly distort sectoral output statistics, but it can also distort trade statistics since goods and services are simply imported by firms for immediate export. As discussed in Section 2, Ireland has a low rate of corporation profit taxes (see also Chapter 4) and so it is thought that intra-firm trade of this kind is common among Irish MNCs. As such, gross exports for sectors with a large presence of foreign-owned firms, such as financial services and computer services, for example, should be treated with some caution, given that some of these exports could simply be imports that are re-exported for this purpose. A crude check on the extent of the distortion to the export statistics as a result of intra-firm trade is to look at the value of net exports (gross exports minus gross imports) at a particular point in time. Although this will not fully pick up the extent of transfer pricing, it will give some indication of the overall contribution of the different sub-sectors. Net exports by sub-sector for 2009 are presented in the last column of Table 9.5. While insurance and financial services remain important export sectors, their impact on the trade balance is much less than what the gross export figures would suggest, due to high levels of imports of these services into Ireland. This is even more the case for other business services that have a large negative trade balance, which, coupled with the high gross export figures for this sub-sector, is suggestive of transfer-pricing activities. Computer services are the single most important sub-sector of the internationally traded services sector with net exports valued at €23 million in 2009 and a negligible level of gross imports. It is also of interest to note the deficit in tourism exports, meaning that more Irish tourists holidayed abroad in 2009 than visited Ireland. Recent proposals to reduce the travel tax will help to stimulate tourism over the coming years.

Table 9.5

Proportion of Gross Exports of Services (%) and
Level of Net Exports (€m) by Disaggregated Sectors

	2004	2005	2006	2007	2008	2009	Net exports 2009
Transport	4.3	4.5	3.4	3.2	3.6	3.6	1,301
Tourism and travel	7.9	8.0	6.2	5.5	5.2	4.3	-2,781
Communications	1.7	0.9	0.6	0.6	0.7	0.6	-582
Insurance	18.7	14.4	12.6	10.8	9.9	9.4	1,274
Financial services	9.3	9.9	9.0	9.2	8.0	7.1	1,462
Computer services	34.3	31.7	26.5	26.8	28.9	29.9	23,534
Royalties licences	0.4	1.0	1.1	1.1	1.2	1.5	-23,836
Other business services	18.7	25.5	22.3	23.5	24.4	25.3	-9,247

Source: CSO, *Service Exports and Imports* (various years), available at: www.cso.ie.

Process of Structural Change – An Irish Case Study

As illustrated in Section 3, the manufacturing sector in Ireland is important both in terms of its contribution to output and employment and also in terms of its contribution to exports and aggregate productivity. Over the last decade, however, the sector has undergone a major structural change in terms of the nature of output produced and the type of labour required. This process of structural change can best be illustrated using the example of a key sector in Irish manufacturing up to the turn of the millennium, the computer hardware sector. In this section, the main findings of a recent case study of this sector are presented.[11]

Over the course of the 1990s, Ireland emerged as a major centre for the production of computer hardware and electronics as a result of foreign investment in the area of computer assembly and the manufacture of computer components. With the arrival of companies like Dell, Gateway, AST and, most notably, Intel, the importance of these sectors to Irish manufacturing in terms of employment and exports grew exponentially. By 2000, the office machinery and computers and the electronic components sectors together accounted for almost 12 per cent of jobs in the manufacturing sector. These sectors were also of significant importance in terms of exports: in 2000 Irish exports of computer hardware and electronic components accounted for 5 per cent and 6 per cent respectively of total global exports and an estimated one-third of all computer sales in the EU were assembled in Ireland. Since then, however, these sectors have experienced significant decline with the relocation of production to China, the Far East and Central and Eastern Europe, which gained comparative advantage in the production of these goods through offering lower-cost production environments, particularly in terms of labour costs. By 2005, Ireland's share of world exports of computer hardware had fallen to 4.6 per cent while China's share exploded from 6 per cent to over 28 per cent in the same period. Ireland's losses were even greater in the electronic components sector, with global export shares falling to 2.5 per cent, with China experiencing similar gains. Similar losses were experienced in employment: by 2003 the share of total manufacturing employment accounted for by these sectors had fallen to 8.6 per cent, equivalent to a loss of over 10,000 jobs.

The closure of computer assembly firms, though, leads to the establishment of related firms in higher-technology segments offering higher wages. These firms underwent significant change, however. For example, Intel has shifted to producing higher value-added manufacturing output through its establishment of successive wafer fabrication plants, while Apple and IBM have transformed their operations from manufacturing to performing high value-added services functions such as technical support and call centres. Further evidence of the process of structural change is the emergence of shared service centres (SSCs).[12] SSCs are managed as separate entities within the corporation and provide the subsidiaries of the corporation with all their service needs. It is a cost-effective way of delivering high-value services such as finance and accounting, IT, human resources, payroll, marketing, etc. in a specialised way. There are currently over a hundred SSCs operating in Ireland. Over 30 per cent are in the electronics and high-technology sectors.

The key lesson to be learned from this experience is that as the manufacturing sector continues to transform and blur into the boundaries of the high value-added services sector, a highly educated and flexible labour force is essential to facilitate the process of change.

5 FOREIGN DIRECT INVESTMENT

Policies aimed at attracting foreign FDI are based on the logic that it brings new investment to the economy that directly boosts national income and leads to the creation of employment. It is also expected that FDI will bring an inflow of knowledge and technology that leads to productivity spill-over effects to the domestic manufacturing sector. In this section, the importance of FDI to Irish manufacturing and internationally traded services relative to other countries in Europe is first examined and the contribution of foreign-owned firms to output and employment analysed. Second, the extent to which productivity spill-over effects have materialised is considered. Third, the increasing role of outward direct investment (ODI) and what this means for Ireland is analysed.

Inward Foreign Direct Investment

Since the 1960s, Ireland's industrial policy has focused on facilitating inward FDI. This has yielded substantial rewards for Ireland in terms of economic growth in the latter half of the last century. Of particular importance have been growth-enhancing economic policies such as fiscal stability, labour market flexibility and science-oriented human capital formation as well as a low corporation tax regime.[13] As a result, Ireland has the most FDI-intensive manufacturing sector of all countries in Europe.

As illustrated in Table 9.6, in 2009 the stock of inward FDI as a percentage of GDP amounted to 87 per cent compared with an average of 45 per cent for the EU. Over the course of the 1990s the ratio of inward FDI stock to GDP grew considerably, despite rapid increases in GDP during this period. Since 2000, however, the overall stock of inward FDI (relative to GDP) has declined almost to its 1990 levels. This decline is due primarily to the outflow of foreign investors in the early 2000s and is also in line with the decline since 2000 in the overall importance of the manufacturing sector in terms of output and employment. This trend can be explained by the increasing attractiveness of developing countries such as China, India and Central and Eastern European countries as locations for investors in labour-intensive manufacturing sectors. In more recent years, positive inflows have returned, but at a more moderate level. These are attributable to an increasing number of investments in high-tech manufacturing sectors and services. The recent global economic downturn is also evident in the level of FDI inflows over the last three years. In 2008, for example, Ireland experienced a net outflow of investment. Inflows, however, appear to have returned to normal levels in 2009.

Table 9.6

FDI Stocks and Flows for Ireland, the UK and the EU

	FDI stocks as a percentage of GDP			Net FDI flows (current $m)		
	1990	2000	2009	2007	2008	2009
Ireland	79.5	131.0	86.9	24,707	-20,030	24,971
UK	20.0	29.6	51.5	186,381	91,487	45,676
EU	10.8	27.3	45.4	923,810	536,917	361,949

Sources: trade flows data sourced from UNCTAD, *World Investment Report 2010*, UNCTAD, Geneva 2007; GDP data sourced from IMF, *World Economic Outlook* (various years).

FDI into Ireland over the last two decades has been on a large scale and this has significantly reshaped the manufacturing sector in Ireland. According to IDA Ireland, over 1,000 foreign firms have chosen Ireland as their European base in a variety of different sectors including engineering, financial and international services, information communications technologies, medical technologies and pharmaceuticals. In addition to Intel, Apple and IBM, other overseas companies with large operations in Ireland include Amazon.com, Google, HP, Microsoft and Yahoo!. In 2008, the internet social networking site Facebook established its European headquarters in Dublin and in 2010, internet professional networking site LinkedIn announced that it too was to use Dublin as the base for its international headquarters.

In 2007, foreign-owned firms accounted for only 10 per cent of local units but 46 per cent of manufacturing employment in the sector and almost 80 per cent of output, while over 95 per cent of the output in the modern manufacturing sector is attributable to foreign-owned firms.[14] Foreign firms exported 94 per cent of their output in 2007 compared with only 47 per cent for domestic firms. This highlights the importance of foreign investment to trade flows in Ireland. The evidence suggests, however, that domestic firms are exporting more over time: between 2003 and 2008 the average annual growth in exports from indigenous companies was almost 9 per cent.[15]

Productivity Spill-over Effects[16]

As discussed in Section 2, a key rationale for industrial policy aimed at promoting FDI is the fact that foreign MNCs establishing in Ireland bring with them knowledge and technology that will spill over into the domestic industrial sector. The extent to which FDI yields benefits to the economy above and beyond the direct contribution to output and employment is an issue that has been extensively debated in the economics literature. The evidence is clear on the fact that foreign-owned firms are larger, have higher labour productivity, higher profits, are more export intensive, employ more skilled workers and spend more on R&D than their domestic counterparts. Thus there is no doubt that the presence of foreign companies in Ireland has contributed to higher aggregate productivity levels and growth rates than would otherwise have been possible.

The measurement of productivity *spill-over* effects is a more complex matter, however, with no consensus about the most appropriate approach. Productivity spill-overs can be horizontal (within a defined sub-sector of manufacturing) or vertical (through backward or forward linkages on the input-supply side). While there is some evidence that the presence of MNCs in Ireland has led to the establishment of an indigenous downstream sector for some industries, most of the empirical literature on the presence of spill-over effects is concerned with the measurement of horizontal spill-over effects from MNCs to Irish firms operating in the same sector. The evidence on the presence of horizontal spill-over effects for Ireland is mixed, however, with positive spill-over effects only evident when sectors are narrowly defined. The strongest evidence for the importance of spill-over effects is found in high-technology sectors.

In order for Irish firms to benefit from productivity spill-over effects they need to have innovative capacity. Ireland performs well by international standards on a range of comparative innovation measures, with a high proportion of firms involved in innovation activity.[17] However, innovation is concentrated amongst larger, foreign-owned firms, with smaller indigenous firms lagging far behind. Overall, the returns to innovations are lower in Ireland than the EU average, suggesting that there are some inefficiencies in the way in which R&D resources are being deployed in enterprises.

In a more general context, the key to innovation is the improvement of the absorption capacity of firms so that they can benefit from technology spill-over effects. This can be achieved through appropriate education and training policies to ensure that the labour force is equipped with the necessary skills to innovate effectively. The National Skills Strategy, developed in 2007, aims to address the changing skills needs of the Irish labour force to increase absorption capacity by 2020, although the focus has shifted somewhat from the original objectives as a result of the changed economic circumstances. A 2007 report published by the Expert Group on Future Skills Needs, which forms the basis for the National Skills Strategy, called for the up-skilling of a substantial proportion of the current workforce to ease the transition process from a manufacturing-base to a high value-added service-driven economy and to help increase absorption capacity.[18] High levels of unemployment, particularly among those previously employed in the construction sector, make these objectives even more important today and are reflected in the government's new Activation Fund, which will target the up-skilling and re-skilling of these groups (see Chapters 6 and 13 for more discussion).

It is clear that FDI has played a crucial role in the success of the Irish manufacturing sector, not only in terms of output and employment, but also in terms of its impact on the domestic industrial sector. MNCs' higher than average productivity levels have raised aggregate productivity levels for the sector as a whole and productivity spill-over effects, particularly in the high-tech sector, have also benefited Irish firms. There is also evidence to suggest that the presence of MNCs has increased domestic firm survival rates and encouraged start-up firms in many downstream supply industries. In the face of declining flows of FDI, the challenge for Irish industrial policy-makers is not only how to continue to attract foreign investment into Ireland and to hold on to the MNCs that are already here, but how better to develop linkages between MNCs and domestic firms in an attempt to fully exploit productivity spill-over effects. This is an even greater challenge in the face of increasing pressure from the EU to harmonise corporation tax rates and increased restrictions on the provision of grants: two important policy tool options in relation to FDI for the Irish government in the past. Of even more importance, however, is the possibility that changes will be made to the corporation profit tax base. For example, if firms are forced to pay taxes on profits in the country where they are earned and can no longer process profits through Irish subsidiaries, not only will this have implications for Irish tax revenues but it may also reduce the attractiveness of Ireland as a place to invest. However, it is also possible that having a low corporation tax in an environment where transfer pricing is no longer permitted could increase the level of actual economic activity that takes place in Ireland, given that firms will be forced to site their real activity in Ireland to avail of the low tax rate. The introduction of transfer pricing rules across the OECD is a clear sign that policy is moving in this direction. In Ireland, the Finance Bill 2010 introduced transfer pricing rules to come into effect in January 2011, endorsing the OECD's Transfer Pricing Guidelines and requiring that 'intra-group transfer prices should be equivalent to those that would be charged between independent persons dealing at arm's length in otherwise similar circumstances'.[19] As well as creating an extra administrative burden on MNCs located in Ireland this will inevitably erode the advantages of transfer pricing for MNCs. For reasons mentioned, it is not clear what overall effect this will have on foreign investment in Ireland.

Outward Direct Investment[20]

A key concern for many developed economies is the extent to which the manufacturing sector can survive in the face of emerging low-cost economies offering an attractive base for manufacturing investment in terms of low input costs and liberal trade and investment policies. From 2003 to 2005, 35 per cent of global FDI was invested in developing countries, with China accounting for almost half of this. Eastern European countries have also experienced significant growth in inward FDI, with Russia experiencing the greatest gains. In Ireland, the increasing importance of ODI is evidenced in Table 9.7. In 2009, the stock of investment by Irish companies abroad amounted to over 86 per cent of GDP with dramatic increases in the flow of ODI experienced since the early 1990s. This ratio is well above the EU average and greater than that of the UK. In fact, ODI now accounts for the same proportion of GDP as FDI (see Table 9.6).

Table 9.7

ODI Stocks and Flows for Ireland, the UK and the EU

| | ODI stocks as a percentage of GDP | | |
	1990	2000	2009
Ireland	31.2	28.8	86.5
UK	22.5	60.1	75.7
EU	11.5	41.0	54.9

Source: as for Table 9.5.

In the mid-2000s, the bulk of manufacturing ODI from Ireland was attributable to a small proportion of long-established Irish companies in the traditional industrial sectors (for example Cement Roadstone Holdings and Greencore). Intuitively, one would expect that, as is the case for foreign-owned firms operating in Ireland, high labour costs make sourcing labour-intensive parts of the production process in Ireland very costly and so sourcing this part of the production chain abroad will improve the competitiveness of Irish producers. Yet early flows of Irish ODI were mainly concentrated in the UK and the USA. It is estimated that Irish companies in the USA employed almost 65,000 people in 1999 compared with just over 100,000 workers employed by US companies in Ireland in the same year. This suggests that low labour costs may not have been the only driver of the decision for Irish firms to invest abroad. In 2009, there appears to have been a shift in the type of Irish ODI. The majority of new Irish investment abroad is in the services sector, and in particular business activities with offshore centres account for an increasing proportion.

A key concern in the face of rising levels of ODI is that it will have a negative impact on the domestic economy in terms of investment, exports and employment. Evidence from countries with a history of ODI suggests that these concerns are unfounded and that high levels of ODI can lead to economic growth. For example, there is evidence to suggest that high levels of ODI are complementary to a strong export base. Traditional exports of finished goods are replaced with exports of high value-added intermediate goods (as has been the case in Ireland in recent years) and the provision of highly skilled services to overseas foreign affiliates by head offices based in the domestic country. The discussion in Section 3 shows that there is evidence to suggest that this type of restructuring, away from low-tech employment to high value-added activities, with corresponding higher wages, is taking place in Ireland. An additional advantage of ODI is that portfolio diversification of this kind may help protect the economy from regional economic downturns at an aggregate level and alleviate some of the pressures associated with export dependence mentioned in the previous section. Finally, high levels of ODI are generally associated with high levels of R&D investment.

Given these advantages, government policy aimed at facilitating outward investments should aim to remove tax and regulatory barriers to investment flows.

This can be achieved through an expansion of Ireland's network of international agreements on double taxation and through support for WTO multilateral agreements on investment rules. An expansion of Enterprise Ireland's current supports to companies wishing to invest abroad, such as Overseas Network, Overseas Incubator Facilities, Acquisition Service, Outsourcing Missions and Foreign Trade and Investment Missions, would also facilitate this process. Ultimately, however, policies aimed at improving Ireland's competitiveness will remain most important, and should aim to re-skill those displaced by these changes and promote high value-added activities in manufacturing and services into the future.

6 CONCLUDING COMMENTS

Major structural change is occurring in the Irish economy: the manufacturing sector, once the backbone of Ireland's economy, is diminishing in importance, to be replaced by a vibrant internationally traded services sector. This raises significant challenges for the Irish economy, particularly in the aftermath of an unprecedented economic crisis of a scale never before experienced in the history of the state. The pace of growth of the internationally traded sector presents real opportunities for growth and job creation as a means of economic recovery. The government's strategy for a smart economy sets the stage for Irish entrepreneurs and foreign investors to engage in emerging sectors such as green technology (see Chapter 10) or advanced computer software industries like cloud computing. A growing internationally traded services sector raises its own sets of challenges that need to be carefully considered, for example the fact that rules governing trade liberalisation are yet to be negotiated and that the dearth of language skills in the labour force may compromise Ireland's ability to attract high-end service companies.

The indigenous sector is also at risk. The banking crisis has had a significant impact on the availability of credit for small to medium-sized enterprises (SMEs) in Ireland (see also Chapters 5 and 7). Since the crisis unfolded in 2008 the Irish Small and Medium Enterprises Association (ISME) has reported significant increases in members being refused applications for new finance. This will have, and may already have had, serious implications for entrepreneurship in Ireland given that it will result in missed opportunities for new ventures and the postponement of investment in existing enterprises, and may ultimately lead to company closures for enterprises experiencing difficult times. Lack of access to credit may also lead to a domino effect within the supply chain: for example, if one firm in a vertically integrated chain of firms has difficulty accessing credit to pay one of its suppliers, it can cause cash flow problems for that supplier, who may in turn also be unable to access credit. The ongoing process of reform of the banking sector will mean that more flexible lending practices to SMEs will eventually be restored; there is some evidence that more enterprises have been accessing credit since late 2010. It will take some time, however, before credit markets are effective in supporting the development of the SME sector, and this could have long-term consequences for economic recovery.

Ultimately, for all sectors to survive, improving competitiveness is of fundamental importance. Falling prices and excess labour supply should help improve Ireland's competitive position, but more is required. For example, an environment must be fostered that promotes innovation and R&D, with greater linkages to the university sector. Recent initiatives in the nanotechnology sector are a good example of how this can work. The issue of human capital also looms large, especially if the Irish labour force is to have the right skills to move up the 'value chain' of production in years to come (see Chapters 6 and 13). A strong pro-competition stance must also be maintained in labour markets (see Chapter 6) and product markets (see Chapter 5), for the benefit of both Irish consumers and Irish businesses.

FDI flows into Ireland have been critical over the last two decades in terms of increasing employment and bringing much-needed technological and managerial skills that eventually pass into other sectors of the economy. Such success was based partly on special tax breaks, something which may have to end as other countries become involved in similar competitive tax-cutting exercises. Such a situation will lead to a zero-sum game overall, with national governments the losers and large MNCs the gainers. There is also now the phenomenon of large investment overseas by Irish companies and this process, as this chapter has emphasised, will have to be managed with care.

There will continue to be a rationale for state support of the manufacturing and internationally traded services sectors, but the nature of that support is changing and will have to change even more in years to come. The emphasis is shifting from tax breaks and direct grants to providing the correct competitive environment in which businesses can, without any direct state aid or tax breaks, flourish.

Endnotes

* My thanks to John O'Hagan for useful comments and feedback on an earlier draft of this chapter.

1 The discussion here draws on F. Barry, 'Foreign direct investment and institutional co-evolution in Ireland', *Scandinavian Economic History Review*, Vol. 55, No. 3, 2007.

2 The discussion here draws on M. Cassidy and E. Strobl, 'Subsidizing industry: an empirical analysis of Irish manufacturing', *Journal of Industry, Competition and Trade*, Vol. 4, No. 2, 2004.

3 Department of the Taoiseach, *Lisbon Agenda. Integrated Guidelines for Growth and Jobs. Implementation of the National Reform Programme, Progress Report*, Government Publications, Dublin 2009.

4 Forfás, *Making it Happen: Growing Enterprise for Ireland*, Forfás, Dublin 2010 and Department of Enterprise, Trade and Innovation, *Trading and Investing in a Smart Economy, A Strategy and Action Plan for Irish Trade, Tourism and Investment to 2015*, DETI, Dublin 2010.

5   Forfás, *Ireland's Nanotechnology Commercialisation Framework 2010–2014*, Forfás, Dublin 2010.

6   The statistics and discussion presented in this section draw on: National Competitiveness Council, *Annual Competitiveness Report 2010*, Forfás, Dublin 2010; National Competitiveness Council, *Costs of Doing Business in Ireland 2010*, Forfás, Dublin 2010; and J. Sexton, 'Trends in output, employment and productivity in Ireland, 1995–2005', in C. Aylward and R. O'Toole (eds), *Perspectives on Irish Productivity*, Forfás, Dublin 2006.

7   Department of Enterprise, Trade and Innovation, *op. cit.*

8   All figures for 2011 are taken from CSO, *External Trade Bulletin*, CSO, Dublin April 2011.

9   The discussion presented in this section draws on Forfás, *Input to the Services Directive: Regulatory Impact Analysis*, Forfás, Dublin 2010.

10 Department of Enterprise, Trade and Innovation, *op. cit.*

11 The data and analysis presented in this section are based on F. Barry and C. Van Egeraat, 'The decline of the computer hardware sector: how Ireland adjusted', *Quarterly Economic Commentary*, ESRI, Dublin 2008.

12 Accenture, *Sustaining High Performance in Shared Services: An Irish Perspective*, Accenture, Dublin 2010.

13 F. Barry, 'Export-platform foreign direct investment: the Irish experience', *EIB Papers*, Vol. 9, No. 2, 2004.

14 CSO, *Manufacturing Enterprises by Industry Sector, Country of Ownership*, 2007, Database Direct, available at www.cso.ie.

15 Department of Enterprise, Trade and Innovation, *op. cit.*

16 This section draws on H. Görg, 'Productivity spill-overs from multinational companies', in Aylward and O'Toole, *op. cit.*

17 Forfás, *Analysis of Ireland's Innovation Performance*, Forfás, Dublin 2011.

18 Expert Group on Future Skills Needs, *Tomorrow's Skills: Towards a National Skills Strategy*, Expert Group on Future Skills Needs, Dublin 2007.

19 Revenue Commissioners, *Finance Bill 2010 Section 38 – Transfer Pricing: Some Questions and Answers*, 2010, p.2, available at www.revenue.ie.

20 This section draws on R. O'Toole, 'Outward direct investment and productivity', in Aylward and O'Toole, *op. cit.*; and Forfás, *Statement on ODI*, 2007, available at http://www.forfas.ie/publications/outward_direct_invest_01/index.html.

CHAPTER 10

Physical Infrastructure, Energy and the Environment

Eleanor Denny and John O'Hagan

1 INTRODUCTION

Physical infrastructure, energy and the environment are strongly interlinked. Physical infrastructure is required not only for transport, but also for energy generation and distribution, and environmental protection. Transport in turn is a major user of energy and in the process a threat to the environment, as transport not only requires physical infrastructure but also fuel for vehicles. Infrastructure is also required to generate energy, particularly electricity, and to deal with air emissions, water provision and quality, and waste. There are no more controversial, or more costly, infrastructural projects, for example, than the construction of a power station (especially if nuclear) or a large incinerator facility.

The most important physical infrastructure projects in Ireland in the last decade or so related to transport, particularly road construction, and to a lesser extent public transport and airports. The focus, therefore, of the first two sections of this chapter, dealing with physical infrastructure in general, will be on large road construction projects. Section 2 will highlight the importance of physical infrastructure to economic activity, indicating that it is an input to production and a part of final consumption. The role of the state in particular is discussed and the contribution of public–private partnerships examined. Some key political economy issues associated with large infrastructural projects are considered. Section 3 outlines some key facts in relation to transport infrastructure in Ireland and highlights the many challenges to be faced, especially in the light of international comparisons and competition. The National Development Plan 2007–2013 has been substantially revised following the recession, but major infrastructural investment is still planned for the years 2011–14 and the *Annual Competitiveness Reports* of the National Competitiveness Council will be there to remind us how well the country has done in the past, and will do in years to come.

These reports also cover energy and the environment and Ireland's performance in this regard. Section 4 looks at the structure of energy demand in Ireland, highlighting the three main sectors: electricity, heating and transport. A detailed discussion of the role of the state in the energy sector is also provided. Section 5 looks at energy supply, in terms of diversity and security. The discussion covers energy infrastructure, renewable energy sources and nuclear energy. The last two, of course, have major environmental dimensions. Section 6 looks at the issue of pricing and competition in the energy sector, relating back to issues discussed in Chapter 5. Section 7 is devoted to three major environmental concerns: air emissions, water pollution and waste disposal. Addressing the potentially disastrous consequences of global warming is the responsibility of all nations, including Ireland. Our obligations under the Kyoto Protocol and, in particular, EU agreements are extensively covered. Together with the question of safe drinking water, there is also the issue of the supply of drinking water, which in the case of Ireland will require substantial new expenditure on infrastructure. The same applies to waste disposal, an issue which raises environmental and infrastructural provision issues.

2 PHYSICAL INFRASTRUCTURE: IMPORTANCE AND PROVISION

Input to Production and Final Consumption

Physical infrastructural investment, or physical capital,[1] consists of large capital-intensive projects, mostly, in the case of Ireland, publicly owned or regulated, which provide the core distribution system for production and consumption for any economy. It includes roads, airports, harbours, railways, utility distribution systems (for example for electricity and gas), water and sewerage systems, and communication networks. No economy can exist without large-scale physical infrastructure and it is crucial to the process of economic development in all countries. One of the great successes of the Roman Empire was the construction of major public infrastructure such as roads and basic water and sewerage works. In the case of Ireland a major programme of canal construction took place in the eighteenth century, when water was the main distribution system for goods. Ports were also built and a basic system of roads existed, particularly in towns. This was followed by the construction of major ports and railroads in the first half of the nineteenth century, which greatly increased the opportunities for trade and economic development. Large-scale investment in water and sewerage systems, energy infrastructure, and telephone networks took place in the twentieth century. These greatly facilitated further advances in economic development. By the end of the twentieth century and the early twenty-first century, the emphasis was on new communication channels, although in the case of Ireland the majority of infrastructural investment has been on the road and energy networks, in an attempt to make up for a major deficit in this regard from the past and also to accommodate the huge increase in employment and economic activity in the last twenty years (see Chapters 6 and 7).

Thus in a very general sense it is clear that infrastructural investment is crucial to economic growth and living standards. Most industries, not only manufacturing, require a good physical distribution system. Not only is it an input to production, it is also part of direct consumption. Thus, for example, roads are required to transport raw materials and other inputs, plus final goods, for manufacturing industry, retail outlets and most other services industries. They are also required by people when commuting to work and travelling for leisure purposes, for example to take a holiday. Not only does the ability to take such trips matter, but safety and time taken also have a strong influence on living standards and well-being.

Industry vitally needs energy as an input and so do households to heat homes, drive cars and provide the electricity required nowadays to facilitate all the household and consumer appliances that one needs to function. Industry needs water and waste disposal, which are also vital to household consumption and comfort. Likewise, Internet connections are needed not only by the manufacturing and services industries but also by individuals – to access knowledge, to 'shop' and consume different forms of entertainment.

Key Factor in Determining Productivity Growth

As seen in Chapter 7, physical capital has for some time been understood by economists as a key determinant of growth, with the Solow model giving it a particularly significant emphasis. But how important is it and how much do changes in physical infrastructure explain changes in productivity growth? As with so many explanations in economics, there is no consensus on the precise impact, with much written on how the road and energy networks in particular impact, either positively or negatively, on growth.[2] Estimating what forces affect productivity is extremely difficult. For example, public investment in transport networks may allow for increased trade, make profitable continued investment and innovation in the motor industry, and eventually allow for the development of efficient and effective supply chain management techniques that greatly increase productivity in industries. But the marginal impact could decline markedly with increasing road construction, and where this happens is very difficult to determine. A further difficulty is that productivity growth and spending on infrastructure are simultaneously determined variables and sometimes it is difficult to isolate the direction of causation. For example, to what extent was the large transport infrastructure investment in Ireland up to 2009 a cause or consequence of the growing economy? There appears to be a firm consensus, though, based on international comparisons (see later) and everyday experiences for many people, that in Ireland the marginal benefits from increased investment in transport infrastructure were considerable, but that now marked reductions in marginal benefits may become evident from any further investment.

The most recent example in relation to this debate is how developments in information technology (IT) contributed to increased productivity growth in the USA. While increased computing speeds and the huge decrease in the price of computing yielded benefits to consumers and producers alike, the benefits of the computer revolution relate in particular to the advent of the Internet, which in a sense can be thought of as the infrastructure of the computing age. As Gramlich states:

> ... like other networks the Internet significantly raised the productivity of each and every computer. The more Internet users there are, the more valuable each Internet connection and the more valuable the information that can be disseminated over the Internet. Thus, it seems likely that the synergies between innovations in computing and innovations in communications have yielded great benefits. And like the interstate highway system, the effects of the Internet on productivity growth are likely to wane over time.[3]

In relation to the productivity impact of increased investment in transport and energy infrastructure, a few general messages appear to apply. First, increased investment is a necessary but not a sufficient condition for increases in productivity. There are many examples of massive wasted investment across the world and over time. Second, the quality and management of the investment are probably more important than its level. Third, the allocation of the total infrastructural budget across the different types of infrastructure listed earlier is an important and difficult policy decision. For example, there is no point in having good IT networks if energy supply cannot be ensured. Likewise there is no point in having good roads if there is no oil for the transport using them. Last, infrastructure is very costly and that it be provided at lowest cost, for a given quality level, is crucial to its success. This leads to the questions of who should fund large capital projects and whether or not there is a strong competitive environment in the tendering for the construction of such projects. A different question relates to the efficient operation of the various infrastructural networks once constructed and the creation of a strong competitive environment for such provision, particularly in the energy area, a topic which is taken up later in the chapter.

Role of the State

Many take it as given that the state should largely fund all major infrastructural projects. This appears to be the case in relation to transport infrastructure, but it should be remembered that the building of the canals in the nineteenth century in Ireland was sometimes financed by private investors. In the USA, the building of the rail network was financed entirely by private companies, although the federal government heavily subsidised the rail network through land grants. The Channel Tunnel between Britain and France was also funded by private investors. Most of the planned investment in energy in Ireland, as shall be seen later, has no exchequer input. Whatever the source of finance, such projects involve huge state involvement, through a strict regulatory environment, subsidies and often major compulsory land purchase.

The first public policy issue revolves around the fact that infrastructure investment has large fixed costs and relatively low marginal costs. In the case of many such projects, the fixed costs are so large that only one firm can feasibly supply the project and hence this results in monopoly provision. Given the dangers of such provision, with regard to abuse of position in terms of pricing, standards, and so on, the state usually steps in and directly provides the infrastructure itself (although it usually hires private companies to carry out the actual work) or heavily regulates the private providers. Transport infrastructure is a good example of this and, as shall be seen later, it receives the largest allocation of state investment funding in Ireland. Construction of roads and rail networks involves huge fixed costs and up to the point of serious congestion the incremental cost of having an additional car or lorry on the road is tiny. Besides, collecting revenues from users may be costly, particularly in city streets (but also on some motorways, as was the case for the M50 in Dublin, with huge costs to commuters in terms of delays at toll booths prior to the introduction of barrier-free tolling). Nonetheless, toll roads are now a feature of Ireland's extensive motorway network, arising from the public–private dimension of such funding.

A second policy issue relates to the network externalities that arise from many large infrastructural projects. A good example here is IT. There are large economies of scale in creating information, as once information is created it can be made available to others without any cost. There are also positive network externalities. The larger and more interconnected the road or rail network the more valuable it is to all, and the same applies to the IT network. Thus the benefits of the whole can be much greater than the sum of its parts and this provides again a strong argument for state intervention to capture such external benefits for all, something a private operator cannot and will not take into account.

It is important, though, not to overstate the value of state intervention. There are cases where government ownership or regulation can actually hamper efficiency and lead to higher prices. State-owned or regulated industries can become entrenched monopolies, innovation can be suppressed, and without competition the quality of services can suffer. As discussed in Chapter 5, deregulation and privatisation can unleash entrepreneurial forces, leading to such innovations as the hub-and-spoke system, following deregulation of the airline industry, and the wide variety of IT services that followed deregulation of the telecommunications sector. As also discussed later in this chapter in relation to the energy sector, deregulation and competition have proved beneficial. This issue relates more to the delivery of services using the infrastructural network than the initial investment per se.

Whatever the debate about the role of the state in infrastructural projects, the reality in Ireland *is* that the state does provide the vast bulk of funding for such projects. Hence the concern should be with how best such projects are managed by the state and that lowest-cost, high-quality provision is assured. One development of importance in this regard in recent years in Ireland has been the idea of public–private partnerships (PPP) in the provision of large infrastructural projects, especially in the transport sector (see also Chapter 3).

Public–Private Partnership[4]

The involvement of private operators in the funding of large-scale infrastructural projects can lead to many benefits, not least the private operators' administrative and operational efficiencies, increased competition and enhanced services to end-users. Examples of efficiencies are the technical expertise and the managerial competencies of commercial operators. Even where the public sector has access to cheaper funding than private concerns, the efficiency gains from private sector participation can outweigh the extra financing costs.

Some states, of course, face fiscal burdens giving rise to liquidity constraints or raising funding costs to such an extent that private funding of infrastructure may appear not just the cheapest but the *only* feasible option. Thus the choice in certain cases may be between privately financed infrastructure and no infrastructure. This will be a matter for sound cost-benefit analysis of all costs and risks over the long run, including an assessment of economic, financial and social consequences.

Such an analysis needs to take into account not only individual contracts but also the impact on the full infrastructural system. As seen earlier, in network industries such as transport infrastructure, linkages between different segments of the networks and the 'actors' involved are critical. Thus the knock-on effects throughout the system must be taken into account. Besides, large transport, energy and other infrastructural projects often have major environmental and social repercussions that need to be properly accounted for and independent sustainability impact assessments commissioned. These issues arise not only when the state is involved but must also be taken into account when there is private involvement. Good cases in point include the controversy surrounding the construction of the M3 motorway near the Hill of Tara site in County Meath, and the Poolbeg incinerator in Dublin.

Thus it is unlikely that there will ever be private sector provision alone; rather there is likely to be some private sector involvement in funding. As such there will always be a high level of public subsidy and therefore clear control and management practices need to be put in place for such projects.

Further Policy Issues

The above are issues that perhaps involve too much detail for a book like this. The main point to make is that the delivery of large infrastructural projects, whether or not private sector financing is involved, is fraught with difficulties. Let us recap the three already discussed.

The first of these is the huge fixed cost involved and hence the need for monopoly provision, at least of the network, if not the use of it. The second is that there are often significant network externalities, which implies that the total could bring benefits considerably greater than the sum of its parts. Third, there is the issue of whether or not to involve the private sector in the financing and management of the infrastructure. Let us turn now to some other more general policy issues.

Many of the benefits of improvements in physical infrastructure are very difficult to estimate, for example in relation to the road network, time savings and reductions in road deaths and accidents. Time savings in travelling for business and leisure purposes is probably the most important benefit of an improved road and rail network in Ireland, yet it can be very difficult to estimate these savings. In particular, the increased future usage of the networks has to be estimated and the problem of severe congestion resulting from increased usage must be taken into account. Likewise, there are considerably fewer road casualties and accidents on wider, multi-carriage roads per kilometre travelled, but the valuation of the costs of a life or of long-term injuries are almost impossible to measure accurately.

There are many environmental and heritage costs/benefits which are also almost impossible to value yet can be crucial to the debate, in particular in relation to road construction, energy provision and waste disposal. Examples of this are noise and air pollution. There may also be damage to important architectural sites or areas of outstanding beauty or important habitats for birds and wildlife. How are these costs/benefits to be established, let alone be evaluated?

Many infrastructural projects are long-term in nature, involving huge sums of money, and the choice of a suitable discount rate to take account of the future benefits/costs is fraught with difficulty, particularly in relation to the environment. The debate about the economics of global warming hinges fundamentally on the discount rate chosen to apply to the costs and benefits of infrastructural and other measures required to deal with expected future environmental concerns twenty to fifty years into the future.

Because the projects are so long-term in nature, there is also often very considerable uncertainty about the benefits/costs into the future, making them difficult to undertake for either the public sector or the private sector. For example, estimating future demand for a major transport facility depends on many uncertainties, such as the price of oil and the development of alternative means of transport in the intervening period. In relation to the environment, for decades there was huge disagreement about the actual scientific evidence of global warming into the future and the consequences of this for the environment, sea levels and ambient temperatures. The debate surrounding the provision of nuclear energy encapsulates all of the above: it requires huge levels of investment, with a very long time horizon and potentially catastrophic but unknown expected external costs (see later).

There is also the issue of considering alternatives, a process that might never end and/or might lead to huge time lags in delivery of major infrastructural projects. Examples of this are roads where, even when construction has commenced, after a consultation process of many years, people object that other routes were not properly considered, although some of the costs they complain about can only be realised once construction begins. A variant of this difficulty is that totally different alternatives were not considered, such as public transport. The building of much-needed airport capacity can often be delayed by many years to take account of the very reasonable concerns of those affected by airport noise and traffic, but these considerations must be set against the benefits to a much larger number of people arising from reduced travel times to/from airports, and better facilities, less crowding and fewer time delays when at the airport.

Finally, there is the huge disruption that can arise during the construction phase. Even when there is broad agreement about the net benefits resulting once the construction phase is completed, there may still be a small number of people so affected during the construction stage that they will, understandably, use every means available to them to prevent the project taking place. Again, though, the possible major benefits to hundreds of thousands of other people must be taken into account.

There is really no scientific way of dealing with all of the issues above arising in relation to large infrastructural projects. At the end of the day they involve major political decisions, which carry many risks to policy-makers. There is also an asymmetry in public reaction to such infrastructural projects. Get them right and the outcome is taken as 'expected'; get them 'wrong' and the outcome is there for all to see, with the result that politicians face obloquy and public outcry. It is no wonder that politicians sometimes defer decisions on infrastructure for as long as possible. Yet tough decisions on infrastructure must be taken, for, as argued above, no economy can function without good infrastructure, be it in transport, energy or the environment. In particular, the business sector requires its provision, not just to function and produce, but to do so in such a way that it can survive in an intensely competitive international environment. Increasingly the provision of good-quality infrastructure, at lowest cost, can be the factor that makes or breaks the success of an industrial concern, although clearly a host of other competitiveness factors apply, as discussed earlier.

3 TRANSPORT AND COMMUNICATIONS INFRASTRUCTURE

Overall
Planned Expenditure
This section now turns to more practical issues, namely the key facts and figures relating to the present state and future plans for infrastructure in Ireland. The main reference point for this was initially the National Development Plan 2007–2013. However, because of the recession the scale of the capital spending envisaged under this plan has been quite dramatically reduced since 2009. The other main source of information is Forfás,[5] the primary state agency assigned with the task of encouraging enterprise in Ireland.

Under the plan, expenditure on transport dominated, with over €33 billion of the total of around €55 billion devoted to this sector. It is interesting to note that, of this €33 billion, only €20 billion was to be funded by the exchequer, €7 billion by PPP and over €2 billion by state bodies. It was planned to spend €8.6 billion on energy infrastructure, most of which was to be funded by state bodies, and €5.8 billion on environmental services (see later sections). The bulk of expenditure on environmental services was to be funded by the exchequer.

The National Recovery Plan 2011–2014 laid out revised priorities and levels of exchequer expenditure for capital investment on infrastructure. In this period, expenditure by the exchequer on transport is planned to be €4.8 billion, way down on the figure envisaged in 2007 but still sizeable. Exchequer expenditure on environmental infrastructure is planned at €3.5 billion, and, as shall be seen later, substantial non-exchequer funding on the energy infrastructure is also planned for the years ahead.

Levels of expenditure of course do not directly relate to importance. For example, in the 'other' category of the National Development Plan, less than €0.5 billion was allocated by the exchequer to communications and broadband. The services provided via this network will be crucially important to producers and consumers in the years ahead, with most of the services being provided privately. Thus, while expenditure on IT networks might be relatively small compared to that on transport, energy and the environment, the provision of adequate IT networks and the enforcement of strict competition in IT service provision may be just as important to industry and consumers as expenditure on other infrastructure.

Quality: International Comparisons

Table 10.1 provides information on the relative quality of the physical infrastructure, in particular that relating to transport, drawing on the World Economic Forum reports which rank each country in terms of the *perceptions* of business.[6] While such measures have their limitations, nonetheless in many cases it is perhaps perceptions rather than the reality that matter. In any case these perceptions correlate closely with the evidence in relation to the value of the public capital stock per person and there is a reassuring stability in the perception rankings between 2001 and 2009 for the countries which did not undergo much change in this period. The main findings in relation to overall infrastructural quality are as follows.

- Denmark, France and Germany received scores greater than 6.0 (of a maximum of 7.0) in 2009.
- Ireland's score was 0.3 below Hungary's and, of the countries listed, only Italy's was lower than Ireland's.
- The OECD average in 2009 was 5.8, down from 6.0 in 2001. The figure for Ireland in the same period improved marginally, up from 3.7 to 4.0, well below the OECD average in both years and way below the figures for France, Germany and the Nordic countries.

Thus there appears to be a perceived very serious overall infrastructural deficit. The picture, though, when you look at the efficiency of the transport network (road, air and sea), which accounts for the vast bulk of public infrastructure, is more encouraging. The other major infrastructural areas are energy, environmental services (such as water provision and waste management), and communications and broadband. While the first two of these are covered later in the chapter, the last will be discussed briefly in this section.

Table 10.1

Ireland's Ranking in Terms of Infrastructure

Country	Perceptions of overall infrastructural quality (score min. 0.0, max. 7.0)		Perceptions of efficiency of transport network (score min. 0.0, max. 10.0)	
	2001	2009	2001	2009
Denmark	6.7	6.2	8.8	9.2
France	6.8	6.6	8.3	9.1
Germany	6.8	6.5	8.8	9.0
Hungary	4.1	4.3	5.1	7.1
Ireland	*3.7*	*4.0*	*3.7*	*6.7*
Italy	3.9	3.8	4.0	4.9
Netherlands	6.2	5.8	7.0	8.0
Poland	n/a	n/a	3.2	6.1
Spain	5.1	5.3	6.1	7.2
UK	5.6	5.2	5.4	7.8
OECD average	6.0	5.8	7.6	8.0

Source: National Competitiveness Council, *Annual Competitiveness Report* 2009 and 2010, Forfás, Dublin, www.competitiveness.ie/media/ncc090818_acr_2009.pdf.

As can be seen in Table 10.1, Ireland ranked very poorly in terms of the perceived efficiency of the transport infrastructure in 2001, getting a score of 3.7 (max 10.0) compared to an OECD average of 7.6 and figures as high as 8.8 in Denmark and Germany. However, by 2009 the situation had improved quite dramatically, with the figure for Ireland rising to 6.7, and this is likely to have risen again in 2010 and 2011 as more major road projects came on stream. Ireland still lagged behind all countries bar Italy and Poland in 2009, but the gap had narrowed substantially and is likely to narrow further, as already mentioned. Two decades of major road construction have brought real dividends.

With the economic downturn, plans for an outer orbital road and eastern bypass for Dublin are distant prospects, although car ownership per thousand of population in Ireland is still below the average of countries with the same level of income per head and as such a further large increase in the total number of cars on the road could occur over the next decade or so. Having a well-developed and interconnected road network *across* the country is also important, given the relatively dispersed nature of economic activity and housing developments, partly due to the fact that tourism and agriculture are important sectors of the economy. This, however, pushes up the unit cost of infrastructure provision, a particularly serious issue in the energy area (see later).

While around €18 billion was to be allocated to roads, €13 billion was also to be allocated to public transport, €2 billion to air transport and around €0.5 billion to seaports. The bulk of the public transport investment was to take place in the Greater Dublin area, with completion of the Metro North line from the city centre to Swords via Dublin Airport planned, as well as a phased development of the Metro West line and extensions to the Luas and a significant expansion of the bus fleet and priority lanes. A key issue is that these systems are integrated, in terms of physical connections, integrated ticketing systems, and park and ride facilities. Most of this, though, has been put on hold and is likely to remain so for many years, until the economy recovers. In the meantime Ireland could fall well behind again, as other countries upgrade their transport networks further; so much continuous investment in infrastructure is required simply to stay level with competitor nations.

This also applies of course to the other important network infrastructure, namely information and communications technology (ICT), which, as discussed earlier, is essential to modern enterprise. Ireland's investment in ICT in 2008 was equal to the euro area average (see also Chapter 7), but behind leading countries such as Japan, the UK and the USA.[7]

Broadband affects not just how enterprises work internally or with each other, but also how they interact with consumers. Despite strong growth since 2003, Ireland continues to perform poorly in terms of broadband take-up per 100 of population. Ireland also has a higher proportion (31 per cent) of fixed connections below 2Mb/s than the euro area (20 per cent); and Ireland remains behind leading countries in terms of upgrading local broadband access networks to fibre and in offering very fast speeds over fibre. These figures can change rapidly, though, as huge increases have been recorded in many countries in the last three to four years and further large changes are likely.[8]

4 ENERGY SECTOR: IMPORTANCE AND PROVISION

One of the most significant infrastructural challenges facing the state is the provision of a secure and sustainable energy supply into the future. This requires not only investment in the underlying capital resources, for example in power stations and networks, but also in the security of energy supply, for example in indigenous fossil fuel production and renewable energy. Both of these areas, the provision of the energy sector physical infrastructure and the security of energy fuel supplies, result in the state traditionally playing a large and important role in the energy sector. This section will first introduce the energy sector and its characteristics and then discuss the importance of the role of the state in the sector.

Importance and Nature of Energy Sector and Demand

Since the 1800s the role of energy in modern society has evolved and today energy is an essential input into almost every aspect of daily life, both for consumption and as an input to production. From lighting, heating and transport at the residential level to production processes, IT systems, communications networks, and retail and services provision, energy is considered a vital necessity without which any developed economy would grind to a halt. In fact, a reliable and safe energy supply at a sustainable cost is considered a basic necessity for economic development.

Energy is generally classified by its mode of application: for electricity, heating/cooling (of space and water) or for transportation. In Ireland, the energy landscape in each of these sectors has changed significantly over the last century as Ireland has grown from a largely agricultural society to a service, industrial and manufacturing-driven economy.

Electricity

The original driver for electricity arose from a desire for people to light their homes cheaply and safely. The subsequent challenge was to develop an electricity system that could create electricity in a central location (at a power plant) and carry it to people's homes (across a network). In 1882 the first power plant in the world was constructed in New York and it supplied eighty-five customers with electricity to light their homes. It wasn't until twenty years later, in 1903, that Ireland's first power station was built at the Pigeon House in Dublin to supply power to the street lights around Dublin city. In 1922 discussions began on a proposal to dam the River Shannon and by 1925 construction had begun on Ireland's first bulk power station, a hydro-electric plant in Ardnacrusha, Co. Clare, to supply electricity to the towns and cities of Ireland. Today the island of Ireland has over thirty power stations operated on coal, gas, oil and peat, 146 wind farms and a variety of smaller installations at businesses and homes. In 2009, electricity accounted for 32 per cent of all energy used in Ireland.

Heating

In terms of energy for heating, Ireland has a strong tradition of open fires in domestic dwellings, which has resulted in coal and peat remaining important heat sources in the residential sector over the past century. Open fires typically have low efficiency and in order to heat the entire house are usually supplemented by oil, electric and, increasingly, gas heating systems. Significant upgrades in building regulations have led to improvements in the efficiency of the building stock in Ireland with a house built in 2010 typically using one-third the heating energy of the average existing home. However, Ireland still has a large stock of inefficient residential dwellings with energy use per dwelling 27 per cent above the UK average in 2005 and 36 per cent above the EU-27 average in 2006. Comparisons with the UK provide a good benchmark as the climates in both countries are similar. Other EU countries have a much higher air-conditioning demand than Ireland, so would tend to have a peak thermal energy demand in the summer months, whereas Ireland would have its peak demand in winter.[9]

Reasons for Ireland's poor performance when compared to the UK and the rest of the EU include larger average dwelling sizes, a higher proportion of solid fuel use and a lack of district heating initiatives. District heating allows heat to be generated efficiently in a central location and then circulated to residential and commercial premises. District heating is prevalent throughout Europe, but its uptake in Ireland has been slow. However, advances in technology and environmental drivers are likely to see an increase in the use of district heating in Ireland in the future. Residential heat demand represents approximately 44 per cent of total heat demand in Ireland, with the remainder from industry, services and agriculture. In 2009, heat demand accounted for 34 per cent of all energy use in Ireland.

Transport
The final third of energy demand is accounted for in the transportation sector, a sector which has seen huge change in the past two decades. Economic activity is the main driver of transport demand and an increase of 190 per cent in economic output in the period 1990–2007 saw transport energy demand increase by 181 per cent in the same period. Much of this increase was seen in freight transportation for the construction industry and an increase in aviation demand, but the residential sector also contributed significantly. In the same period, the number of licensed private cars increased from 796,408 in 1990 to 1,882,901 in 2007, an increase of 136 per cent.

Role of the State
As discussed in Section 2, large infrastructural projects often necessitate the intervention of the state due to their significant capital costs and the importance of the assets to sustaining economic growth. The expected lifetime of investments in the energy sector is forty years or more, thus the wisdom of any investment decisions, for example investment in a coal-fired power station versus a nuclear station, must be considered within a similar time frame. Investments in the underlying network have even longer lifetimes. Similarly, policy decisions with a view to increasing competitiveness or decreasing emissions today must take account of the long-term legacy of these decisions.[10] The energy sector displays many types of market failure, such as monopolies, externalities and public goods, each of which prompts a role for the state in the sector (see also Chapter 3).

Monopolies
The first form of market failure in the energy sector is the presence of monopolies. Due to the importance of maintaining the security of energy supply, the state traditionally took a role in sourcing, generating, transmitting and supplying electricity and gas to end-users. In other words, the state created state-owned vertically integrated monopolies such as the Electricity Supply Board (ESB) and

Bord Gáis Éireann (BGE). While the energy sector has evolved significantly in recent years with the introduction of new players and increased competition (see also Chapter 5), the role of the state in all aspects of the energy industry continues to be large.

Across Europe, the provision of electricity and gas requires extensive network infrastructure and, because of the significant economies of scale, these networks are considered to be natural monopolies. In 1996 the EU initiated common rules on the internal markets for electricity and gas, intended to open up electricity and gas markets to competition in all the member states. However, these EU directives recognise that the networks element of the industry is a natural monopoly and so allow member states to continue to have a monopoly in network provision, but this company cannot participate in any other aspects of the industry. Thus, the electricity and gas networks are now separated from the traditional vertically integrated monopolies and are operated and maintained by companies which are ring-fenced from other aspects of the industry. In Ireland, these companies are EirGrid (high-voltage electricity network), ESB Networks (low-voltage electricity networks), and Bord Gáis Networks (gas interconnectors and network).

While EirGrid, ESB Networks, and Bord Gáis Networks are now independent companies, they continue to remain under the ownership of the state. In fact, a recent report's recommendations included that the high-voltage electricity and gas networks should remain under state ownership, as these are the most critical elements of the energy infrastructure.[11]

While the electricity and gas networks are recognised to be natural monopolies, the EU directive does require an increase in competition in the generation of electricity and the supply of both electricity and gas to end-users. With this in mind, Ireland has seen a number of new independent participants, such as Airtricity and Flogas, enter the electricity and gas markets in recent years (competition in the energy sector is discussed further in Section 6 and also in Chapter 5). However, the state remains the dominant player in both sectors.

In fact, the ESB remains by a significant margin the largest undertaking in state ownership, accounting for one half of the state's commercial sector when measured by net assets. The state participation in the energy sector also includes Bord Gáis Éireann (through the gas infrastructure but also in the electricity sector and more recently in wind power developments), Bord na Móna (with involvement in peat production, power generation and wind) and also in Coillte (which provides wood to the power generation sector and has also begun to develop interests in wind farms). Thus, the state owns three companies (ESB, Bord Gáis and Bord na Móna) that have competing interests in the electricity generation sector and one (Coillte) that is developing interests in this area. While state participation in the energy sector was traditionally required in all aspects of the industry to ensure the provision of a secure energy supply, the necessity to have such a large and competing involvement is now questionable. With this in mind, and with a view to raising additional revenues for the state, a recent report recommends that ESB, Bord Gáis Éireann, Bord na Móna and Coillte should all be privatised.[12]

While formerly dominated by vertically integrated monopolies, the energy sector now displays increased competition (see also Chapter 5). However, it is far from perfectly competitive. Natural monopolies remain in the network aspect of the energy sector and the generation and supply elements of the industry are more like oligopolies (which retain a high level of state ownership). The potential for strategic behaviour on the part of participants in the sector remains high and thus the sector must be heavily regulated. The state-run Commission for Energy Regulation in Ireland undertakes this role in both the electricity and gas sectors. In fact, the energy sector is one of the most highly regulated of all industrial sectors. Thus, while the state's role in the provision of electricity and gas may diminish in the coming years through the sale of state assets, it will continue to play an important role in the networks element of the sector and crucially in the regulation of all aspects of the industry.

Externalities

A second reason for the involvement of the state in the energy sector is due to the fact that the energy sector is the largest contributor to greenhouse gas emissions in Ireland. The presence of externalities, such as emissions, prompts a role for government in the energy sector. In Ireland this has taken the form of subsidies for renewable generation and energy efficiency measures as well as penalties for producers of carbon dioxide (such as carbon taxes and mandatory participation in the EU Emissions Trading Scheme). Environmental issues are discussed later in Section 7.

Public Goods

A third reason for the involvement of the state in the energy sector is the theory that security of energy supply is an example of a marketable public good. Energy supply is considered a basic necessity and when provided for all, it promotes greater standards of living for all. A secure energy supply results in a lower risk of blackouts and supply interruptions, which is a necessity to promote commercial activity and economic development. Thus, the benefits of a secure energy supply are enjoyed by all, even those who do not pay directly for it.

However, investments in energy infrastructure have long lead times (up to ten years when planning delays are taken into account) and exceptionally high capital costs. Once a power station is built it improves the security of energy supply for all, but the cost is so high that no individual customer can afford to pay to incentivise an increase in generation capacity. In addition, providing energy from a single source (e.g. oil) is a threat to supply security, whereas providing energy from a diverse range of sources reduces the risk of supply interruption and increases energy security. However, market incentives are unlikely to be present to encourage private investment in a diverse range of fuels. All of these factors prompt a role for government in securing the provision of energy security from a diverse range of fuel sources. This can be done by direct involvement through the establishment of state-run vertically integrated monopolies or through regulation and incentive schemes.

Energy and Spatial Planning

In examining Ireland's energy consumption patterns, the state's role in spatial planning is a key issue. Compared to other EU countries, Ireland's planning legacy has resulted in a historical trend of low-density housing, leading to urban sprawl around major cities and large numbers of one-off houses in rural areas. In 2009, just 3.1 per cent of Ireland's population lived in apartments, the lowest figure in the EU-27, where the average is 41.7 per cent.[13] This planning legacy of low-density and one-off housing has important knock-on implications for energy usage in all sectors.

The most obvious implication is for the transport sector; when people live closer to their workplace, commuting distances are shorter, and a public transport system can be optimised to meet the needs of the population more efficiently. In the electricity sector, our dispersed population has led to Ireland having four times the EU average length of power lines per customer.[14] While unsightly and more costly to construct, longer lines also have the disadvantage that more energy is lost in transmission. A history of poor spatial planning decisions also has consequences for the development of new power stations, with the routing of power lines more challenging when houses are distributed widely outside towns and villages. In the heating sector, our distributed housing impacts on the availability of mainline gas, one of the most efficient fuels available for domestic use. One-off and dispersed housing also reduces the potential for district heating.

The provision of electricity, heating and transportation are considered basic necessities in any developed society. Thus, in an era of rising oil prices, environmental concerns and competitive pressures, energy policy is a critical concern for policy-makers, and decisions in this area have far-reaching consequences. Energy policy is generally driven by three main goals: security of supply; sustainability of prices for end-users; and environmental concerns. Each of these components will be discussed in detail in the following sections.

5 PERFORMANCE AND POLICY ISSUES IN ENERGY SUPPLY

As one of the key inputs to economic activity, the security of energy supply into the future is a key concern. Interruptions in supply, even for short periods of time, can have very serious economic consequences. Security of supply can be considered under a number of metrics: for example, how reliant is the country on an individual fuel source, and how diverse are its energy fuel needs? How dependent is the country on imported fuel and how exposed is it as a result to price fluctuations and interruptions in imported fuel supplies? Does the country have the physical infrastructure in place to ensure delivery of energy to the end-user into the future?

Fuel Diversity

Table 10.2 illustrates the breakdown of energy demand in Ireland in 2008 by fuel type. It can be seen that Ireland's dominant fuel source is oil, which accounts for around 55 per cent of total energy use. This demand is primarily driven by the transport and heating sectors. Natural gas is increasing in importance, mainly driven by its usage in electricity generation and domestic heating.

Table 10.2

Ireland's Percentage Energy Usage by Type, 2008

	Total	Electricity	Heating	Transport
Oil[1]	55	4	54	99
Natural gas	27	57	31	–
Coal	9	18	7	–
Peat	5	12	5	–
Renewable sources	4	7	4	1
Electricity imports	0.2	1	–	–

Source: Sustainable Energy Authority of Ireland, *Energy in Ireland 1990–2009*, Energy Policy Statistical Support Unit, 2010.
[1] Includes oil products such as diesel, petrol, and kerosene.

As mentioned in Section 4, policy-makers generally try to encourage as much diversity as possible so that each sector is protected should there be an interruption in the supply of one fuel source. In each of the energy sectors, though, Ireland has a heavy reliance on at least one fuel type. This is particularly pertinent for the transport sector, where 99 per cent of fuels are oil-based, and thus this sector is heavily exposed to any potential interruptions in oil supply.

The electricity sector, as can be seen in Table 10.2, uses the most diverse range of fuel types, although it has a heavy and growing reliance on natural gas. The existing oil-fired power stations are gradually being decommissioned due to age and any new fossil fuel-based power stations planned are expected to be natural gas fired. While coal and oil can be stored (albeit at a cost), natural gas storage is much more complex. Thus, this heavy reliance on natural gas for electricity production can be seen as a threat to supply security into the future. The sources of energy for the heating sector are more diversified and reflect that of the economy as a whole (see earlier), with a heavy dependence likewise on oil.

Indigenous Fuels and Import Dependency

Twinned with the challenge of diversity of fuel supplies is the reliance of a country on imported fuels. When a country can produce energy locally it provides a hedge against fluctuations in international fuel prices and interruptions in fuel supplies. It also saves on important foreign exchange outlays. Thus, policy-makers try as much as possible to encourage the production of energy domestically.

Ireland had an import dependency of 89 per cent in 2009, the fourth highest dependency in the EU-27 and well above the EU average. The trend has been upward, the figure having been around 70 per cent twenty years ago, and reflects the fact that Ireland is not endowed with significant indigenous fossil fuel resources and has, to date, not harnessed significant quantities of renewable resources.

Oil, as seen in Table 10.2 above, is by far the most dominant energy source in Ireland, and 100 per cent is imported. The transport sector has the heaviest reliance on imported fuels with 99 per cent dependence on imported oil. The bulk of Ireland's oil, however, is sourced from politically stable countries such as Norway, Denmark and the UK.

Arising from membership of the EU and the International Energy Agency (IEA), Ireland must hold 90 days of oil stocks based on the previous year's imports. Under the European Communities (Minimum Stocks of Petroleum Oils) Regulations, this responsibility has been vested in an Irish state body called the National Oil Reserves Agency (NORA). NORA receives no exchequer funding and its ongoing activities are 100 per cent funded by a levy imposed on certain oil products. According to the Department of Communications, Energy and Natural Resources, if there were a 10 per cent reduction in world oil supplies (a level of disruption unprecedented since the Suez War of 1956–57), it is estimated that the required 90-day reserves would last over two years, even without taking into account any demand reduction measures.[15] Thus, in the short term, Ireland is hedged against fluctuations in oil supply. However, in the medium to long term, in order to protect itself from fluctuating supply and prices, Ireland needs to diversify further its energy mix away from oil, particularly in the transport and heating sectors.

Given Ireland's large oil stocks, interruptions to gas supply are of greater concern in the short to medium term. In 2009, just 8 per cent of Ireland's gas was produced domestically (at the Kinsale gas field) with the remaining 92 per cent imported via a pipeline to Britain. The majority of Ireland's imported gas is sourced from politically stable locations in the North Sea. It is anticipated that Ireland's production of natural gas will increase in the coming years through the development of the Corrib gas field and a proposed liquefied natural gas development in Co. Clare. Besides, a number of gas storage facilities are planned in Larne and Ballycotton.

In addition to domestic gas, Ireland also has an indigenous peat resource which is currently used to generate electricity at three power stations. The Irish government supports the use of peat for electricity generation through a Public Service Obligation levy on all electricity bills (see later). The justification for this support is for security of supply reasons (to reduce Ireland's dependence on imported fuels) and to support jobs in rural areas.

In a further effort to reduce Ireland's reliance on imported fuels (as well as for environmental and sustainability reasons), the Irish government has set targets for renewable energy in each of the energy consumption sectors. In the electricity sector Ireland has an ambitious target of achieving 40 per cent of its electricity from renewable sources by 2020, exceeding the targets of any other country worldwide. In the heating sector the target is 12 per cent by 2020 and for transport 10 per cent. Given the centralised nature of electricity supply, it is relatively easier to integrate renewable sources into this sector, hence the higher target.

Renewable Energy

Hydro generation was the earliest renewable technology used for electricity generation and it underwent rapid development throughout the last century. Across the developed world few, if any, suitable economic sites remain for the further development of hydro-electricity. After hydro, wind generation is one of the most advanced forms of renewable energy and output has grown rapidly in the last fifteen years. As the market for wind energy has grown, the costs have reduced dramatically. Ambitious renewable energy targets together with reducing costs and successes to date are likely to ensure that wind energy continues to grow in electricity networks worldwide.

Given its location on the edge of the Atlantic Ocean, Ireland has a vast wind resource potential. It is anticipated that the bulk of Ireland's renewable target in the electricity sector will be met through wind generation. In 2010, wind generation represented over 11 per cent of electricity generation and the island of Ireland, as a single synchronous power system, has arguably the largest penetrations of wind power in the world at present.

Solar technology for electricity generation requires direct sunlight, and as such is not considered an economically viable option for Ireland. Ireland does, however, have large ocean energy resources for the development of wave and tidal turbines. Nevertheless, the development of ocean technology has been relatively slow with just a small number of devices at the commercial prototype stage. While the vast majority of wind turbines follow the same general design (three blades on a vertical tower), no single ocean device has emerged as the leading design. Operational challenges and access issues in the marine environment have been among the main barriers to ocean energy development to date.

Renewable technologies such as wind generation, solar, tidal and wave generation have a 'variable' output. The output of these units depends upon weather conditions, which cannot be controlled by the operator of the generator. For example, the amount of electricity generated by a wind turbine fluctuates as wind speed changes and that of a solar panel with the intensity of sunlight. Thus, the control of their output is limited. When significant penetrations of these forms of generation are connected to an electricity network, it can increase the challenge of providing a secure and reliable electricity supply at all times. This is a challenge that must be addressed by electricity system operators into the future as wind and other renewable penetrations in Ireland increase further.

In the heating and transport sectors, the integration of renewable sources of energy is more challenging as these sectors do not generally use centralised energy supplies. For heating, just 3.8 per cent of energy came from renewable sources in 2008, with the main contributor being the use of waste wood biomass. In the transport sector, renewable energy represented 1.2 per cent of transport energy in 2008. The share of bio-fuels grew to 1 per cent by 2008 following the introduction of tax breaks in 2006. The use of electricity in the transport sector (for the Dart and Luas) is also considered to be 'renewable' as the electricity can be generated through renewable sources.

Energy Infrastructure
In order to ensure the security of energy supply it is important to examine not only the sustainability of the fuels used (renewable versus fossil fuel) but also the adequacy of the energy infrastructure. As mentioned in Section 4, adequate infrastructure requires the intervention of the state, not only in incentivising the provision of infrastructure but also through regulation.

The main infrastructural challenges in the heating energy sector are the poor-quality existing housing stock and the availability of mains gas. While advances have been made in recent years regarding the energy usage of new-build housing (for example Part L of the Building Regulations 2008), unfortunately in many cases these came too late and did not apply to houses built at the height of the housing boom. Retro-fitting existing houses with improved insulation, glazing and efficient boilers is likely to be the predominant source of infrastructural improvements in residential heating in the future.

Natural gas is one of the most efficient forms of heating. However, access to the natural gas network is required. Gas supply in Ireland is delivered via a network of approximately 12,300km of pipelines. There are two main gas entry points, one at Inch in Co. Cork to service the Kinsale and Seven Heads gas fields and the other from Moffat in western Scotland, which connects Ireland to the main British gas network. The primary source of future indigenous production of gas is the Corrib gas field in Co. Mayo. To date, five oil wells are completed and ready for production at the Corrib site and the 83km offshore pipeline was completed in 2009. The final section of the pipeline is onshore, which has led to much local opposition. Planning permission for this final onshore section was granted in January 2011 and, assuming no further delays, the Corrib gas field is expected to be online in 2012/2013, leading to a third entry point. When operational, the output of this gas field is anticipated to meet approximately 73 per cent of Irish annual gas demand in 2012/2013, declining in later years.[16]

In the *electricity* sector, a formula known as 'generation adequacy' is used to measure the relationship between the output of electricity that can be supplied, and predicted demand. A statistic known as the 'loss of load expectation' (LOLE) measures any imbalance between projected supply and demand. In Ireland, the accepted LOLE is eight hours per year. In other words, Ireland is considered to have enough supply potential (power stations, renewable generators, etc.) to meet demand if the predicted number of hours when customers lose power is equal to or less than eight hours per year. When examining future demand and supply options, we must ensure that this LOLE criterion continues to be met.

Currently Ireland has only one electrical interconnector to the system in Britain. This interconnector allows Ireland to import electricity from Scotland when needed and to export power when Ireland has excess generation. A second interconnector, to Wales, is currently under construction; it will significantly enhance the reliability of the Irish electricity system and allow for continued operation with a LOLE of eight hours per annum.

The electricity system operator of Ireland, EirGrid, predicts that the adequacy situation is strongly positive until at least 2016. A surplus of electricity supply is predicted for each year with a LOLE of not more than eight hours per year being comfortably met. This is due to projected investment in new generation capacity (both conventional and renewable), increased interconnection, and low demand growth, arising from the marked slow-down in economic activity. It should be noted, however, that any new generation capacity will require the servicing and upgrade of the existing electricity network. To this effect, in 2010 the Commission for Energy Regulation announced plans to invest €3.76 billion in the Irish electricity network. The purpose of this investment is to improve the quality of electricity to customers, to allow for the development of new energy projects (such as remote wind farms) and to help attract new foreign direct investment into regions which would traditionally have been poorly serviced by the electricity network. This network upgrade plan will be financed through revenues earned by ESB networks and EirGrid. Again, the issue of spatial planning arises in regard to the upgrade of the electricity network. Ireland's legacy of ribbon development greatly increases the challenge of routing power lines, often resulting in lengthy planning delays.

Nuclear Energy

A highly controversial topic relating to energy supply security and energy infrastructure is the potential for nuclear energy in Ireland. The international nuclear debate has heightened in recent months, following the events in 2011 at the Fukushima nuclear plant in Japan, with widespread re-evaluation of nuclear programmes. Current Irish legislation bans the generation of electricity from nuclear sources, and it is unlikely that any Irish government would be elected with a mandate for nuclear energy in the foreseeable future. The infrastructural aspects of nuclear power for Ireland will be discussed in this section and the environmental aspects in a later section.

Nuclear fission energy is the energy that is released when an atom is split in two. In most nuclear power stations, the atom that is split is a uranium atom. The splitting uranium atoms react with each other to split more atoms, creating a chain reaction. Each of these reactions releases energy in the form of heat, which can then be used to generate electricity. Uranium is in abundant supply across the world, with large stocks in politically stable countries such as Canada and Australia.

The infrastructural challenges of integrating nuclear energy into the Irish electricity system are very challenging. First, the majority of nuclear power stations are large at over 1,000MW. A power station of this size would represent over 22 per cent of Ireland's peak electricity demand in 2010. In order to operate the electricity system in a reliable fashion, the system operator is required to carry a certain amount of electricity in 'back-up' mode to guard against any contingencies (similar to having a doctor on call). This 'back-up' electricity is known as reserve and the amount carried is equal to the size of the largest unit on the system. Currently the largest unit is at Poolbeg in Dublin and is 460MW in size. The introduction of a nuclear unit would increase the amount of back-up capacity required to 1,000MW, which would have significant cost and operational implications. In addition, any power station of 1,000MW in size would require significant electricity network reinforcement.

Another infrastructural challenge to nuclear power generation is that it is relatively inflexible in nature. Once a nuclear plant is in operation its output cannot be varied easily due to safety concerns. This lack of flexibility would cause a challenge for the reliable operation of the Irish electricity system. With a large and growing wind penetration, what Ireland needs are flexible power stations to accommodate the variable wind output, i.e. power stations which can increase their output when renewable generation is low and decrease output when renewable generation is high. Thus, as Ireland is actively pursuing the promotion of renewable energy, it needs complementary flexible conventional power stations. Nuclear power stations are not flexible in their operation and thus are not complementary to renewable generation. Thus, Ireland can either pursue nuclear or renewable sources of energy, but probably not both.

6 END-USER ENERGY PRICES AND COMPETITION

The second pillar of energy policy is the sustainability of end-user energy prices. As a key input in almost every production process, energy costs have a direct impact on Ireland's international competitiveness and indeed on living standards in Ireland, as the cheaper the energy the better off are consumers. The provision of electricity and heating is also considered to be a basic necessity and thus it is important to protect the financially disadvantaged from excessively high prices. However, prices must also be high enough to attract investment in the energy infrastructure in Ireland into the future. Thus, energy prices are generally discussed as being sustainable: low enough so as not to adversely impact on competitiveness, living standards, and vulnerable users; but high enough to ensure continued investment in supply. Table 10.3 illustrates Ireland's end-user energy prices compared to the EU-15 countries listed.

Table 10.3

End-User Energy Prices (Including Taxes) in EU-15 Countries

	Electricity prices €2009 per 100kWh		Gas prices €2009 per GJ[1]		Transport prices (March 2011) € per litre	
	Industrial	Domestic	Industrial	Domestic	Unleaded	Diesel
Austria	8.82	19.09	–	–	1.35	1.35
Belgium	11.11	19.16	9.04	16.82	1.51	1.37
Denmark	8.59	26.98	15.43	25.55	1.66	1.52
Finland	6.89	12.96	8.50	–	1.60	1.37
France	7.02	12.73	10.01	15.29	1.58	1.46
Germany	11.32	22.82	11.98	18.00	1.61	1.44
Greece	9.48	11.54	–	–	1.59	1.39
Ireland	*12.06*	*20.30*	*9.30*	*17.89*	*1.49*	*1.45*
Italy	14.35	20.93	10.79	21.04	1.53	1.42
Luxembourg	11.57	18.82	11.21	13.68	1.31	1.20
Netherlands	11.30	19.00	10.64	23.13	1.69	1.41
Portugal	8.94	15.08	9.81	16.78	1.53	1.38
Spain	11.54	15.77	8.73	16.98	1.32	1.30
Sweden	6.67	16.02	10.96	24.77	1.54	1.37
UK	11.17	14.66	8.35	11.84	1.52	1.59

Source: electricity and gas prices are from Sustainable Energy Authority of Ireland, 'Understanding electricity and gas prices in Ireland', SEAI, Dublin 2009; unleaded and diesel prices were obtained from the AA website, www.aaireland.ie, in April 2011.
[1] Gas prices unavailable for Austria and Greece; domestic gas prices unavailable for Finland.

It can be seen that end-user *electricity* prices in Ireland are among the highest in the EU. Electricity prices in Ireland are made up of four components: generation; networks; retail; and the public service obligation (PSO) levy. Looking at each of these components in turn can help explain Ireland's high electricity prices.

Generation Costs and the Single Electricity Market
The largest component of the electricity bill for a company is accounted for by generation costs, i.e. the cost of generating electricity. The energy industry has traditionally been dominated by statutory monopolies that control the network and the supply of energy products, e.g. ESB in the electricity sector and Bord Gáis in the gas sector. However, EU directives aimed at increasing competition (in order to reduce end-user prices) in the electricity and gas sectors have increased competition in both of these sectors in recent years.

In order to promote investment, the EU directed each member state to create an open and transparent market for wholesale electricity generation. In Ireland this prompted the development of the single electricity market (SEM) which went 'live' in November 2007 and is a single market across the Republic and Northern Ireland. It is a supply-side auction where power stations bid on the basis of how much electricity they can provide in any hour and their marginal cost. The system operator then selects the cheapest units to meet the demand in any hour. The marginal cost of the last unit selected is the market price for the hour, also known as the pool price. There are also two other payment mechanisms called the uplift and the capacity payment mechanism, designed to allow generators recover their longer-term costs.

The SEM mechanism is generally considered to be operating efficiently and in March 2011 Ireland had fifty-three registered companies generating electricity through the market. While Ireland has some relatively inefficient generating stations with higher costs, international fuel prices are the key driver of the cost of generation. Ireland has close to the highest reliance on imported fossil fuels for electricity of all EU countries (at 80 per cent in 2010). In fact, of the countries listed in Table 10.3, only the Netherlands has a higher reliance on imported fossil fuels for electricity generation. It is this exposure to international fuel price fluctuations that is the main driver of Ireland's high electricity prices.

Network, Retail and Levy Costs
The second largest component of end-user prices is network costs. These are charges which are used to maintain and upgrade the electricity network. This is essential in order to encourage foreign direct investment into areas with relatively weak network connection. Also, without investment in the electricity network the achievement of Ireland's renewable targets will not be possible. However, as mentioned previously, Ireland's spatial planning legacy has resulted in Ireland having four times the EU average length of power line; thus network costs are higher than those experienced elsewhere in the EU.

The retail component of the end-user bill covers the administrative, accounting and services costs of the electricity supplier. In Ireland, the electricity supply companies buy electricity from the SEM at the pool price, which varies on an hourly basis, and then sell this electricity to end-use customers, usually at a fixed-rate tariff. The retail component accounts for the mark-up between the pool price at which suppliers buy electricity and the fixed tariff at which it is sold. The Commission for Energy Regulation has been successful in promoting competition in the electricity supply business and Ireland now has eight electricity supply companies.

The final component of electricity bills is the PSO levy. This levy is designed to support the use of indigenous peat and renewable energy sources in electricity generation. In 2010/11 the PSO levy was €2.73 per month for residential customers and €8.25 per month for business customers. The PSO is justified for reasons of security of supply, but it is one of the most contradictory policies of the Irish government in the energy area. Peat is the most inefficient fuel for electricity

285

generation and is the highest emitter of carbon dioxide (CO_2) of all fuels used in electricity generation in Ireland. Thus, while on the one hand the government has developed ambitious targets for renewable sources of energy to reduce emissions, on the other hand it is financially supporting the use of peat, the highest emitter of CO_2.

Heating and Transport Costs
The Commission for Energy Regulation has also been actively promoting competition in the heating sector through deregulation of the gas market. In 2011, residential customers could purchase their gas from one of four suppliers (Airtricity, Bord Gáis Energy, ESB Electric Ireland and Flogas) and business customers from eight suppliers. Competition in this market has ensured that, since 2008, gas prices in Ireland for business customers have been below the EU average (Table 10.3).

In the transport sector, the main driver of end-user prices is international fuel price fluctuations, with other factors such as exchange rates, production, and refining costs also playing a role. In 2011 political uncertainty in North Africa and the Middle East has contributed to rising oil prices internationally. In March 2011 the average price of unleaded petrol in the EU was €1.46 per litre, marginally below the average price in Ireland of €1.49 (see Table 10.3). The price of petrol is determined by transportation costs and the excise rates charged by governments. The excise rates (including the carbon charge) in Ireland on motor fuels in 2011 are 57.6 cent of the price of a litre of petrol and 46.6 cent of a litre of diesel.

7 ENVIRONMENTAL ISSUES

So far two of the pillars of energy policy have been discussed: security of supply; and sustainable end-user prices. The third energy policy pillar is environmental sustainability. Unfortunately, Ireland's record of compliance with EU environmental standards is not exemplary and in 2009 Ireland had the highest number of environmental infringements as declared by the European Court of Justice across the whole of the EU.[17] Environmental policy is discussed under three headings in this section: emissions; water; and waste.

Emissions
Due to international concern about climate change, policy-makers worldwide have introduced numerous instruments to help curb global emissions. Obviously, a goal of zero pollution is unrealistic and undesirable since pollution is a by-product of day-to-day living. Thus, the key for policy-makers is to decide upon an optimal level of operation where the costs do not exceed the benefits of pollution (material standard of living).

The Kyoto Protocol and the EU Trading Scheme

The most wide-reaching agreement on climate change is the Kyoto Protocol, which sets binding targets for thirty-seven industrialised countries and the EU to reduce greenhouse gas (GHG) emissions. The Protocol is currently in Phase II and signatories have committed to an average GHG reduction of five per cent against 1990 levels over the period 2008–12.

Under the Kyoto Treaty, each country must meet its targets primarily through national measures. In order to meet the EU commitment, Ireland has been set one of the most stringent targets in the EU of limiting annual GHG emissions to 13 per cent above 1990 levels in the period 2008–12. In order to assist in meeting these emissions targets, the EU Emission Trading Scheme (EU ETS) commenced operation in January 2005. The EU ETS is now the largest multi-country, multi-sector GHG emissions trading scheme in the world.

In accordance with the EU ETS, each member state was required to develop a national allocation plan which stated the total quantity of allowances that it intended to allocate to polluters in the member state and how it proposed to allocate them. Over a hundred major industrial and institutional sites in Ireland are covered by the EU ETS. These include power generation, other combustion, cement, lime, glass and ceramic plants and oil refining. Also included are large companies in areas such as food and drink, pharmaceuticals and semi-conductors.

While it was established to meet the Kyoto targets, the EU ETS scheme is now fully operational and is intended to extend beyond 2012 to meet EU targets of reducing GHG emissions to 20 per cent below 1990 levels by 2020. In fact, from 2012 the mechanism will be opened up further to include emissions from airlines and in 2013 to allow trading of other emission types.

Combustion of fossil fuels is the largest source (approximately 68 per cent) of GHG emissions in Ireland in 2009, with 27 per cent of these regulated under the EU ETS. The *agriculture sector* (due to emissions from livestock) remains the single largest contributor to overall emissions, at 29 per cent of the total, followed by the *energy sector* (primarily power generation) and the *transport sector*, both with a 21 per cent share. The remainder is made up by the *industrial and commercial, residential and waste* sectors.

While only 27 per cent of Ireland's emissions are currently covered by the EU ETS, a second, and different, target is proposed for Ireland under the EU Commission's Energy and Climate Package, currently being debated at a European level. This package will cover emissions not included in the EU ETS, such as agriculture and transport. The EU Commission's proposals initially require Ireland to deliver a 20 per cent reduction in emissions, relative to 2005 levels, by 2020 and this may be increased to 30 per cent by 2020, if a new global climate change agreement is reached. These are considered to be onerous targets and the Economic and Social Research Institute predicts that these EU targets for 2020 are out of domestic reach if current policy is continued.[18]

Renewable energy has been discussed previously and our ambitious national targets form part of Ireland's measures aimed at reducing GHG emissions.

Improvements are also planned on the demand side with the 2007 government White Paper, *Delivering a Sustainable Energy Future for Ireland*, setting a target for a 20 per cent improvement in energy efficiency across the whole economy by 2020.

Nuclear Energy

Omitted from Ireland's emissions reduction plans is the potential for nuclear generation. In 2005, Ireland had the fifth highest CO_2 emissions per capita in the EU, whereas France, with the largest nuclear programme, had one of the lowest CO_2 levels. However, it should be noted that nuclear energy is not 100 per cent emission-free as CO_2 is released during uranium mining, transportation, decommissioning and waste treatment. Also, nuclear energy can contribute to emissions reduction in the electricity sector but alone does not assist in meeting targets in the heating and transport sectors. Nevertheless, the fact that nuclear energy allows for the generation of large amounts of electricity with minimal levels of CO_2 is the most compelling argument for nuclear power generation.

Nuclear waste and issues surrounding waste storage and disposal are among the most concerning aspects of nuclear power generation. Nuclear waste is categorised into three classes based on its radioactivity: low-level, intermediate-level and high-level waste. Final disposal methods currently exist for low- and intermediate-level waste. However, there are presently no operating facilities in the world for the final disposal of high-level nuclear waste products. Current practice is to store all high-level waste in intermediate storage facilities based on site at the nuclear power stations.

Used uranium fuel must be stored for ten to twenty years before its heat levels and radiation are sufficiently low to handle. After this period it is generally stored in intermediate dry storage for a further fifty to a hundred years to allow for additional cooling and to decrease radioactivity further. These interim storage facilities range from bunkers able to withstand aeroplane crashes (such as the Habog facility in the Netherlands) to open-air canisters. As mentioned, there currently exist no final storage facilities for used uranium and nuclear waste. However, facilities are being planned for 2020–25 in a number of EU countries.

In the event that a nuclear power station is built in Ireland, one of the main areas of concern would be the nuclear waste issue. Compared to other nuclear nations, Ireland would produce a relatively small amount of high-level waste. This is due to the fact that Ireland would only operate a nuclear station of approximately 1,000MW in size. This figure is small compared to other European countries such as France (63,000MW), Germany (20,000MW), Sweden (9,000MW) and Belgium (5,800MW). Thus, the most likely outcome for any nuclear waste produced in Ireland would be for it to be transported to a reprocessing facility in either the UK or mainland Europe once it had reached temperature and radiation levels low enough for transportation (after approximately twenty to forty years in storage in Ireland).[19]

Following the events at Japanese nuclear stations in 2011 the debate about nuclear energy has refocused on the potential safety concerns. New nuclear power stations have far superior safety precautions than old stations, with much of the operation now automated. However, the potential for accidents should be considered when examining nuclear energy. The environmental impact of an accident in Ireland is likely to be catastrophic. The prevailing winds are south-westerly so an explosive accident would almost certainly see radioactive clouds spread over land rather than towards the Atlantic. If the power station were located on Ireland's west coast, it is likely that the majority of the island would be affected by the spread of radioactivity, with the radioactive clouds then spreading across Britain and into mainland Europe.

While a fully informed scientific debate about nuclear energy is warranted in Ireland, it is unlikely, as mentioned earlier, that any Irish government would be elected with such a mandate in the foreseeable future. However, despite Ireland's legislative ban on nuclear energy, electricity generated by nuclear power is used in Ireland through the use of electrical imports from Britain. This use of nuclear power is likely to increase into the future as further interconnection to Britain is planned.

Water

One of the primary environmental challenges facing Ireland over the next decade is water quality and preservation. Ireland is fortunate in having a relatively abundant supply of fresh water with approximately 50 per cent of the land area of the state drained by just nine river systems. In 2000 the EU developed the Water Framework Directive (WFD) in response to the increasing threat of pollution and growing demand from the public for cleaner rivers, lakes and beaches. This directive is unique as it establishes a framework for the protection of all waters including rivers, lakes, estuaries, coastal waters and groundwater, and their dependent wildlife/habitats, under one piece of environmental legislation.

Under the WFD, Ireland must achieve 'good water status' for all waters by 2015. Currently, much of Ireland's water does not meet this quality status and it is envisaged that substantial measures will be needed for Ireland to comply with this directive by 2015. For example, just over 50 per cent of Ireland's surface waters currently meet the ecological status required in this directive.

One of the reasons for Ireland's poor performance is the proliferation of construction during the housing boom. Construction was permitted without due regard for discharge into surrounding rivers and lakes and as a result Ireland is potentially facing significant fines for non-compliance with EU legislation. Other sources of water pollution are nutrient inputs from agriculture and municipal sources. Table 10.4 illustrates Ireland's poor performance against the requirements set down by the WFD.

Table 10.4

Ireland's Water Standards According to the Requirements
of the EU Water Framework Directive, 2009 (%)

	Good status	Unsatisfactory status
Groundwater	85	15
Rivers	52	48
Lakes	53	47
Lake bathing quality	67	33
Estuarine and coastal water	64	36
Seawater bathing	93	7

Source: Environmental Protection Agency, *Water Quality in Ireland 2007-2009*, EPA Report No. 12/10/500, Ireland 2010.

In Ireland the majority of drinking water originates from surface water (82 per cent) and the remainder from groundwater (10 per cent) and springs (8 per cent). The most important health indicator of drinking water quality in Ireland is the presence of microbiological particles, in particular *E. coli*. The presence of *E. coli* in drinking water indicates that the treatment process at the water treatment plant is not operating adequately or that contamination has entered the water distribution system after treatment. In Ireland in 2009, a total of 200 supplies (6.6 per cent) failed to meet the standard for *E. coli* at one time or more during the year. The majority of supplies where *E. coli* was detected were private group water schemes, e.g. from local wells.

Once water is extracted, it requires treatment in order to make it fit for consumption. As mentioned previously, given Ireland's legacy of ribbon development the water networks are radial in nature and experience high losses. It is estimated that over 34 per cent of Ireland's water supply is lost in transmission, one of the highest levels in Europe.[20] In an effort to ease pressure on water supplies it was announced in Budget 2009 that domestic water charges are to be introduced in the coming years. Water charges are currently in place for all commercial premises across Ireland.

Ireland has undergone significant investment in improving the water services infrastructure (for drinking water and urban waste water), with over €4.6 billion invested over the last decade. This has resulted in a dramatic improvement in the level of treatment of urban waste water. However, as Table 10.4 indicates, it is apparent that Ireland has a long way to go before it can meet its required water standards.

A related issue which has loomed large in the public consciousness in recent years is flooding. Floods are a natural and inevitable part of life in Ireland and are usually caused by a combination of events, including overflowing river banks, coastal storms, or blocked and overloaded ditches. Numerous severe floods have occurred throughout the country in the last decade and it is widely anticipated that changes in rainfall patterns and rises in sea levels resulting from climate change may make such flooding incidents more frequent and severe in the future. In 2008, the government announced new flooding guidelines and all new developments must adhere to these procedures. However, this initiative is unfortunately a classic example of closing the stable door after the horse has bolted, as the proliferation of development before 2008 did not adhere to these guidelines, with much construction taking place on natural flood plains.

Waste

Waste generation and resource use have increased in Ireland over the past decade in parallel with increasing production and consumption of goods and services. Ireland has made progress in meeting many EU waste recycling/recovery targets but challenges remain in relation to reducing the level of waste generated and waste management (see Table 10.5).

Table 10.5

Ireland's Compliance with EU Waste Legislation

	Target date	Indicator
EU Packaging Directive	2011	Achieved
WEEE Directive	2008	Achieved
End of Life Vehicles Directive	2006	Not achieved
	(2015)	(At risk)
Batteries Directive	2012	At risk
Landfill Directive	2013 and 2016	At risk
New waste framework directive	2020	Achieved

Source: Environmental Protection Agency, *National Waste Report 2009*, EPA Report No. 02/11/350, Ireland 2011.

The bulk of Ireland's waste is municipal waste, which is defined as household waste, commercial waste and cleaning waste. Packaging waste includes materials such as cardboard, paper, glass, plastic, steel, aluminium and wood. Since 2001 Ireland has been compliant with all statutory packaging recovery targets and is expected to comfortably exceed the EU target of 60 per cent recovery rate of packaging for 2011. The Waste Electrical and Electronic Equipment (WEEE) Directive has been highly successful in Ireland with an average collection of 9kg per capita in 2009, well in excess of the EU target of 4kg.

Currently 35 per cent of Ireland's municipal waste is recycled, with the majority exported to Britain. There has been a significant improvement in Ireland's attitude towards recycling and a two-bin service (general waste bins and mixed dry recyclables bins) was provided to 96 per cent of serviced households in 2009. According to the Environmental Protection Agency (EPA), in 2009 there were almost 2,000 bring banks in operation for collecting dry recyclables such as glass, clothes and beverage cans.

While Ireland has outperformed its waste targets in many areas, the main threat to the sustainability of waste management is infrastructural capacity.

Ireland's waste infrastructure relies heavily on landfill. There are currently twenty-nine active landfill sites for municipal waste disposal and, at current fill rates, sixteen of these sites will have reached their full capacity by 2012. In addition, landfill capacity is not distributed evenly throughout the state and some regions are already reaching a critical capacity shortage. The Irish government has a target of diverting 50 per cent of current household waste away from landfill by the end of 2013. However, this target is unlikely to be achieved as Ireland continues to produce among the highest levels of municipal waste per capita in the EU.

There is currently no incineration capacity, either for municipal waste or other forms of waste, in Ireland. In 2005 the EPA granted licences for two commercial incinerators in Carranstown in Co. Meath and Ringaskiddy in Co. Cork and in 2008 a third licence was issued for an incinerator at Poolbeg in Dublin. All of these developments have undergone lengthy planning delays and none of the facilities is yet in operation, although construction is well advanced at the Carranstown facility.

Ireland is at an important juncture in waste management, with impending EU targets and penalties on the horizon. With this in mind, one of the significant developments in the waste sector in recent years has been the introduction of refuse charges in an effort to manage and reduce waste. Domestic waste charges are now levied on almost all households that use an organised refuse collection service. These charges were brought in at different times by different local authorities and are not uniform across the state. However, without a concerted and significant effort towards a reduction in total waste production, a reduced reliance on landfill and the development of further waste management infrastructure, Ireland is likely to face significant EU non-compliance fines in relation to waste in the coming years.

8 CONCLUSIONS

This chapter has examined the development of Ireland's infrastructure, energy provision and environmental measures over the past decade and has highlighted some of the challenges facing each of these sectors. One of the real success stories of the economic boom has been the huge improvement in the transport infrastructure in Ireland, with major improvements seen in both road networks and public transport infrastructure. Unfortunately, however, this improvement is twinned with missed opportunities in terms of spatial planning. The housing boom did little to address the dispersed nature of the population and the poor quality of housing stock relative to our EU neighbours. The period of rapid construction has also left a negative legacy in terms of our environmental goals in the areas of water quality and waste management. In fact planning issues are a recurring theme throughout this chapter, from costly time lags in the construction of necessary road networks, to the high average length of our electricity lines, to the security of future gas supplies at the Corrib field and the sustainability of waste management with delays in incinerator construction. Thus, looking to the future, Ireland is facing significant challenges in keeping up with competitors in terms of the quality of physical infrastructure, end-user energy prices and in meeting many EU environmental targets. Unfortunately these challenges are likely to be heightened should the current economic downturn not be reversed in the coming years.

Endnotes

1 There is also investment in human capital, such as education, and social capital, such as housing and hospitals, both of which will be looked at in later chapters; and the non-built physical capital of a country, such as mountains, rivers and lakes, as well as cultural capital, such as national museums, historical buildings, etc., all of which are important in the functioning of a successful economy and society.

2 See E. Gramlich, 'Infrastructure and economic development', Texas Trade Corridors New Economy Conference, San Antonio, August 2001, available at www.federalreserve.gov/boarddocs/speeches/2001/20010803/default.htm.

3 Ibid., p. 2.

4 This section draws heavily on H. Christiansen, 'The OECD principles for private sector participation in infrastructure', IMF International Seminar on Strengthening Public Investment and Managing Fiscal Risks from Public–Private Partnerships, Budapest, March 2007, available at www.federalreserve.gov/boarddocs/speeches/2001/20010803/default.htm.

5 The National Policy and Advisory Board for Enterprise, Trade, Science, Technology and Innovation. All Forfás publications are available at their website: www.forfas.ie/publications/index.html.

6 See National Competitiveness Council, *Review of International Assessments of Ireland's Competitiveness*, Forfás, Dublin 2010, available at www.forfas.ie/ncc/reports/ncc071220/index.html. International assessments of Ireland's competitiveness have become very important, given that they have such high visibility among international investors and commentators. In the case of the World Economic Forum Report, which is the one drawn on most in this chapter, 126 indicators of competitiveness are used in total, 69 per cent of which are based on the surveyed opinions of executives. For the 2007–8 report, over 11,000 business leaders were polled in 131 economies, 42 of whom were from Ireland. The main advantage of an approach based on executive opinions is that they are ultimately what business decisions are based on. They are also timelier than internationally comparable official statistical data, but sample sizes for individual countries can be small.

7 National Competitiveness Council, *op. cit.*

8 Ibid.

9 This section draws heavily on Sustainable Energy Authority of Ireland, *Residential Energy Roadmap*, SEAI, Dublin 2010, available at www.seai.ie.

10 A good evaluation of Ireland's energy policy in each of these areas can be found in J. FitzGerald, 'A review of Irish energy policy', ESRI Research Series No. 21, Dublin 2011.

11 Department of Finance, *Report of the Review Group on State Assets and Liabilities*, Department of Finance, Dublin 2011, available at www.finance.gov.ie/viewdoc.asp?DocID=6805.

12 Ibid.

13 Housing statistics are from Eurostat, the European Commission statistical database.

14 J. Shine, 'A road map for smart networks', *Engineers Journal*, Vol. 63, No. 5, June 2009.

15 See Department of Communications, Energy and Natural Resources, *Oil Stock Policy*, at http://www.dcenr.gov.ie.

16 This section draws on data from the Commission for Energy Regulation, *Joint Gas Capacity Statement* 2010, CER Report No. 10121, Dublin 2010, available at http://www.cer.ie.

17 European Commission Legal Enforcement Section, *Statistics on Environmental Infringements*, at http://ec.europa.eu.

18 P. Gorecki, S. Lyons and R. Tol, 'EU climate change policy 2013–2020: using the clean development mechanism more effectively in the non-EU-ETS sector', *Energy Policy,* Vol. 38, No. 11, 2010.

19 This section draws significantly on a research report into nuclear energy in Ireland by P. Richardson, 'The feasibility of nuclear power in Ireland', ERC Working Paper No. 10, Dublin 2008 (available at www.ucd.ie/erc).

20 European Environment Agency, *Losses from Urban Water Networks*, available at www.eea.europa.eu.

CHAPTER 11

The Agri-Food Sector

Alan Matthews

1 INTRODUCTION

This chapter discusses the role of the agri-food sector in the Irish economy. The agri-food sector is a complex value chain which links the procurement of agricultural raw materials produced on farms, through their processing and distribution, to final consumption. The industry consists of multiple players such as farmers, input suppliers, manufacturers, importers, packagers, transporters, wholesalers, retailers and final customers. The agri-food sector of the Irish economy has traditionally been treated as a distinct sector for economic and policy analysis, in part because of its importance as one of the key indigenous sectors in the economy and in part because of the extent of policy intervention, which sets it apart from other traded sectors.

Although agriculture no longer has the dominant role in economic activity which it once had, when the contribution of the food industry is factored in, the agri-food sector remains a significant player. In 2009, it accounted for 6 per cent of Irish gross national product (GNP) and 8 per cent of employment. The agricultural sector remains important in other ways. Together with forestry, it occupies over 70 per cent of the land area of the country; it thus has a significant impact on the physical environment and the protection of biodiversity. It is the largest single contributor to Ireland's greenhouse gas emissions, accounting for 28 per cent of the total over the 2008–12 period, ahead of transport (responsible for 21 per cent). It remains the single most substantial contributor to the economic and social viability of rural areas. The food and drink industry is Ireland's most important indigenous sector, accounting in 2009 for approximately half of sales by Irish-owned manufacturing industries. It has a turnover approaching €22 billion (2009) and supplies most of our domestic food needs. Agri-food exports contributed 9 per cent of total merchandise exports in 2009 and 64 per cent of manufacturing exports by indigenous companies. Food and drink expenditures accounted for 17 per cent of household consumption expenditure (not including meals out). Thus agricultural and food policy is intimately linked to debates on economic competitiveness, rural development, the environment and consumer well-being.

Another reason for the interest in agricultural and food policy is the decisive influence of government interventions on the fortunes of the industry. This dependence can be highlighted in a single statistic: the income accruing to farmers from agricultural activity arises entirely from public policy transfers from both EU and Irish consumers and taxpayers. Agricultural production in the EU is highly protected from world market competition. EU tariff levels on agricultural and food imports average around 18 per cent, compared to 4 per cent for non-agricultural goods, and for some agricultural products they exceed 100 per cent. This substantial government intervention in favour of a particular industry raises a series of questions. What objectives is it designed to achieve? Are these objectives justified? Is the support provided achieving these objectives? Is the support being provided efficiently? These are questions which economists are well placed to answer.

These questions are particularly pertinent at present because agricultural and food policy faces challenges on a number of fronts. Agricultural commodity prices, having fallen steadily in real terms for several decades, have suddenly increased dramatically; in February 2011 the UN Food and Agricultural Organisation's global food price index reached its highest point in decades. Rising food prices, along with increased energy prices, are now causing a serious headache for central banks trying to prevent inflationary expectations gaining hold. Higher prices, of course, encourage farmers to increase production, but ensuring that this increased production is sustainable in environmental terms will be a major challenge. High prices have also raised again the spectre of food insecurity and focused attention on the appropriate balance between producing food at home and relying on imports from other countries. This debate is central to the ongoing negotiations on agricultural trade liberalisation under the auspices of the World Trade Organisation (WTO). High food prices reflect in part ambitious government mandates to promote the production of renewable energies and, in particular, bio-fuels. Whether it makes sense to use agricultural land resources to produce food or fuel is a hotly contested issue. Higher food prices also throw into relief the increasing levels of concentration in the food marketing chain and the possible abuse by supermarkets, in particular, of their growing market power. At the same time, there is evidence of growing concern among consumers about the safety and quality of food being produced.

The purpose of this chapter is to describe these challenges in more detail and to discuss the appropriate policy responses. Section 2 provides a brief overview of some salient characteristics of the Irish agricultural sector. Section 3 discusses the changing policy context for agriculture at EU and international levels. Section 4 describes the food processing and distribution sectors. Section 5 explores the growing emphasis given to food safety regulation, the promotion of food quality, and the control of market power throughout the food chain. Section 6 concludes the chapter by summarising some of the conflicting tendencies at work as the agri-food sector faces into a more market-oriented and uncertain environment.

2 AGRICULTURAL SECTOR

Structural Characteristics

In 2010 the agricultural industry produced food products and raw materials valued at €5.3 billion at producer prices. Its GNP share was an estimated 1.9 per cent in that year (down from 6.3 per cent in 1996). Around 89,500 persons worked in agriculture in 2010, accounting for 5 per cent of total employment. The discrepancy between the share of the labour force in agriculture and its share of GNP is a first indication that labour productivity and thus farm income might be relatively lower in the sector than in the economy at large.

Income from Agriculture

A closer look at the sources of agricultural factor income shows the high dependence of farming on transfers from the non-farm sector. Table 11.1 derives the income arising in agriculture starting with the market value of the output of agricultural commodities produced on farms. This is initially valued at producer prices, which are farm gate prices or the prices received by the farmer. Agricultural output is then valued at basic prices, which include subsidies directly linked to the production of particular commodities minus any taxes on products. Subtracting intermediate consumption gives gross value added at basic prices. Subtracting the estimated depreciation on the capital used in agriculture (mainly machinery and buildings) gives net value added at basic prices. Agricultural income is the sum of this item plus net subsidies paid to farmers. The most important subsidy is the single farm payment, paid as a support to farm incomes (see Section 3). Other subsidies include agri-environment payments and compensatory payments to farmers in less favoured farming areas, which might be seen as remuneration for the 'public goods' that farming provides, such as a varied landscape or continued agricultural land use in remote areas.

The figures are rather astonishing, even if 2009 was a disastrous year for farm incomes due to the combination of a collapse in milk prices and high input costs. Nonetheless, even in 2010, income from commercial farming activity accounted for only 30 per cent of agricultural income, with the remaining 70 per cent coming in the form of direct payments. In fact, including expenditure on farm investment schemes, installation aid for young farmers and afforestation grants and premia, which are not included by the CSO in the calculation of agricultural income, brings all payments to farmers in 2010 to €2.1 billion. When it is recalled that the value of farm output at producer prices is also supported by high tariffs on lower-cost imports from outside the EU (see Section 3), the vulnerability of farm incomes to policy changes which might lead to lower support and protection is underlined. The other issue which jumps out from Table 11.1 is the year-on-year volatility of farm incomes, reflecting fluctuations in both output and input prices. Helping farmers to cope with price and income volatility has always been an important justification for farm policy and this objective has re-emerged at the top of the policy agenda in recent years.

Table 11.1

Output, Input and Income in Agriculture, 2009 and 2010 (€ million)

	2009	2010	% change 2010/2009
Goods output at producer prices	4,728.4	5,348.0	13.1
Contract work	268.7	268.7	0.0
Subsidies less taxes on products	15.1	17.0	12.6
Agricultural output at basic prices	5,012.2	5,633.7	12.4
Intermediate consumption	4,070.9	4,104.6	0.8
Gross value added at basic prices	941.4	1,529.0	62.4
Fixed capital consumption	780.6	744.5	-4.6
Net value added at basic prices	160.8	784.5	387.9
Other subsidies less taxes on production	1,841.5	1,710.2	-7.1
Agricultural income	2,002.3	2,494.7	24.6

Source: Department of Agriculture, Fisheries and Food, *Annual Review and Outlook for Agriculture, Fisheries and Food 2010/2011*, Dublin 2011.

Production

Climatically, Ireland is better suited to grassland than to crop production. Of the total agricultural area of 4.2 million hectares in 2009, over 90 per cent was devoted to grass and rough grazing. Livestock and livestock products accounted for 66 per cent of total output at producers' prices in 2010 (Table 11.2). The table also highlights the growing share of material and service inputs as a proportion of

Table 11.2

Composition of Agricultural Outputs and Inputs, Selected Years (% of Gross Agricultural Output by Value)

	1996	2006	2010
Total outputs			
Cattle	28.7	28.6	28.0
Milk	29.8	25.3	28.7
Crops	24.6	27.9	6.2
Pigs	6.9	6.1	3.1
Sheep	4.7	3.6	28.0
Other	5.3	8.4	5.9
Gross agricultural output at producer prices	100.0	100.0	100.0
Total inputs	*60.0*	*74.4*	*76.8*
Feed, fertiliser and seed	24.4	27.5	29.4
Other current inputs	35.6	46.8	47.3

Source: CSO, *Agricultural Output, Input and Income*, www.statcentral.ie [accessed 21 April 2011].

gross agricultural output. While this is due partly to the fall in the value of output arising from reform of the EU's Common Agricultural Policy (CAP) (see Section 3), it also reflects the increasing intensification of agricultural production, a phenomenon which has given rise to concern about agriculture's impact on the environment.

An important characteristic of Irish agriculture is its export orientation. The export market absorbs more than 80 per cent of dairy and beef output. Around 45 per cent of Irish agri-food exports go to the UK, around 35 per cent to the rest of the EU and 20 per cent are exported outside the EU. Sales to third country markets outside the EU were heavily dependent on export subsidies, but with the rise in global food prices these now play a much less important role. The continued use of export subsidies is under challenge from other trading countries in the WTO negotiations on agricultural trade liberalisation (see Section 3).

Price Developments
Long-Term Decline in Relative Price
The real price of agricultural output, measured as the ratio of output prices to the consumer price index, is a good indicator of the purchasing power of farm products relative to consumer goods and services. This ratio more than halved over the period 1980 to 2010. Even with the recent spike in food prices, the cost of inputs has risen even faster. This fall in the relative price of food over time, which is not unique to Ireland but has been a general phenomenon in all industrialised economies, is crucially important in understanding the adjustment pressures on agriculture and hence the reasons for government intervention in the sector.

The fall in relative food prices reflects the interplay of the supply of and demand for farm products. On the one hand, the supply potential of the farm sector has increased as the scientific revolution gathered pace, making available to farmers a range of productive new inputs such as improved seed varieties, better fertilisers, more powerful machinery, and more effective chemicals and pesticides. Because of this technological innovation, the supply of agricultural products has increased rapidly. However, the market for this increased output did not grow to the same extent. Growth in demand is dependent on growth in population and in per capita incomes. But the rate of population growth in industrialised countries has slowed down and in some cases has virtually ceased. While per capita incomes continue to grow, a smaller and smaller proportion of this increase is spent on food. The consequence has been a downward pressure on the aggregate price level for agricultural products relative to other commodities.

Impact on Incomes and Structure
This in turn puts a downward pressure on farm incomes and has encouraged farm family members to take up non-farm job opportunities. In all industrialised countries, the share of the farm workforce in total employment has fallen significantly. In Ireland, the numbers at work in agriculture fell from 330,000 in 1960 to 89,500 in late 2010. If this adjustment process proceeds smoothly, the

reduction in the numbers engaged in agriculture should ensure that farm incomes, on average, stay in line with average non-farm incomes. For various reasons, however, some farmers may find it difficult to leave farming in the face of this downward pressure on farm incomes. Unemployment may be high in the non-farm sector, or their age and skill profile can make it difficult for them to find off-farm employment. Many farmers appear trapped in agriculture, with low incomes. Government transfers to agriculture have been justified in the past as a response to this perceived problem of low average farm incomes relative to the rest of society.

The process of adjustment to falling real farm prices is reflected in ongoing structural change in agriculture. In 2007, there were around 128,000 farms in Ireland. Their average size in terms of land area is 32 hectares, although there is considerable diversity around this average. This average area farmed is large in EU terms, but because of the relatively low intensity of land use the average size of farm business in Ireland is at the smaller end of the EU spectrum. There is an important regional dimension to differences in farm size, with a predominance of smaller farms in the west and the north-west, and a greater proportion of larger farms in the south and east. Small farm size is frequently associated with a low-margin farming system (mainly dry-stock) and a predominance of older farmers, many of whom are unmarried. The number of farms is falling over time, at a rate of about 2 per cent per annum. A more disaggregated analysis shows that the decline is concentrated among smaller farms (less than 20 hectares), whose number fell from 85,000 to 55,000 between 1992 and 2007, while the number of larger farms is more stable at around 73,000.

Recent Large Price Rises
The persistence of this long-term decline in real food prices makes the sudden increase in food prices in 2007 even more striking. The key question is whether this is just a flash in the pan, the outcome of a series of chance events such as drought in major producing countries, or whether it represents the start of a new era in which farmers will receive more for their production. There is much evidence to support the latter view. We can use the same supply and demand framework to understand this phenomenon. On the demand side, rapidly rising per capita incomes in emerging economies are leading to shifts in diet preferences, with greater demand for meat and dairy products. Food and energy markets have become increasingly interlinked, not only on the cost side (where modern agriculture is a heavy energy consumer) but also on the output side (as agricultural land is diverted to the production of energy crops for biomass and bio-fuels). On the supply side, the increasing scarcity of water and land and, in the longer term, the likely impact of climate change, are putting increasing pressure on supply capacity. Public and private investment in agricultural research, which was behind the productivity growth that drove the secular decline in food prices in the past, has been cut back or diverted to non-production areas such as the environment, animal welfare and the development of more sophisticated foods. Some of the new technologies available to increase food supply, such as aspects

of biotechnology, have met substantial consumer resistance. It is thus very likely that the market environment for the Irish agri-food sector will be very different in the next ten years from what it has been in the past. As a net food exporter, not only farmers but the national economy stands to gain.

Farm Household Income

The changing composition of income sources in farm households can be tracked over time using data from the Household Budget Surveys and the annual Surveys of Income and Living Conditions conducted by the Central Statistics Office (CSO). Whereas in 1980, 58 per cent of farm household income was derived from farming, this had fallen to 27 per cent in 2008 (Table 11.3). Income from farming in this table includes the direct payments which farmers receive under EU agricultural policy (discussed in Section 3). Income from farming compares unfavourably with average industrial earnings, although comparisons are difficult for statistical and conceptual reasons. For example, the average family farm income estimated in the Teagasc National Farm Survey for 2009, admittedly an appalling year for farm incomes, was €11,968 (the 2008 figure was €16,993) compared to 2008 average earnings of €41,600 for unskilled operatives in the construction industry. However, this comparison is not comparing like with like. The average family farm income on the 40 per cent of full-time farms in the Teagasc survey was €24,214 in 2009 (€37,590 in 2008) (bear in mind, however, that this figure must remunerate the capital invested in the farm and that there may be more than one labour unit engaged on full-time farms, so it is not directly comparable to the industrial earnings figure either). Conversely, the average income from farming on the remaining 60 per cent of part-time farms in the Teagasc survey in 2009 was only €7,899. Clearly, this level of income is inadequate on its own to support a farm family. However, on around 53 per cent of all farms, either the holder and/or the spouse have an off-farm job. The increasing importance of off-farm income means that average farm *household* incomes are now close to average incomes in the non-farm economy.

Table 11.3

Percentage of Total Farm Household Income from
All Sources, 1980–2008

	1980	1987	1994	1999/2000	2005	2008
Farm income	58.3	54.2	51.3	39.0	34.3	27.0
Non-farming income	26.3	17.6	37.0	50.3	49.7	53.9
State transfers	15.2	28.3	11.7	10.6	16.0	19.1
Gross income	100	100	100	100	100	100

Sources: CSO, *Household Budget Survey*, Stationery Office, Dublin (various issues); 2005 and 2008 data from the CSO, *EU Survey of Income and Living Conditions* (EU-SILC), www.statcentral.ie [accessed 21 April 2011].

Table 11.4 compares the average incomes of farm households with those of urban households, other rural households, and the state average.[1] Average household income is a good measure of living standards, although it does not take account of differences in the effort or resources required to generate this income. On average, farm household incomes were around 10 per cent lower than for the state as a whole in 2008. However, poverty levels among farm households are not that different from those of non-farm households. EU-SILC data show that consistent poverty is generally lower among farm households than other household groups, indicating a low rate of enforced deprivation among farm families.

Table 11.4

Average Annual Household Income, 2008 (€)

Income source	Farm households	Other rural households	Urban households	State average
Farming income	16,502	–	–	1,328
Non-farm employment	22,890	27,582	45,058	38,081
Other direct income	9,991	7,740	7,356	7,683
State transfers	11,670	13,827	13,561	13,488
Gross income	61,053	49,149	65,975	60,579
less total direct taxation	9,064	8,165	13,561	11,537
Disposable income	51,988	40,085	56,911	51,515
Persons per household	3.15	2.83	2.96	2.94
Gross income per person in household	19,367	17,367	22,279	20,627
Disposable income per person in household	16,492	14,164	19,218	17,541

Source: CSO EU-SILC data, reported in Department of Agriculture, Fisheries and Food, *Annual Review and Outlook for Agriculture, Fisheries and Food 2010/2011*, Dublin 2011.

3 AGRICULTURAL POLICY

Common Agricultural Policy (CAP)

Most countries intervene in their agricultural markets in pursuit of the objectives of price stabilisation and income support. This is also true for EU agricultural policy, the objectives of which are spelled out in Article 33 (formerly 39) of the Treaty of European Union and are worth quoting in full:

- To increase agricultural productivity by promoting technical progress and by ensuring the rational development of agricultural production and the optimum utilisation of all factors of production, in particular labour;

- Thus, to ensure a fair standard of living for the agricultural community, in particular by increasing the individual earnings of persons engaged in agriculture;
- To stabilise markets;
- To provide certainty of supplies;
- To ensure that supplies reach consumers at reasonable prices.

These five objectives of efficient agricultural production, fair incomes for farmers, stable markets, food security and reasonable consumer prices would be broadly acceptable to most people, though the sharp-eyed will note the ambiguity of the wording (what is a fair standard of living for farmers? What is a reasonable price for consumers?) and the potential for conflict between different objectives. However, the mechanisms put in place to achieve these objectives have prioritised the farm income objective at considerable cost to the EU budget and consumers.

The mechanisms used have changed over time. The original CAP was strongly interventionist. Farm prices in the EU were supported by a combination of policy instruments, including import tariffs, market intervention and export subsidies. *Import tariffs* ensure a high domestic price as long as there is a net deficit on the EU market. Originally, the EU's import tariffs took the form of variable levies designed to help stabilise internal EU prices, but these were transformed into fixed amounts following the WTO Agreement on Agriculture in 1995 (see below). Price support to producers was further strengthened in the event of excess EU supplies by a guarantee that government agencies would buy farm products at a minimum support price (called the *intervention price*). Intervention was intended to deal with temporary surpluses of supply. Once the market had recovered and prices had risen, intervention stocks could be sold. As the EU became more than self-sufficient in many temperate-zone foods, greater reliance was placed on *export subsidies* or *refunds*. These export refunds bridge the gap between the high internal market prices and the lower world prices in most years and make possible the export of higher-priced foodstuffs from the EU. High import tariffs, intervention purchases and export refunds were the principal means of supporting prices to farmers under the classical CAP.

The operation of the CAP price support policy ensured a greater degree of internal price stability than in other countries and meant higher per capita incomes for a greater number of farmers than would otherwise have been the case. However, these achievements were bought at a price. The resulting increase in output could not be absorbed by the natural growth in demand, leading to the accumulation of intervention stocks and to dumping on international markets. Thus the EU, which was initially a deficit producer of many agricultural products, became a major net exporter. An obvious consequence of this was the escalating budget cost of purchasing surplus production for intervention storage and of financing export refunds; and growing calls for reform.

Reform of CAP

MacSharry and Agenda 2000 Reforms

A number of half-hearted attempts were made to limit the budgetary cost of the CAP during the 1980s, of which the introduction of milk quotas in 1984 was the most important. The first successful attempt to tackle the malfunctioning CAP was pushed through in 1993 by EU Agriculture Commissioner Ray MacSharry. The MacSharry reform initiated a significant reduction in support prices for the first time. Farmers were compensated by increased direct payments which were tied (coupled) to the level of output on each farm. These payments were accompanied by measures designed to control supply: for example, arable farmers over a certain size were required to set aside (idle) a proportion of their land, and ceilings were placed on the number of livestock which could qualify for payments. These market regime reforms were accompanied by new agri-environment, forestry and early retirement schemes for farmers, part of an expanded rural development emphasis in the CAP.

A further round of CAP reform was agreed in March 1999 as part of the negotiations on the Agenda 2000 agreement to prepare the EU for eastern enlargement. This pursued the same model of reductions in support prices while compensating farmers by further increasing direct payments. Notably, reductions in milk support prices were included for the first time. The Agenda 2000 reform also consolidated various socio-structural measures to encourage farm modernisation as well as agri-environment payments into a single Rural Develop-ment Regulation, which became known as Pillar 2 of the CAP.

The MacSharry and Agenda 2000 direct payments required that a farmer must plant sufficient arable land (in the case of cereals, oilseeds and protein crops) or keep a sufficient number of animals in order to draw down these payments. Such payments are called *coupled payments* because they are linked to the amount each farmer produces. Because the rules differed for each payments scheme (with respect to payment dates, inspection requirements, etc.), claiming these payments involved farmers (or their advisers) in a great deal of paperwork and administration. A second criticism, as demonstrated by the fact that on many farms the value of income from farming was less than the direct payments received, was that many farmers were keeping livestock or growing crops simply to collect the subsidies, rather than responding to market demand.

Fischler and Health Check Reforms

Under Franz Fischler, the EU Commissioner for Agriculture in the period 1999–2004, the EU embarked on a further CAP reform in 2003. The most important change in the Fischler reform was to replace all premia and arable aid payments with a single farm payment to each farmer. This single farm payment is based on the level of assistance received by each farm in the reference period 2000–2. Farmers are entitled to receive this payment regardless of changes in the area planted to crops or the number of livestock on their farm, or indeed regardless whether they produce on their farm at all (subject to the conditions specified below). This *decoupling* of the payment from production means that farmers now make their production decisions based on the relative market returns from each enterprise rather than the size of the subsidy available. The single farm payment is linked to respect for standards in the areas of the environment, food safety, plant health and animal welfare, as well as a requirement to keep all farmland in good agricultural and environmental condition, or so-called 'cross-compliance'.

The Fischler reform also strengthened the CAP rural development pillar by reducing the amount of direct payments that farmers received and transferring these savings to rural development programmes (a process known as the *modulation* of direct payments). It also continued the *reform of the market regimes* by lowering support prices and increasing direct payments in compensation. Subsequently, a rolling programme of reform was implemented which extended the Fischler reforms to a variety of other market regimes (cotton, tobacco, olive oil, bananas, sugar). Now, only some limited coupled payments linked to beef and sheep production continue in some member states. A consequence of the sugar market reform, in which support prices for sugar were reduced and incentives provided to encourage the closure of refining capacity, was that Ireland's only sugar processor, Greencore, ceased production at the end of the 2006 season.

The most recent reform was the 2008 'Health Check', which introduced some minor adjustments to the Fischler reforms. Importantly, it confirmed an earlier decision to phase out milk quotas from the beginning of the 2015 season, a move from which Ireland, with its strong base in dairying, hopes to benefit. Greater flexibility was given to member states to target some of their direct payments on assistance to sectors with special problems (so-called Article 68 measures). Another milestone, given the food price spike that occurred in that year, was the abolition of arable set-aside.

As a consequence of these successive reforms, the CAP is now a very different animal from its classical guise. It now consists of two Pillars: Pillar 1 refers to the market support regimes and single farm payment which contribute to the support of farm incomes, while Pillar 2 refers to rural development measures. Pillar 1 continues to take the lion's share of the CAP budget, accounting for over 75 per cent of CAP expenditure. However, most of Pillar 1 expenditure is now decoupled and does not provide the same incentive to over-produce as before. Nonetheless, farmers continue to benefit from high levels of external protection which in normal years keep food prices on the internal EU market considerably higher than world market levels. These high protection levels have come under sustained criticism from the EU's trading partners in negotiations on trade liberalisation under the auspices of the WTO.

WTO Disciplines on Agricultural Support

The WTO Agreement on Agriculture which came into force in 1995 establishes rules on the manner and amount of government support to agriculture. All border restrictions, including measures such as quotas and variable import levies, were converted into fixed tariffs which are bound at a maximum rate. Furthermore, these bound tariffs were, over a six-year period, reduced by 36 per cent on average compared to their levels in 1986–90. There is also an obligation to ensure that a minimum of 5 per cent of the domestic market is open to foreign competition, which is achieved through the use of tariff rate quotas. These allow imports from third countries at a preferential duty rate but only for the quota quantity. For countries which use export subsidies, these subsidies had to be reduced by 36 per cent in value and 21 per cent in volume relative to the average for the period 1986–90; no new export subsidies can be introduced. With regard to domestic support to agriculture, the agreement distinguishes between permitted and non-permitted forms of support. Support that does not influence, or only minimally influences, farmers' incentives to produce is permitted and there are no disciplines applied (support of this kind is considered decoupled from production and therefore not to cause distortions to trade). Trade-distorting support, such as market price support, is capped and had to be reduced by 20 per cent compared to the base period 1986–88.

A new round of negotiations to liberalise agricultural trade began in March 2000, as foreseen in the WTO Agreement on Agriculture. In November 2001, these negotiations were folded into the general round of trade negotiations launched by the WTO Ministerial Council at its meeting in Doha, Qatar, and known as the Doha Round. The negotiations have proved difficult, not least because of disagreements between developed and developing countries over agricultural subsidies. There was an important breakthrough in May 2004 when, for the first time, the EU indicated that it was prepared to negotiate an end date for the elimination of export subsidies provided all other forms of export support used by other countries were eliminated in parallel and provided there was a satisfactory agreement reached in the other areas of the negotiations. However, disagreement on the extent of tariff cuts for both agricultural and non-agricultural products continued, and negotiations were suspended in December 2008. Attempts since then to continue with behind-the-scenes negotiations in Geneva have proved fruitless, and at the time of writing (April 2011) the Doha Round appears close to collapse. Irish farmers will breathe a sigh of relief if this happens, even if an agreement would bring benefits to the non-farm sector. The fact that the single farm payment has been decoupled from production would protect it even if further subsidy cuts were agreed in the Doha Round. However, the significant tariff reductions for beef and dairy products under discussion would certainly mean lower prices for Irish farmers. Perhaps anticipating the failure of the Doha Round, the EU is pursuing a more aggressive programme of free trade agreements with its trading partners. These also require agricultural concessions in terms of greater market access on the part of the EU. Of particular concern to Irish farmers are the trade agreement negotiations with Mercosur, the common market of South America in which Brazil is the leading player. Brazil is seeking additional access for its beef exports, which would compete directly with Irish farmers.

Energy from Agriculture

The significant increase in energy prices (with oil prices increasing from $40 per barrel in mid-2004 to $110 per barrel in 2008 and, although dropping to under $50 in 2009, soaring again to $120 per barrel in early 2011) as well as the need to reduce carbon dioxide emissions has renewed interest in agriculture and forestry as a provider of renewable energy. Ireland is hugely reliant on imported energy to cover over 90 per cent of its requirements and, under prompting from EU legislation, ambitious targets to increase the contribution of renewable energy have been set (see Chapter 10). The majority of biomass energy in Ireland is derived from wood products which are converted into heat, although there is growing interest in using wood for electricity production through combined heat and power plants.

Great hopes are held for bio-energy in Ireland both in providing a new set of market opportunities for Irish agriculture (and forestry) as well as helping to redress Ireland's dependence on fossil fuels and to reduce greenhouse gas emissions. Ireland's interventions to meet the bio-fuels target have been limited to date, restricted to providing excise duty relief for a number of pilot bio-fuels projects (even though this is estimated to cost some €200m over the 2006–10 period) and some limited support to farmers for growing energy crops. To meet the bio-fuels targets, a bio-fuels obligation scheme was introduced in 2010 that obliges fuel distributors to achieve a specific target percentage use of bio-fuels (on an energy basis) in their total annual fuel business each year. However, most of the fossil fuel on the Irish market comes via the UK and is already pre-blended with bio-fuel so the fuel distributors have no need to purchase Irish supplies. Irish liquid bio-fuel production has as a result come to a standstill. On the production side, additional incentives have been put in place to encourage farmers to grow more energy crops.

The growth in public support for energy production from agriculture has been justified because of its contribution to energy security, to helping meet greenhouse gas reduction targets and to providing an alternative revenue stream to farmers as traditional forms of agricultural support are wound down. However, the transfer of agricultural resources from food to fuel production has contributed to the recent rise in food prices and has led some voices to question the sustainability of this strategy. Relying on domestic production of feedstock to meet the bio-fuel targets in the EU, and Ireland, would mean that most of the arable area would be required for fuel rather than food production. The climate change advantages of the first generation of bio-fuels (largely rapeseed for bio-diesel and sugar beet and wheat for bio-ethanol in Europe) as compared to fossil fuels are increasingly being questioned. Developing countries can produce bio-fuels much more cheaply than we can in Europe, although there are worries that a large-scale expansion of the land area devoted to bio-fuels in tropical countries may have other adverse environmental impacts, such as the destruction of rainforest. For these reasons, a number of scientific and advocacy bodies have called for the bio-fuels targets at EU level to be rescinded. In Ireland, solid-fuel energy crops such as willow and miscanthus, used for the production of energy and heat, are likely to be more economically attractive, have better energy input/output ratios, and contribute more to greenhouse gas (GHG) emission savings.

CAP after 2013

In November 2010, the European Commission published a Communication, *The CAP Towards 2020*, which sets out options for the further reform of the EU's CAP after 2013. The context of this communication is the debate on the size and composition of the next EU medium-term financial framework. The financial framework establishes the main budgetary parameters (revenue sources and expenditure headings) within which the EU must operate and is normally agreed for a seven-year period. The current financial framework runs from 2007 to 2013 and sets out the budget available for agricultural spending up to 2013. Spending limits after that date must be agreed in the context of the next financial framework, whose duration remains to be decided but which is expected to cover the period 2014–20. Even by 2013 the CAP will continue to be the largest single element in the EU budget. As a significant beneficiary of CAP spending, Ireland has an obvious interest in the size of the budget to be allocated to the CAP in the coming period.

The budget negotiations are difficult because of the economic crisis in Europe, which limits the fiscal resources available to governments. The EU has adopted a growth strategy for the years to 2020 with ambitious targets for employment, innovation, education, social inclusion and climate/energy, and significant investment will be required to support these objectives. It also faces major external challenges and there is a need to provide resources to support the stabilisation and economic development of its neighbours in the western Balkans, Eastern Europe and North Africa. Given the likely opposition to increasing the overall size of the EU budget, cutting the size of the CAP budget would be one way of providing additional resources for these new EU priorities.

This is the context within which the Commission's proposals for CAP reform need to be assessed. There is an awareness in agricultural policy-making circles of growing criticism of agricultural spending as being unfocused, untargeted and hard to justify on any rational criteria. Direct payments were originally introduced as compensation for price cuts which took place as long ago as 1995. The significant disparities between the amounts that the old member states receive per hectare and the amounts received by the new member states are hard to justify on any explicit criteria. The new member states are pressing to have this issue addressed. It is a certainty that greater equity in the distribution of direct payments between member states will be one outcome of the next CAP reform. Others argue that direct payments should be targeted more to reward farmers who are producing environmental public goods. Farmers and their supporters warn against the adverse consequences of reducing support to agriculture just at the time when world food supplies are tightening and global food prices are soaring. Although it is hard to imagine European consumers going hungry because of higher food prices (the share of EU consumer expenditure on raw material food costs is around 3–4 per cent), and high prices in themselves should provide the incentive for farmers to increase production without the need for further public support, the rhetoric around food security is playing an important part in the debate on the future CAP. The Commission's legislative proposals are expected in November 2011 following the publication of its proposals for the next medium-term financial framework in June 2011. It is expected that final agreement on reforms will be reached in early 2013 for implementation in the following year. As a result of the Treaty of Lisbon, this will be the first CAP reform in which the European Parliament will have equal powers with the Council of Ministers in determining the outcome. It is as yet unclear how the involvement of the Parliament is likely to influence the outcome of the debate.

4 FOOD PROCESSING AND DISTRIBUTION

Food Industry

Few agricultural products are sold direct to the consumer – vegetables, fruit and eggs sold at farmers' markets being the main examples. Most agricultural products are purchased by food processors which prepare food for final consumption for either the domestic or export market. Output of the Irish food industry (including drinks) in 2008 amounted to €24 billion, or almost five times that of primary agriculture. The contribution of the different sub-sectors is shown in Table 11.5. Gross value added (which subtracts the value of raw materials purchased by the industry and gives a better idea of its contribution to the overall economy) amounted to €7.7 billion, equivalent to 6 per cent of GNP at market prices. The industry provides direct employment for around 43,000 people, or one-fifth of the total industrial workforce.

Globally, the food industry consists of a fairly limited number of well-known multinational food companies (Nestlé, Unilever, Kraft, Kellogg, etc.) as well as a myriad of much less well-known small and medium-sized enterprises which supply a wide variety of food products. This is reflected in the food industry structure in Ireland, which consists of subsidiaries of multinational firms (for example, there is an impressive cluster of international firms in Ireland, such as Abbott, Danone and Pfizer, which together produce 15 per cent of the world's supply of infant milk formula), some larger Irish-owned firms which have themselves become multinationals (Kerry Foods, Glanbia, Greencore, etc.) and then a large number of small and medium-sized firms which are a crucial source of employment and potentially innovation for the sector as a whole. While there are over 640 individual plants in the industry, the 40 largest firms, each with over 250 employees, account for around 40 per cent of the employment and almost 60 per cent of the output. The existence of the multinational sector creates the same need for caution in interpreting statistics on value added and productivity levels as for manufacturing as a whole. There is a pronounced dualism in the sector, to which the phenomenon of transfer pricing may contribute.

Table 11.5

Key Indicators for the Irish Food Processing
and Drink Industry, 2008 (€m)

Industrial sector	Turnover (€m)	Gross value added (€m)	Persons engaged
Food products	*21,413*	*6,417*	*36,727*
Meat and meat products	4,366	594	12,868
Fish, crustaceans and molluscs	414	108	2,041
Fruit and vegetables	299	69	1,642
Vegetable, animal oils and fats	19	5	68
Dairy products	3,870	911	5,317
Grain mill products, starches and starch products	121	17	333
Bakery and farinaceous products	846	333	5,615
Other food products	10,391	4,218	6,469
Prepared animal feeds	1,087	161	2,374
Beverages	*2,745*	*1,320*	*4,049*

Source: CSO, *Census of Industrial Production*, CSO, Dublin 2008. Results are presented for industrial enterprises with three or more persons engaged, so total employment in the food and drink industry is somewhat underestimated in this table.

Distribution

The final element of the food chain consists of distribution, comprising wholesalers, retailers and food service firms, which provide the link between the food industry and consumers. Wholesaling involves the purchase of goods from suppliers and importers for resale to retailers and food service customers. Wholesalers provide a range of services such as storage, distribution and other services in connection with the sale of goods. The principal innovation of modern wholesaling is the emergence and growth of wholesaler-franchisors, that is, wholesalers that sell predominantly to retailers which are affiliated to them (symbol groups such as SuperValu, Londis, etc.). Retailers decide whether their outlets will operate more profitably if run as an independent retailer or under the brand of a wholesaler-franchisor. Thus, modern wholesaling is very much involved with developments at the retail level.[2]

The wholesale level of the grocery supply chain is highly concentrated. The Competition Authority estimates that over 95 per cent of the wholesale turnover in the Irish grocery sector is attributable to seven groups of operators. Just two firms, Musgrave and BWG Foods, together account for almost 80 per cent of grocery wholesale turnover. Six of the seven groups are wholesaler-franchisors which engage in the traditional function of buying goods from suppliers for resale to retailers and which license one or more retail brands to retailers that are part of their symbol groups. The remaining group combines independent cash-and-carry wholesalers which are engaged in the traditional function of buying goods from suppliers for resale to retailers (and by definition, do not license a brand to retailers).

The grocery retail sector in Ireland is made up of the major multiples, symbol groups, independent retailers and speciality independents, e.g. greengrocers, butchers, etc. The number of multiples has grown steadily, as well as their size, facilitated by the emergence of out-of-town shopping centres. The main multiples operating in the Irish market have been Tesco, Dunnes Stores, Superquinn and Marks & Spencer. Recent years have also seen the arrival of the German cut-price own brand chains Aldi and Lidl into the Irish market. While the overall share of the discount stores is still low, they have achieved significant market share in some geographic and product markets. The market share of the symbol groups has also grown and the market share of the independents is on a continuing downward trend. The fastest-growing segment of the grocery market is garage forecourt shops. This reflects increased car ownership, the convenience of accessing forecourt outlets and the increased demand for convenience foods.

The Competition Authority estimates that the six multiples together account for 46 per cent of retail turnover in grocery goods in the state. The retailers which are affiliated to the four largest wholesaler-franchisors account for a further 40 per cent of retail grocery turnover while the other retailers, independent retailers and retailers affiliated to smaller wholesaler-franchisors account for the remaining 14 per cent of grocery sales. From a supplier's perspective, buying power is even more concentrated. Just three grocery purchasers, Dunnes Stores, Tesco and Musgraves/Supervalu, account for 70 per cent of all retail sales. This higher figure is explained by the fact that Musgraves/Supervalu is a centralised buying group that owns the symbol group franchise for a large number of independent retailers who individually have a very small market share.

The other main channel for food distribution is the food service sector, defined as 'food consumed away from home', the importance of which has also been growing over time. An Bord Bia estimates that the Irish food service market was worth €6.5 billion at consumer prices in 2009, and €2.2 billion at operator buying prices. This accounts for over one-fifth of all expenditure on food. The channel is made up of fast-food restaurants, full service restaurants, pubs and coffee shops, hotels and institutional catering. Food is now more important than drink in sales terms for pubs and the collapse of the lunchtime trade during the recession hit many pubs hard. The food service market in Ireland is less developed than in other European countries, where the sector accounts for around one-third of consumer expenditure on food, or in the United States, where the share is 50 per cent.

Structural Changes in the Food Chain

The market for food is changing rapidly due to changing consumer demands and market structures. Changing consumer lifestyles are having a decisive influence on food demand. Increased numbers of working women, reduced leisure time and the decline in the traditional family unit are changing eating habits and increasing the demand for convenience foods. Thus important growth areas for the food industry are the food ingredients business (such as dairy ingredients, meat, by-products such as pizza toppings and meat flavourings, and other ingredients such as colourings, flavourings and malt) for pre-prepared foods, as well as the food service sector (embracing all forms of catering and eating out). Other important changes in consumer preferences are the growing concern over food safety, interest in nutrition/health/obesity management issues as well as the growing importance of ethical and food quality concerns, e.g. organic, fair trade, shop local, food miles, and animal welfare (see Section 5).

In the traditional view of the food supply chain, it comprised three clearly identifiable and distinct levels: retail, wholesale and supply. These divisions have become increasingly blurred over time. Some operators are active across more than one level. For example, some retailers combine the retail and wholesale levels. Other retailers operate across all three levels, selling own-branded products and having very close relationships with suppliers. The other important trend is the growing importance of retail concentration, which is shifting market power to the giant retailers. Just twenty-five retailers in Europe now account for 45 per cent of food sales. In Ireland, we have seen that just three buyers account for 70 per cent of retail grocery purchases. This concentration of buying power gives the large retailers substantial power to dictate terms to their suppliers, including not only price but also quality and safety characteristics (see Section 5).

Food and drink exports in 2010 amounted to almost €8 billion, around two-thirds of the total from indigenous manufacturing industry, and the government has set ambitious targets to increase this level in its *Food Harvest 2020* report published in 2010. Because of the importance of the UK market, sales are heavily influenced by the euro–sterling exchange rate. Any sharp appreciation in the value of the euro makes it difficult for the industry to increase, let alone maintain, its market share in the UK. Shifting sales to the euro zone would limit this exchange rate risk and is a policy objective. Beyond this, the food industry faces significant challenges to improve its competitiveness, including reducing key input costs such as energy and waste, as well as improving its innovation capacity to benefit fully from emerging consumer trends.

5 FOOD POLICY

Growing Concern over Food Safety

From the earliest times food has been particularly susceptible to exploitation, and there is a long history of food legislation with the purpose of preventing consumers being either cheated or poisoned! Measures for the protection of the consumer against the adulteration of food and drink are among the earliest examples of social legislation. Since then the scope of food law has been greatly widened. Examples of some of the matters now covered by legislation include: the produce of diseased animals posing a threat to human health; sanitary conditions in food preparation, packaging and handling; pesticide and hormone residues in food; packaging materials which may pose a threat to health; food additives; the labelling requirements for food products; and weights and measures legislation.

Despite the undoubted improvement in food purity and in merchandising practices brought about by this legislation, consumers are increasingly uneasy about the safety and quality of the modern food supply. Issues of recent concern include agrochemical residues in food, the increasing number and diversity of food additives, the use of illegal substances in livestock production, the existence of nitrates in drinking water, and genetically engineered foods. There have been sharp falls in the consumption of particular foods caused by publicity given, for example, to bovine spongiform encephalopathy (BSE) in cattle, listeria in soft cheeses and salmonella in eggs. Consumer concerns also extend beyond the safety of food products to their production methods, including genetic modification, animal welfare, and environmental and ethical concerns.

The risk of food-borne diseases has increased for a number of reasons. Best hygiene practices are not always followed in commercial and domestic kitchens. Fewer people are preparing their own food, and more eating outside the home means a higher proportion of people are at risk from outbreaks of disease. The increasing demand for ready-to-go foods has resulted in food being served in a growing number of non-traditional outlets such as garage forecourts. The global distribution of food has lengthened the food chain. The increased competition between and price constraints on food producers has led the food sector to seek cost reductions through ever more complex food processing and may sometimes encourage suppliers to adopt practices which have adverse health effects (the dioxin contamination of Irish pig meat in 2008, which cost the taxpayer over €100 million, was the result of an animal feed compounder using contaminated fuel oil sold as food-grade oil by a Northern Ireland supplier).

Fortunately, in Ireland, food problems have not emerged to the dramatic extent reached elsewhere. However, the increase in food poisoning notifications (*E. coli*, for instance) suggests that vigilance is essential. Food production and tourism are major elements in the economy, and both depend crucially on a favourable international perception of the safety of Irish food. So along with the issue of the health and lives of its own citizens, Ireland has a vital economic interest in becoming a centre of excellence in food safety.

Economic Considerations

In economic terms, the need for governments to regulate for food safety is the result of a market failure. This arises because consumers are not necessarily in a position to determine the safety characteristics of food they consume on the basis of visual inspection alone. There is thus an asymmetry of information between the producer and consumer of food. In this, the market for food safety is like the market for used cars. Sellers have more information than buyers about the quality of the car. Because buyers often cannot tell the difference between a good and a bad used car, both good and bad cars must sell at the same price and the seller of a good car is unable to extract a premium for quality. In the same way, there is a tendency for food safety to be undersupplied by the market because consumers are not always able to distinguish between high and low food standards.

Of course, if we go to a restaurant and subsequently experience illness due to food poisoning, we are unlikely to patronise that restaurant again. Where there is the likelihood of repeat purchases, food businesses have an incentive to maintain high standards in order to maximise the likelihood of retaining our custom. The development of brand names, or supermarkets that monitor quality on our behalf, are other ways in which market institutions can respond to the asymmetry of information. However, sometimes firms themselves may be unaware of, say, the carcinogenic risk associated with a particular additive or production process. There may also be strong externalities that justify government intervention, either on the production side (one rogue producer who fails to meet adequate food standards can put the reputation of an entire national food industry at risk) or on the consumption side (an infectious food-borne illness imposes wider costs on society that transcend those incurred by the individual consumer). This is the economic case for governments to step in to ensure that minimum food standards are maintained.

While the failure to observe adequate food standards can impose economic costs on both individuals and society at large, maintaining and enforcing these standards is also a costly exercise. For economists, this raises the question whether the benefits from a particular food regulation (in terms of the avoided cost of food illnesses or, for an exporting country, the loss of market reputation in export markets) exceed its costs. The idea that we should try to balance benefits and costs in setting food regulations suggests that trying to achieve zero risk is not the optimal strategy. Removing all risk from eating food is likely to be hugely expensive, and the economic benefit from lowering risk from a minimal to a zero risk of contracting an illness may not justify taking this extra step. There may also be an alternative and more efficient instrument available to achieve the same degree of risk reduction, for example by introducing more stringent product liability legislation which allows consumers to claim damages if harmed by consuming unsafe food. Governments, of course, should not take such decisions on the basis of cost benefit studies alone; moral and ethical criteria must also be taken into account. However, the economist's framework of balancing the expected benefits from risk reduction against the costs of achieving such reductions should be an important adjunct to the decision-making process in food safety regulation.

EU Food Safety Framework
These growing concerns prompted the incoming European Commission in October 1999 to make food safety a top priority. In January 2000, the Irish Commissioner for Health and Consumer Protection, David Byrne, produced a White Paper on Food Safety which outlined a comprehensive strategy to restore consumers' confidence in their food supply. There were three elements to the strategy: new legislation on the safety of food and animal feed; a new agency to offer scientific advice on food-borne threats; and more stringent control and enforcement.

A new General Food Law which brought together the general principles of food and animal feed safety was agreed in 2002. Until then, EU food law had been motivated mainly by the desire to facilitate the free movement of foodstuffs throughout the internal market, by removing technical barriers such as differences in standards. The new law made food safety and consumer protection the cornerstone of the regulatory regime. Including animal feed in its provisions was a major advance as animal feed has been the source of many food scares in the past decade. This was supplemented by new food hygiene legislation passed in 2004 and which has come into effect since 2006. This modernises, consolidates and simplifies the previous EU food hygiene legislation and introduces a 'farm to fork' approach to food safety, by including primary production (farmers and growers), for the first time in the majority of cases, in food hygiene legislation.

The general principles which now underlie food safety policy emphasise a whole food chain approach (food safety must be ensured at all stages of the food chain, from the producer through to the consumer), risk analysis (meaning that the policy is based on a scientific understanding of risk with due account for the need for precaution when scientific opinion is not yet clear), operator liability (all food sector operators are now responsible for ensuring the safety of the products they import, produce, process or sell), traceability (from 1 January 2005 all foodstuffs, animal feeds and feed ingredients must be traceable right through the food chain) and openness (citizens have the right to clear and accurate information on food and health risks from public authorities). The General Food Law is supplemented by a large number of targeted regulations addressing specific food safety issues, such as the use of pesticides, food supplements, colouring, antibiotics and hormones in food production; rules on hygiene; food labelling; and legislation setting down procedures for the release, marketing, labelling and traceability of crops and foodstuffs containing genetically modified organisms.

The second Commission initiative was the creation of the European Food Safety Authority (EFSA) in 2002 to provide a source of independent, objective scientific advice on food-related risks. The new Authority has responsibility for the EU Rapid Alert System, which links EU countries in cases of food-borne threats. The Commission explicitly rejected the option of modelling it on the US Food and Drugs Administration, which has responsibility not only for risk assessment (i.e. quantifying the risk associated with a potential food hazard) but also risk management (i.e. taking the necessary decisions to respond to a perceived food-borne risk, such as strengthening existing regulations). The Authority's role is limited to giving its opinion, and it is up to the Commission (in conjunction with the Council and the Parliament) to initiate the required action. EFSA works through a series of Scientific Panels composed of independent experts who are responsible for providing scientific opinions to the Authority. Of course, scientists may disagree, and in the legislation establishing EFSA member states were reluctant to grant it the power to act as the ultimate source of food safety information. In the event of a disagreement between the EFSA and a national food safety agency, for example, it would be up to the courts to resolve this conflict. However, there are encouraging signs that EFSA has developed strong working relationships with national agencies to develop a common approach to risk assessment throughout the EU.

The third initiative was to improve the EU framework for control and enforcement of food safety legislation. Enforcement of food regulations is the responsibility of national governments, albeit under the oversight of the EU. An EU framework directive lays down norms and procedures relating to inspection and enforcement, and the Food and Veterinary Office of the European Commission, which is based in Grange, County Meath, controls the performance of national authorities and makes recommendations aimed at improving national control and inspection systems. The Commission's powers to ensure enforcement in member states have been criticised in the past as slow and unwieldy. An important enforcement change was the extension during 2000 of the EU Product Liability Directive to primary agricultural products such as beef, milk, fruit and vegetables. This makes farmers liable for damages if consumers take legal proceedings against them and if there is proof that they are responsible for putting unsafe food into the food chain.

Irish Responses

In Ireland, the Food Safety Authority (FSA) was set up in 1999 to ensure that food produced, distributed or marketed in the state meets the highest standards of food safety and hygiene and to co-ordinate food safety activities 'from farm to fork'. The FSA has functions in relation to research, advice, co-ordination of services and certification of food. It operates the national food safety compliance programme by means of service contracts with the agencies involved in the enforcement of food legislation (including government departments, health boards, local authorities and the Radiological Protection Institute). Around 2,300 persons in total are involved in the inspection and control of food. In addition, the Authority works with industry and training bodies to improve, harmonise and co-ordinate food safety and hygiene training through the country. The FSA is required to operate on the basis of scientific principles and with the primacy of consumer interests in mind.

Initiatives such as the National Beef Assurance Scheme and the National Sheep Identification System have been launched to ensure the identification and traceability of animals/meat. Controls on BSE remain in place to ensure that meat from confirmed cases and from herds in which cases have been located does not enter the food or feed chains. Another priority area concerns residue testing, which is focused particularly on detecting illegal growth promoters in cattle and antibiotic residues in pigs. A new cross-border food safety promotion board known as Safefood has been established under the Good Friday Agreement to contribute to the improved co-ordination of food safety activities on the island as a whole. Its functions include food safety promotion; research into food safety; communication of food alerts; surveillance of food-borne diseases; and the promotion of scientific co-operation and linkages between laboratories.

316

Food Quality

Alongside food safety, consumers are showing a greater interest in food quality. What constitutes quality is very much a subjective matter, especially where food is concerned. Food quality was traditionally associated with its organoleptic properties, or properties that can be assessed by the senses (taste, smell, sight and touch). These attributes, such as freshness, colour, degree of blemish or shape, are readily ascertained by consumers. However, consumers increasingly seek to make purchases based on lifestyle or ethical considerations. They demand information on specific product or process characteristics, including the place of origin, carbon footprint, whether the farming practices are organic or not, whether the product has been modified by biotechnology, whether it meets 'fair trade' standards, and whether high animal welfare standards were adopted. Because the consumer cannot make an informed decision on these issues just by looking at a food product, he or she depends on accurate labelling. But because of the potential for fraud (e.g. passing off a non-organic product as organic in order to obtain the premium price), labelling claims are either regulated by the state or may be substantiated by a credible third party (as where an environmental non-governmental organisation certifies that a product has been sustainably produced).

Both public authorities and the food industry have an interest in communicating food quality characteristics to consumers. Ireland is a high-cost food producer and cannot compete on cost alone with major agricultural exporters. However, by targeting food quality characteristics where consumers have a demonstrated willingness to pay, the Irish food industry can hope to attract a premium price and thereby improve its competitiveness. Similarly, food retailers seek to use quality attributes as a means of product differentiation, both to attract more customers to their stores and to persuade them to part with more money when they are there. As a result, there has been an explosion of quality assurance schemes, both private and public, aiming to provide information to consumers. Indeed, one of the problems in this area is information overload, such that consumers are confused rather than informed by the plethora of labels and logos that have emerged.

An Bord Bia, as the state body charged with the marketing of Irish food abroad, operates a number of quality assurance schemes for beef, lamb, chicken, pig meat, eggs and horticulture, which are associated with particular production standards. A Bord Bia survey conducted in early 2009 found that more than four in five consumers in Ireland recognised its Quality Mark and almost half of respondents said that they would be much more likely to buy a product bearing the mark. It also sees an opportunity for the Irish industry to emphasise its environmental sustainability credentials as markets increasingly factor climate change considerations into their businesses. It is supporting research to demonstrate that Irish grass-fed beef has a much lower carbon footprint than beef produced under more intensive feedlot conditions or under extensive conditions in some developing countries such as Brazil.

The growing demand for food safety and improved animal welfare will increasingly impact on farmers. Even in the absence of government regulation, the private sector and particularly the large retail chains are insisting that their suppliers meet stringent hygiene and safety standards. These demands will require farmers to undertake additional investments and will accelerate the process of structural change in the industry. However, they also open up additional marketing opportunities. Instead of selling beef as a commodity product, for example, it becomes possible to produce beef for particular niche markets and to guarantee consumers that their particular requirements have been met. One fast-growing market is for organic produce. Organic production in Ireland is relatively limited, with 1,400 registered producers and 53,000 hectares (1.3 per cent of the agricultural land area) in organic production or in conversion in 2010. The government objective is to have 5 per cent of agricultural land under organic farming by 2012. An Organic Farming Action Plan 2008–12 seeks to develop the organic market and to increase production in line with market trends. Farmers who wish to convert to organic production are eligible for aid under the EU agri-environment scheme.

Market Power in the Food Chain
Concentration of Buying Power

A major issue in the food chain, not only in Ireland but across Europe, is whether the concentration of buying power in the hands of retailers gives them excessive market power to set prices and trading conditions at the expense of suppliers and farmers. Concern about the abuse of market power in the food chain is not a new issue. Since the beginning of the last century farmers have attempted to increase their collective bargaining power in negotiating prices with creameries, meat factories and grain millers. One outcome of these attempts was the co-operative movement, which still plays an important role in the Irish dairy industry. With the rise of supermarkets these concerns have now moved further down the food chain. In a situation where it is not unusual that the top three retailers control 50 per cent or more of a country's grocery trade, there is a noticeable asymmetry in bargaining power between retailers and their suppliers. The largest food companies account for only 1–2 per cent of a retailer's business at national level, but conversely a retailer may represent 20–30 per cent of those companies' business.

There are frequent allegations that retailers have taken advantage of this situation of unequal dependence to increase their profit margins at the expense of consumers and of suppliers and farmers further back the food chain through anti-competitive practices. There are in fact two separate issues here – buyer power vis-à-vis suppliers and seller power vis-à-vis consumers. These are separate markets and the degree of competition is not necessarily the same in each. Suppliers often complain about unfair practices such as the practice of seeking 'hello money'. This is the name given to the practice where supermarkets seek payments from suppliers to have their goods stocked. Processors and suppliers may be compelled to carry the cost of product discounting campaigns by retailers. Retailers may seek to use exclusive supply agreements with suppliers to withhold supplies from price-cutting rivals. Growth in the sales of own-label brands is also highlighted as another possible factor leading to an increase in buyer power.

Evidence from Food Prices

Other evidence that the food chain may not be fully competitive comes from the behaviour of food prices. Farmers are often angry when they see prices falling at farm level but increasing to the consumer at retail level, and blame the food chain intermediaries, particularly supermarkets, for pocketing the difference. Indeed, the farmers' share of the retail price of food has steadily decreased over time, even for relatively simple products such as a litre of milk or a standard loaf of bread. Between 1995 and 2009 the farmers' share of the retail price for liquid milk fell from 42 to 33 per cent. For cheese, the share fell from 34 to 20 per cent, for pig meat from 51 to 27 per cent, and for beef from 60 to 50 per cent.[3] The retail price, of course, includes the cost of the marketing services (processing, transport, assembly, packaging, storage and distribution) added to the raw material provided by the farmer. There may be good reasons why the cost of these marketing services increases at a difference pace from the cost of the raw material. But the generally high price of food in Ireland relative to other EU countries reinforces the suspicion that competition in the retail food market is less aggressive than it should be.

Successive surveys by the National Consumer Agency have shown that grocery prices are higher in the Republic than in Northern Ireland. Retailers claimed that higher costs of doing business in the Republic of Ireland contributed to the price differential. Forfás published a study in December 2008 which found that, while the cost of doing business in the Republic of Ireland was 25 per cent higher than in Northern Ireland, this would only account for a 5–6 per cent price difference, approximately. The price differentials were particularly marked following the sharp depreciation of sterling against the euro in 2008. Supermarkets were accused of not passing on the benefits of a stronger euro in terms of lower prices for imported goods, and there was a significant increase in cross-border shopping to take advantage of the considerably lower prices for food items in the North. The then Minister for Enterprise, Trade and Innovation commissioned a report from the Competition Authority to examine the operation of the import and distribution sector and to investigate whether this was evidence of excessive profit-taking at the expense of consumers.

The Competition Authority study found a number of other explanations for the higher cost of imported food in the Republic.[4] All grocery goods supplied in Northern Ireland come from the UK multiples' supply chain. This has two main effects. First, as the UK multiples have a national pricing policy, Northern Ireland retail stores' goods are priced to a much larger market. They therefore benefit from volume sale discounts that the Republic's retailers and wholesalers cannot get. Second, because there is a national pricing policy, the costs of distributing goods to Northern Ireland are absorbed with the rest of the UK, whereas in the Republic these extra costs are internalised. In effect, stores in Northern Ireland are subsidised by the UK market structure. Third, price comparisons ignore the impact on take-home prices of promotions, widely used in the Republic to attract customers to stores. In periods without promotions the price is high and during promotions the price is low. The rebates offered by suppliers during promotions reduce the effective net price of goods to supermarkets. In the UK, there is less promotional activity and prices to retailers are closer to the net price. Fourth, the Competition Authority also highlighted the absence of retail planning caps in Northern Ireland. Retail planning guidelines in the Republic introduced in 1982 under pressure from the independent retailers mean that there are no large-scale low-cost grocery retailers such as exist in Northern Ireland. The report failed to find any behaviour or practice relating, for example, to the buyer power of retailers that adversely affected the normal competitive dynamics of supply chains.

Proposed Code of Practice

Despite this conclusion the Fianna Fáil–Green government announced its intention in 2009 to introduce a Code of Practice on either a voluntary or statutory basis intended to achieve a balance in the relationships between actors in the food supply chain. The proposed Code of Practice for Grocery Good Undertakings appears to be modelled on a similar code of conduct which was first introduced in the UK in 2002. It would be accompanied by an independent Ombudsman who would arbitrate in disputes between parties in the supply chain. The Fine Gael–Labour government similarly included a commitment in its Programme for Government in 2011 to enact a Fair Trade Act, which would ban a number of unfair trading practices, such as 'hello money', in the retail sector. The Competition Authority is sceptical that such initiatives would lead to better prices for consumers. It notes that there is inevitably a degree of tension between supermarkets and their suppliers because one party seeks the highest possible price and the other the lowest price, and that regulation could lead to higher prices to consumers. It points out that the unfair practices complained of were already outlawed in the 2006 Competition Act, but only where their objective or effect is the prevention, restriction or distortion of competition. If this 'competition test' is not included, it argues that conduct which could be pro-competitive and ultimately pro-consumer could be prohibited. It notes that the major problem with implementing the existing competition provisions (which also applies to the UK Code of Practice) is the reluctance of suppliers to make a complaint for fear that it would lead to their de-listing by the multiple. The Authority proposes to strengthen the existing provisions in the Competition Act to make it easier for suppliers to make complaints, as well as prohibiting retaliatory de-listing for not paying hello money. It would also seem desirable, given their role in the economy, that the large vertically integrated retailers should be obliged to report details of their profitability and turnover in Ireland, which is not the case at present.

6 CONCLUSIONS

The agri-food sector is one of the key sectors of the Irish economy, accounting for around 6 per cent of GNP and 8 per cent of employment. This chapter has emphasised the way in which the sector is heavily influenced by government policies promoting specific objectives. The substantial protection provided to EU agriculture means that almost all the income generated by agricultural production arises because of transfers either from consumers or taxpayers resulting from the operation of the CAP. The share of budget transfers from taxpayers, which now accounts for 70 per cent of Irish farm income, is particularly striking.

Farming faces both challenges and opportunities in the future. The system of transfers is threatened by further WTO trade commitments, by changing EU budget priorities and by an increasingly powerful environmental lobby concerned about the negative impact of intensive agricultural production on the environment. The future justification for the single farm payment, so important to incomes on many farms, is unclear, with many inequities between farmers themselves. On the other hand, food prices are hardening, driven upwards by growing demand for meat and dairy products in the rapidly growing emerging economies, by the competition between food and fuel for agricultural resources, and by constraints on increasing global supply capacity. There has rarely been a more propitious time to wean farming off protectionism and to encourage a greater market orientation. Over the next decade, more emphasis must be put on strengthening the competitiveness of farm production while ensuring that it lives up to ever-higher consumer demands for safety and environmental sustainability.

In 2010 the government published its *Food Harvest 2020* report, which set ambitious targets for the contribution of the agri-food sector to economic recovery. It proposed a 33 per cent increase in the value of agricultural output (including fisheries and forestry) compared to 2007–9, a 40 per cent increase in food industry value added and a 42 per cent increase in export earnings. Higher food prices (see Section 2) will make some contribution towards meeting these targets, but their achievement will also require a step-change in trend growth rates for the sector. Although the abolition of milk quotas from 2015 should help to release the competitive dynamism of that sector, the prospect that direct payment support might be reduced in the next CAP reform will reduce the profitability of dry-stock production, in particular. There is undoubtedly the technical potential to increase output significantly from current resources – there is an enormous gap in efficiency between the most productive and less productive farms. But unless ways can be found to transfer the use of land more quickly into the hands of younger and more skilled operators it is unlikely that this technical potential will be fully realised.

The paradox should be noted that, at a time when government intervention in agricultural markets is being reduced, the demand for greater regulation of food markets has never been greater. While the rationale for continued agricultural support becomes less and less persuasive as food prices increase and farm incomes approach equality with incomes in the non-farm sector, the growing complexity of the food chain and fear of the consequences of new technological advances is fuelling consumer demands for greater food regulation. While a perfectly sound case for regulation can be made, it is important to bear in mind that all regulation imposes costs as well as benefits and that the task of the regulator is to find the appropriate balance (see Chapter 5). Economists are particularly well trained to assist in finding this balance through assessing the costs and benefits of alternative regulatory policies.

Endnotes

1   The farm household figures in this section take a broad definition of a farm household as any household with income from farming. If farm households are defined more narrowly as households whose principal income comes from farming, the comparison with non-farm households would be less favourable.

2   Competition Authority, *A Description of the Structure and Operation of Grocery Retailing and Wholesaling in Ireland: 2001 to 2006*, Grocery Monitor Report No. 1, 2008.

3   Irish Farmers' Association, *Equity for Farmers in the Food Supply Chain*, Dublin 2010.

4   Competition Authority, *Retail-related Import and Distribution Study*, Dublin 2009.

POLICY ISSUES IN THE NON-MARKET SECTOR

CHAPTER 12

Health: Funding, Access and Efficiency

Anne Nolan[*]

1 INTRODUCTION[1]

This chapter examines the health sector, a key component of Irish economic activity and the subject of much recent policy discussion. In terms of its economic impact, expenditure on the health services accounted for 12.1 per cent of gross national income (GNI) and 12.4 per cent of total employment in 2009. The public sector accounts for approximately 80 per cent of total health expenditure in Ireland. After years of expenditure growth barely in line with inflation during the 1980s and early 1990s, public health expenditure increased sharply from the mid-1990s (see Figure 12.1). Indeed, over the period 2000–9, public health expenditure more than doubled in real terms. However, the effect of the sharp deterioration in the public finances since then is reflected in public health expenditure, which declined from €15.5 billion in 2009 to €14.8 billion in 2010; further reductions in public health expenditure of approximately 8 per cent are required for the period 2011–14 under the terms of the National Recovery Plan.

The challenges facing the Irish health service today are therefore very different from those of just a few years ago. In the latter part of the last decade, the sustainability of ever-increasing levels of health expenditure was a major concern, and issues such as long waiting lists (and the consequent impact on health outcomes), A&E overcrowding and deteriorating outcomes in certain areas (suicide, obesity and binge drinking) dominated public discussion of the Irish health service. In just a few years the environment has changed dramatically. The wider fiscal and banking crisis and its impact on the resources available for the public health sector is an immediate challenge. In particular, the focus is now on ensuring that existing service levels and quality are maintained in a period of declining public health expenditure. This will require increased efficiencies across the health sector, with recent initiatives focusing on some of the largest components of public health expenditure, namely labour and pharmaceuticals. In addition, the recent general election campaign highlighted ongoing concerns with access to health services in Ireland.

Figure 12.1

Public Health Expenditure in Ireland, 1990–2010, € million (Deflated by CPI)

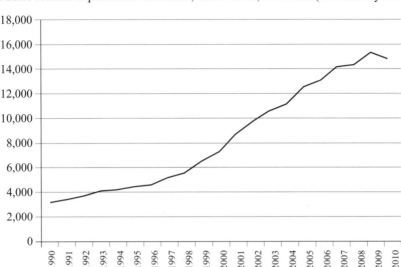

Sources: for expenditure data see Department of Health and Children, *Health Statistics*, Stationery Office, Dublin (various issues) and Department of Health and Children, *Health in Ireland: Key Trends*, Stationery Office, Dublin (various issues); for consumer price index data see CSO, *Consumer Price Index*, Stationery Office, Dublin (various issues).

The remainder of this chapter focuses on the themes of access and efficiency in the context of discussions on key issues with regard to the health services in Ireland. Section 2 discusses the rationale for government intervention in the financing and delivery of health services (see also Chapter 3), outlining the various efficiency and equity justifications for government intervention in the sector. Section 3 outlines the key features of the Irish health service, in terms of governance and organisational structure, entitlement, financing and delivery. This section also discusses proposed changes to the structure and financing of the health service, most notably those outlined in the recent *Government for National Recovery* document. Section 4 looks at the Irish health sector in a comparative context, discussing how the Irish experience in terms of expenditure, outcomes, financing and delivery structures compares with other OECD countries. Sections 5 and 6 focus on the two key issues facing the Irish health services at present: access and efficiency. Section 5 focuses on the financing of primary care services in Ireland, as well as the current role of private health insurance in the Irish healthcare system. In the context of declining levels of public health expenditure over the next few years, Section 6 discusses the issue of cost containment in the health sector, with a particular focus on two areas of recent concern: labour costs and pharmaceuticals. Section 7 concludes the chapter.

2 WHY GOVERNMENT INTERVENTION?

Despite the fact that the private sector accounts for approximately 20 per cent of healthcare finance (see Section 3), and is heavily involved in the provision of health services in Ireland, the public sector remains the main agent responsible for the finance and delivery of health services in Ireland. Chapter 3 discusses the rationale for government intervention in the economy in general. In terms of the health services, efficiency concerns relating to asymmetric information, uncertainty and the existence of externalities, as well as equity or distributional concerns, motivate government involvement in healthcare. Where the government does not directly involve itself in the provision of healthcare services, it may have a role in terms of financing, regulation, pricing (taxation and subsidies) and information provision.

While asymmetric information, uncertainty and externalities are the most readily identifiable indicators of market failure in the health sector, healthcare markets also suffer from imperfect competition in the sense that many of the conditions for perfectly competitive markets are absent or deficient. Many services, e.g. hospital services, are subject to economies of scale; producers can often influence the level of demand and/or price; and price signals are often absent, particularly where third-party reimbursement systems (e.g. insurance) are in operation. Most importantly, however, the assumptions of perfectly informed consumers, the absence of uncertainty and the absence of externalities are violated in healthcare markets.

Asymmetric Information
The nature of the relationship between producers and consumers in healthcare is distorted by asymmetric information. Patients are essentially buying the provider's knowledge and/or information when they consume healthcare. In comparison with other goods and services, information acquisition on the part of the consumer in healthcare markets is made more difficult by the nature of the product. Learning by experience is complicated by the fact that every illness episode is different, the consumer cannot sample the service before purchase and is unlikely to have had prior experience of the same service. In addition, the information is often technically complex, involving many years of study.

The relationship has often been characterised as a principal agent one; due to the high costs of acquiring such technical information, the patient relies on the healthcare provider to act in their best interests in terms of diagnosis and treatment decisions. The presence of asymmetric information justifies a role for government in improving consumers' information and regulating the behaviour of doctors and other healthcare professionals. For example, governments intervene in terms of the licensing and accreditation of providers, the authorisation of pharmaceuticals that can be prescribed to patients and the provision of information to consumers (e.g. the Medical Council recently removed restrictions on advertising on the part of doctors in Ireland, including the display of price information). However, it does not follow that government intervention in either the financing or provision of healthcare is necessary.

Uncertainty

Healthcare markets are also characterised by uncertainty, i.e. lack of information about the future. This necessitates a role for insurance in offering the consumer protection against uncertainty. Ill-health is inherently unpredictable, both in terms of financial costs and physical and emotional suffering. However, the problems of adverse selection, moral hazard and cream-skimming may arise in a private health insurance market, leading to efficiency and equity failings. Adverse selection arises when the insurer cannot distinguish between low and high risks, because individuals purchasing health insurance have better information about their risk status than the insurer. Insurers must therefore base the premium on the risk pool that includes both low and high risks. Low-risk individuals will not purchase health insurance because the premium does not reflect their risk status, leaving only high-risk individuals in the risk pool. This can make the fund unsustainable. The solution is to have compulsory insurance or differential (i.e. risk-related) premiums. However, due to concerns that high-risk individuals would be denied access to healthcare under a private health insurance system with differential premiums on the basis of age and health status, most governments intervene to provide compulsory health insurance for most basic health services.

Moral hazard behaviour, where an individual's behaviour is affected by their insurance status, may arise in the form of excessive utilisation of services on the part of the patient. It may also arise in the form of fewer preventive activities, and there is some empirical evidence from the USA that shows that eligibility for Medicare (which starts automatically at age 65 years) results in a reduction in preventive activities and an increase in unhealthy behaviours among men.[2] User fees, which aim to make patients more aware of the resource implications of their decisions, are often used to temper the moral hazard effects of free or heavily subsidised healthcare. However, the degree to which user fees are effective in changing behaviour has been questioned, and there are well-documented adverse impacts on access (see also Section 5).

A final problem associated with a private insurance market is that of cream-skimming. Insurers seek to encourage low-risk persons to insure with their company. In the market for car insurance, for example, premia are substantially higher for high-risk groups such as young males. Once again, due to equity concerns about certain groups being denied medical treatment, governments intervene, either to offer compulsory insurance or to regulate the sector. In Ireland, the government strictly regulates the behaviour of the three major private insurers in an attempt to prevent cream-skimming through the principles of open enrolment (no one can be refused cover), community rating (all individuals face the same premium) and lifetime cover (once insured, an individual's policy cannot be terminated). The continued stability of the community rating system means that a risk-equalisation scheme (which aims to remove differences in insurers' costs that result from differing risk profiles among members) is necessary. Section 5 discusses risk equalisation and the role of private health insurance in the Irish healthcare system in greater detail.

Externalities

The healthcare sector may also be characterised by the presence of externalities when private costs or benefits are out of line with social costs or benefits. For a positive/negative externality, private benefits/costs are less than social benefits/costs, meaning that output is below/above the socially optimal level. The standard solution to an externality is to levy a Pigouvian tax in the case of goods or services that produce negative externalities or to offer a subsidy in the case of goods or services that produce positive externalities. Free childhood vaccinations against infectious diseases and excise taxes on cigarettes are the most obvious examples of government intervention in the health sector due to the presence of externalities. A vaccinated population confers a positive externality on society, while second-hand cigarette smoke confers a negative externality on society; in the absence of government intervention vaccination levels would be less than the socially optimal level due to higher social benefits than private benefits, while smoking levels would be greater than the socially optimal level due to higher social costs than private costs. Of course, the efficacy of taxes in changing behaviour to reflect the socially optimal level depends on the price elasticity of demand for the good/service, the availability of substitutes, its budget share, etc. (see also Chapter 4).

Equity

Apart from efficiency concerns, the desire to ensure that healthcare should be distributed equitably across the population motivates government intervention in the sector. However, there is much discussion over what is meant by equity in the context of the health services.[3] Is the objective equality of opportunity (i.e. access to healthcare) or equality of outcome (i.e. health status)? Many governments intervene to smooth out differences in health outcomes that are not related to need factors such as age, gender or health status, but rather to socio-economic characteristics such as income, area of residence, level of education, etc. For example, a recent study found that perinatal mortality rates in Ireland among the unskilled manual/unemployed group were 1.85 times higher than those among the professional group.[4] However, most governments also subscribe to the notion of equality of opportunity in the sense that access to healthcare should be distributed on the basis of need for care, not on the basis of non-health-related attributes, such as ability to pay (which is the case for many other commodities). But how do we define access? Most studies proxy access by utilisation, arguing that access to health services is equitable if utilisation rates are similar, even after controlling for need factors such as age, gender and health status. However, it is obvious that even if everyone enjoys the same access to healthcare, persons in equal need may end up consuming different amounts of care (and types of care) due to differing tastes and preferences, differing ability to navigate the system, etc. Nonetheless, the principle of access according to need rather than ability to pay is an accepted principle in most countries, and the recent debate in the USA about extending insurance cover to the significant proportion of the population who are currently uninsured highlights the widespread concern about individuals being denied medical treatment simply due to financial circumstances.

An additional issue concerns the progressivity of funding sources, i.e. most governments subscribe to the view that health services should be financed in relation to ability to pay (those on higher incomes should pay a higher proportion of their incomes in taxation, social insurance contributions, etc.). Such thinking motivates government involvement in the financing of healthcare services, offering free or subsidised services to those on low incomes or in particularly vulnerable situations.

Government Intervention in Practice

In practice, the public sector uses a variety of instruments to intervene in the healthcare sector. While in Ireland the government intervenes heavily in terms of regulation, information provision and financing, it mainly leaves the provision of health services to private operators, who consequently receive much of their funding from public sources (e.g. GP services and voluntary hospital services). Due to concerns over the ability of the private market to deliver insurance efficiently and equitably (in particular, adverse selection, moral hazard and cream-skimming behaviours must be absent), governments in Europe have tended to intervene by providing compulsory insurance for most basic health services (e.g. in France and Germany all individuals are compulsorily insured for most health services and the system is funded through the social insurance scheme, with the contributions of those on low incomes or who are economically inactive paid by the state). In Ireland, the state intervenes by providing compulsory insurance for certain services (mainly hospital services) to the full population, providing compulsory insurance for all services to certain vulnerable sections of the population (e.g. those on low incomes) and strictly regulating conduct in the private insurance market (the Health Insurance Authority was established in 2001 to act as regulator of the private health insurance market in Ireland).

While government intervention to correct market failures is an accepted feature of modern economies, government failure may itself lead to efficiency or equity failings. In particular, government intervention in terms of provision may lead to inefficiency, as government-owned and operated facilities face a loose budget constraint. In addition, regulatory capture by vested interests may result in regulations that lead to an inefficient level of output, e.g. the restrictions on pharmacy locations which existed prior to the revocation of the 1996 Health Regulations Act in 2001. Ensuring that public funding sources are progressive in their impact is also an important concern.

3 KEY FEATURES OF THE IRISH HEALTH SERVICE

Governance and Organisational Structure

In June 2003, the government announced its commitment to a major reform of the health service. The Health Service Reform Programme aimed to implement the recommendations contained in three major reports on the health system: the *Report of the National Task Force on Medical Staffing* (the Hanly Report), the *Report of the Commission on Financial Management and Control Systems in the Health Service* (the Brennan Report) and the *Audit of Structures and Functions in the Health System* (the Prospectus Report). The key bodies in the health service are the Department of Health and Children, the Health Service Executive (HSE) and a regulatory agency, the Health Information and Quality Authority (HIQA).

The main role of the Department is to advise the minister and government on the strategic development of the health system. The preparation of legislation in accordance with health policy is a key responsibility of the Department. In March 2011, further restructuring of government departments was undertaken, with a separate Department of Children established in addition to the Department of Health. HIQA was fully established in 2007. It is an independent agency responsible for developing standards, monitoring compliance and carrying out investigations in residential services for children, older persons, and persons with disabilities. It is also responsible for carrying out health technology assessments (HTAs) in Ireland (e.g. it carried out the HTA for the cervical cancer vaccine that was subsequently adopted for 12-year-old girls in 2010).

The HSE, which was established in January 2005, is responsible for the delivery of health and social care services in Ireland. Prior to its establishment, services were delivered through a complex structure of ten regional Health Boards, the Eastern Regional Health Authority and a number of other different agencies. As a result of further restructuring in October 2010, the Integrated Services Directorate (ISD) of the HSE incorporates the previously separate directorates of Primary, Community and Continuing Care (PCCC) and the National Hospitals Office (NHO). Four regional directors of operations (Dublin Mid-East, Dublin North-East, West and South) are responsible for the provision of health and social services in their area. Many services are provided directly (e.g. district nurses and public nursing homes), while others are provided under contract with the HSE by self-employed health professionals, private health service providers, voluntary hospitals and voluntary/community organisations. Many other advisory agencies and voluntary organisations under the authority of the HSE play a role in service delivery, regulation and development in the health system, e.g. An Bord Altranais (the Nursing Board) is responsible for the regulation of the nursing profession in Ireland.

The HSE is the largest employer in the state, employing nearly 110,000 staff in 2009, and its budget of €15.1 billion in 2009 is the largest of any public sector organisation in Ireland.[5] As illustrated in Table 12.1, the largest components of HSE expenditure in 2009 were the (then) PCCC and NHO directorates (accounting for 56.4 per cent and 35.6 per cent of total HSE expenditure respectively). Over time, expenditure on PCCC services has been increasing at a faster pace than expenditure on acute hospital services. Much of this is driven by large increases in expenditure on payments to GPs, pharmacists and other primary care providers for services delivered under the various state schemes providing free or subsidised primary healthcare services. Further details on these schemes are provided below.

Table 12.1
HSE Expenditure by Directorate 2006–2009 (€ million)

Programme	2006	2007	2008	2009
National Hospitals Office	4,585	5,088	5,332	5,380
Primary Community and Continuing Care	7,045	7,880	8,492	8,531
Population Health	69	82	95	197
Corporate and Shared Services	613	667	759	934
Health Repayment Scheme[1]	–	120	236	79
Gross HSE expenditure	12,312	13,837	14,915	15,122

Source: A. Brick, A. Nolan, J. O'Reilly and S. Smith, *Resource Allocation, Financing and Sustainability in Healthcare: Evidence for the Expert Group on Resource Allocation and Financing in the Health Sector*, Department of Health and Children and ESRI, Dublin 2010.
[1] The Health Repayment Scheme (which provides for the refund of those who were charged for services in nursing homes even though there was no legal basis for the charges) came into effect in 2007.

Eligibility for Free Public Health Services
All individuals who are ordinarily resident in Ireland are granted either full or limited eligibility for public healthcare services. Individuals with full eligibility, termed 'medical card holders' or 'public patients', are entitled to receive all health services free of charge under the General Medical Services (GMS) Scheme. This includes GP services, prescribed medicines, all dental, ophthalmic and aural services, maternity services, in-patient services in public hospitals and specialist treatment in outpatient clinics of public hospitals. However, from 1 October 2010, medical card holders are required to pay a charge of 50¢ per prescription (subject to a maximum charge of €10 per family). At the end of December 2010 approximately 36 per cent of the population had a medical card (see Table 12.2).

The remainder of the population, those with limited eligibility ('non-medical card holders' or 'private patients'), are entitled to free maternity services, in-patient services in public hospitals (subject to a €75 charge per day up to an annual maximum of €750), specialist services in outpatient clinics (again, subject to a €75 charge per day up to an annual maximum of €750), assistance towards the cost of prescribed medicines over a monthly limit (under the Drugs Payment

(e.g. GP fees by non-medical card holders) account for a further 14 per cent. Despite the fact that nearly 50 per cent of the population hold private health insurance, it accounts for only 8 per cent of total financing in Irish healthcare. Since 1990, the proportion accounted for by public resources has increased, while that contributed by direct out-of-pocket payments by individuals and private health insurance has fallen.

Delivery of Health Services

While the state is heavily involved in the financing of health services in Ireland, it mainly leaves the delivery of health services to the private sector, with the hospital and primary care sectors providing particularly good examples of the intermix between the public and private sectors in the financing and delivery of health services in Ireland. There are three different types of hospital in Ireland: voluntary hospitals, which are run on a not-for-profit basis by private organisations (usually religious institutions) but which receive most of their funding from the state; HSE hospitals, which are owned and operated by the HSE; and privately owned, operated and funded hospitals. Public hospital services are provided in voluntary and HSE hospitals and most of these hospitals also provide private healthcare. Consultants employed in public hospitals may treat private patients in the same public hospital (depending on their contract). While there are controls on the proportion of beds that may be used by private patients (nationally, 20 per cent for in-patients and 30 per cent for day patients) and consultant activity is monitored to ensure that they do not exceed their private activity cap, there are concerns that acute public hospitals and consultants are sidestepping restrictions on their private practice, resulting in public hospital resources potentially being diverted away from public patients towards their private counterparts.[7]

Primary care services are mainly provided by independent professionals (e.g. GPs, pharmacists, dentists, etc.), who may be contracted to provide services in the public sector in addition to services provided to private patients (approximately 75 per cent of GPs also have contracts to provide services to medical card holders).[8] The Primary Care Reimbursement Service (PCRS) undertakes the reimbursement of providers for GP, dental, optical and pharmaceutical services supplied to medical card holders as well as the reimbursement of pharmacists for services provided to non-medical card holders under the various community drugs schemes.

The Irish healthcare system therefore has a mixture of a universal public health service and a fee-based private system. Some services are publicly funded and delivered (e.g. treatment as a public patient in a public hospital), some are publicly funded but privately delivered (e.g. GP consultations by medical card holders), some are privately funded and delivered (e.g. GP consultations by non-medical card holders), while some are privately funded but publicly delivered (e.g. non-medical card holders must pay a modest charge for treatment in public hospitals). This complex mixture has implications for the allocation of resources, both between the public and the private sector and between different types of care (see Section 5 for further discussion).

Proposals for Reform

The *National Recovery Plan 2011–2014* and *Government for National Recovery* documents provide some details on the proposed future direction of the Irish health service. Any future developments need to be seen in the context of the substantial reduction in public health expenditure of 8 per cent over the period 2011–14 that is required under the terms of the National Recovery Plan. One of the most significant changes proposed by the new coalition government is the abolition of the HSE. HSE ownership and management of public hospitals would end, and the purchasing role of the HSE would transfer to a new purchasing agency. The HSE has been frequently criticised in recent years as being inefficient and unresponsive; much of the criticism has focused on the proportion of administrative staff within the organisation. Recent research found that while much of the growth in the 'management and administration' component of HSE staff occurred prior to the establishment of the HSE in 2005, most of the growth over the 2005–9 period occurred in the higher management and administrative grades.[9]

By far the most significant recent proposal concerns the commitment of the new coalition government to move towards a system of universal health insurance (UHI) for Ireland. The precise details of the UHI scheme have to be worked out. Indeed, while the two coalition parties both proposed UHI as their preferred method of healthcare financing during the election campaign, they differed in how the system would be organised (Fine Gael favoured the Dutch system of competing private insurers, while Labour favoured a single public insurer). The proposed solution is a combination of the two positions in offering individuals a choice between a public or a private insurer. Despite this ambiguity, the core features of the proposed UHI system, namely a system in which the purchase of health insurance is compulsory (although paid by the state for those on low incomes), and in which private practice in public hospitals is no longer a feature, would represent a major change in Irish healthcare financing. In other countries with UHI, the purchase of supplementary private health insurance is not prohibited, but the provision of private healthcare is completely separate under such a system and individuals are generally not eligible to opt out of the public system.

In addition, the proposal to move towards the provision of free primary care services for the entire population represents a major departure in the financing of primary care services in Ireland. Free primary care for all would be introduced on a phased basis, with free care extended to those on the Long Term Illness Scheme in year one and to those on the High Tech Drugs Scheme in year two, with subsidised care extended to all in the next phase, followed by access to free care to all in the final phase. The importance of removing access barriers to primary care services has been highlighted repeatedly in previous research on the Irish healthcare system.[10] As the first point of contact with the health service in most cases, and as an important source of preventive healthcare, it is important that individuals are incentivised to register with a primary care provider, to seek care with a primary care provider in the first instance wherever possible, and to seek care at the earliest possible stage of illness. In the current system, such incentives only exist for the population who have a medical card or GP Visit card.

Major changes in the financing of Irish healthcare would also have major implications for how healthcare in Ireland is delivered. The coalition government has signalled its intention to establish all public hospitals as independent, not-for-profit entities, and so if this change is implemented the current system, whereby the HSE owns and operates the majority of public hospitals, will end. In addition, the co-location policy favoured by the previous administration would cease. In 2006, the government invited expressions of interest for the co-location of private hospitals on eleven existing public hospital sites, with the aim of freeing up beds in public hospitals allocated to private patients. Generous tax incentives were available to encourage the establishment of these and other private facilities.

While the current system of provision of primary care services is compatible with UHI (i.e. private, self-employed GPs contracting with the state for the provision of GP services to the population), a new GP contract will be necessary if free primary care is extended to the full population. The Government for National Recovery programme makes a number of commitments in relation to a new GP contract, including that remuneration will be reduced, that incentives for the provision of services to chronically ill patients will be introduced, and that GPs will be paid on a predominately capitation basis. Potentially more contentious, although also necessary, is the commitment to re-negotiate the consultants' contract. The current contract dates from 2008, and was introduced only after a long and protracted period of negotiation. The coalition government simply makes a commitment to re-negotiate the contract, and to reduce the remuneration of hospital consultants.

4 THE IRISH HEALTHCARE SYSTEM IN COMPARATIVE CONTEXT

Health Expenditure[11]

In 2009, total health expenditure in Ireland amounted to €19.7 billion, of which approximately €15 billion was accounted for by expenditure by the HSE. Table 12.4 illustrates that Ireland, along with most other OECD countries, experienced an increase in the share of national income devoted to health over the period 2000–8. However, the sharp decline in national income in Ireland since 2008 is reflected in a significant worsening in the total health expenditure/GNI ratio over the last two years. It is estimated that total health expenditure accounted for 12.1 per cent of GNI in Ireland in 2009. How this ratio will evolve in the next few years is crucially dependent on what assumptions are made about national income growth.

Table 12.4
Health Expenditure as a Percentage of GNI[1], 2000 and 2008

	2000	2008[2]	% aged over 65
Australia	8.3	8.4	13.2
Austria	10.1	10.0	17.1
Canada	9.1	9.8	13.6
Denmark	8.4	9.3	15.7
Finland	7.3	7.9	16.6
France	9.9	10.6	16.5
Germany	10.4	10.0	20.2
Ireland	*7.1*	*9.3*	*11.5*
Netherlands	7.8	9.5	14.9
New Zealand	8.2	9.6	12.6
Sweden	8.2	8.4	17.6
UK	7.1	8.0	15.7
USA	13.2	15.3	12.7

Sources: OECD, *op. cit.*; European Commission, *AMECO Macro-Economic Database 2011*, available at http://ec.europa.eu/economy_finance/db_indicators/ameco/index_en.htm [last accessed 21/04/11].
[1]While health expenditure is usually expressed as a proportion of GDP, the large divergence between Irish GDP and GNP/GNI figures means that, for comparative purposes, it is more appropriate to express health expenditure as a proportion of GNP/GNI.
[2] Data for Australia relate to 2007.

Healthcare Financing

Table 12.5 presents the sources of finance for selected OECD countries for 2008. In terms of public sources of finance, countries such as France and Germany rely much more heavily on social insurance contributions than general government sources, such as taxation, for their revenue. Social insurance contributions, which are compulsory and generally shared between the employer and employee, tend to be earmarked for specific purposes; in Ireland the 'health levy' (which has since been replaced by the Universal Social Charge) contributed less than 1 per cent of total healthcare finance in 2008. However, it was a minor source of health sector finance in Ireland. As in other countries, revenue from general taxation in Ireland is not earmarked specifically for the health services, which means that it must compete with other areas for public funds.

Due to universal eligibility for free public health services in many countries, the share of total expenditure funded through private sources (out-of-pocket payments by individuals, private insurance payments and other sources of finance, e.g. voluntary donations) is much smaller than that accounted for by public sources. The exception is the USA, which provides free healthcare only for the old and those on low incomes (through the Medicare and Medicaid schemes respectively) and consequently relies more heavily on private sources of finance, particularly insurance.

Table 12.5

Sources of Finance for Total Health Expenditure for
Selected OECD[1] Countries (Percentage of Total Health
Expenditure, 2008)

	General government	Social insurance	Out-of-pocket payments	Private insurance	Other private sources
Australia[2]	67	0	18	8	7
Austria	33	44	15	5	4
Canada	70	1	15	13	2
Finland	60	15	19	2	4
France	5	73	7	13	2
Germany	9	68	13	10	1
Ireland	*76*	*1*	*14*	*8*	*1*
New Zealand	70	10	14	5	0
Sweden	82	0	16	0	2
UK	83	0	11	1	4
USA[2]	33	13	12	35	8

Source: OECD, *op. cit.*
[1] Data for Denmark and Netherlands are incomplete.
[2] Data for Australia and the USA relate to 2007.

The prevalence of universal entitlement to free public health services across Europe results in monetary costs for healthcare consultations that are effectively zero, meaning that there is little incentive to control utilisation. User fees, in the form of co-payments, co-insurance or deductibles, can help to control utilisation, although there are concerns that such initiatives may reduce necessary as well as unnecessary utilisation. Nonetheless, most countries levy minimal user fees on consumers in an attempt to make them more aware of the resource implications of their behaviour. For example, in Ireland, a fee of €75 per day applies to individuals without medical cards for treatment as an in-patient in the public hospital sector. As Table 12.5 illustrates, out-of-pocket payments are now more important than private insurance as a source of finance for all countries examined except France and the USA. However, there are concerns that as governments come under increasing pressure to fund public health programmes, and out-of-pocket payments become more important as a source of revenue, a greater share of the funding burden will fall on those in ill health (see Section 5 for a discussion of equity issues surrounding user fees in healthcare).

Health Outcomes[12]

Levels of expenditure provide no guidance as to whether this expenditure is efficiently and effectively spent or distributed equitably across different sectors of the population. As the ultimate objective of health policy is to improve population health, it is useful to examine where countries rank in terms of health outcomes and whether there is any correlation between such measures and health expenditure.

Table 12.6 confirms the weak association between health expenditure and health outcome indicators such as life expectancy and infant mortality. However, a recent study of the effect of health expenditure on life expectancy and infant mortality across the EU-15 over the period 1980–95 found no effect of expenditure on life expectancy but a significant effect on infant mortality. The literature highlights the fact that social, environmental and cultural factors such as diet, exercise, genetic inheritance, lifestyle, education, social status, income distribution, social support and housing, and their complex interactions, may be more important in determining the level and distribution of health outcomes than simple health expenditure. The recent increases in resources devoted to health promotion and prevention (e.g. through the smoking in the workplace ban, breast cancer screening, promotion of healthy eating, etc.) reflects this realisation that lifestyle factors are also crucial in influencing population health outcomes.

Table 12.6

Total Health Expenditure
Per Capita and Health Outcome Rankings, 2008

	Expenditure	Male life expectancy	Female life expectancy	Infant mortality
Australia	9	1	2	9
Austria	4	7	3	4
Canada	2	3	5	12
Denmark	7	11	12	7
Finland	12	12	4	2
France	6	8	1	5
Germany	5	9	7	6
Ireland	*8*	*10*	*10*	*3*
Netherlands	3	5	8	8
New Zealand	13	4	9	10
Sweden	10	2	6	1
UK	11	6	11	11
USA	1	13	13	13

Source: for data on expenditure (total health expenditure per capita expressed in USA $ PPP), male and female life expectancy (at birth) and infant mortality (per 1,000 live births), see OECD, *op. cit.*

In an attempt to quantify more accurately the contribution of the health sector, the concept of amenable or avoidable mortality has been developed to assess the quality and performance of health systems. Amenable mortality refers to deaths from conditions considered amenable to healthcare, such as treatable cancers, diabetes and cardiovascular disease. A 2003 study found that rankings of countries according to amenable mortality were substantially different from those using other measures such as disability-free life expectancy. For example, while the UK was ranked tenth out of nineteen countries in terms of disability-free life expectancy in 2003, it dropped to eighteenth place when assessed in terms of amenable mortality.

A related strand of research concentrates on the pitfalls involved in using single measures of health status to assess health sector performance. A 2004 ESRI report used a methodology developed in Canada to assess overall health system performance by ranking countries on their achievement in relation to nineteen broad indicators (such as life expectancy, premature mortality for various conditions and immunisation rates). Of the countries of the old EU-15 and Australia, Canada, Japan, New Zealand and the USA, the top three performing countries in terms of overall health system performance were Sweden, France and Italy, while their rankings in terms of expenditure in that year were tenth, third and twelfth respectively.

5 HEALTH SECTOR FINANCE AND ACCESS

While the proportion of private financing in Irish healthcare is not unusual internationally, what sets Ireland apart from other OECD countries is the large proportion of the population who must pay out of pocket for primary care. In addition, despite its relatively small contribution to overall health sector financing in Ireland, private health insurance has important implications for equity in the Irish system, particularly in terms of the interaction of public and private care in public hospitals.

User Fees and Access to Primary Care

While the proportion of the population eligible for free GP services has increased recently with rising unemployment, and currently stands at approximately 36 per cent of the population, the fact remains that over 60 per cent of the Irish population must pay out of pocket for GP (and other primary care) services. The effect of user fees on healthcare utilisation has been extensively studied. User fees are payments at the point of use and can take a number of different forms, including co-payment (a fixed fee per service), co-insurance (a fixed percentage of the cost of the service) and deductible (full cost of the service up to a certain threshold).

The primary motivation for user fees is to reduce moral hazard behaviour among consumers of healthcare services (i.e. the unnecessary use of healthcare services by patients). A secondary motivation is to generate revenue. However, there is extensive empirical evidence that user fees discourage both necessary as well as unnecessary healthcare utilisation. The most comprehensive study of the impact of user fees on healthcare utilisation and outcomes is the Health Insurance Experiment which was carried out in the USA in the late 1970s and early 1980s by the RAND Corporation. Individuals were randomly assigned to a number of health insurance plans which differed in the degree of co-payments for healthcare services. The experiment found that user fees were just as likely to reduce necessary healthcare utilisation as unnecessary healthcare utilisation, and while the impact on health outcomes was negligible for the average participant, significant negative effects were found for certain vulnerable groups (e.g. blood pressure was lowered for those receiving free care relative to those on co-payments).[13] This research also highlights the negative equity implications of user fees. While demand for healthcare is relatively price inelastic, those on lower incomes have a higher price elasticity than those on higher incomes. Therefore, any increase in the cost of healthcare will have a greater deterrent effect on the poorer sections of society.

In the Irish system of primary care, non-medical card holders pay a co-payment for each GP visit, while they pay for all prescriptions up to a monthly deductible of €120. Medical card holders receive free GP visits, and pay a 50¢ charge per prescription, up to a monthly deductible of €10. Notwithstanding the current proposals in relation to free GP care for all by 2014 (see Section 3), the current system has been criticised on a number of grounds, principally in relation to those just above the income threshold for a medical or GP Visit card. The sharp distinction between those with and without eligibility for free GP care means that a relatively small increase in weekly income can render an individual ineligible for a medical or GP Visit card and thus liable for the full cost of GP care. Previous research has indeed found that GP visiting rates are lowest among those just above the income threshold for a medical card (even controlling for differences in health need), although the deterrent effect of user fees for GP services among non-medical card holders has been found to persist throughout the income distribution.[14]

Role of Private Health Insurance
Private health insurance in Ireland is primarily taken out by non-medical card holders to cover the costs of private or semi-private hospital care in public and private hospitals. However, increasingly, the major insurers have started to offer (limited) cover for primary care expenses, usually in the form of a fixed amount per visit (subject to an annual maximum number of visits). It is difficult to gather data on the proportion of private health insurance plans that cover primary care expenses, but data from the recently released *Growing up in Ireland* survey show that approximately 25 per cent of 9-year-old children live in households with private health insurance that provides some cover for primary care expenses.[15] Notwithstanding the recent proposals in relation to a system of UHI for Ireland,

341

there is still considerable uncertainty about the operation of the private health insurance market in Ireland (principally, the continued absence of risk equalisation). In addition, access issues associated with private health insurance-funded care in public hospital remain of concern.

Apart from a small number of restricted membership private health insurance schemes, there are three main private health insurance companies in Ireland: VHI, Quinn Healthcare and Aviva Health. At the end of 2009, VHI Healthcare accounted for 64 per cent of the private health insurance market, while Quinn Healthcare had a 22 per cent share, Hibernian Aviva had 10 per cent and the restricted membership schemes accounted for the remaining 4 per cent.[16] The government strictly regulates the behaviour of the three major private insurers in the Irish market via the principles of open enrolment (no one can be refused cover), community rating (all individuals face the same premium) and lifetime cover (once insured, an individual's policy cannot be terminated). The continued stability of the community rating system means that a risk equalisation scheme (which aims to remove differences in insurers' costs that result from differing risk profiles among members) must be implemented. The government's attempts to introduce a risk equalisation scheme in Ireland suffered a serious setback in July 2008 with the Supreme Court ruling that the government's legal interpretation of risk equalisation in the Irish context was incorrect.

Following the Supreme Court judgement, the Minister for Health and Children announced the introduction of interim measures to support the cost of health insurance for older customers. While insurers must still abide by the principles of open enrolment, community rating and lifetime cover, the absence of risk equalisation payments could lead to insurers offering a more diverse set of plans which charge different premiums or offer different benefits to different sections of the population. The interim measures, which consist of a 'community rating levy' and additional tax relief for customers over the age of 50 years (restricted since January 2011 to those over the age of 60 years only), and which in combination are revenue neutral, are in place until such time as an alternative risk equalisation scheme can be devised. The tax credits are currently set to equal 50 per cent of the higher costs of insuring older people and, in this way, insurers of older people are partially compensated for the extra costs arising. Therefore, insurers are still incentivised to seek out younger, healthier customers and there is some evidence of differential pricing in terms of different policies aimed at younger customers.

Notwithstanding these recent developments, the broader question of the role of private health insurance in Irish healthcare remains. Private health insurance in Ireland essentially provides cover for services already available free of charge (or heavily subsidised) in the public sector. It therefore fulfils a duplicate role, in contrast to other countries where its role is strictly supplementary to that of the public system (e.g. Canada). The recently announced UHI scheme is in part a response to the frequent criticisms of the two-tier system of care in public hospitals that is supported by the current role of private health insurance in Ireland. In addition, it is unclear whether the current rates of high private health

manner in which Irish health services are financed and delivered, with important implications for equity and efficiency in the system.

Endnotes

* The author would like to thank Carol Newman and John O'Hagan for comments on an earlier version of the chapter. All views expressed are those of the author and are not necessarily shared by the Economic and Social Research Institute (ESRI).

1 This section draws on: A. Brick and A. Nolan, 'The sustainability of Irish health expenditure', Chapter 5 in T. Callan (ed.) *Budget Perspectives 2011*, FFS and ESRI, Dublin 2010; CSO, *Quarterly National Household Survey (Quarter 4 2010)*, CSO, Dublin 2011; A. Brick, A. Nolan, J. O'Reilly and S. Smith, *Resource Allocation, Financing and Sustainability in Healthcare: Evidence for the Expert Group on Resource Allocation and Financing in the Health Sector*, Department of Health and Children and ESRI, Dublin 2010; Government of Ireland, *The National Recovery Plan 2011–2014*, Stationery Office, Dublin 2010.

2 D. Dave and R. Kaestner, 'Health insurance and ex-ante moral hazard: evidence from Medicare', *International Journal of Healthcare Finance and Economics*, Vol. 9, No. 4, 2009.

3 See also S. Smith, *Equity in Healthcare: A View from the Irish Healthcare System*, Adelaide Hospital Society, Dublin 2009.

4 R. Layte and B. Clyne, 'Perinatal mortality in Ireland', *Economic and Social Review*, Vol. 41, No. 2, 2010.

5 Health Service Executive, *Annual Report and Financial Statements 2009*, HSE, Dublin 2010.

6 Calculated from Health Service Executive, *December 2010 Performance Report on NSP 2010*, HSE, Dublin 2011.

7 See J. O'Reilly and M. Wiley, 'Who's that sleeping in my bed? Potential and actual utilization of public and private in-patient beds in Irish acute public hospitals', *Journal of Health Services Research and Policy*, Vol. 15, No. 4, 2010.

8 Competition Authority, *Competition in Professional Services: General Practitioners*, Competition Authority, Dublin 2009.

9 Brick, Nolan, O'Reilly and Smith, *op. cit.*

10 See, *inter alia*, F. Ruane, *Report of the Expert Group on Resource Allocation and Financing in the Health Sector*, Department of Health and Children, Dublin 2010; R. Layte, A. Nolan and B. Nolan, *Poor Prescriptions: Poverty and Access to Community Health Services*, Combat Poverty Agency, Dublin 2007.

11 Further details and discussion on Irish health expenditure are available in: Brick, Nolan, O'Reilly and Smith, *op. cit.*; Brick and Nolan, *op. cit.*

12 For further reading see J. Nixon and R. Ulmann, 'The relationship between healthcare expenditure and health outcomes: evidence and caveats for a causal link', *European Journal of Health Economics*, Vol. 7, No.1, 2006; E. Nolte and M. McKee, 'Measuring the health of nations: analysis of mortality amenable to healthcare', *British Medical Journal*, Vol. 327, 2003; A. Nolan and B. Nolan, 'Ireland's healthcare system: some issues and challenges', Chapter 4 in T. Callan, A. Doris and D. McCoy (eds), *Budget Perspectives 2005*, FFS and ESRI, Dublin 2004.

13 J. Newhouse and Insurance Experiment Group, *Free for All? Lessons from the RAND Health Insurance Experiment,* Harvard University Press, Cambridge MA 1993.

14 A. Nolan, 'The impact of income on private patients' access to GP services in Ireland', *Journal of Health Services Research and Policy,* Vol. 13, No. 4, 2008.

15 Calculated from ESRI, *Growing up in Ireland – Nine Year Old Cohort Microdata,* ESRI, Dublin 2010.

16 Health Insurance Authority, *Submission of the Health Insurance Authority to the Oireachtas Joint Committee on Health and Children,* HIA, Dublin 2009.

17 Health Insurance Authority, *Health Insurance Authority News March 2011,* HIA, Dublin 2011.

18 Sources for this section include: Congressional Research Service, *US Healthcare Spending: Comparison with other OECD Countries,* CRS, Washington 2007; European Commission, *Benchmarking ICT use among General Practitioners in Europe (Final Report),* European Commission, Brussels 2008; U. Gerdtham, J. Sogaard, F. Andersson and B. Jonsson, 'An econometric analysis of healthcare expenditure: a cross-section of the OECD countries', *Journal of Health Economics,* Vol. 11, No. 1, 1992; B. Starfield and L. Shi, 'Policy relevant determinants of health: an international perspective', *Health Policy,* Vol. 60, 2002; B. Starfield, L. Shi and J. Macinko, 'Contribution of primary care to health systems and health', *Millbank Quarterly,* Vol. 83, No. 3, 2005.

CHAPTER 13

Education: Market Failure and Government Interventions

*Carol Newman**

1 INTRODUCTION

A key assumption underpinning public support for the education system is that education equips individuals with the knowledge and skills necessary to participate in the economy at both an economic and a social level. The role of government is to ensure that education provision occurs in an efficient and equitable way. The government may achieve this either through the direct provision of the service or the regulation of some aspects of its provision.

In Ireland, education is largely publicly provided with a small private component. There are three core layers to the Irish education system: primary; second level; and third level or the tertiary sector. In recent times, the pre-primary and fourth-level sectors have also become increasingly important. The responsibility for the government's role in the provision of education at primary and second level rests with the Department of Education and Skills, while the Higher Education Authority (HEA), an independent statutory body, largely manages provision at third and fourth level while remaining answerable to the Minister for Education and Skills. Unlike many other countries, pre-primary education is predominantly privately funded with a minimal role for government. While in Ireland the Early Years Education Policy Unit falls under the remit of the Department, it is co-located with the Office of the Minister for Children and Youth Affairs and is viewed as a component of the overall strategic policy framework for children.

In 2010, there were 3,165 primary schools and 730 second-level schools aided by the Department, and seven universities, fifteen institutes of technology (ITs), seven teacher training colleges and four other types of third-level institution supported by the HEA.[1] In total, 23 per cent of the population, or just over one million students, were enrolled in full-time education in 2010 (up from 927,000 in 2006). While the total number of students at primary level declined during the 1990s, the last decade has seen a surge in the numbers, due to both high birth rates and high levels of immigration in the late 1990s and 2000s (see Chapter 6), with 62,000 more students in primary schools in 2010 compared with 2002. This, of course, given that education at this level is predominantly state funded, will place extra pressure on the public finances. Part of this increase has filtered through to second-level education, which has seen an increase of 11,500 students in the same period, but significant increases are expected in the next decade (though part of this may be eased by immigrants with young families returning to their home countries). Between 2002 and 2010 the numbers at third level increased by over 20 per cent, mainly into the expanded IT sector, but there have also been large increases in the number of places available at the universities.

As with all other sectors in the Irish economy, the education sector has not been unaffected by the current economic crisis. At grassroots level, budget cuts have meant that class sizes have increased at both primary and second level and many support services have been cut. A moratorium on recruitment in the third-level sector, coupled with the need to make substantial budget savings, means that, at least in the short term, the third-level sector will also be placed under increased pressure in the delivery of teaching and research. This chapter focuses on the broader policy issues associated with government provision of education services. We do, however, consider the challenges facing the Irish government in delivering an efficient and effective education service that can contribute significantly to economic recovery in the current economic climate.

The chapter begins by providing the economic justifications for government intervention in the provision of education in Section 2. Section 3 examines government education policy in an Irish context, focusing on recent policies aimed at promoting growth through various education initiatives; and equity, both within the system and as an end-goal in the wider distributional context. Section 4 examines the effectiveness of government in delivering an efficient and equitable education service, covering issues relating to the level of expenditure and the allocation of funds across different levels of education, the efficiency of the system, and the extent to which inequities exist within the system. Educational outcomes are also compared across OECD countries. Section 5 concludes the chapter.

2 ECONOMIC PERSPECTIVES OF EDUCATION

In the absence of an education system, citizens will lack the basic social skills necessary to participate in the economy and, more important perhaps, in society in general: for example, an illiterate individual may be unable to follow basic rules and regulations imposed by government, such as reading road signs or informing themselves on key personal items like medicine dosages or the terms and conditions of a loan application. A properly functioning education system performs an important social engineering function by facilitating the transfer of common values and morals. Government policy on education can cover a wide range of issues. In most developed economies, government regulation requires that all individuals remain in education up to some minimum age: in Ireland education is compulsory up to the age of 16. A large part of education policy is concerned with easing the financial constraints associated with purchasing education services by providing free schooling, for example. The government also has a say in the quality of service provision (e.g. curriculum design, training of teachers, monitoring the performance of teachers and schools). It is also common that governments have in place education policies for individuals with special needs to ensure that the most vulnerable in society are given the opportunity to fully participate in the labour force and integrate into society more generally.

In most developed economies the state plays a very direct role in the provision and funding of compulsory education. There is no dispute in Ireland, or other developed nations, about state funding of education up to compulsory level. There is a vast body of research which highlights the efficiency improvements that could be achieved in public spending by diverting human capital investment toward the young, including both pre-school and primary levels. However, that said, in Ireland at least, the state increasingly takes a very proactive role in higher education up to and including the funding of postgraduate students and postdoctoral researchers. In this section, the extent to which the government has a necessary role in the provision of education is explored. Government intervention in any market can be justified where the market fails to optimally provide the good or service. Intervention may also be justified on equity grounds to promote distributional objectives. The arguments for intervention differ depending on the level of education, a factor also considered in this section.

Education as an Investment: Private and Social Returns
Education is an investment in human capital that yields both private and social returns. The decision to invest in human capital accumulation, like any other investment, will depend on the investor's evaluation of the expected present value of the stream of costs and benefits flowing from that investment. A parent deciding whether or not to send their child to school will compare the expected costs, such as tuition fees, books, cost of travel to school, etc., with the expected benefits for the child, for example the ability to function in society, and better job and earnings prospects. They may also consider the benefits that accrue to themselves, such as reduced childcare costs or the possibility that their children, if successful, might be able to look after them financially when they are older. At higher levels of education, these decisions are taken by individuals or firms. An individual's decision to invest in personal human capital, such as a third-level degree for example, will also involve a comparison of the costs with the benefits. As well as the cost of tuition fees and books, etc., the cost of forgone earnings will also be considered. At this level individuals may also place more or less weight than their parents on the personal benefits, such as greater employability and higher earnings. A firm making a decision to invest in training courses to improve the human capital of its workers will undertake the investment if the present value of the expected future returns to that investment, in the form of higher productivity and reduced costs, is greater than the cost of the investment.

Investment in education, however, may also confer *positive externalities* on the rest of society that will not be taken into account by parents, individuals or firms. At a fundamental level, the most significant social return to education, as mentioned earlier, is having a population who can function at a basic level in society and understand basic rules and regulations. For higher levels of education, social returns can take the form of productivity improvements which will contribute to economic growth above and beyond those for which an individual/firm is remunerated through higher wages/profits; improvements in the quality of services, for example the health or legal professions; or other social benefits such as increased political participation and a healthy democratic system. These arguments also apply to early years education and care, which is linked with immediate benefits such as better school readiness and cognitive outcomes, but also with long-term effects such as lower rates of lone parenthood and lower crime rates. By ignoring these social returns, parents, individuals and firms will under-invest in education and training (i.e. education will be provided below the socially optimal level), thus providing justification for government involvement in its provision.

Returning to the investment decision-making process, and with this in mind, it is clear that the government, when making a decision on whether and how much to invest in the education system, will weigh up the cost of the investment (including the actual cash outlay, the opportunity cost of people not contributing to production while in full-time education and any efficiency losses associated with the financing of education through the tax system) with the aggregate economic returns to the economy of having a well-educated workforce (such as the extent to which it will contribute to the more productive use of resources, higher levels of output and faster economic growth) but also the other social returns mentioned here, such as greater equality in terms of opportunities, social inclusion, improved cultural and political participation, etc.

Placing an economic value on intangible social returns is notoriously difficult. Nevertheless, even though the social returns to primary and second-level education are unobservable, it is well established that they will far exceed the private returns, thus justifying government provision. At higher levels of education, however, it is more difficult to reach this conclusion, given that the private returns are known to be significantly higher than those at first and second level, raising questions about the justification for government provision of third-level education, at least on these grounds. In what follows, the empirical evidence on the private and social returns to education is evaluated.

Empirical Evidence on Private Returns
An extensive literature exists on quantifying the private individual returns to education. In particular, there is an enormous econometric literature estimating the impact of education on earnings. Studies typically show that the returns to education are around 6 to 8 per cent per school year for men and 9 to 11 per cent for women.[2] These so-called Mincer returns (after the pioneering labour

economist Jacob Mincer, who first formulated the empirical structure for estimating human capital models) apply to all levels of education but are generally larger for higher education. The earnings return to education has been well documented in the Irish context with evidence suggesting not only a positive relationship between earnings and educational attainment but also that this earnings advantage increases with the length of time spent in the labour market. Higher levels of education are also found to be associated with higher levels of labour force participation and lower unemployment risk. Evidence from the ESRI's Living in Ireland Panel Survey supports this result, highlighting the implications of a low level of education attainment on long-term labour market integration.[3] The unemployment rate for early school leavers in the 18 to 24 age group was 19 per cent in 2006 compared with an unemployment rate of 8.2 per cent for all persons in the same age group. The evidence suggests that in the Irish case, like many other OECD countries, the individual returns to education are significant in terms of earnings, labour market participation and unemployment risk.

While findings suggest that education leads to higher private returns, the link between educational attainment and productivity has been more difficult to quantify. An alternative to the human capital view is the screening theory of education, which suggests that there is no link between individual educational attainment and productivity improvements, and that the only purpose of education is to serve as a signalling device to employers as to who the most productive employees are likely to be. This argument is based on the observation that those with the greatest ability, which is determined by unobservable factors such as family background, opportunities, access to quality schools, etc., are more likely to be educated but are also more likely to be productive. Employers will choose to recruit and pay higher salaries to well-educated individuals who through attaining an education have signalled their productive ability.

From an empirical point of view, no consensus has been reached on which theory holds: does education lead to more productive individuals or are more productive individuals likely to stay in education for longer? One reason for this is that it is statistically very difficult to disentangle the two theories as the end result is the same – more educated persons earn more. In any case, where there are private returns to education, be they a reward for productivity improvements or otherwise (personal fulfilment or satisfaction, for example), the investment should be undertaken by the individual themselves with no justification for government intervention on these grounds.

Empirical Evidence on Social Returns
The social returns to first- and second-level education are undeniably important for any functioning economy. For this reason, most of the attention in the literature focuses on the social returns to third-level education in an attempt to justify public provision. However, any attempts to quantify the social returns to education investment (at any level) are faced with serious difficulties in

establishing causal relationships between education attainment and socially desirable outcomes.

For example, political scientists have highlighted correlations between voter participation and education for many years and have used this to argue that education leads to more informed voters, and hence a more democratic society. Some of the most rigorous evidence suggests that *entrance* into higher education increases the probability of voter participation by 21 to 30 per cent. However, correlation does not imply causation. There may be unobservable characteristics of people who value schooling which make them more likely to value civic duties and responsibilities. If this is the case, estimates of the correlation between education and civic participation such as voting behaviour may overstate the true civic returns to education and mislead policy-makers into thinking that policies that improve access to higher education will necessarily increase the probability of active civic participation. The literature on the impact of education on health status again suffers from problems of establishing causation. For example, ability clearly affects an individual's success in schooling, but healthier people will generally be more productive and more able. Similarly initial assets or family wealth may affect an individual's access to both education and health care.

Much less documented but equally significant is establishing the extent to which investment in ongoing training and education by firms or individuals yields benefits to society in excess of those that firms are rewarded for in terms of productivity improvements, lower costs and higher profits, or that individuals are rewarded for in terms of higher earnings or better employment prospects. For example, continuous education and training will prevent skills shortages, create a more adaptable labour force with greater innovative ability, and make the economy more attractive to outside investors, all of which will facilitate economic growth. In addition, lifelong learning may create a happier, more personally fulfilled society. The OECD have long acknowledged that improving the skills of the workforce on an ongoing basis (an area where the Nordic countries perform particularly well) will be important for economic growth by facilitating the development of an adaptable and flexible labour force (see Chapter 6).[4] They find a positive link between continuous education and training and workers' performance in terms of productivity, employment opportunities and earnings. More recently, there has been some emerging empirical work which has found causal links between lifelong learning and earnings, but also social returns in the form of social position.[5]

Despite the dearth of empirical evidence, the existence of social returns is the key argument made for government intervention in education provision. The social capital developed at primary and second level (for example, respect for social norms and rule of law) are fundamental to the functioning of any economy. There is also no doubt that higher levels of education lead to a more skilled and productive labour force, capable of producing greater levels of output, facilitating technological advancement and attracting investment. In relation to lifelong learning, it is clear that investment can help to create an adaptable and flexible workforce, an important advantage for any economy undergoing major structural change.

Market Failures

In addition to justifying state involvement in the provision of education on the grounds that the social rate of return exceeds the private rate of return, other market failures may prevent education from being optimally provided in the absence of government intervention.

Credit Market Failure

Education would be unaffordable for large segments of the population if it were privately provided. While at first and second level the burden of tuition fees would lie with parents, at higher levels of education individuals would rely on credit markets to finance schooling. Credit markets will fail to operate efficiently in this environment for two reasons. First, most students applying for loans to pay for their studies will lack collateral of any kind to guarantee the loan, and second, the benefits of education will vary substantially across individuals with no guarantee of success and hence no guarantee that the student will be able to repay the loan in the future. In the absence of collateral and a means of repayment, banks will be unwilling to finance individuals to pay for private education. This failure of credit markets to finance private education may warrant government intervention in the provision of education services, especially at third level, where government involvement usually comes in the form of direct financial assistance to students (for example free tuition fees, government-guaranteed loan schemes, etc.). At first and second level education would become a luxury service for the wealthy or for those to whom banks are willing to lend money. While this does not constitute a credit market failure it would be undesirable on equity grounds (see later).

Imperfect Information

Aside from credit market failure, the provision of education itself is characterised by imperfect information, resulting in sub-optimal outcomes in the absence of government intervention. First, it can be argued that parents and individuals do not have full information on the benefits of schooling and will under-invest in education. Furthermore, the extent of this knowledge gap may be unevenly distributed across the population, depending on factors like social class and family background. To overcome this failure, the government can introduce regulations to ensure children reach a certain minimum level of education (i.e. compulsory schooling age) and at higher levels of education can provide incentives to encourage participation through, for example, free fees or maintenance grants for those living below a certain income threshold. Second, individuals lack information regarding the quality of the education service being provided. In the case of primary and second-level education, if all parents could afford to pay fees for their children to attend private schools, market forces would operate in the standard way, with higher fees potentially signalling better-quality institutions.

However, in most cases parents cannot afford to pay for their children to receive a private education and so the choice of school becomes limited. In the absence of government intervention to ensure certain quality standards are met, there will be no incentive for schools to deliver an efficient service.

An alternative to the regulation of quality standards is to allow schools to be privately run and for the government to regulate the credit markets used to finance education. For example, the government could grant vouchers to all individuals that can be spent at their own discretion, allowing them to freely choose the schools that suit their preferences and meet their standards. A possibility at third level is for the government to guarantee loans to students to pay for their tuition fees, which they must repay once their studies have been completed. Of course, this can lead to similar problems to those outlined at the start of this section as there is no guarantee that students will be in a position to repay these loans at a later stage. Many OECD countries operate publicly secured student loans to finance tuition fees or living costs associated with third-level education. For example, in the UK all students are eligible for government-funded loans for tuition and maintenance at a nominal interest rate, that do not have to be repaid until after graduation with the option of holding off repaying until after earnings have reached more than £15,000. In Australia, Iceland, New Zealand, Norway and Sweden student loans amount to 0.2 per cent of GDP or more.[6]

Equity

Government intervention in the provision of education is also justified on equity grounds. As argued earlier, education is a key determinant of earnings and employment prospects and so plays an important role in determining not only the level of income in society but also the distribution of that income. A key role for government is therefore to promote *equality of opportunity* by attempting to ensure equal access to education for all its citizens (see also Chapters 2 and 8).

Governments attempt to achieve this through various initiatives such as free compulsory education up to a certain age or financial support for third-level education. Many governments also ensure that discrimination on gender, race, ethnic, disability or any other grounds does not take place within the education system by ensuring equal access to all groups in society. However, since individuals' educational prospects and information on the benefits of education are unevenly distributed across the population, it is more likely that specific socio-economic groups, usually those at the lower end of the income distribution, will underachieve in relation to educational attainment. Therefore, on *horizontal equity* grounds it is justified for the government to target education expenditure and programmes at potentially educationally disadvantaged socio-economic groups. In fact, this is also justifiable on efficiency grounds if the extent of the information problems outlined above is more pronounced among these groups, justifying targeted higher levels of expenditure. Intervention on these grounds will also satisfy the principle of *vertical equity*. Since education determines future earnings, by redistributing tax revenues to poorer socio-economic groups in the form of education investments, a more equal outcome will result once the returns to these investments have been realised.

3 EDUCATION POLICY IN IRELAND

Irish education policy was slower to evolve than was the case for many other OECD countries. The seminal development in Irish education policy took place in 1967 with the introduction of free second-level education for all. Since the 1960s, education expenditure as a percentage of national income has doubled and since the early 1990s, the Irish government has demonstrated an increased level of commitment to investment in education and training, recognising its importance for economic, social and cultural development

Education policy in Ireland can be divided into two strands, each of which attempts to achieve different objectives for the economy. First, education policy aims to facilitate the accumulation of human capital in the economy with the aim of fuelling economic growth. Second, education policy aims to contribute to the government's policy objective of equity by ensuring equal access to and opportunities within the system for all. Much co-operation also happens at an EU level in the development of education and training policies. For example, most EU countries, including Ireland, signed up to the Bologna Declaration in 1999, under which they agreed to co-operate on achieving a range of objectives for higher education in the EU, including comparable degree programmes, a system of credit transfers to aid student mobility and the promotion of inter-institutional co-operation in research. In this section the focus is on specific Irish policy initiatives, but bearing in mind the fact that many are motivated by recommendations made at higher levels of governance.

Policies Aimed at Promoting Economic Growth

As discussed in Section 2, a key rationale for government intervention in education provision is the importance of education for the creation of a skilled labour force. Thus, a key role of education is to produce a well-educated workforce that can meet the demands of an expanding economy. A more skilled and productive labour force will produce more output, facilitate the development and diffusion of new technologies, further fuelling growth, and will make the economy a more attractive place to invest, particularly if the skills of the labour force match labour demand. This is the assumption underlying the notion that modern-day economies are both 'knowledge based' and 'knowledge driven', where the ability to innovate is the key to successful economic development.

Much of the current and proposed education policy in Ireland in this regard is targeted at achieving outcomes that will contribute to Ireland's Smart Economy Framework and will target innovation-driven areas in high-technology sectors (see Chapter 9). The idea that education initiatives should be industry-led is not new. Acknowledging the fact that a well-educated and skilled labour force is a key determinant of competitiveness, in 1997 the Irish government established an Expert Group on Future Skills Needs to assist in the development of national strategies to ensure a flexible and adaptable labour force. Since its establishment, the Expert Group has produced a range of reports monitoring trends in Ireland's skills supply and making recommendations as to how education and training should best be oriented towards improving labour productivity, minimising unemployment and developing a labour force that can support high-value knowledge-based industries. These have ranged from sector-specific reports (for example, *Future Skills Needs of Enterprise within the Green Economy in Ireland* and *Future Skills Requirements of the Biopharma-Pharmachem* in 2010) to more general reports focusing on the skills needs of the labour market in a broader context. Research of this kind is particularly important at present where there is a mismatch of skills between those who are unemployed and the types of highly skilled jobs that are increasingly in demand, particularly in the internationally traded services sector (see Chapters 6, 7 and 9). The extent to which policy initiatives deliver on these objectives is discussed in Section 4. It is clear, though, that future education policy aimed at achieving economic growth objectives will be strongly guided by the needs of industry.

Initiatives at Primary and Second Level

As discussed in Section 2, one of the key functions of primary and second-level education is to set the foundations for the development of a labour force equipped with the necessary social capital to contribute to the economy and the society more generally. However, the quality of primary and second-level education will play a huge part in determining standards at third level, given that most students at third-level universities and colleges in Ireland have come through the Irish education system. Therefore any policies aimed at improving the level of preparedness of school leavers for the challenges of third-level education will fall under this umbrella. For example, in recent years the Irish government has introduced initiatives such as better career guidance at second level, particularly in the junior cycle when students begin making career choices, and initiatives aimed at promoting the application of new technology in teaching methods.

There are also an increasing number of initiatives being introduced at primary and second level that are specifically focused on preparing the future labour force to meet the needs of Ireland's smart economy. The strategy for developing Ireland as a smart economy will require increasing numbers of graduates in finance, science and engineering. One major problem that has emerged, however, is the deterioration in the mathematical ability of Irish school leavers. Between 2005 and 2009 the proportion of students who sat Higher Level Mathematics at Leaving Certificate fell from 19 per cent to 16 per cent and is very much out of line with participation at Higher Level in other subjects. Another worrying issue is the recent OECD education indicators, which revealed that the level of mathematics of Irish students is significantly below the OECD average and is on a downward trajectory (see later).

In an attempt to address the issue, Project Maths, an alternative approach to the teaching of mathematics at second level that aims to better prepare students for careers in science, engineering and finance, was introduced on a pilot basis in twenty-four schools in 2008 and was rolled out to all second-level schools in September 2010. Recently (2010), there have been further proposals for reforms to improve literacy and numeracy with particular emphasis placed on how literacy and numeracy are taught, how outcomes are assessed and progress is monitored.[7] These proposals also call for better links between schools and parents in supporting the development of literacy and numeracy skills in children.

The impact of initiatives and reforms at first and second level aimed at improving economic growth can take quite some time to realise. For example, the first cohort of primary school children to engage fully in the 1999 reform of the primary school curriculum are only now reaching second-level education. Similarly, the benefits, or otherwise, of initiatives like Project Maths will take another five or six years to be realised at third level, and a number of additional years beyond that before any impact will be seen in the job market. This is not to say that initiatives at first and second level aimed at improving and developing education services to meet the needs of the economy are not important, but given that their benefits are not realised for many years, attention is often focused on initiatives at third level, where more immediate benefits can potentially be realised.

Initiatives at Third Level

The higher education sector in most developed economies plays an important role in achieving economic growth objectives, both in terms of educating well-qualified graduates with the skills demanded in the labour force, but also in terms of contribution to high-level research and innovation. In January 2011, the Department of Education and Skills in Ireland published the *National Strategy for Higher Education to 2030*, which emphasises the importance of higher education for economic recovery. The proposals are wide ranging, covering teaching and learning, research, the engagement of the higher education sector with the wider society and the internationalisation of education at third level.

While a number of detailed proposals relating to the quality of the teaching and learning experience at third-level institutions are included, a notable emphasis is placed on the internationalisation of the third-level sector.[8] The rationale for internationalisation is twofold: first, it is expected that increased exposure internationally will improve the quality of learning, teaching and research by introducing the third-level sector in Ireland to new ideas and practices; and second, education should be viewed as an internationally traded service that can make a significant contribution to the output of the economy (see Chapter 9). Ensuring that the third-level sector delivers a high-quality and internationally competitive learning experience for students will be an important component of any successful internationalisation strategy and this in turn will depend to a large extent on the level of resources available to achieve this.

Another key feature of the strategy is the emphasis placed on research, both in terms of its importance for teaching but also more generally for the generation of ideas and innovation. Linkages between higher education institutions and industry are also highlighted as potentially playing an important role in facilitating economic recovery. A notable example of this is the Innovation Alliance, a partnership between two of the main universities in Ireland (Trinity College Dublin and University College Dublin), the state and business communities that aims to develop a culture and framework for innovation in Ireland that, it is hoped, will help to deliver on the goals set out under Ireland's Smart Economy Framework.

These, of course, are not new ideas. Government support for research through third-level institutions began in a real way with the establishment of Science Foundation Ireland (SFI) in 2000. The role of SFI is to support research in science and engineering. In 1998 the Programme for Research in Third-Level Institutions (PRTLI) also provided a new general source of research funding and in 1999 and 2001, respectively, the Irish Research Council for Humanities and Social Sciences and the Irish Research Council for Science, Engineering and Technology were established, providing new and significant sources of funding for individual researchers and research projects in these fields. Much of the funding from these sources is targeted at funding doctoral students and postdoctoral researchers, commonly referred to as 'fourth-level' education.

The shift in focus of expenditure on research, from providing direct financial supports to industry to diverting resources through third-level institutions, provides a clear indication of the government's view that higher education is important for economic growth. A causal relationship, however, between the different elements of higher education (formation and production of graduates and research and development (R&D)) and economic growth have yet to be established in a formal and convincing way.

Policies Aimed at Promoting Equity

As discussed in Section 2, an important rationale for government intervention in the provision of education is to promote equality of opportunity by ensuring equal access to the education system for all. While participation rates in education have increased significantly in Ireland over the last number of decades, up to the 1990s education policy in Ireland focused on increasing the overall level of participation in education with few attempts to promote equity in access to the system. Inequalities in education can manifest themselves in two ways, either through inequalities in educational achievement or the level of education attainment across different groups. These inequities are not confined to educational divides on the basis of social class but can manifest themselves as inequities across ethnic divides, as affecting people with disabilities, or in terms of gender or race.

With the introduction of free second-level schooling in the 1960s and compulsory education up to the age of 16, participation in schooling is almost universal across all groups in society. In 2009 this was extended to early years education, with all children in Ireland now entitled, under the Early Childcare and Education Scheme, to one year of free pre-schooling in the year before they begin primary school. However, the provision of compulsory and free schooling does not necessarily mean that all individuals will realise their true potential in the schooling system and this is often a function of circumstances or social background. Increased levels of funding can go some way to alleviating these inequalities in the education system; however, targeting expenditure at the most vulnerable groups will be more effective.

Initiatives at Primary and Second Level
Specific policy initiatives aimed at promoting equity within the education system have largely targeted compulsory education, since the main determinants of post-compulsory education achievement are educational background and the foundations laid at an early stage of educational development. Over the years a range of different schemes have been put in place to target educational disadvantage at first and second level. The current initiative, Delivering Equality of Opportunity in Schools, specifically targets disadvantaged schools and through the Schools Support Programme delivers a range of interventions aimed at eliminating educational disadvantage. Many of these initiatives and programmes have been in place for a long time, such as the School Completion Programme, Giving Children an Even Break, Breaking the Cycle, the Home School Community Liaison Scheme, and Literacy and Numeracy Schemes.[9]

Initiatives at Third Level
By far the most significant development in higher education policy aimed at promoting equality of access to third-level education was the introduction of free tuition fees for full-time third-level undergraduate EU students in 1996. Over the last number of years the increase in the number of places at third-level institutions has also aimed to improve access to third-level education. The government also provides specific financial incentives to individuals participating in third-level education, such as the Higher Education Grants Scheme and the Vocational Education Committee's Scholarship Scheme (which provide maintenance grants on a means-tested basis). In addition, third-level institutions themselves operate programmes to encourage participation by all groups in society (e.g. the Trinity Access Programme). The promotion of equal opportunities in third level falls under the remit of the HEA, which recognises the promotion of social inclusion as a key national policy objective. The *National Plan for Equity of Access to Higher Education 2008–2013* sets out a range of targets for improving access to third-level education in the coming years.[10] The plan includes targets for increased representation at third level of lower socio-economic groups, mature

students and students with disabilities, and highlights the importance of access programmes, lifelong learning and the introduction of non-traditional entry routes as a means to achieving this.

4 DELIVERY AND EFFECTIVENESS OF EDUCATION SERVICES

Evaluating the performance of government in the provision of a service like education is complicated by the fact that many of the returns to education are intangible, as discussed in Section 2. This makes traditional cost-benefit analysis very difficult as often the benefits are impossible to quantify. This also creates problems in attempting to compare outcomes across countries.

In this section, the level of provision of education services is examined by looking at public expenditure on education in Ireland and how this relates to other OECD countries. How funds are allocated at different levels of the education system is also analysed, both relative to other OECD countries and within a specific Irish context. Notwithstanding the difficulties in measuring outcomes in the education sector, how education outcomes in Ireland relate to those in other OECD countries is analysed. From an efficiency point of view it is important that the government achieves value for money in its spending decisions and so the trade-off between achieving quality outcomes and productivity improvements is discussed. The section concludes with some discussion on the extent to which the system offers equal opportunities or improves the distribution of income by leading to more equal outcomes.

Public Expenditure on Education

In 2010, total government expenditure by the Department of Education and Skills was estimated to amount to almost €8.7 billion, 14.5 per cent of total government expenditure. The increased importance of education expenditure in Ireland is highlighted by the fact that in 1995 it only accounted for 12.2 per cent of total government expenditure. Table 13.1 presents statistics on the proportion of education expenditure in gross domestic product (GDP) (gross national income (GNI) for Ireland) for a selection of OECD countries. In 2007, the most recent year for which comparable data are available, expenditure on education as a percentage of GNI in Ireland was 5.5 per cent, down from 6.4 per cent in 1995. With a declining birth rate and a reduction in the proportion of the population of school-going age, the demand for education expenditure will fall over time. As a result, across most OECD countries a stabilisation or even a fall in spending on education is expected. This was the case for most countries between 1995 and 2000 but since then some increases have been observed. This may in part be explained by slow growth in GDP in many European countries since 2000, but it may also be due to increasing expenditure levels in response to new EU targets as set out in the Lisbon Agenda. Also illustrated in Table 13.1 is the relatively small level, except in the USA, of private expenditure on educational institutions.

Table 13.1

Expenditure on Educational Institutions
as a Percentage of GDP/GNI

| | 1995 | 2000 | 2007 | | |
	Total	Total	Total	Public[1]	Private
Austria	6.1	5.5	5.4	4.9	0.5
Denmark	6.2	6.6	7.1	6.6	0.5
Finland	6.3	5.6	5.6	5.5	0.1
Germany	5.4	n/a	4.7	4.0	0.7
Ireland[2]	*6.4*	*5.2*	*5.5*	*5.1*	*0.3*
Netherlands	4.8	4.5	5.6	4.7	0.9
UK	5.5	5.0	5.8	4.0	1.8
USA	6.6	7.0	7.6	5.0	2.6
EU-19 average[3]	–	–	5.3	4.8	0.6
OECD average[3]	–	–	5.5	4.5	1.0

Source: OECD, *Education at a Glance, OECD Indicators 2010*, OECD, Paris 2010.

[1] Public expenditure includes public expenditure on educational institutions plus public subsidies to households.

[2] Expenditure on educational institutions expressed as a percentage of GNI. Public/private disaggregation based on 2006 data.

[3] Averages are not available for 1995 and 2000.

In Table 13.2 the level of expenditure (both private and public) on educational institutions by student in 2007 is presented. In all countries spend per student increases across education level with the highest spend per student at third level, although once research expenditure is excluded from these figures the levels of expenditure at third level are for the most part similar to those at second level. European countries lag behind US investment in education at all levels, but particularly at third level. It should be noted, however, that while these figures are adjusted for differences in purchasing power across countries they are not adjusted for differences in costs of education. Ireland spends slightly above the EU and OECD average per student at primary and second level ($6,901 and $9,375 respectively), while expenditure at third level ($8,907) is at the OECD average and above the EU average. These figures include both public and private expenditure and highlight the fact that Ireland performs well on spend per student when compared to the average.

While Ireland lags behind some of the countries represented in the table, it should be noted that even this gap is narrowing, particularly at primary and second level: in 2000, spend per student in Ireland was 24 per cent lower for primary and 15 per cent lower for secondary than the OECD average. In contrast, expenditure at third level in 2000 was at the OECD average. This suggests a slower pace of growth in third-level expenditure in Ireland compared with our EU neighbours, and relative to primary and second level within Ireland. Of course the level of expenditure tells us nothing about the quality of service provision, which is dealt with later in this section. It is also difficult to ascertain whether it is more efficient for the government to allocate funds to one level of education over another without understanding the full returns to each type of investment; the difficulties in doing this are highlighted in Section 2. In what follows, the allocation of funds at different levels in Ireland is discussed.

Table 13.2

Expenditure on Educational Institutions per Student by Level of Education in 2007 (Expressed in Equivalent US$ Converted using PPPs)

	Pre-primary	Primary	Secondary	Tertiary	Tertiary (excluding research)
Austria	6,409	8,664	8,840	15,039	10,552
Denmark	5,594	9,176	9,675	16,466	–
Finland	4,789	6,234	7,829	13,566	8,178
France	5,527	6,044	9,532	12,773	9,001
Germany	6,119	5,548	7,841	13,823	8,534
Ireland	*4,948*[1]	*6,901*	*9,375*	*12,631*	*8,907*
Netherlands	6,130	6,552	10,248	15,969	10,421
UK	7,598	8,222	8,892	15,463	9,023
USA	9,394	10,229	11,301	27,010	24,230
EU-19 average	5,468	6,752	8,346	12,084	7,899
OECD average	5,447	6,741	8,267	12,907	8,970

Source: as for Table 13.1.

Note: figures include expenditure on both public and private institutions.

[1] Pre-primary school figure for Ireland is based on 2006 data.

Allocation of Funds at Primary and Second Level

The government adopts a centralised approach to allocating resources to primary and second-level schools with some variation across different types of school such as vocational, community and comprehensive schools. Private fee-paying schools are allocated resources to cover teachers' salaries. The allocation of teachers to schools is also important and is based on the government's targeted student to teacher ratio. Teachers are currently allocated on the basis of student enrolment, but there may also be a number of ex-quota posts, such as guidance teachers, deputy principals or home–school liaison officers allocated on the basis of school size or need (for example, if the school is located in a disadvantaged area it may qualify for more ex-quota posts). In some cases there may also be lower student–teacher ratios linked to certain programmes aimed at tackling disadvantage.

Overall, student–teacher ratios were reduced at both primary and second level over the 1990s. In 2008, the number of students to teaching staff in primary schools in Ireland was 17.8, compared with an EU average of 14.6, while for secondary schools the student–teacher ratio was 12.8, slightly above the EU average of 12.0.[11] Recent budget cuts aimed at reducing the number of teachers on the payroll have, however, eroded some of the gains achieved in reducing class sizes in Ireland over the last few years. This, coupled with cuts in other ex-quota posts and in the number of Special Needs Assistants, means that many teachers find themselves in front of classes of well in excess of thirty students.

The main motivation for cuts in the number of teachers is that a significant proportion of government expenditure on education is made up of wages and salaries (see later). Capital expenditure makes up 8 per cent of total expenditure on education, while some resources are allocated directly to students, such as book grants, free school meals, Back to School Clothing Allowances, etc. However, these types of individual transfer play a much more significant role in the third-level sector in the form of maintenance grants to third-level students.

Allocation of Funds at Third Level
The higher education system in Ireland is predominantly publicly funded. The HEA is responsible for the allocation of funding to universities, ITs and some other higher education and research institutions. As already mentioned, in 1996 free tuition fees were introduced for eligible full-time undergraduate EU students. These fees are paid to higher education institutions by the state and the HEA manages the allocation of grants in respect of the Free Fees scheme along with the core recurrent grants to the various institutions. The HEA is also responsible for the capital building and equipment programme and administers various research programmes including the PRTLI (see above), the Programme for Strategic Co-operation between Irish Aid and Higher Education and Research Institutes 2007–2011, and European Funding for Research Infrastructure and Technology Sector Research, which is a funding programme directed at the ITs.[12] While research funding for higher education has increased in recent years, higher education institutions still rely to a very large extent on the recurrent grants. The vast majority of funding for higher education comes from the exchequer.

By far the most contentious issue in relation to the allocation of third-level funding, and an issue that is currently very much up for debate, is government expenditure on student transfers, both in the form of tuition fees and maintenance grants, which form a significant component of expenditure on third-level education. As discussed in Section 2, the private returns to third-level education are significant in terms of higher earnings, higher labour force participation rates, and lower unemployment risk. In addition, statistics show a high correlation between third-level participation and social class of parents. It is therefore difficult to justify the use of taxation income, collected from the general public, to finance individual participation in the accumulation of human capital which may yield significant private returns to those individuals in the future. Given the current public finance crisis and the very large predicted increases in student numbers in the future, it appears that the introduction of student contributions is inevitable.

There are many possible mechanisms for introducing student contributions for tuition fees.[13] It is clear from the discussion presented in Section 2 that both the individual and the wider economy will benefit from a student engaging in third-level education. It would therefore seem appropriate for the state to continue to supplement the cost of tuition. On the principle of equity, however, it is also important that the system is designed to ensure that all potential students have access to the education system and that none is excluded because they are unable to pay. The introduction of means-tested grants for tuition fees or free fees for those on low incomes, a reform of the maintenance grant system and offering state-guaranteed loans to students are all options that are under consideration by the government.

The final issue for consideration is at what level the fees should be set. The introduction of fees could create an opportunity to foster more competition between third-level institutions if they are allowed a say in the level of fees. For example, if one university offers a better quality of service than another, this can be reflected in the price of the courses on offer. The price of similar 'student experiences' in other countries would also have to be considered in setting the level of the fees, given that education is now an internationally traded service.

Benchmarking Education Performance
While Ireland was late to make any substantial investments in the education sector, with free second-level education only introduced in the 1960s, the previous analysis highlights the fact that the level of investment in education in Ireland is now comparable to many other EU and OECD countries. Overall, in terms of access to education, there is some evidence that education outcomes are also improving in Ireland. In Table 13.3 the percentage of upper-secondary and tertiary graduates in the population at the typical age of graduation are presented. The most remarkable improvement for Ireland was the increase in the proportion of the population aged 17–18 who graduated from upper-second level, from only 74 per cent in 2000 (below the EU average) to 96 per cent in 2008, well above the EU average of 80 per cent. Ireland also performs well on the proportion of the population aged 21 with a tertiary-level qualification, at 46 per cent in 2008, above the EU average of 38 per cent and up from only 30 per cent in 2000.

On the basis of these numbers it is clear that public investment in education is leading to an improvement in graduation rates. However, these gains are not borne out in measures of literacy and numeracy among Irish students. The recent results of the OECD Programme for International Student Assessment (PISA) reveals a marked decline in the performance of Irish students (15-year-olds) on a number of different measures. The rankings for reading, mathematics and science are presented in Table 13.4. Ireland experienced a huge decline in reading scores between 2000 and 2009, by far the greatest decline of all OECD countries. Ireland now ranks sixteenth in the OECD in terms of reading compared with fifth in 2000. Of even more concern is the fact that Ireland ranks twenty-sixth in terms of mathematics, down from fifteenth in 2000, and is at a level that is statistically significantly below the OECD average. Ireland did not decline by as much in sciences, though, falling from a position of ninth in 2000 to fourteenth in 2009, with scores in science still significantly above the OECD average.

Table 13.3

Upper Second-Level and Tertiary-Level Graduates as a Percentage of Population at Typical Age of Graduation[1]

	Second level			Tertiary level		
	2000	2005	2008	2000	2005	2008
Denmark	90	82	83	37	46	47
Finland	91	94	93	41	48	63
Germany	92	99	97	18	20	25
Ireland	*74*	*91*	*96*	*30*	*38*	*46*
UK[2]	–	86	91	37	39	35
USA	70	75	77	34	34	37
EU-19 average	75	80	80	27	35	38
OECD average	77	83	83	28	36	38

Source: as for Table 13.1.

[1] Data are not available for Austria, France and the Netherlands.

[2] Data for second-level graduation rates in the UK prior to 2005 are not available.

Overall, these results suggest that rising investment levels in education are not being translated into improved outcomes, raising serious questions as to whether government funds are being put to efficient use. In fact, if the countries represented in Table 13.2 are ranked in terms of expenditure levels on education there appears to be no correlation between investment and outcomes. For example, Finland spends below the OECD and EU-19 averages on second-level education and ranks first of all EU countries in terms of performance. In contrast, Denmark, France and Ireland, which rank highly in terms of spend per student (Table 13.2), are consistently among the poorly performing countries.

Table 13.4

Ranking of OECD Countries on Student Performance, 2000 and 2009

Reading 2009 (2000)		Mathematics 2009 (2000)		Science 2009 (2000)	
Finland	1 (1)	Korea	1 (2)	Finland	1 (3)
Canada	2 (2)	Finland	2 (4)	Japan	2 (2)
New Zealand	3 (3)	Switzerland	3 (7)	Korea	3 (1)
Japan	4 (8)	Japan	4 (1)	New Zealand	4 (6)
Australia	5 (4)	Canada	5 (6)	Canada	5 (5)
Netherlands	6 (–)	Netherlands	6 (–)	Estonia	6 (–)
Belgium	7 (11)	New Zealand	7 (3)	Australia	7 (7)
Norway	8 (13)	Belgium	8 (9)	Netherlands	8 (–)
Estonia	9 (–)	Australia	9 (5)	Germany	9 (20*)
Switzerland	10 (17)	Germany	10 (19*)	Switzerland	10 (18)
Poland	11 (23*)	Estonia	11 (–)	UK	11 (4)
Iceland	12 (12)	Iceland	12 (13)	Slovenia	12 (–)
USA	13 (15)	Denmark	13 (12)	Poland	13 (21*)
Sweden	14 (9)	Slovenia	14 (–)	*Ireland*	*14 (9)*
Germany	15 (21*)	Norway	15 (16)	Belgium	15 (17)
Ireland	*16 (5)*	France	16 (10)	Hungary	16 (15)
France	17 (14)	Slovak Rep.	17 (–)	USA	17 (14)
Denmark	18 (17)	Austria	18 (11)	Czech Rep.	18 (11)
UK	19 (7)	Poland	19 (22*)	Norway	19 (13)
Hungary	20 (22*)	Sweden	20 (14)	Denmark	20 (22*)
Portugal	21 (25*)	Czech Rep.	21 (17)	France	21 (12)
Italy*	22 (20*)	UK	22 (8)	Iceland*	22 (16)
Slovenia*	23 (–)	Hungary	23 (20*)	Sweden*	23 (10)
Greece*	24 (24*)	Luxembourg*	24 (26*)	Austria*	24 (8)
Spain*	25 (18*)	USA*	25 (18)	Portugal*	25 (25*)
Czech Rep.*	26 (19*)	*Ireland**	*26 (15)*	Slovak Rep.*	26 (–)

Source: rankings for 2009 are extracted from OECD, *Pisa 2009 at a Glance,* OECD, Paris 2010; rankings for 2000 are extracted from OECD, *Knowledge and Skills for Life: First Results from the OECD Programme for International Student Assessment 2000*, OECD, Paris 2001.

* indicates statistically significantly below the OECD average.

Efficiency of Education Expenditure

It is difficult to draw conclusions on the performance of the sector on the basis of the level of government expenditure; as is clear from the previous analysis. Higher levels of government expenditure do not automatically imply a higher-quality service. In general, the empirical evidence is mixed on whether increased expenditure per pupil positively impacts student achievement and the evidence presented here suggests that it may not. In contrast to other sectors of the economy, where productivity improvements are often associated with using fewer labour inputs to achieve the same level of output, in the education sector, where the objective is achieving a higher-quality service, increasing the number of labour inputs (i.e. reducing student–teacher ratios) is inevitable as over time the public demand higher-quality education services (Wagner's Law, see Chapter 3). There is much debate, however, on whether reduced student–teacher ratios result in improved academic achievement, with many empirical studies supporting the notion that class sizes matter but many others providing little evidence of such a relationship. Achieving productivity improvements (or value for money) is further impeded by the phenomenon known as Baumol's disease (see Chapters 3 and 12) where inflationary cost increases lead to high wages in the non-productive sectors (primarily public services) of the economy. This is particularly the case for education as it is such a labour-intensive service where the majority of the budget is absorbed by salaries and wages.

At first and second level, salaries and wages account for almost 80 per cent of current education expenditure in Ireland. The salary levels of Irish teachers are very much out of line with the rest of the EU, as is revealed in Table 13.5. In 2008, the average salary for a primary school teacher in Ireland with 15 years' experience was $54,100, compared with an EU average of $38,982 (adjusted for PPP). While the EU average for lower and upper secondary schooling is higher than for primary, Irish teachers are still paid more. Recent public sector pay cuts and a cap on the starting salaries of new teachers will have closed some of this gap, although the 2011 Croke Park Agreement guarantees that the salaries of teachers will not be cut any further (see Chapter 3). While it is argued that the freeze in pay cuts will be in exchange for changes in work practices and improvements in productivity, it is difficult to see what improvements can be made to justify such a significant difference in salaries as is evident from Table 13.5. Finland, for example, is the top performing country in Europe in terms of comparable educational outcomes (Table 13.4) but the annual salaries of teachers in Finland are approximately $10,000 lower than in Ireland at all levels.

Academic salaries in Ireland have also come under scrutiny in recent years. In particular, a number of high-profile media stories have tracked the evolution of 'superstar' academics in the Irish university sector. In general, higher academic grades, such as professor, in Ireland are comparatively highly paid, but this is mainly due to the relativity maintained between professorial and higher civil service grades at assistant secretary level. It is, however, commonplace in other countries to top up salaries of top academics, particularly in market-sensitive disciplines such as economics, law, medical sciences and business. For example, in the USA the contractual arrangements for salaries are on a one-to-one basis, while in the UK scales exist up to the level of professor, whereafter personal contracts and agreed salaries that reflect market norms and competitive pressures take effect. So while in terms of salary scales it appears that Irish academics fare well internationally, it is difficult to make comparisons due to differences in hiring practices. It is unlikely that any change to the current system of remuneration of academics in Ireland will happen in the short to medium term, given the current constraints on academic hiring rules and the proposals for future controls on the way in which higher education institutions recruit academic staff.

Table 13.5

Teachers' Salaries after 15 Years of Experience
in 2008 (Expressed in Equivalent US$ Converted using PPPs)

	Primary	Lower secondary	Upper secondary
Austria	37,914	40,993	42,177
Denmark	42,308	42,308	51,034
Finland	38,217	40,953	44,919
France	31,927	34,316	34,593
Germany	54,184	59,156	63,634
Ireland	*54,100*	*54,100*	*54,100*
Netherlands	45,916	50,227	67,105
USA	44,172	44,000	47,317
EU-19 average	38,982	45,519	45,043
OECD average	39,426	41,927	45,850

Source: as for Table 13.1.
Note: figures for the UK are not available.

Given the disproportionately high wage and salaries bill in the education sector in Ireland, the extent to which the taxpayer achieves value for money is questionable. There are, however, some productivity improvements that could be realised. For example, as discussed in Chapter 9, advances in technology and communications increasingly reduce the need for consumers to be physically present at the point of delivery of services. This is also the case for education services, most of which can be delivered online, for example via a live online classroom where teachers speak to hundreds or thousands of students across the world at one time. There are very successful examples of this at third level, such as the Open University and Hibernia, an online teacher training college in Ireland. There is, however, an extensive ongoing debate on the extent to which this may affect the quality of education services provided, although part of this opposition may be fuelled by a resistance to change and technological improvements, as emphasised in other parts of this book (see Chapters 3 and 12).

At third level, other productivity improvements are possible. For example, higher education institutions could benefit from economies of scale by merging together. In some ways this is already happening, for example, with the TCD–UCD Innovation Alliance previously mentioned and the creation of the Innovation Academy, a collaborative joint venture in PhD education. Of course, merging all universities and other higher education institutions may not be desirable as it would stifle competition within the sector.

Equity

Since earnings are a key determinant of well-being, a lower probability of participating in the labour force, a higher probability of unemployment and lower average earnings of those with lower levels of education attainment together imply that inequalities in educational opportunities will have serious implications for the distribution of income in the economy. This does not take into account the other negative welfare effects associated with early school leavers, such as social exclusion or crime, for example, which exacerbate the need for government education policies that target such inequities.

Across countries, evidence suggests that those who fail to complete upper second-level education are more likely to come from disadvantaged backgrounds. In an Irish context research has shown that those from working-class and unemployed families are more likely to underperform in Junior and Leaving Certificate examinations relative to their initial ability compared with other social groups. In addition, participation in tertiary education is highly correlated with the educational attainment and social background of parents (see below).[14]

At primary and second level, government policy has focused on the retention and achievement of students, particularly from disadvantaged backgrounds. Declining student–teacher ratios are part of these measures, but so are targeted initiatives aimed at tackling educational disadvantage (see Section 3). However, it will be a number of years before the benefits of these measures are fully realised. At second level, there have been substantial increases in the provision of, and numbers taking, the special Junior Certificate School Programme and the Applied Leaving Certificate Programme, which were introduced to target inequality in second-level education for all. The benefits of interventions of this kind are evidenced by the increasing rates of second-level completion: as revealed in Table 13.3, 96 per cent of students (of typical graduation age) completed second-level education in Ireland in 2008.

Of more significance, however, is the extent to which this follows through to equality of access and achievement at third level. The evidence suggests that equality of access to third level has improved in Ireland over the last number of years, but there is still evidence of inequities within the system.[15] For example, the socio-economic groups that are least likely to enter higher education are those from non-manual and semi-skilled and unskilled manual households and these groups are particularly under-represented at the universities. There has been some evidence of improvements in access for other targeted groups, though. For example, the number of adult learners in higher education increased from less than 2 per cent of new entrants in 1986 to almost 13 per cent of new entrants in 2006, while the proportion of students with disabilities in higher-level education increased from 0.6 per cent in 1994 to over 3 per cent in 2006. Overall, however, there is a clear need for continued government efforts to promote equity at all levels of the education system.

5 CONCLUSION

Education plays a very important role in the economic, social and cultural development of all economies. Not only is education a key to economic development in the contribution it makes to the enhancement of the skill level, productivity and competitiveness of the economy, but it plays a vital role in determining the income level and social status of individuals and will directly impact on the distribution of income in an economy. Due to the failure of private markets to optimally provide education, the government has a crucial role to play in ensuring education services are provided in such a way as to optimally meet these objectives.

In an Irish context, education policy attempts to ensure the delivery of an efficient and equitable service. While funding levels are high by international standards, evidence suggests that the Irish education system falls short of delivering an effective, efficient and equitable service. The statistics presented in this chapter are worrying, particularly given the emphasis on education and skills in the government's National Reform Programme. The Irish government has continually emphasised that a key component of Ireland's economic recovery will be the creation of jobs in new and emerging high value-added sectors that require a skilled and flexible labour force (see Chapters 6, 7 and 9). The education sector will play an important role in this process both in terms of re-skilling those, particularly from the construction sector, who have lost their jobs and in conducting research with commercial potential through links between academia and industry. However, the resources available to government to even maintain the current level of service delivery are significantly constrained. The deterioration in the basic skill levels of numeracy and mathematics also needs to be addressed at first and second level and this will be challenging with significantly fewer resources for schools in terms of funding and teachers. Careful consideration needs to be given to the way the activities of the education sector are funded at all levels to ensure value for money and that an appropriate balance between improving educational outcomes, delivering an equitable service and supporting higher education is achieved.

Endnotes

* This chapter builds on Chapter 12 in the tenth edition of this book, which was co-authored with Colm Harmon: some of the same material is included in this version. I would like to thank John O'Hagan for his comments and suggestions on an earlier draft of this chapter.

1 See Department of Education and Skills, *Key Statistics 2009–2010*, 2010 (www.education.ie).

2 See C. Harmon, H. Oosterbeek and I. Walker, 'The returns to education: microeconomics', *Journal of Economic Surveys*, Vol. 17, No. 2, 2003; and J. Heckman,

L. Lochner and P. Todd, 'Fifty years of Mincer earnings regressions', NBER Working Paper 9732, National Bureau of Economics Research 2003.

3 For examples, see A. Barrett, J. FitzGerald and A. Nolan, 'Earnings inequality, returns to education and immigration into Ireland', *Labour Economics*, Vol. 9, No. 5, 2002; OECD, 'Investment in human capital through upper-secondary and tertiary education', *OECD Economic Studies No. 34*, OECD, Paris 2002; and S. McCoy and S. Smyth, 'Educational expenditure: implications for equality', *Budget Perspectives 2004*, ESRI, Dublin 2004.

4 OECD, *Improving Workers' Skills: Analytical Evidence and the Role of the Social Partners*, OECD, Paris 2003.

5 J. Blanden, F. Buscha, P. Sturgis and P. Urwin, 'Measuring the returns to lifelong learning', Centre for the Economics of Education, LSE, DP 110, 2010.

6 OECD, *OECD Economic Survey of the United Kingdom: Graduate Contributions for Higher Education,* OECD, Paris 2004.

7 For details on each of these programmes see Department of Education and Skills, *Report of the Project Maths Implementation Support Group*, Department of Education and Skills, Dublin 2010, and Department of Education and Skills, *Better Literacy and Numeracy for Children and Young People: A Draft National Plan to Improve Literacy and Numeracy in Schools*, Dublin 2010.

8 See also Department of Education and Skills, *Investing in Global Relationships: Ireland's International Education Strategy 2010–15*, Dublin 2010.

9 For details of these schemes see www.education.ie.

10 Higher Education Authority, *National Plan for Equity of Access to Higher Education 2008–2013*, National Office of Equity of Access to Higher Education, Higher Education Authority, Dublin 2008.

11 OECD, *Education at a Glance 2010*, OECD, Paris 2010.

12 For details of these programmes see www.hea.ie.

13 The discussion presented here draws on Department of Education and Skills, *Policy Options for New Student Contributions in Higher Education: Report to the Minister for Education and Science*, Dublin 2009.

14 McCoy and Smyth, *op. cit.*

15 Statistics presented are taken from Higher Education Authority, *op. cit.*

Index